The Unforgettable Story of an Unforgettable Woman.

"Inspired . . . passionate . . . compelling . . . reads like an adventure novel."

—*Chicago Tribune*

"Deeply moving, thoroughly candid . . . Mrs. Meir's story is both a personal one and a public one."

—*Los Angeles Times*

"Mrs. Meir speaks from the heart—about herself as wife and mother, concerning which she feels she could have done better, and about her country, to which she unstintingly gave what others might have given their families . . . her nation can be grateful to this remarkable woman whose combination of strength with compassion, wisdom with fortitude are so transparently mirrored in these pages."

—*John Barkham Reviews*

MY LIFE
by
Golda Meir

A DELL BOOK

Published by
DELL PUBLISHING CO., INC.
1 Dag Hammarskjold Plaza
New York, New York 10017

First American Edition 1975
Copyright © 1975 by Golda Meir

Dell ® TM 681510, Dell Publishing Co., Inc.

ISBN: 0-440-15656-4

Reprinted by arrangement with G. P. Putnam's Sons
Photos courtesy of Shabtai Himmelfarb
and the Israeli Government Press Agency.
Printed in the United States of America
First Dell Printing—November 1976
Second Dell Printing—January 1977
Third Dell Printing—February 1977
Fourth Dell Printing—May 1978
Fifth Dell Printing—January 1979

To my sisters, Sheyna and Clara,
to our children,
and to our children's children

Contents

1. My Childhood 11
2. A Political Adolescence 27
3. I Choose Palestine 49
4. The Start of a New Life 71
5. Pioneers and Problems 95
6. "We Shall Fight Hitler" 124
7. The Struggle Against the British 155
8. We Have Our State 193
9. Minister to Moscow 235
10. The Right to Exist 272
11. African and Other Friendships 305
12. We Are Alone 336
13. The Prime Minister 366
14. The Yom Kippur War 405
15. The End of the Road 438
    Index 445

I have never kept diaries, nor have I ever been a writer of letters, and I certainly never expected to write the story of my life. But today, in the hope that perhaps those who read this book will learn and understand a little more about Israel, Zionism and the Jewish people, I have told of some of the men and women whom I have known, some of the places I have seen and, above all, some of the incredible events in which I have participated.

G. M.

Ramat Aviv
June, 1975

1. My Childhood

In a way, I suppose that the little I recall of my early childhood in Russia, my first eight years, sums up my beginnings, what now are called the formative years. If so, it is sad that I have very few happy or even pleasant memories of this time. The isolated episodes that have stayed with me throughout the past seventy years have to do mostly with the terrible hardships my family suffered, with poverty, cold, hunger and fear, and I suppose my recollection of being frightened is the clearest of all my memories. I must have been very young, maybe only three and a half or four. We lived then on the first floor of a small house in Kiev, and I can still recall distinctly hearing about a pogrom that was to descend on us. I didn't know then, of course, what a pogrom was, but I knew it had something to do with being Jewish and with the rabble that used to surge through town, brandishing knives and huge sticks, screaming "Christ killers" as they looked for the Jews, and who were now going to do terrible things to me and to my family.

I can remember how I stood on the stairs that led to the second floor, where another Jewish family lived, holding hands with their little daughter and watching our fathers trying to barricade the entrance with boards of wood. That pogrom never materialized, but to this day I remember how scared I was and how angry that all my father could do to protect me was to nail a few planks together while we waited for the hooligans to come. And, above all, I remember being aware that this was happening to me because I was Jewish, which made me different from most of the other children in the yard. It was a feeling that I was to know again many times during my life—the fear, the frustration, the consciousness of being different and the profound instinctive belief that if one wanted to survive, one had to take effective action about it personally.

Also, I remember all too clearly how poor we were. There was never enough of anything, not food, not warm clothing, not heat at home. I was always a little too cold outside and a little too empty inside. Even now, from that very distant past, I can summon up with no effort at all, almost intact, the picture of myself sitting in tears in the kitchen, watching my mother feed some of the gruel that rightfully belonged to me to my younger sister, Zipke. Gruel was a great luxury in our home in those days, and I bitterly resented having to share any of it, even with the baby. Years later I was to experience the dread of my own children's hunger and to learn for myself what it is like to have to decide which child is to receive more food, but, of course, in that kitchen in Kiev, I knew only that life was hard and that there was no justice anywhere. I am glad that no one told me then that my older sister, Sheyna, often fainted from hunger in school.

My parents were newcomers in Kiev. They had met and married in Pinsk, where my mother's family lived, and it was to Pinsk that we all returned within a few years—in 1903, when I was five. My mother was very proud of her romance with my father and told us about it often, but although I came to know the story by heart, I never tired of hearing it. My parents had married very unconventionally, without the benefit of a *shadchan,* the traditional matchmaker.

I don't know exactly how it happened that my father, who was born in the Ukraine, had to report for military duty in Pinsk, but it was there that my mother once saw him in the street. He was a tall, handsome young man, with whom she instantly fell in love and about whom she even dared tell her parents. A matchmaker was called in eventually, but only for what might be termed the technical arrangements. What was even more impressive—in her and our eyes—was the fact that she managed to persuade her parents that love at first sight was enough, even though my father, who had been orphaned of his father, had no money at all and his family could claim very little distinction. There was one saving fact, however. He was not an ignoramus. In his very early teens, he had studied for a while in a yeshiva, a Jewish religious seminary, and he knew the Torah. My grandfather duly took this fact into account, although I have always suspected that he was also influenced by the fact that my mother had never been known to change her mind about anything substantive.

My parents were very different from each other: My father, Moshe Yitzhak Mabovitch, was a slender, delicately featured, fundamentally optimistic man, much given to believing in people—unless and until proved wrong—a trait that, on the whole, was to make his life a failure in worldly terms. In short, he was what you might call an innocent, the kind of man who would probably have been more successful if circumstances had ever been just slightly easier. Blume, my copper-haired mother, was pretty, energetic, bright and far more sophisticated and enterprising than my father, but, like him, a born optimist and very sociable. Despite everything, on Friday nights our house was always full of people, members of the family mostly. I remember swarms of cousins, second cousins, aunts and uncles. None of them was to survive the Holocaust, but they live on in my mind's eye, sitting around our kitchen table, drinking tea out of glasses and, on the Sabbath and holidays, singing for hours—and I remember my parents' sweet voices ringing out above the others.

It was not a particularly religious household. My parents, of course, observed Jewish tradition. They kept a kosher kitchen and celebrated all the Jewish holidays and festivals. But religion as such—to the extent that it can be separated from tradition for Jews—played very little role in our lives. I can't remember as a child ever having thought very much about God or praying to a personal deity, although when I was older—we were already in America—I sometimes argued about religion with my mother. I remember that once she wanted to prove to me that God existed. She said, "Why does it rain or snow, for instance?" So I explained what I had learned in school about rain, and then she said to me, *"Nu, Góldele, du bist aza chachome, mach du zol gein a reignel"* (So, Goldele, if you're so clever, *you* make it rain!) Since no one had heard of cloud seeding in those days, I couldn't think of an answer. As for the Jews being a chosen people, I never quite accepted that. It seemed, and still seems to me, more reasonable to believe, not that God chose the Jews, but that the Jews were the first people that chose God, the first people in

history to have done something truly revolutionary, and it
was this choice that made them unique.

At any rate, we lived in this—as in other respects—in
the way most Jews lived in the towns and villages of Eastern Europe. We went to *shul* (synagogue) on festivals and
fast days, we blessed the Sabbath, and we kept two calen-
dars: one Russian, the other relating to that far-off land
from which we had been exiled 2,000 years before and
whose seasons and ancient customs we still marked in Kiev
and Pinsk.

My parents had moved to Kiev when Sheyna (who was
nine years my senior) was still very small. My father
wanted to better his situation, and although Kiev was beyond the Pale of Settlement and in that part of Russia in
which Jews were normally forbidden to live, he was an ar-
tisan, and as such, if he could prove that he was a skilled
carpenter by passing the necessary examination, he might
receive the precious permit to move to Kiev. So he made a
perfect chess table, passed the test, and we packed our bags
and left Pinsk, filled with hope. In Kiev Father found work
for the government, making furniture for school libraries,
and even got an advance. With this money, plus money my
parents borrowed, he built a little carpentry shop of his
own, and it seemed as though all would be well. But in the
end the job fell through. Perhaps, as he said, it was because
he was Jewish, and Kiev was noted for its anti-Semitism.
At all events, very soon there was no job, no money and
debts that had to be paid somehow. It was a crisis that was
to recur throughout my childhood.

My father began desperately to look for work everywhere; he would be out all day and much of the night, and
when he came home in the bitter dark of a Russian winter,
there was rarely enough food in the house to make him a
meal. Bread and salt herring had to do.

But my mother had other troubles. Four little boys and a
girl all fell ill: Two of them died before they were a year
old, two of them went within one month. My mother
mourned each one of her babies with a broken heart, but
like most Jewish mothers of that generation, she accepted
the will of God and drew no conclusions about child rear-
ing from the row of little graves. Then, right after the last
of the babies had died, a well-to-do family who lived near
us offered my mother a job as wet nurse to their new baby.

They made one condition: My parents and Sheyna were to move from their miserable, damp little room to a larger, lighter, airier one, and a nurse was to come teach my poor young mother the rudiments of child care. So it was thanks to this "foster child" that Sheyna's life improved and that I was born into relative order, cleanliness and health. Our benefactors saw to it that my mother always had enough to eat, and soon my parents had three children, Sheyna, Zipke and me.

In 1903, when I was about five, we went back to Pinsk. Father, never one to give up, had a new dream now. Never mind the failure of Kiev, he said. He would go to America, to the *goldene medina*—the "land of gold," as the Jews called it—and make his fortune there. Mother, Sheyna, Zipke (the new daughter) and I would wait for him in Pinsk. So he gathered up his few belongings again and left for the unknown continent, and we moved to my grandparents' house.

I don't know to what extent any of my grandparents influenced me, although in Pinsk I lived with my mother's parents for a long time. Certainly it is hard for me to believe that my father's father played any role at all in my life, since he died before my parents met. But somehow or other he became one of the personalities that people my childhood, and now, going back into the past, I feel he belongs to this story. He had been one of the thousands of "kidnapped" Jewish children of Russia, *shanghaied* into the czar's army to serve for twenty-five years. Ill-clothed, ill-fed, terrified children, more often than not they were under constant pressure to convert to Christianity. My Mabovitch grandfather had been snatched by the army when he was all of thirteen, the son of a highly religious family, brought up to observe the finest points of Orthodox Jewish tradition. He served in the Russian army for another thirteen years, and never once, despite threats, derision and often punishment, did he touch *treife* (nonkosher) food. All those years he kept himself alive on uncooked vegetables and bread. Though pressed hard to change his religion and often made to pay for his refusal by being forced to kneel for hours on a stone floor, he never gave in. When he was released and came back home, he was nonetheless haunted by the fear that inadvertently he might somehow have broken the Law. So to atone for the sin he may have committed, he slept for years on a bench in an unheated synagogue with only a stone at his head for a pillow. Little wonder that he died young.

Grandfather Mabovitch was not my only tenacious—or, to use a more fashionable word applied frequently to me by people who are not great admirers of mine, "intransigent"—relative. There was also my maternal great-grandmother, whom I never knew and for whom I was named. She was known for her will of iron and for her bossiness. No one in the family, so we were told, ever dared take a step without consulting her. For instance, it was my Bobbe Golde who was really responsible for the fact that my parents were allowed to marry each other. When my father came to Grandfather Naiditch to ask for my mother's hand in marriage, my grandfather shook his head unhappily and heaved great sighs at the idea that his darling Blume was to marry a mere carpenter, even if that carpenter could be described as a cabinetmaker. But my great-grandmother came to the rescue at once: "What matters most of all," she said firmly, "is whether or not he is a *mensch*. If he is, then a carpenter too can become a merchant one day. . . ." My father was to remain a carpenter all his life, but thanks to Bobbe Golde's ruling, my grandfather gave his blessing to the marriage. Bobbe Golde lived to be ninety-four and one of the stories I remember most distinctly about her is that she always took salt instead of sugar in her tea because, she said, "I want to take the taste of the *Goless* [Diaspora] with me into the other world." Interestingly enough, so my parents told me, we bore a striking resemblance to each other.

They are all gone now, of course: they and their children and their children's children: they and their way of life. The *shtetl* of Eastern Europe has gone, too, destroyed in flames, its memory preserved accurately only in the Yiddish literature to which it gave birth and through which it expressed itself. That *shtetl*, reconstructed in novels and films, which has become known today in places my grandparents never even heard of, that gay, heart-warming, charming *shtetl* on whose roofs fiddlers eternally play sentimental music, has almost nothing to do with anything I remember, with the poverty-stricken, wretched little communities in which Jews eked out a living, comforting themselves with the hope that things would somehow be better one day and with their belief that there was a point to their misery.

They were God-fearing and brave people, most of them, but their lives, like my Mabovitch grandfather's, were essentially tragic. And I myself have never felt—not even for a minute—any nostalgia for the past into which I was born, though it deeply colored and affected my life and my convictions, about the way in which all men, women and children, everywhere and whoever they are, are entitled to spend their lives—productively and free of humiliation—and, even more, about the way in which Jews, in particular, should live. I have often told my own children, and more recently my grandchildren, about life in the *shtetl* as I myself dimly remember it, and there is nothing that makes me happier than the certain knowledge that for them it is only a history lesson. A very important lesson about a very important part of their heritage, but not something with which they can ever really identify themselves because their lives were so totally different from the start.

Anyhow, Father spent three lonely difficult years in America. He had painfully scraped together the money to get there, and like many thousands of the Russian Jews who streamed into the *goldene medina* at the turn of the century, he had thought of America as the one place where he would surely make the fortune that would allow him to return home, to Russia, and to a new life there. Of course, it didn't work out like that—not for him or for the thousands like him—but the idea that he would come back to us made our three years without him easier to bear.

Although the Kiev of my birth is lost to me in the fog of time, I have retained some sort of inner image of Pinsk, perhaps because I have heard and read about it so much. Many of the people I was to meet in later life came originally from Pinsk or from the townlets that clustered around it, including the families of Chaim Weizmann and Moshe Sharett.

Many years later I twice nearly went back to Pinsk. In 1939, when I was in Poland on a mission for the labor movement, I fell ill on the very day I was to visit the town, and the trip was canceled. Then, in the summer of 1948, when I was appointed Israel's minister to the Soviet Union, I was seized by a sudden desire to go back to Pinsk to see for myself if any of my relatives had survived the Nazis, but the Soviet government refused to permit me to go. I hoped that in the course of time I would be allowed to make the journey; but in the beginning of 1949 I had to return to Israel, and my visit to Pinsk was postponed indefinitely. Perhaps it was just as well; I learned later that only one very distant relative out of our whole large family was still alive.

The town that I remember was filled with Jews. Pinsk was one of the most celebrated centers of Russian-Jewish life and at one time even had had a Jewish majority. It was built on two great rivers, the Pina and the Pripet—both of which flow into the Dnieper—and it was these rivers that supplied most of the Jews of Pinsk with their livelihoods. They fished, unloaded cargo, did porterage, broke the giant ice floes in winter and dragged the ice to huge storage cellars in the houses of the well-to-do, where they served to create cooling facilities all through the summer. At one time my grandfather, who was fairly well off compared to my parents, owned such a cellar to which neighbors brought their Sabbath and holiday dishes when it was very hot and from which they took ice for the sick. The richer Jews dealt in timber and in the salt trade, and Pinsk even had nail, plywood and match factories that were owned by Jews and, of course, gave employment to dozens of Jewish workers.

But I remember mostly the *Pinsker blotte,* as we called them at home, the swamps that seemed to me then like oceans of mud and that we were taught to avoid like the plague. In my memory those swamps are forever linked to my persistent terror of the Cossacks, to a winter night when I played with other children in a narrow lane near the forbidden *blotte* and then suddenly, as though out of nowhere, or maybe out of the swamps themselves, came the Cossacks on their horses, literally galloping over our crouching, shivering bodies. "Well," said my mother later, shivering and crying herself, "what did I tell you?"

Cossacks and the black, bottomless swamps, however, were not the only terrors Pinsk held for me. I can remember a row of big buildings on a street that led to the river and the monastery that stood opposite the buildings on a hill. In front of it, all day, sat or lay numbers of wild-haired, wild-eyed cripples who prayed aloud and begged for alms. I tried to avoid passing them, and when I had to,

I closed my eyes and ran. But if Mother really wanted to frighten me, she knew that all she had to do was mention the beggars and I would abandon all defiance.

Still, not everything could have been so fearful. I was a child, and like all children, I played and sang and made up stories to tell the baby. With Sheyna's help, I learned to read and write and even do a little arithmetic, although I didn't start school in Pinsk, as I should have. "A golden child, they called you," my mother said. "Always busy with something." But what I was really busy doing in Pinsk, I suppose, was learning about life—again, chiefly from Sheyna.

Sheyna was fourteen when Father left for the States, a remarkable, intense, intelligent girl who became, and who remained, one of the great influences of my life—perhaps the greatest, apart from the man I married. By any standard, she was an unusual person, and for me she was a shining example, my dearest friend and my mentor. Even late in life, when we were both grown women, grandmothers, in fact, Sheyna was the one person whose praise and approval—when I won them, which was not easy—meant most to me. Sheyna, in fact, is part of the story of my life. She died in 1972; but I think of her constantly, and her children and grandchildren are as dear to me as my own.

In Pinsk, although we were so pitifully poor and Mother only barely managed (with my grandfather's help) to keep us going, Sheyna refused to go to work. The move back to Pinsk had been very hard on her. She had gone to a wonderful school in Kiev, and she was bent on studying, on acquiring knowledge and getting an education, not only so that she herself would have a fuller and better life, but, even more, so that she could help change and better the world. At fourteen, Sheyna was a revolutionary, an earnest, dedicated member of the Socialist-Zionist movement, and as such doubly dangerous in the eyes of police and liable to punishment. Not only were she and her friends "conspiring" to overthrow the all-powerful czar, but they also proclaimed their dream to bring into existence a Jewish socialist state in Palestine. In the Russia of the early twentieth century, even a fourteen- or fifteen-year-old schoolgirl who held such views would be arrested for subversive activity, and I still remember hearing the screams of young men and women being brutally beaten in the police station around the corner from where we lived.

My mother heard those screams, too, and daily begged Sheyna to have nothing to do with the movement; she could endanger herself and us and even Father in America! But Sheyna was very stubborn. It was not enough for her to want changes; she had to participate in bringing them about. Night after night, my mother kept herself awake until Sheyna came home from her mysterious meetings, while I lay in bed, taking it all in silently: Sheyna's devotion to the cause in which she believed so strongly; Mother's overwhelming anxiety; Father's (to me, inexplicable) absence; and the periodic and fearful sound of the hooves of Cossack horses outside.

On Saturdays, when Mother went off to the synagogue, Sheyna organized meetings at home. Even when Mother found out about them and pleaded with Sheyna not to imperil us, there was nothing she could do about these meetings except nervously walk up and down outside the house when she got back on Saturday morning, patrolling it like a sentry so that when a policeman approached, she could at least warn the young conspirators. But it wasn't only the idea that an ordinary policeman might swoop down at any moment and arrest Sheyna that so worried my poor mother. What really gnawed at her heart throughout all those months was the fear (always rampant in the Russia of those days) that one or another of Sheyna's friends might turn out to be an *agent provocateur*.

Of course, I was much too small to understand what the arguments and tears and door slammings were about, but I used to squeeze myself onto the flat top of our big coal stove (which was built into the wall) and sit there for hours on those Saturday mornings, listening to Sheyna and her friends and trying to make out what it was that they all were so excited about and why it made my mother cry so. Sometimes when I pretended to be engrossed in drawing or in copying the strangely shaped letters in the siddur (the Hebrew prayer book), which was one of the few books in our house, I tried to follow what Sheyna was fervently explaining to my mother, but all I gathered was that she was involved in a special kind of struggle that concerned not only the Russian people, but also, and more especially, the Jews.

A great deal has already been written—and much more will certainly be written in the future—about the Zionist movement, and most people by now have at least some notion of what the word "Zionism" means and that it has to do with the return of the Jewish people to the land of their forefathers—the Land of Israel, as it is called in Hebrew. But perhaps even today not everyone realizes that this remarkable movement sprang up spontaneously, and more or less simultaneously, in various parts of Europe toward the end of the nineteenth century. It was like a drama that was being enacted in different ways on different stages in different languages but that dealt with the same theme everywhere: that the so-called Jewish problem (of course, it was really a Christian problem) was basically the result of Jewish homelessness and that it could not, and would not, be solved unless and until the Jews had a land of their own again. Obviously, this land could only be Zion, the land from which the Jews had been exiled 2,000 years before but which had remained the spiritual center of Jewry throughout the centuries and which, when I was a little girl in Pinsk and up to the end of World War I, was a desolate and neglected province of the Ottoman Empire called Palestine.

The first Jews who made the modern return to Zion came there as early as 1878 to found a pioneering village which they named Petach Tikva (the Gate of Hope). By 1882 small groups of Zionists from Russia who called themselves the Hovevei Zion (Lovers of Zion) had arrived in the country determined to reclaim the land, farm it and defend it. But in 1882 Theodor Herzl, who was to be the founder of the World Zionist Organization and thus, essentially, the father of the State of Israel, was still quite unaware of what was happening to the Jews in Eastern Europe and of the existence of the Hovevei Zion. The successful and sophisticated Paris correspondent of the important Viennese newspaper the *Neue Freie Presse,* Herzl became interested in the fate of the Jews only in 1894, when he was assigned to cover the trial of Captain Dreyfus. Shocked by the injustice done to this Jewish officer—and by the open anti-Semitism of the French army—Herzl, too, came to believe that there was only one possible permanent solution to the situation of the Jews. His subsequent achievements and failures—the whole amazing story of his attempt to create a Jewish state—are part of the history learned by all Israeli schoolchildren and should be studied by anyone who wants to understand what Zionism is really all about.

Although my mother and Sheyna knew about Herzl, the first time I can remember hearing his name was when an aunt of mine (who lived in the same house as the Weizmann family and who was therefore often the bearer of important tidings, both good and bad) came in one day, her eyes brimming with tears, to tell my mother that the unthinkable had happened: Herzl was dead. I have never forgotten the stunned silence that greeted her announcement. As for Sheyna, she decided—typically—to wear only black clothes in mourning for Herzl from that afternoon in the summer of 1904 until we reached Milwaukee two long years later.

Although the yearning of the Jews for their own land was not the direct result of pogroms (the idea of the Jewish resettlement of Palestine had been urged by Jews and even some non-Jews long before the word "pogrom" became part of the vocabulary of European Jewry), the Russian pogroms of my childhood gave the idea immediacy, especially when it became clear to the Jews that the Russian government itself was using them as scapegoats of the regime's struggle to put down the revolutionary movement.

Most of the young Jewish revolutionaries in Pinsk, although united in their determination to press for an end to the czarist regime and in their immense enthusiasm for education as a tool with which to liberate Russian's exploited and oppressed masses, were divided at that point into two main groups. There were the members of the Bund (Union), who believed that the solution to the plight of the Jews in Russia and elsewhere would be found when socialism prevailed. Once the economic and social structure of the Jews was changed, said the Bundists, anti-Semitism would totally disappear. In that better, brighter, socialist world, the Jews could still, if they so desired, retain their cultural identity, go on speaking Yiddish, maintain whatever customs and traditions they chose, eat whatever food they wanted to eat. But there would be no reason at all for clinging to the obsolete idea of Jewish nationhood.

The Poalei Zion (Labor Zionists), like Sheyna, saw it all differently. They believed that the so-called Jewish problem had other roots, and its solution therefore had to be more

far-reaching and radical than merely the righting of economic wrongs or social inequalities. In addition to the
shared social idea, they clung to a national idea based on
the concept of Jewish peoplehood and the reestablishment
of Jewish independence. At the time, although both these
movements were secret and illegal, ironically enough the
bitterest enemies of Zionism were the Bundists, and most of
the debates that whirled about my head whenever Sheyna
and her friends got together in our house had to do with
the conflict between the two groups.

Sometimes, when Sheyna and I got into a fight and I lost
my temper, I used to threaten to tell Maxim, the big, red-
faced policeman in our neighborhood, all about her political activities. Of course, I never did, and of course, Sheyna
knew that my threats were empty; but they worried her all
the same. "What will you tell Maxim?" she asked. "I'll tell
him that you and all your friends want to do away with the
czar," I would shriek.

"Do you know what will happen to me then? I'll be sent
away to Siberia, where I'll die of cold and never come
back," she'd say. "That's what happens to people who are
exiled."

Truth to tell, I was always very careful to keep out of
Maxim's way. Whenever I saw him lumbering in my direction, I took to my heels and fled. Years later Sheyna told
me that although Maxim had never arrested anyone himself, she was quite sure that he provided the authorities regularly with plenty of information about all the youngsters
with whom she associated.

On second thought, I must also have learned at least one
very important nonpolitical lesson on top of the stove: that
nothing in life just happens. It isn't enough to believe in
something; you have to have the stamina to meet obstacles
and overcome them, to struggle. I must have begun, when I
was about six or seven, to grasp the philosophy that underlay everything that Sheyna did. There is only one way to
do anything: the right way. Sheyna was already a perfec-
tionist at fifteen, a girl who lived according to the highest
principles, whatever the price, a severe taskmaster and very
austere.

Even after we had both been living for years in what was
first Palestine, then Israel, and she could have afforded
some of the things that make life a little easier, she did

without them because she felt they represented a standard of living that was too high for the country. As late as the 1960s, when she was old and not well, her sole luxury was a refrigerator, nothing else. She did without an oven, cooked all her life on a gas burner and thought that an electric mixer was more than she could permit herself to own, considering where she was living. Had she been more flexible, less strict with herself and with others, she might have understood what those meetings of hers in Pinsk cost my mother in terms of dread and sorrow and perhaps have compromised a little. But she was relentless about the things that really mattered to her, and the political meetings in our house went on, despite the never-ending battles about them. Once Sheyna even left home and went to live for a while with an aunt of ours; but that household turned out to be even less tolerant than our own, and she reluctantly came back.

It was around this time that Sheyna met Shamai Korngold, her husband-to-be, a strong, clever, gifted boy who had given up the great joy of studying and his burning interest in mathematics in order to join the revolutionary movement. A close-to-wordless romance blossomed between them, and Shamai also became and stayed part of my life. He was one of the leaders of the young Zionists, nicknamed Copernicus in the movement. Shamai was the only grandson of a well-known Torah scholar, in whose house he and his parents lived and on whom they were financially dependent. He visited us often, and I can remember his whispered conversations with Sheyna about the increased revolutionary ferment in town and the regiment of Cossacks that were on their way to subdue Pinsk with their flashing swords. It was from these conversations that I gathered that something frightful had happened to the Jews of Kishinev and that in Pinsk the Jews were planning to defend themselves with arms and homemade bombs.

In response to the worsening situation, Sheyna and Shamai did more than merely hold or attend conspiratorial meetings; they did their best to bring other young people into the movement, even, to his horror, the only daughter of our white-bearded *shochet,* the ultra-Orthodox ritual slaughterer from whom we rented the room in which we lived. Eventually, Mother's anxiety for Sheyna and Zipke and me became intolerable, and she began to write frantic letters to my father. It was out of the question, she wrote, for us to stay in Pinsk any longer. We must join him in America.

But like many things in life, this was far easier said than done. My father, who had by now moved from New York to Milwaukee, was barely making a living. He wrote back that he hoped to get a job working on the railway and soon he would have enough money for our tickets. We moved out of the *shochet's* house to a room in a bagel baker's flat. The bagels were baked at night, so the flat was always hot, and the baker gave my mother a job. Then, late in 1905, a letter came from Milwaukee. My father was working, so we could start getting ready to leave.

The preparations for our journey were long and complicated. It was not a simple matter then for a woman and three girls, two of them still very small, to travel all the way from Pinsk to Milwaukee by themselves. For my mother, relief must have been combined with new anxieties, and for Sheyna leaving Russia meant leaving Shamai and everything for which they had worked so hard and risked so much. I can remember only the hustle and bustle of those last weeks in Pinsk, the farewells from the family, the embraces and the tears. Going to America then was almost like going to the moon. Perhaps had my mother or aunts known that one day I would be back in Russia as a representative of a Jewish state—or that, as prime minister of Israel, I would one day welcome to that country hundreds upon hundreds of Russian Jews with embraces and tears—they might have cried less bitterly, although God knows the intervening years were to bring more than tears to the family we left behind. And perhaps if we had known that throughout Europe thousands of families like ours were on the move, headed toward what they, too, firmly believed would be, and was indeed a better life in the New World, we would have been less frightened. But we knew nothing about the many women and children who were traveling then under similar conditions from countries like Ireland, Italy and Poland to join husbands and fathers in America, and we were very scared.

Not many of the details of our voyage to Milwaukee in 1906 have remained in my memory, and most of what I think I remember is probably made up of stories my mother and Sheyna told to me. What I do recall is that we had to cross the border into Galicia secretly because, three years earlier, my father had helped a friend reach America by taking that man's wife and daughters with him on his papers and pretending that they were members of his family. So when our turn came to leave, we also had to pretend to be other people. Although we obediently memorized false names and details about our make-believe identities and Sheyna sternly drilled us all until we were letter-perfect— even Zipke—our actual crossing was effected by bribing the police with money mother had somehow managed to raise. In the confusion most of our "luggage" got lost—or perhaps it was stolen. Anyhow, I remember that early one icy spring morning we finally entered Galicia and the shack in which we waited for the train that would take us to the port. We lived in that unheated shack for two days, sleeping on the unheated floor, and I remember that Zipke cried most of the time until the train finally arrived and distracted her. Then we moved on past a series of unremembered stops, first to Vienna and then to Antwerp, where we spent another forty-eight hours in an immigration center, this time waiting for the ship that was to take us to America and to my father.

It was not a pleasure trip, that fourteen-day journey aboard ship. Crammed into a dark, stuffy cabin with four other people, we spent the nights on sheetless bunks and most of the days standing in line for food that was ladled out to us as though we were cattle. Mother, Sheyna and Zipke were seasick most of the time, but I felt well and can remember staring at the sea for hours, wondering what Milwaukee would be like. The ship was packed with immigrants from Russia—pale, exhausted and just as scared as we were. Sometimes I would play with some of the other children who, like us, were traveling steerage, and we would tell each other stories about the unimaginable riches that awaited us in the *goldene medina*. But I suspect that they, too, knew that in fact we were all bound for places about which we knew nothing at all and for a country that was totally strange to us.

2. A Political Adolescence

My father met us in Milwaukee, and he seemed changed: beardless, American-looking, in fact a stranger. He hadn't managed to find an apartment for us yet, so we moved, temporarily and not comfortably, into his one room in a house that belonged to a family of recently arrived Polish Jews. Milwaukee—even the small part of it that I saw during those first few days—overwhelmed me: new food, the baffling sounds of an entirely unfamiliar language, the confusion of getting used to a parent I had almost forgotten. It all gave me a feeling of unreality so strong that I can still remember standing in the street and wondering who and where I was.

I suppose that being together with his family again after so long was not easy for my father either. At any rate, even before we really had time to rest up from the journey or get to know him again, he did a most extraordinary thing: Refusing to listen to any arguments, on the morning after our arrival he determinedly marched all of us downtown on a shopping expedition. He was horrified, he said, by our appearance. We looked so dowdy and "Old World," particularly Sheyna in her matronly black dress. He insisted on buying us all new clothes, as though by dressing us differently he could turn us, within twenty-four hours, into three American-looking girls. His first purchase was for Sheyna—a frilly blouse and a straw hat with a broad brim covered in poppies, daisies and cornflowers. "Now you look like a human being," he said. "This is how we dress in America." Sheyna immediately burst into tears of rage and shame. "Maybe that's how you dress in America," she shouted, "but I am certainly not going to dress like that!" She absolutely refused to wear either the hat or the blouse, and I think perhaps that premature excursion downtown marked the actual start of what were to be years of tension between them.

Not only were their personalities very different, but for three long years Father had been receiving complaining letters from Mother about Sheyna and her selfish behavior, and in his heart of hearts he must have blamed Sheyna for his not having been able to go back to Russia again and the family's having to come to the States. Not that he was unhappy in Milwaukee. On the contrary, by the time we came he was already part of the immigrant life there. He was a member of a synagogue, he had joined a trade union (he was employed, off and on, in the workshops of the Milwaukee railroad), and he had accumulated a number of cronies. In his own eyes, he was on the way to becoming a full-fledged American Jew, and he liked it. The last thing in the world he wanted was a disobedient, sullen daughter who demanded the right to live and dress in Milwaukee as though it were Pinsk, and the argument that first morning in Schuster's Department Store was soon to develop into a far more serious conflict. But I was delighted by my pretty new clothes, by the soda pop and ice cream and by the excitement of being in a real skyscraper, the first five-story building I had ever seen. In general, I thought Milwaukee was wonderful. Everything looked so colorful and fresh, as though it had just been created, and I stood for hours staring at the traffic and the people. The automobile in which my father had fetched us from the train was the first I had ever ridden in, and I was fascinated by what seemed like the endless procession of cars, trolleys and shiny bicycles on the street.

We went for a walk, and I peered, unbelieving, into the interior of the drugstore with its papier-mâché fisherman advertising cod-liver oil, the barbershop with its weird chairs and the cigar store with its wooden Indian. I remember enviously watching a little girl of my own age dressed up in her Sunday best, with puffed sleeves and high-button shoes, proudly wheeling a doll that reclined grandly on a pillow of its own, and marveling at the sight of the women in long white skirts and men in white shirts and neck-ties. It was all completely strange and unlike anything I had seen or known before, and I spent the first days in Milwaukee in a kind of trance.

Very soon we moved to a little apartment of our own on

Walnut Street, in the city's poorer Jewish section. Today that part of Milwaukee is inhabited by blacks who are, for the most part, as poor as we were then. But in 1906 the clapboard houses with their pretty porches and steps looked like palaces to me. I even thought that our flat (which had no electricity and no bathroom) was the height of luxury. The apartment had two rooms, a tiny kitchenette, and a long corridor that led to what was its greatest attraction for my mother, though I must say not for anyone else: a vacant shop that she instantly decided to run. My father, whose feelings were undoubtedly hurt by her obvious lack of faith in his ability to support us and who was not about to give up his carpentry, announced at once that she could do whatever she wanted, but that he would have nothing to do with the shop. It became the bane of my life. It began as a dairy store and then developed into a grocery; but it never prospered, and it almost ruined the years I spent in Milwaukee.

Looking back at my mother's decision, I can only marvel at her determination. We hadn't been in Milwaukee for more than a week or two; she didn't know one word of English; she had no inkling at all of which products were likely to sell well; she had never run or even worked in a shop before. Nonetheless, probably because she was so terrified of our being as abjectly poor as we had been in Russia, she took this tremendous responsibility on herself without stopping to think through the consequences. Running the shop meant not only that she had to buy stock on credit (because obviously, we had no surplus cash), but also that she would have to get up at dawn everyday to buy whatever was needed at the market and then drag her purchases back home. Fortunately, the women in the neighborhood rallied around her. Many of them were new immigrants themselves, and their natural reaction was to assist another newcomer. They taught her a few English phrases, how to behave behind the counter, how to work the cash register and scales and to whom she could safely allow credit.

Like my father's ill-fated shopping trip, my mother's hasty decision about the shop was almost certainly part of my parent's reaction to finding themselves in such alien surroundings. Unfortunately, both these precipitous steps were to have a serious effect not only on Sheyna's life, but

also on mine, although in very differing degrees. As far as I
was concerned, my mother's enforced absence every morning meant that somebody had to mind the store while she
was gone. Sheyna, like my father, refused to help out in
any way. Her socialist principles, she declared, made it impossible. "I did not come to America to turn into a shop-
keeper, into a social parasite," she declared. My parents
were very angry with her, but characteristically, she did
what her principles dictated: She found herself a job. Before we took it in, Sheyna was in a tailorshop making but-
tonholes by hand. It was difficult work, which she did
badly and she hated, even though she was now entitled to
consider herself a real member of the proletariat. After she
had earned the grand total of thirty cents for three days'
work, my father made her give up the job and help
Mother. Still, she managed to get away from the shop
whenever she could, and for months I had to stand behind
the counter every morning until mother returned from the
market. For an eight- or nine-year-old girl, this was not an
easy chore.

I started school in a huge, fortresslike building on
Fourth Street near Milwaukee's famous Schlitz beer factory, and I loved it. I can't remember how long it took me
to learn English (at home, of course, we spoke Yiddish,
and luckily, so did almost everyone else on Walnut Street),
but I have no recollection of the language ever being a real
problem for me, so I must have picked it up quickly. I
made friends quickly, too. Two of those early first- or
second-grade friends remained friends all my life, and both
live in Israel now. One was Regina Hamburger (today
Medzini), who lived on our street and who was to leave
America when I did; the other was Sarah Feder, who became one of the leaders of Labor Zionism in the United
States. Anyhow, coming late to class almost every day was
awful, and I used to cry all the way to school. Once a policeman even came to the shop to explain to my mother
about truancy. She listened attentively but barely understood anything he said, so I went on being late for school
and sometimes never got there at all—an ever greater disgrace. My mother—not that she had much alternative—
didn't seem to be moved by my bitter resentment of the
shop. "We have to live, don't we?" she claimed, and if my
father and Sheyna—each for his and her own reasons—

would not help, that didn't mean *I* was absolved of the task. "So it will take you a little longer to become a *rebbetzin* [a bluestocking]," she added. I never became a bluestocking, of course, but I learned a lot at that school.

More than fifty years later—when I was seventy-one and a prime minister—I went back to that school for a few hours. It had not changed very much in all those years except that the vast majority of its pupils were now black, not Jewish, as in 1906. They welcomed me as though I were a queen. Standing in rows on the creaky old stage I remembered so well, freshly scrubbed and neat as pins, they serenaded me with Yiddish and Hebrew songs and raised their voices to peal out the Israeli anthem "Hatikvah" which made my eyes fill with tears. Each one of the classrooms had been beautifully decorated with posters about Israel and signs reading SHALOM (one of the children thought it was my family name), and when I entered the school, two little girls wearing headbands with Stars of David on them solemnly presented me with an enormous white rose made of tissue paper and pipe cleaners, which I wore all day and carefully carried back to Israel with me.

Another of the gifts I got that day in 1971 from the Fourth Street School was a record of my grades for one of the years I had spent there: 95 in reading, 90 in spelling, 95 in arithmetic, 85 in music and a mysterious 90 in something called manual arts, which I cannot remember at all. But when the children asked me to talk to them for a few minutes, it was not about book learning that I chose to speak. I had learned a lot more than fractions or how to spell at Fourth Street, and I decided to tell those eager, attentive children—born, as I myself had been, into a minority and living, as I myself had lived, without much extravagance (to put it mildly)—what the gist of that learning had been. "It isn't really important to decide when you are very young just exactly what you want to become when you grow up," I told them. "It is much more important to decide on the way you want to live. If you are going to be honest with yourself and honest with your friends, if you are going to get involved with causes which are good for others, not only for yourselves, then it seems to me that that is sufficient, and maybe what you will be is only a matter of chance." I had a feeling that they understood me.

At all events, apart from the shop and being aware of

Sheyna's evident misery about having to live at home—and having had to part from Shamai, who was still in Russia and whom she missed terribly—I think back on those five years in Milwaukee with great pleasure. There was so much to see and do and learn that the memory of Pinsk was almost erased. Almost but not entirely. In September, when we had been in America just over three months, my father told us to be sure and watch the famous Labor Day parade in which he, too, would be marching. Dressed up in our new clothes, Mother, Zipke and I took our places at the street corner he recommended and waited for the parade to begin, not knowing exactly what a parade was, but looking forward to it anyway. Suddenly Zipke saw the mounted police who led the parade. She was absolutely terrified. "It's the Cossacks! The Cossacks are coming!" she screamed, and sobbed so hard that she had to be taken home and put to bed. But for me, that parade—the crowds, the brass bands, the floats, the smell of popcorn and hot dogs—symbolized American freedom. Police on horseback were actually escorting the marchers, instead of dispersing them and trampling them underfoot, as they were doing in Russia, and I felt the impact of a new way of life. I didn't know or care about it then—or for some time to come—but it occurs to me now that both Wisconsin in general and Milwaukee in particular were blessed by extremely liberal administrations. Milwaukee was a city of immigrants and had a strong socialist tradition, a socialist mayor for many years and America's first socialist congressman, Victor Berger. But of course, we would have responded in much the same way to any kind of parade in any American city; or maybe there really was some special vitality about Labor Day then, in Milwaukee, a city to which so many German liberals and intellectuals had fled after the unsuccessful Revolution of 1848 and which was as well know for its vigorous trade unions as for its beer gardens. In any case, to see my father marching on that September day was like coming out of the dark into the light.

Of course, it would have been better if Mother hadn't had to work so hard, if Sheyna had got along with my parents more easily, if we had had just a little more money. But even as it was, even with my secret sorrow about and loathing for the store, those early years in Milwaukee were full and good years for me. But they were less so for

Sheyna. Almost everything was going wrong for her: She found it extremely hard to adjust, to learn English, to make friends. She was inexplicably tired, even listless, much of the time, and the constant conflict at home didn't help— particularly my parents' rather clumsy attempts to find her a husband as though Shamai didn't exist. At eighteen, her life had suddenly narrowed itself down to almost nothing.

Then—it seemed like a miracle—she heard about an opening in a big men's clothing factory in Chicago and was taken on there. But for some reason that didn't work out either, and she started work as a seamstress in a smaller factory—a sweatshop really—for women's clothing, where she finally settled down. After a while, however, she was back in Milwaukee with a badly infected finger. Had she been less run-down, it would have undoubtedly healed faster, but as it was, she had to stay at home for several weeks. My parents were triumphant about her return; but I felt very sorry for her, and during those weeks when I helped take care of her, comb her hair and dress her, we grew closer.

One day Sheyna told me that she had received a letter from our aunt in Pinsk about Shamai. He had been ar- rested but had escaped from jail and was now on his way to New York. Thoughtfully our aunt enclosed his address, and Sheyna wrote to him at once. By the time she heard from him her finger was completely healed, she had found another job, and she was busily planning Shamai's arrival in Milwaukee.

Needless to say, I was delighted that her spirits had lifted at last. Perhaps now that Shamai was coming, Sheyna would always be happy, and perhaps the atmosphere at home would change. I couldn't remember much about Sha- mai, but I looked forward to his arrival with a heart almost as full as Sheyna's. Unfortunately my parents, especially my mother, greeted the news very differently. "Marry Sha- mai? But he has no prospects at all," my mother said. "He is a pauper, a greenhorn, a young man with no means and without a future." And—never mind the logic—at the same time he was too good for Sheyna; he came from a well-to-do family which would never give its approval. The match would be a disaster, however one looked at it.

As usual, Sheyna went ahead and did as she thought best. She rented a room for Shamai and summoned him to

Milwaukee. He arrived depressed and unsure of himself, but Sheyna was confident that together they could overcome any and all obstacles. Eventually he got a job in a cigarette factory, and they set about learning English at night.

Then Sheyna fell ill, and this time it was serious: The diagnosis was TB. She would have to go to a sanatorium, and it was questionable whether she would ever be allowed to get married. Her entire world caved in. She gave up her job and her room and reluctantly came home again. My parents hid their worry for her under a storm of rebuke and nagging, and I did my childish and not very effective best to cheer up both Sheyna and Shamai and to intervene on their behalf with my mother and father whenever the tension seemed about to explode into a crisis.

Within a few weeks everything had changed: Sheyna left for the Jewish Hospital for Consumptives in Denver, Shamai left for Chicago and began forlornly to look for a job there, and I started saving up my meager lunch money for stamps that I sent to Sheyna so she could write to me. Once or twice I even "borrowed" the stamp money from Mother's till, but since there was no correspondence at all between Sheyna and my parents, I was really her only link with the family—which I thought justified the crime.

In my letters to Sheyna, which to my surprise she kept for years, I told her about my life at home. "I am very good in school," I wrote in 1908. "I am now in third high and in June I am going to pass in fourth low." And: "I can tell you Pa does not work yet and in the store it is not very busy and I am glad you are out of bed."

The truth of the matter was that work of the kind my father could do was very scarce in Milwaukee then, and even when he did get a job, it was usually only for twenty or twenty-five cents an hour. The shop was also doing very badly, and to make matters worse, my mother suffered a miscarriage and the doctor made her stay in bed for several weeks, so I cooked and scrubbed, hung laundry and minded the store, choking back tears of rage all the time because I was forced to miss even more school. But I didn't want Sheyna to have to worry about us. She was having a hard enough time herself in Denver, and I saw to it that my letters remained rather terse, though I never deliberately misled her regarding the state of affairs at home.

I missed Sheyna terribly, but the years without her went by quickly. School absorbed me, and in the little time I had left over from the shop (and helping my mother at home and Zipke—who had now been renamed Clara by Mr. Finn, the school principal—with her lessons) I read and read. Every now and then, Regina Hamburger and I got tickets (perhaps through the school) for a play or a movie. Those were very rare treats, and to this day I remember one of them distinctly—seeing *Uncle Tom's Cabin* and suffering through every moment of it with Uncle Tom and Eva. I can still recall jumping to my feet in the theater, literally beside myself with hatred for Simon Legree. I think it must have been the first thing I ever saw on a stage, and I told my mother and Clara the story over and over again. It had a kind of special reality for all of us.

One important (to me) event took place when I was in the fourth grade. I got involved in my first "publc work." Although school in Milwaukee was free, a nominal sum was charged for textbooks, which many of the children in my class could not afford. Obviously, someone had to do something to solve the problem, so I decided to launch a fund. It was to be my very first experience as a fund raiser, but hardly the last!

Regina and I collected a group of girls from the school, explained the purpose of the fund, and we all painted posters announcing that the American Young Sisters Society (we were particularly proud of the name we had made up for our nonexistent organization) was to hold a public meeting on the subject of textbooks. Then, having appointed myself chairman of the society, I hired a hall and sent invitations out to the entire district. Today it seems incredible to me that anyone would agree to rent a hall to a child of eleven but the meeting took place as scheduled one Saturday evening, and dozens of people came. The program was very simple: I spoke about the need for all children to have textbooks whether they had money or not, and Clara, who was then about eight, recited a socialist poem in Yiddish. I can see her now, a very small redheaded child, standing in front of the audience in Packen Hall, gesturing dramatically as she declaimed. The result of the meeting was twofold: A considerable amount of money (by our standards) was raised, and my parents showered praise on Clara and me while walking home that evening. I only wished that Sheyna had been there. But at least I could send her the clipping together with a picture of me, from a Milwaukee paper that referred to the meeting:

> A score of little children who give their playtime and scant pennies to charity, and charity organized on their own initiative, too. . . . And it is worthy of comment that this charity is itself a loud comment on the fact that little children may go to the public schools without proper provision of books. Think what that means. . . .

The letter I wrote to Sheyna about the meeting was almost as dramatic as Clara's poem. "Dear Sister," it read, "Now I can tell you that we had the greatest success that there ever was in Packen Hall. And the entertainment was grand. . . ."

My mother had begged me to write out my speech, but it made more sense to me to say what I wanted to say, what was in my heart. And considering it was my first public address, I think I did rather well. At any rate, with the exception of major policy statements at the United Nations or the Knesset, I never got into the habit of using a written text, and I went on for the next half century making "speeches from my head," as I described it to Sheyna in that letter I wrote her in the summer of 1909.

Eventually, during the summer vacation, Regina and I got our first real jobs: very junior salesgirls at a department store downtown. What we really did, for the most part, was wrap packages and run errands; but we made a few dollars each week, and I was released from having to stand in our shop all day. My father, very much against his will, took my place there, and it was with a sense of great independence that I pressed my skirt and blouse each evening and set out at dawn each day to walk to work. It was a long walk, but the carfare I saved went toward a winter coat—the first thing I ever bought with my own earnings.

When I was fourteen, I finished elementary school. My marks were good, and I was chosen to be class valedictorian. The future seemed very bright and clear to me. Obviously I would go on to high school and then, perhaps, even become a teacher, which is what I most wanted to be. I thought—and still think today—that teaching is the nob-

lest and the most satisfying profession of all. A good
teacher opens up the whole world for children, makes it
possible for them to learn to use their minds and in many
ways equips them for life. I *knew* I could teach well, once I
was sufficiently educated myself, and I wanted that kind of
responsibility. Regina, Sarah and I talked endlessly about
what we would do when we grew up. I remember on those
summer evenings how we sat for hours on the steps of my
house and discussed our futures. Like teenage girls everywhere, we thought these were the most important decisions
we would ever have to take—other than marriage, and that
certainly seemed much too remote to be worth our talking
about.

My parents, however—as I ought to have understood
but did not—had other plans for me. I think my father
would have liked me to be educated, and at my Fourth
Street graduation ceremony his eyes were moist. He understood, I believe, what was involved; but in a way his own
life had defeated him, and he was unable to be of much
help to me. My mother, as usual and despite her disastrous
relationship with Sheyna, knew exactly what I should do.
Now that I had finished elementary school, spoke English
well and without an accent and had developed into what
the neighbors said was a *dervaksene shein meydl* (a fine,
upstanding girl), I could work in the shop full time and
sooner or later—but better sooner—start thinking seriously
about getting married, which, she reminded me, was forbidden to women teachers by state law.

If I insisted on acquiring a profession, she said, I could
go to secretarial school and learn to become a shorthand
typist. At least, I wouldn't remain an old maid that way.
My father nodded his head. "It doesn't pay to be too
clever," he warned. "Men don't like smart girls." As
Sheyna had done before me, I tried in every way I knew to
change my parents' mind. In tears, I explained that nowadays an education was important, even for a married
woman, and argued that in any case I had no intention
whatsoever of getting married for a very long time. Besides,
I sobbed, I would rather die than spend my life—or even
part of it—hunched over a typewriter in some dingy office.

But neither my arguments nor my tears were of any
avail. My parents were convinced that high school, for me
at least, was an unwarranted luxury—not only unneces-

sary, but undesirable. From the distance of Denver, Sheyna (now convalescent and out of the sanatorium) encouraged me in my campaign, and so did Shamai, who had joined her there. As they wrote to me often, sending their letters to Regina's house so my parents wouldn't find out about the correspondence, I knew that Shamai had first washed dishes in the sanatorium and had then been taken on to work in a small dry-cleaning plant that served one of the big Denver hotels. In his spare time he was studying book-keeping, and most important of all, in the face of repeated warnings from Sheyna's doctor, they were going to be married. "Better we should live less," Shamai had decided, "but live together." It was to be one of the happiest marriages I ever knew, and despite the doctor's grim prediction, it lasted forty-three years and resulted in three children.

My parents were very upset at first, especially my mother. "Another lunatic with grand ideas and not a cent in his pocket," she sniffed. *That* was a husband for Sheyna? *That* was a man who could support and take care of her? But Shamai not only loved Sheyna, but understood her. He never argued with her. When he was sure that he was right about something, he went ahead and did it, and Sheyna always knew when she was beaten. But when she wanted something and it was really important to her, Shamai never stood in her way. To me, the news of their marriage meant that Sheyna now had what she most needed and wanted— and that I at last had a brother.

In my secret letters to Denver I wrote in detail about the continuing fights over school that were making my life at home almost intolerable and were leading me to decide to become independent as soon as possible. That autumn, the autumn of 1912, I defiantly began my first term at Milwaukee's North Division High School and in the afternoons and on weekends worked at a variety of odd jobs, determined never again to ask my parents for money. But none of this helped; the disputes at home went on and on.

The last straw was my mother's attempt to find me a husband. She didn't want me to get married at once, of course, but she very much wanted to be sure not only that I would get married at what she considered a reasonable age, but that, unlike Sheyna, *I* at least would marry somebody substantial. Not rich—that was out of the question— but at least solid. In actual fact, she was already discreetly

negotiating with a Mr. Goodstein, a pleasant, friendly, relatively well-to-do man in his early thirties, whom I knew
because he used to come into the store now and then to
chat for a while. Mr. Goodstein! But he was an old man!
Twice my age! I sent a furious letter to poor Sheyna. The
reply came from Denver by return mail. "No, you
shouldn't stop school. You are too young to work; you
have good chances to become something," Shamai wrote.
And with perfect generosity: "My advice is that you should
get ready and come to us. We are not rich either, but you
will have good chances here to study, and we will do all we
can for you." At the bottom of his letter, Sheyna wrote her
own warming invitation: "You must come to us immediately." There would be enough of everything for all of us,
she assured me. All together, we would manage. "First,
you'll have all the opportunities to study; second, you'll
have plenty to eat; third, you'll have the necessary clothes
that a person ought to have."

I was very touched then by their letter, but reading it
today, I am even more moved by the readiness of those two
young people, still so far from being established themselves,
to take me in and share whatever they had with me. That
letter, written from Denver in November, 1912, was a
turning point in my life because it was in Denver that my
real education began and that I started to grow up. I suppose that if Sheyna and Shamai had not come to my rescue, I would have gone on fighting with my parents, crying
at night and still somehow going to high school. I can't
imagine that I would have agreed under any circumstances
to stop studying and marry the probably much-maligned
Mr. Goodstein; but Sheyna and Shamai's offer was like a
lifeline, and I grabbed at it.

In the years that have passed since that November, I
have also often thought of Sheyna's last letter to me before
I joined her in Denver. "The main thing," she wrote, "is
never to be excited. Always be calm and act coolly. This
way of action will always bring you good results. Be
brave." That was advice about running away from home;
but I never forgot it, and it stood me in good stead within a
few years when I came to what was to be my real home,
the land in which I was prepared to fight to the death in
order to stay.

Getting to Denver was not easy. I couldn't possibly expect my parents to agree to my leaving home and going to live with Sheyna. They would never have permitted it. The only solution was not to tell them anything at all, simply to leave. It might not be the bravest course, but it would certainly be the most efficient. Sheyna and Shamai sent me some money for a railway ticket, and Regina and I planned my flight down to the last detail. The first problem to be solved was how to get together enough money to pay for the rest of my ticket. I borrowed some of it from Sarah (which was certainly a very "cool" action considering that I had no idea how I would ever pay it back), and Regina and I persuaded a number of new immigrants on the street into taking English lessons from us for ten cents an hour. When we had collected enough money, we set about plotting the details of my departure.

Regina was a marvelously devoted ally. Not only was she absolutely trustworthy and could be relied on not to tell either my parents or her own anything about my plans, but she was also very imaginative—although now that I write about it, I have an idea that she must have mixed up my escape with an elopement. What she proposed—and what I very gladly accepted—was that since we lived above the store then, I should make a bundle of my clothes (just as well that it wouldn't be a very large bundle) and lower it the evening before my departure to Regina, who would spirit it away to the baggage department of the railway station. Then, in the morning, instead of going to school, I could go right to the train.

When the fateful evening arrived, I sat in the kitchen with my parents as though it were just an ordinary night, but my heart was very heavy. While they drank tea and talked, I scribbled a note for them to read the next day. It was only a few words and not very well-chosen ones at that. "I am going to live with Sheyna, so that I can study," I wrote, adding that there was nothing for them to worry about and that I would write from Denver. It must have hurt them terribly to read that note the next morning, and if I were to write it today, I would do so only after much thought and with very great care. But I was under extreme pressure then and only fifteen. Before I went to sleep that night, I went over to Clara's bed and looked at her for a minute. I felt very guilty about leaving her without even saying good-bye, and I wondered what would happen to

her now that both Sheyna and I were out of the house, as I
thought, for good. Clara was growing up to be the most
"American" of us all, a quiet, shy, undemanding little girl,
whom everyone liked but to whom I had never paid much
attention and whom I didn't really know very well. Now
that I was going to leave her, I remember feeling a sudden
sense of responsibility. It turned out, though I couldn't
have known it then, that being the only child at home was
actually to make her life easier. My parents were far more
lenient with Clara than they had ever been with Sheyna or
with me, and my mother even spoiled her sometimes. We
weren't a demonstrative family, but that night I stroked her
face and kissed her, although she slept through my farewell.

Very early the next morning, I left home as planned and
went to the station to board the train for Denver. I had
never traveled alone before, and the idea that trains run
according to a timetable had never occurred either to me
or to my fellow conspirator, so I was still sitting nervously,
with a pounding heart, on a bench in the station when my
parents opened and read the note I had written for them at
home. But as the Yiddish saying goes, I had considerably
more luck than brains, and somehow or other, in the confusion, no one looked for me until the train had left and I was
on my way to Sheyna, knowing that I had done something
that deeply wounded my mother and father, but that was
truly essential for me. In the two years that I was to spend
in Denver, my father, unforgiving, wrote to me only once.
But from time to time my mother and I exchanged letters,
and by the time I came back I no longer had to battle for
the right to do as I wanted.

Both Regina and Clara sent me vivid descriptions of the
reaction at home to my leaving. Clara's letter was full of
accusations. My mother had wept bitter tears, then dried
her eyes and gone to see Regina's mother. By the time Regina came back from school feeling very pleased with herself her mother had heard all about her "disgraceful" assistance to me, and Regina was given a sound hiding. Good
friend that she was, she avoided any recriminations in her
own letter to me. On the contrary, it was rather apologetic.
"I hope I won't hurt your feelings, but everyone thought
you had eloped with an Italian. How they got the idea, I
can't get at . . . Now, dear Goldie, don't get angry at me
for writing this, but I can't help it, you asked. . . . I

burned with anger and resentment, but what could I do?"

In Denver, life really opened up for me, although Sheyna
and Shamai proved to be almost as strict as my parents and
we all had to work very hard. Shamai was now employed
as a part-time janitor at the local telephone company, as
well as worked in his own dry-cleaning shop, and the arrangement was that when I got through with school in the
afternoons, I would take over for him in the shop so that
he could go on to his second job. I could do my homework
at the shop, and if a customer wanted something pressed, I
could do that, too.

In the evenings, after supper, Sheyna badgered me to go
on with my schoolwork, but I was fascinated by the people
who used to drop into their home and sit around talking till
late at night. I found the endless discussions about politics
much more interesting than any of my lessons. Sheyna's
small apartment had become a kind of center in Denver for
the Jewish immigrants from Russia who had come out west
for treatment at Denver's famous Jewish Hospital for Consumptives (in which Sheyna herself had spent so much
time). Almost all of them were unmarried. Some of them
were anarchists, some were socialists, and some were Socialist Zionists. They all had either been ill or were still ill;
they all were uprooted; they all were passionately and vitally concerned with the major issues of the day. They
talked, argued and even quarreled for hours about what
was happening in the world and what ought to happen.
They talked about the anarchist philosophy of Emma Goldman and Peter Kropotkin, about President Wilson and the
European situation, about pacificism, the role of women in
society, the future of the Jewish people—and they drank
cup after cup of tea with lemon. I blessed those rounds of
tea because although Sheyna so strongly disapproved of the
hours I was keeping, I managed to stay up most nights by
volunteering to disinfect the cups afterward—an offer
which was rarely turned down.

Of course, I was always the youngest person in the room,
and my Yiddish wasn't as literary as that of many of the
debaters; but I hung on their words as though they would
change the fate of mankind and sometimes, after a while,
even voiced opinions of my own. Much of that nightly conversation was way over my head. I didn't know what dia-
lectical materialism was or who exactly Hegel, Kant or

Schopenhauer was, but I knew that socialism meant democracy, the right of workers to a decent life, an eight-hour workday and no exploitation. And I understood that tyrants had to be overthrown, but dictatorship of any kind—including that of the proletariat—held no appeal for me at all.

I listened raptly to everyone hold forth, but it was to the Socialist Zionists that I found myself listening most attentively, and it was their political philosophy that made the most sense to me. I understood and responded fully to the idea of a national home for the Jews—one place on the face of the earth where Jews could be free and independent—and I took it for granted that in such a place no one would be in want or be exploited or live in fear of other men. I was much more interested in the kind of Jewish national home the Zionists wanted to create in Palestine than I was in the political scene in Denver itself or even in what was then going on in Russia.

The talk at Sheyna's—almost all of it in Yiddish, since very few of the talkers spoke English well enough to express themselves properly on these urgent ideological matters—was very free-ranging. There were evenings in which most of the discussion was about Yiddish literature—Sholom Aleichem, I. L. Peretz, Mendele Mocher Sforim—and other evenings that were devoted to specific questions such as women's suffrage or the future of trade unionism. I was interested in all of it, but when they talked about people like Aaron David Gordon, for instance, who had gone to Palestine in 1905 and helped found Degainia (the kibbutz established three years later on the deserted tip of the Sea of Galilee), I was absolutely fascinated and found myself dreaming about joining the pioneers in Palestine.

I can't remember which of the young men it was who first spoke about Gordon at Sheyna's, but I do remember how fascinated I was by what he told us about the middle-aged man with a long white beard that made him look like Father Time, a man who had never done any physical work before and who came to Palestine with his family when he was almost fifty to till its soil with his own hands and write about the "religion of labor," as his credo came to be known by his disciples. The building of Palestine, Gordon believed, was to be *the* greatest Jewish contribution to humanity. In the Land of Israel the Jews would find

their way to the making of a just society through their own
physical labor—provided that each and every individual
made a massive personal effort in this direction.

Gordon died in 1922—one year after I myself came to
Palestine—and I never met him. But I think that of all the
world's great thinkers and revolutionaries about whom I
heard so much at Sheyna's, he is perhaps the one I would
most have wanted to know myself—and would most like
my grandchildren to meet.

I was enthralled also by the romantic story of Rachel
Bluwstein, a delicate girl from Russia who came to Palestine at about the same time as Gordon and was deeply influenced by him. A remarkably gifted poet, she went to
work on the soil in a new settlement near the Sea of Galilee, where some of her most beautiful poems were written.
Although she didn't know a word of Hebrew before she
came to Palestine, she was to become one of the first modern Hebrew poets, and many of her poems have been set to
music and are still sung in Israel. Eventually she became
too ill (with the TB that killed her at forty) to work the
land she loved so much, but she was still alive and young
when I was in Denver and heard her name for the first
time from someone who had known her in Russia.

Years later, when it became fashionable for young people to deride my generation for its rigidity, conventionality
and loyalty to the Establishment, it was about intellectual
rebels such as A. D. Gordon and Rachel and dozens of
others like them that I used to think. No modern hippie, in
my opinion, has ever revolted as effectively against the Establishment of the day as those pioneers did at the beginning of the century. Many of them came from the homes of
merchants and scholars; many even from prosperous assimilated families. If Zionism alone had fired them, they could
have come to Palestine, bought orange groves there and
hired Arabs to do all the work for them. It would have
been easier. But they were radicals at heart and deeply believed that only self-labor could truly liberate the Jews
from the ghetto and its mentality and make it possible for
them to reclaim the land and earn a moral right to it, in
addition to the historic right. Some of them were poets,
some were cranks, some had stormy personal lives; but
what they all had in common was a fervor to experiment,
to build a good society in Palestine, or at least a society

that would be better than what had been known in most parts of the world. The communes they founded—the kibbutzim of Israel—have endured, I am sure, only because of the genuinely revolutionary social ideal that underlay and still underlies them.

At all events, to the extent that my own future convictions were shaped and given form, and ideas were discarded or accepted by me while I was growing, those talk-filled nights in Denver played a considerable role. But my stay in Denver had other consequences, too. One of the less articulate young men who came to Sheyna's often was a gentle, soft-spoken friend of theirs, Morris Meyerson, whose sister had met Sheyna in the sanatorium. Morris' family had immigrated to America from Lithuania and, like ours, was very poor. His father had died when he was just a boy, and he had gone to work early in life in order to support his mother and three sisters. At the time we met, he was working sporadically as a sign painter.

Although he never raised his voice, even during the stormiest of the nightly sessions, I think I first noticed Morris because although he was almost entirely self-educated, he was so well versed in the kind of things that neither I nor most of Sheyna and Shamai's friends knew anything at all about. He loved poetry, art and music and knew and understood a great deal about them, and he was prepared to talk at length on the merits of a given sonnet or sonata to someone as interested (and as ignorant) as I was.

When Morris and I came to know each other better, we started to go to free concerts in the park together, and Morris patiently introduced me to the joys of classical music, read Byron, Shelley, Keats and the *Rubáiyát* of Omar Khayyám to me and took me to lectures on literature, history and philosophy. To this day I associate certain pieces of music with the clear, dry mountain air of Denver and the wonderful parks in which Morris and I walked every Sunday in the spring and summer of 1913.

One of those concerts left an indelible impression on me, not so much because of the music—which I barely heard—but because of the threateningly clouded sky. I had wanted to look my best for Morris, so the day before I had gone off to a five-and-ten-cent store and bought myself a new straw hat. The only color in stock was bright red, so I took it, a little reluctantly because it seemed rather too frivolous; but it was very becoming, and I hoped that Morris would like it. I still remember with horror the first afternoon I wore it. It was a cloudy, dark day, and Morris didn't even notice my hat; but I was so terrified that it would rain and that the red would trickle all over me that I spent the entire time worrying about the weather.

I admired Morris enormously—more than I had ever admired anyone except Sheyna—not only for his encyclopedic knowledge, but for his gentleness, his intelligence and his wonderful sense of humor. He was only five or six years my senior, but he seemed much older, much calmer and much steadier. Without at first being aware of what was happening to me, I fell in love with him and couldn't help realizing that he loved me, too, although for a long time we said nothing to each other about the way we felt.

Sheyna was very fond of Morris, too, and luckily approved of my seeing him so often. Still, that was not, she informed me sternly, why she had helped me run away from home. I had come to Denver to study, she said, not to listen to music or learn poetry. She took her mission of being my guardian very seriously, which meant watching me like a hawk, and after several months I began to feel that I might just as well have stayed in Milwaukee. Shamai put much less pressure on me; but the reins had definitely tightened, and I began to feel very restive. One day, after Sheyna had been particularly bossy, ordering me about and scolding me as though I were still a child, I decided that the time had come for me to try to live alone, without a mother hen and without being nagged all the time, and I marched out of the apartment in the black skirt and white blouse I had been wearing all day without taking anything else with me, not even a nightgown. If I was leaving Sheyna's home and authority, I was not entitled, I thought, to keep anything that Sheyna or Shamai had bought for me. I closed the door behind me, and that, I thought, was that: I was on my own at last.

It was something of a comedown to realize ten minutes later that now I had to find somewhere to live until I could support myself. A little crestfallen but very grateful, I accepted the invitation extended by two of Sheyna's friends who had always been especially nice to me and to whom I confided that for the moment I was homeless. Unfortunately, it was not exactly the best choice of a haven. Both my hosts were in a fairly advanced stage of TB, and to this day I can offer no explanation other than what my mother used to call *a na'ar's mazel* (the luck of a fool) for the fact that I remained free of the disease. They lived in rather cramped quarters that consisted of a room (with a niche at one end of it) and a kitchen. The niche was mine for as long as I wanted it, they told me; but since they both were so sick, I felt I had to let them go to bed early, and I didn't dare switch the light on over my couch when it grew dark. In fact, the only place I could read without bothering them—or be disturbed myself by their nightlong coughing—was the bathroom, where wrapped up in a blanket and armed with Morris' current reading list (which was always terrifyingly long) and a pile of books, I used to spend most of my nights.

At sixteen, of course, one can do without almost everything, including sleep, and I was delighted with my setup—and even more, to be quite honest, with myself. Not only had I found myself somewhere to live, but I had also come to the conclusion that high school would have to wait after all. It was even more important for me to learn to cope with life alone, I told myself, than to acquire the schooling for which I had so longed. The first thing to do now that I had my niche was to find a job. My father used to say, fatalistically, "When you chop wood, you get splinters," so I was now preparing myself for the splinters; a job might be hard to get. But within a day or two I found work in a shop where my chief responsibility was to take measurements for custom-made skirt linings. It wasn't exactly a stimulating or elevating job, but it kept me going and soon made it possible for me to rent a tiny, but at least germ-free, room of my own. Incidentally, one by-product of that job is that even today I find myself automatically giving a quick glance at the hems of skirts and can run one up with total confidence.

I may have felt, and looked, very grown-up for my age, but the truth was that there were many moments when I would have preferred to have been back living with Sheyna, Shamai and their new baby, Judith. I had Morris, of course, about whom I had by now even written to Regina ("He isn't very handsome, but he has a beautiful soul!"), and several other friends—in particular a most extraordinary young man from Chicago called Yossel Kopelov, who chose to be a barber because he was convinced that this was the only profession that would leave him enough time to read and with whom Morris and I spent a lot of time. But friends and family are very different things, and I was sometimes almost as lonely as I was independent, particularly when Morris wasn't around. However, since neither Sheyna nor I was very good at admitting to error or apologizing, it took several months before we finally made up.

Then, after I had been on my own for about a year, I got a letter from my father, the only one he wrote to me during this period. It was very short and to the point: If I valued my mother's life, he wrote, I should come back home at once. I understood that for him to write to me at all meant swallowing his pride and he would only have done so if I were really needed at home. So Morris and I talked it over, and I decided that I should go back—to Milwaukee, to my parents and Clara and to high school. To be quite frank, I was not sorry to return, although it meant leaving Morris, who had to stay on in Denver for a while till his sister recovered. One night, before I left, Morris told me shyly that he was in love with me and wanted to marry me. I explained happily and just as shyly that I loved him, too, but that I was still much too young for marriage, and we agreed that we would have to wait. In the meantime, we would keep our relationship a secret and write to each other all the time. So I left for Milwaukee in what I told Regina the next day was a blissful state of mind.

3. I Choose Palestine

I found our home quite changed. My parents had mellowed a lot, their economic situation had improved, and Clara was already a teen-ager. The family had moved to a new and nicer apartment on Tenth Street, and it bustled with people and activity. My mother and father now took it for granted that I would be going to high school, and even after I had been graduated from high school and registered in October, 1916, at the Milwaukee Normal School (the Teachers' Training College, as it was then called), they made no protest at all. I don't think that they really ever believed I needed any more education; but they let me have my way, and our relationships improved beyond recognition—although my mother and I still fought sometimes. One of those rows was about Morris' letters to me. My mother felt that it was her duty to know all about my romance in Denver (about which someone, perhaps Sheyna, had written to her), and once she even made Clara read a bunch of them and translate them into Yiddish for her (Morris and I wrote to each other in English, which my mother found hard to read). Aware of the fact that she had done something dreadful, Clara told me about it later, swearing that she had left out what she tactfully called "the more personal bits," and from then on Morris sent his letters to Regina's house.

As their life grew easier, my parents had become much more active in the community. My mother—who, I think, was probably never aware of the need to express herself beyond the immediate family circle or the routine of family duties—had nonetheless developed what must have been a natural talent for good works, perhaps through the people she met in the shop and the problems they unfolded before her while she weighed rice and sugar for them. At all events, she was now busier than ever, but much more relaxed, despite her habit (which annoyed me tremendously) of claiming that nothing in Milwaukee was as good as Pinsk. Take the fruit, for instance. Who ate fruit in Pinsk? Certainly not my family! Still my mother went on praising the invented delights of "home" and I eventually learned not to explode each time she did it.

Mother was forever cooking and baking, listening to some stranger's troubles or helping run a neighborhood bazaar or raffle. She was a very good cook and taught me how to make plain, nourishing Jewish food, the kind that I prepare and like to this day—although my son and one of my grandsons, who consider themselves gourmet cooks and make everything with wine, turn up their noses at my "unimaginative" food. (Not that they ever refuse it!) On Friday evenings, when we sat down for the Sabbath meal—chicken soup, gefilte fish, and meat braised with potatoes and onions, with a carrot-and-prune tzimmes on the side—in addition to Father, Clara and me, there would almost always be guests from out of town, whose visits frequently lasted for several weeks.

During World War I my mother turned our house into a make-shift depot for the boys who had volunteered for the Jewish Legion and were going to fight under the Jewish flag within the framework of the British army to liberate Palestine from the Turks. Most of the young men from Milwaukee who joined the legion (immigrants exempt from conscription) left our house equipped with little bags embroidered by my mother in which they kept their prayer shawls and phylacteries and much larger bags full of cookies still warm from her oven. With an open heart, she ran an open house, and when I try to remember her at this period, I hear the sound of her laughter in the kitchen as she fried onions, peeled carrots and chopped fish for Friday night, talking to one of the guests who would be sleeping on our living-room couch for the weekend.

My father, too, had become deeply involved with Jewish life in the city. Most of the people who slept on our famous couch during those years were socialists (Labor Zionists) from the East, Yiddish writers on lecture tours or out-of-town members of the B'nai B'rith (the Jewish fraternal order to which my father belonged). My parents, in short, had become completely integrated, and their home had turned into a kind of institution, as far as the Jewish community in Milwaukee and its visitors were concerned. Of the many people whom I first met or first heard speak in public then, some were to become major influences not only on my life, but, much more important, on the Zionist movement, particularly on Labor Zionism. And some of them were later to be numbered among the founding fathers of the Jewish state.

If I pause now to recollect the men who made the strongest impression upon me as they passed through Milwaukee when I was in my late teens, I think first of all of such Jews as Nachman Syrkin, who was one of the most fiery ideologists of Labor Zionism. A Russian Jew who had studied philosophy and psychology in Berlin, Syrkin returned to Russia after the 1905 Revolution and then emigrated to the United States, where he became the leader of the American Poalei Zion (Labor Zionists). Syrkin believed that the sole hope of the Jewish proletariat (which he labeled the "slave of slaves" or the "proletariat of the proletariats") lay in mass immigration to Palestine, and he wrote and spoke brilliantly on this subject throughout Europe and the States. My favorite story about Syrkin (whose daughter Marie became my close friend and later my biographer) has to do with a debate that took place between him and Dr. Chaim Zhitlovsky, a celebrated protagonist of Yiddish as the Jewish national language, who believed primarily in the civil-rights aspects of the Jewish problem, while Syrkin was a passionate Zionist and an advocate of the revival of the Hebrew language. In the course of the debate Syrkin said to Zhitlovsky, "All right, let's come to an agreement to divide it all up. You take everything that already exists, and I'll take everything that doesn't exist yet. For example, *Eretz Yisroel* [The Land of Israel] as a Jewish state does *not* exist, so it's mine; the Diaspora exists, so it's yours. Yiddish exists, so it's yours, but since Hebrew isn't spoken yet in everyday life, it'll be mine. Whatever is real and concrete will be yours, and whatever you call empty dreams will be mine."

Shmarya (his full name was Shmaryahu) Levin was another. He was without doubt one of the greatest Zionist orators of the day, a man whose wit and charm captivated thousands of Jews all over the world. Since those days, like Syrkin, he has somehow joined the company of the shadow figures of Zionism, known to most young Israelis, if at all, only because even the smallest town in Israel has a street named after him. But for my generation, he was one of the giants of the movement, and to the extent that my friends and I idolized anyone, it was the elegant, persuasive, deeply intellectual Shmarya. His humor was typically Yiddish, so much so that it is hard to translate any of its subtlety into English. For instance, he used to say sardonically of the Jews, "True, we are a very small people, but remarkably hard to take." Or, equally ironically, he described Palestine as a marvelous country where the winters can be spent in Egypt (where it rarely rains) and the summers in the mountains of Lebanon. Once at a Zionist congress in Switzerland, he came up to me excitedly. "Golda," he said, "I have a splendid moral for a fable. All I need now is the fable itself." In 1924 Shmarya settled in Palestine, and our paths crossed frequently; but my own vivid memory of him still has to do with the sheer dread that once seized me in Chicago in 1929, when I was asked to speak in public, for the first time at a very large meeting, and to my horror spotted Shmarya in one of the very first rows. "My God," I thought, "how can I open my mouth when Shmarya is sitting there?" But I did and afterward was overwhelmed with pleasure when he told me how well I had spoken.

The first Palestinians I ever encountered were Yitzhak Ben-Zvi, who was to become Israel's second president; Ya'akov Zerubavel, a well-known Labor Zionist and writer, and David Ben-Gurion. Ben-Zvi and Ben-Gurion came to Milwaukee to recruit soldiers for the Jewish Legion in 1916, soon after they had been expelled from Palestine by the Turks and ordered never to return. Zerubavel, whom the Turks sentenced to prison, had succeeded in escaping but was sentenced *in absentia* to fifteen years of penal servitude.

I had never met people like those Palestinians before or heard stories like those they told about the *yishuv* (the small Jewish community of Palestine, which had by then been reduced from some 85,000 to only 56,000). This was my first clue to how terribly it was suffering from the brutality of the Turkish regime, which had already brought normal life in the country to a virtual standstill. They were in a fever of anxiety about the fate of the Jews of Palestine and convinced that an effective Jewish claim could be made to the Land of Israel after the war only if the Jewish people played a significant and visible military role, *as Jews,* in the fighting. In fact, they spoke about the Jewish Legion with such feeling that I immediately tried to volunteer for it—and was crushed when I learned that girls were not being accepted.

I knew much about Palestine by then, of course, but my knowledge was rather theoretical. These Palestininans, however, talked to us not about the vision or theory of Zionism, but about its reality. They told us in detail about the fifty-odd Jewish agricultural settlements that had already been established there and described Gordon's Settlement, Degania, in a way that made it seem real and populated by flesh-and-blood people, not mythical heroes and heroines. They told us also about Tel Aviv, which had just been founded on the sand dunes outside Jaffa, and about Hashomer, the *yishuv's* Jewish self-defense organization, in which both Ben-Zvi and Ben-Gurion were active. But most of all, they talked about their hopes and dreams for an Allied victory over the Turks. They all had worked very closely together in Palestine, and Ben-Zvi often talked about a fourth member of their group, Rachel Yanait, who was later to become his wife. As I listened to him, I began to think of her as typical of the women of the *yishuv,* who were proving that it was possible to function as wives, mothers and comrades-in-arms, enduring constant danger and hardship, not only without complaining, but with a sense of enormous fulfillment, and it seemed to me that she, and women like her, were doing more—without the benefit of publicity—to further the cause of our sex than even the most militant of suffragists in the United States or England.

I listened spellbound to the Palestinians, and I took every opportunity to hear them speak, although it was months before I actually dared approach them myself. Ben-Zvi and Zerubavel were much easier to talk to than Ben-Gurion; they were far less dogmatic and warmer. Ben-Zvi came to Milwaukee—and to my parents' house—several times and would sit around, sing Yiddish folk songs with us and patiently answer all our questions about Palestine. He was a tall, rather gawky young man with a sweet smile and a kindly, hesitant manner that drew people to him at once.

As for Ben-Gurion, my first recollection is actually of

not meeting him. He was due to visit Milwaukee, and it had been arranged for him to give a speech on Saturday night and to have lunch at our home on Sunday. But that Saturday night the Chicago Philharmonic was in town. Morris (who had come to Milwaukee by then) had invited me to the concert weeks earlier, and I felt duty bound to go with him, although I can't say that I enjoyed the music much that night. The next morning the Labor Zionists informed me that the lunch was off. It wasn't proper, they said, that a person who couldn't be bothered to hear Ben-Gurion speak—and of course, I was too embarrassed to explain the extremely personal reason for my absence—should have the privilege of entertaining him for lunch. I was heartbroken but thought that they were perfectly right, and I accepted their verdict stoically. Later, of course, I did meet Ben-Gurion, and I remember remaining in awe of him for a very long time. He was one of the least approachable men I ever knew, and there was something about him even then that made it hard for one to get to know him. But more about Ben-Gurion later.

Slowly, Zionism was beginning to fill my mind and my life. I believed absolutely that as a Jew I belonged in Palestine and that as a Labor Zionist I could do my full share within the *yishuv* to help attain the goals of social and economic equality. The time hadn't quite come yet for me to decide to live there. But I knew that I was not going to be a parlor Zionist—advocating settlement in Palestine for others—and I refused to join the Labor Zionist Party until I could make a binding decision.

In the meantime, there was school and Morris. While he was still in Denver, we corresponded regularly, and through those letters—read again after so many years—I see that there were also the small, private tragedies and doubts of every girl's life. Why didn't I have black hair and big, lustrous eyes? Why wasn't I more attractive? How *could* Morris love me? *Did* he really love me? I must have peppered my letters to him with ill-concealed requests for assurance and the assurance always came—although it was not always phrased very gallantly. "I have repeatedly asked you not to contradict me on the question of your beauty," he wrote once. ". . . You pop up every now and then with these same timid and self-deprecating remarks which I cannot bear."

In other letters we tried rather awkwardly to plan a joint future and inevitably ended up by writing to each other about Palestine. Morris was much less sure then about Zionism than I was, and he had a more romantic, more speculative nature. He dreamed of a world in which every-one would live in peace, and national self-determination held little attraction for him. He didn't really think that a sovereign state would help the Jews much. It would just be one more state with the usual burdens and penalties of statehood. One letter from him dated 1915 reads in part:

> I don't know whether to be glad or sorry that you seem to be so enthusiastic a nationalist. I am altogether passive in this matter, though I give you full credit for your activity, as I do to all others engaged in doing something toward helping a distressed nation. The other day I received a notice to attend one of the meetings. . . . But since I do not care particularly as to whether the Jews are going to suffer in Russia or in the Holy Land, I didn't go. . . .

By 1915 Jews were suffering in many places, and my father and I started to work together on a variety of relief activities, which were incidentally to bring us closer together. As was true in World War II most of the relief work for the Jews of Europe during World War I was handled by the newly formed Joint Distribution Committee. But unlike the situation in the 1940s, this remarkable organization was then being run badly from New York by a handful of bureaucrats, and it had become the target of much sharp criticism. One result of this situation was that the Jewish labor groups decided to found their own organization, which they called the People's Relief Committee, and that was the organization my father and I joined. We worked very well together and today it fills me with joy to recall our cooperation—although I think it came as somewhat of a shock to my father that I was now on my way to becoming an adult. Father represented his trade union in the new organization and I was the spokesman of a small Labor Zionist literary group which I attended after school. Although I no longer even remember its undoubtedly fancy name, I was very active on its behalf. We had a lecture program for which we invited speakers from Chicago. They would come out to Milwaukee every two weeks and we would hold what would now be called seminars on various facets of Yiddish literature. We were chronically short of money to pay the speakers' expenses and rent a hall, so we used to charge our members twenty-five cents per lecture—which was quite a lot in those days. I remember one man who appeared at each lecture but refused to pay anything. "I'm not coming for the lecture," he explained, "I am coming to ask a question."

Toward the end of the war another major Jewish movement was born: the American Jewish Congress, which was to play a leading role in the formation of the World Jewish Congress in the 1930s. In those days, although the Bund (which had been transplanted in the United States) didn't object to the formation of the congress, it violently opposed its pro-Palestine orientation. In 1918, when elections to the congress were held in all the large Jewish communities of the United States (this was the first time that the Jews of America held elections of their own), feelings ran high. The Zionists pulled one way; the Bundists pulled the other. Both my father and I were actively involved in that election campaign and felt strongly that the congress must put itself on record as favoring Zionism.

If you wanted to campaign among Jews, I decided, the logical place to locate yourself was the neighborhood synagogue, particularly around the time of the Jewish High Holidays, when everyone went to the synagogue. But since only men were allowed to address the congregation, I put up a box just outside the synagogue, and people walking out on their way home had no alternative other than to hear at least part of what I had to say about the Labor Zionist platform. I suppose I had more than my fair share of self-confidence in this respect, if not in others, and when a great many people actually stopped to listen to me outside the synagogue, I thought I ought to try it again in another place. But this time my father learned about my plans, and we had a terrible row. Moshe Mabovitch's daughter, he stormed, was not going to stand on a box in the street and make a spectacle of herself. It was out of the question, a *shandeh* (a disgrace). I tried to explain that I had committed myself to going, that my friends were waiting for me in the street, that it was a perfectly acceptable thing to do. But my father was so angry that he didn't listen to a word I said. My mother stood between us like a referee at a fight, and we went on arguing at the top of our voices.

In the end neither of us gave in. My father, red in the face with fury, said that if I insisted on going, he would come after me and publicly pull me home by my braid. I had no doubt that he would do so, because he generally kept his promises. But I went anyway. I warned my friends on the street corner that my father was on the war path, got up on my soapbox and made my speech—not without some panic. When I finally got home, I found my mother waiting up for me in the kitchen. Father was already asleep, she told me, but he had been at the street corner meeting and had heard me speak. "I don't know where she gets it from," he said to her wonderingly. He had been so carried away listening to me perched on my soapbox that he had completely forgotten his threat! Neither of us referred to the incident again but I consider that to have been the most successful speech I ever made.

Around this time I began to do some real teaching. The Labor Zionists had started a part-time *folkschule*, a Yiddish school in the Jewish Center of Milwaukee. Classes were held on Saturday afternoons, Sunday mornings and one other afternoon during the week. I taught Yiddish: reading, writing and some literature and history. Yiddish, it seemed to me was one of the strongest links that existed between the Jews, and I loved teaching it. It wasn't what the Milwaukee Normal School was preparing me for, but I found it exceedingly satisfying to be able to introduce some of the Jewish children of the city to the great Yiddish writers I so admired. English was certainly a fine language, but Yiddish was the language of the Jewish street, the natural, warm, intimate language that united a scattered nation. In retrospect, I can see that I was a bit of a prig then about Yiddish; there was no greater crime in my eyes at that stage than, for instance, for one of the children to mix Yiddish with English, and I even thought for a while that the Jews should have two languages in Palestine—Hebrew and Yiddish. How could one think of doing away with Yiddish there, of all places? When the Labor Zionists wanted to start an English-speaking branch and asked me to take it over, I would have nothing to do with it. If people wanted to belong to the Paolei Zion, they should at least

know Yiddish! It turned out, of course, that I would have
been better off applying myself to Hebrew, but who knew it
then? Eventually, when we went to Palestine, I learned Hebrew, of course, but my Hebrew has never really been as
good as my Yiddish.

I enjoyed teaching in the *folkschule*. I liked the children,
they liked me, and I felt useful. When the weather was
good, on Sunday evenings, after the *folkschule*, my family,
some of my pupils and Morris (whenever he was in Milwaukee) used to go on picnics. My mother made mounds
of food, and we sat under a tree in a park and sang. I
didn't smoke in those days, and I sang at the drop of a hat.
Then my parents would fall asleep on the grass, their faces
covered by the weekend edition of one of the Yiddish newspapers published in the East—which they read every weekend from start to finish—and the rest of us would talk
about life, liberty and the pursuit of happiness until the sun
set. Then we would go home, and my mother would give
the whole crowd of us supper.

Right after the war, when anti-Semitic pogroms broke
out in the Ukraine and Poland (those in the Ukraine being
largely the responsibility of the notorious commander of the
Ukrainian army, Simon Petlyura, whose units did away
with whole Jewish communities), I helped organize a protest march down one of Milwaukee's main streets. The
Jewish owner of a big department store in town got wind of
my plans and asked me to come and see him. "I understand that you intend to lead a demonstration down Washington Avenue," he said. "If you do so, I want you to know
that I shall leave town." I told him that I had no objection
at all to his leaving town and that I had every intention of
going on with the plans for the march. However unwise he
thought it might be, I wasn't at all worried about what people would think or say. There was nothing for the Jews to
be ashamed of; on the contrary, I told him, I was sure that
by showing how we felt about the murder and maiming of
Jews overseas, we would earn the respect and sympathy of
the rest of the city.

It turned out to be an extremely successful parade.
Hundreds of people took part in it, although it seemed impossible that there were so many Jews in Milwaukee. Incidentally, it came as a surprise to me (despite my brave
words to the store owner) that so many non-Jews partici-

pated in that demonstration, and I can remember looking into the eyes of the people who lined the street watching us and feeling how supportive they were. There weren't many protest marches in those days, and we got publicity all over America. Perhaps this is the place to mention that I myself never once encountered any anti-Semitism in Milwaukee. Although I lived in a Jewish district and mingled almost entirely with Jews, both in school and out of it, I had non-Jewish friends, of course—as I was to have all my life. But even though they were never quite as close to me as were the Jews, I felt entirely free and at home with them.

I think it was while we were marching through town that day that I realized I could no longer postpone a final decision about Palestine. However hard it might be for those who were dearest to me, I could no longer put off making up my mind about where I was going to live. Palestine, I felt, not parades in Milwaukee, was the only real, meaningful answer to Petlyura's murderous mobs. The Jews must have a land of their own again—and I must help build it, not by making speeches or raising funds, but by living and working there.

First I formally joined the Labor Zionist (Poalei Zion) Party and thus took what for me was the first step on the road to Palestine. At that time the Labor Zionists didn't have a youth movement. According to the constitution of the party, only people over the age of eighteen were accepted. I was only seventeen, but I was already known to the membership and they let me enter the party ranks. Now I had to persuade Morris to come to Palestine with me, for it was unthinkable to me that we should not be together. I knew that even if he agreed to come, we would still have to wait for a year or two—until we raised enough money for the fare, among other things—but it was imperative that before we got married, Morris should know that I was determined to live there. I didn't present the situation to him as an ultimatum, but I did make my position clear. I wanted very much to marry him, *and* I was set on going to Palestine. "I know that you don't feel as strongly about living in Palestine as I do," I told him, "but I beg you to come with me." He loved me very much, Morris answered, but regarding Palestine, he wanted to think things over and arrive at a decision himself. Today I understand that Morris, who was far more perceptive and far less impulsive than I, wanted time not only to weight the matter of moving to Palestine, but also perhaps to consider whether we were really suited to each other after all. In one of his letters to me from Denver, just before he came to Milwaukee, he had written: "Have you ever stopped to think whether your Morris has the one attribute without which all other refinements are worthless, namely, 'the indomitable will'?" It was one of those questions that lovers ask each other without expecting or wanting an answer, and I, for my part, had no doubt at all. But Morris was wiser, and he must have sensed that in some ways we were very different and that, one day, those differences between us might be important.

So we parted for a while. I left school (how strange that it had lost its great importance for me) and went to Chicago, where, on the strength of my having worked briefly as a librarian in Milwaukee, I was taken on by the public library. Sheyna, Shamai and their two children had also moved to Chicago, and Shamai was working on a Jewish newspaper there. Regina came to Chicago, too, and I saw all of them quite often, although I stayed with another friend. But I wasn't at all happy. The idea that I might have to choose between Morris and Palestine made me miserable, and for the most part I kept to myself, working for the Labor Zionists in my free time—making speeches, organizing meetings, raising funds. There was always something that took precedence over my private worries and therefore served to distract me from them—a situation that was not to change much in the course of the next six decades.

Fortunately, though he still had reservations about Palestine, Morris was sufficiently drawn to the idea of living there to agree to go with me. His decision was undoubtedly influenced to some extent by the fact that in November, 1917, the British government announced that it favored "the establishment in Palestine of a National Home for the Jewish People" and that it would use "its best endeavours to facilitate the achievement of this objective." The Balfour Declaration—so named because it was signed by Arthur James Balfour, who was then Britain's foreign secretary—was couched in the form of a letter addressed by Lord Balfour to Lord Rothschild. It came just at the time that British forces, under General Allenby, had begun to conquer

Palestine from the Turks, and although in years to come the ambiguous way in which it was worded was to be responsible for virtually endless bloodshed in the Middle East, in those days it was greeted by the Zionists as laying the foundations at last for a Jewish commonwealth in Palestine. It goes without saying that the announcement filled me with elation. The exile of the Jews had ended. Now the ingathering would really begin, and Morris and I together would be among the millions of Jews who would surely stream to Palestine.

It was against the background of this historic event that we were married, on December 24, 1917, at my parents' home. Our marriage was preceded by a familiarly long and emotional argument with my mother. We wanted a civil ceremony, no guests and no fuss. We were socialists, tolerant of tradition, but in no way bound by ritual. We neither wanted nor needed a religious ceremony. But my mother informed me in no uncertain terms that a civil marriage would kill her, that she would have to leave Milwaukee at once, and that I would be shaming the entire family, to say nothing of the Jewish people, if I didn't have a traditional wedding. Besides, would it harm us? So Morris and I gave in; indeed, what damage would fifteen minutes under the *chuppah* (bridal canopy) do to our principles? We invited a few people, my mother prepared refreshments, and Rabbi Scheinfeld, one of the true Jewish scholars of Milwaukee, officiated. To her dying day, my mother talked with pride about the fact that Rabbi Scheinfeld had come to our house for my wedding, had made a short speech wishing us well and even—though he was known for his strictness in religious matters and as a rule refused to drink, let alone eat, anything outside his home—had tasted a piece of her cake. I have often thought about how much that day meant to her and how I nearly ruined it for her by wanting to be married at city hall.

Once again I was starting out on a new life; Pinsk, Milwaukee, Denver all had been stations of a sort. Now I was nearly twenty, a married woman and on my way to the only place that had any real call on me. But since the war had not ended yet, it was still impossible for us to go. There wasn't any room in my parents' house for us, nor did we particularly want to live with anyone, so we moved to a place of our own for a couple of years. I traveled a lot for the Labor Zionists during those years and seem to have been away from Milwaukee almost as much as I was there. I suppose that I was in demand because I was young, I could speak both English and Yiddish fluently, and I was prepared to travel anywhere and to make speeches without much prior notice.

A few months after our marriage, for instance, the party decided to publish a national newspaper and asked me to help sell shares. My father was furious. "Who leaves a new husband and goes on the road?" he shouted, outraged at the idea that I had agreed to be away from Milwaukee for more than a day or two. But Morris understood that I couldn't say no to the movement, and I went. I was away for several weeks. The arrangement was that I was paid $15 a week and all my expenses, which meant my meals—except for dessert. I paid for ice cream myself. No one in the party stayed in a hotel then. I slept over at the homes of other party members, sometimes even in the same bed with my hostess.

I went as far as Canada, and then it turned out that I didn't have a passport. Morris wasn't an American citizen yet, and married women couldn't take out their own citizenship then. My father's passport would have helped, but he was still very angry with me for going and refused to send it to me. So I tried to cross into Canada without a passport. Of course, when we reached Montreal, I was taken off the train, marched to the immigration office and politely but firmly questioned as to what I thought I was doing. Not only did I come from Milwaukee—a socialist town—but I was Russian-born! I suppose the Canadian authorities thought for a minute that they had caught a Bolshevik agent, but in the end a prominent Labor Zionist came to my rescue, and I was finally allowed into Canada. I sold a lot of shares for that paper (it was called *Die Zeit* [The Times]), and when we moved to New York, I sold it on the streets in the evenings. But for all my efforts, it didn't survive long.

For Morris my frequent absences must have been very difficult, but he was immensely patient and understanding, and I can see now that in a way I took advantage of his forbearance. Whenever I was out of town, I wrote long letters to him, but they tended to be more about the meeting I had just addressed or the one I was about to address, the situation in Palestine or the movement than about us or our relationship. Morris consoled himself for my being away so much by turning our tiny apartment into the real home that awaited me whenever I was in Milwaukee. He cut out pictures from magazines and framed them to brighten the walls. And although we had no money and he was often without a job (he worked as a sign painter whenever he could), there were always a few flowers in the house when I came back. He spent his free time when I was on the road reading, listening to music and helping Clara weather out some of the storms and stresses of adolescence. They went for long walks together, and Morris took her to concerts and the theater. He was really the only member of the family to spend any time with her, and she adored him and told him all her secrets.

In the winter of 1918 the American Jewish Congress held its first convention in Philadelphia. The main purpose was the formulation of a program (to be presented at the Peace Conference in Versailles) for the safeguarding of the civil rights of the Jews in Europe. To my astonishment and delight, I was chosen to be one of the delegates fom Milwaukee. It was a marvelously stimulating experience; I can still remember how proud I was to have been chosen to represent my own community and what it was like sitting with the rest of the delegation in the overheated train on our way to Philadelphia. I was (as always in that period) the youngest in the group and, in a way, everyone pampered me—except when it came to giving me assignments. Today when journalists ask me when my political career actually began, my mind always flashes back to that convention, to the smoke-filled hall in a Philadelphia hotel where I sat for hours listening, completely absorbed, to the details of the program being thrashed out, to the excitement of the debates and of being able to cast my own vote. "I tell you that some moments reached such heights that after them one could have died happy," I scribbled ecstatically to Morris.

From Chicago, Sheyna wrote less ecstatic letters warning me that I was becoming much too involved in matters of public—rather than private—concern. "As far as personal happiness is concerned, grasp it, Goldie, and hold it tight," she wrote in one troubled letter. "The only thing I heartily wish you is that you should not try to be what you *ought* to be but what you are. If everybody would only be what they are, we would have a much finer world. . . ." I was quite sure, however, that I could cope with everything and assured Morris that when we got to Palestine at last, I would no longer be constantly on the move.

By the winter of 1920 it began to look as though we might soon really be able to depart. We rented an apartment in Morningside Heights in New York and started to prepare for the trip. Regina and a Canadian couple called Manson (who didn't go to Palestine in the end) and Yossel Kopelov joined us in the flat. In the early spring, we bought tickets for the SS *Pocahontas* and began to rid ourselves of those of our meager possessions that seemed unsuitable for the life we were now going to lead as pioneers. Despite everything we had heard and read about Palestine, our ideas of life there were somewhat primitive; we expected to live in tents, so I cheerfully sold all our furniture, our curtains, the iron, even the fur collar of my old winter coat (because we rather unrealistically believed that there was no need for winter clothes in Palestine). The only thing we agreed to take with us, in fact, was our record player and our records. The record player was the kind you wound by hand—so it could be played even in a tent—and we would at least have music in the wilderness for which we were headed. For the same reason, I stocked up on blankets, of all things. If we were going to sleep on the ground, better we should be prepared for it.

Then we began a round of farewells. On our way to Milwaukee to say good-bye to my parents and Clara, we stopped off in Chicago to part from Sheyna and Shamai. I felt a little anxious about the visit since I knew that Sheyna didn't really approve of our going to Palestine ("Goldie, don't you think there is a middle road for idealism, right here on the spot?" she had asked in one of her recent letters). I remember how we sat in their tiny living room with their children—ten-year-old Judith and three-year-old Chaim—and told them all about the ship, what we were taking with us and so forth. Sheyna listened so attentively to all the details that at one point Shamai said with a smile, "Maybe you'd like to go, too?" To my utter astonishment—and probably hers also—Sheyna suddenly replied, "Yes, I would." For a moment, we thought she was joking, but she was absolutely serious. If we were going because we felt that it was necessary for us to go, then by the same token, it was no less necessary for her to go, too. What's more, she said, if Shamai were willing to stay behind in order to earn the money without which she wouldn't be able to keep them in Palestine, she would take the children with her.

In one sense, it cannot be said that Sheyna's abrupt announcement that day was entirely unexpected. She had been a Zionist since she was a young girl, and although she was much more cautious than I in certain respects, she was fundamentally and profoundly committed to the same cause. Of course, I don't really know just what it was that triggered her actual decision, but I would like to make the point that neither Morris nor Sheyna went to Palestine as my escort. Both of them went because both of them had come to the conclusion that Palestine was where they should be.

I can think of no greater compliment to Sheyna or to the quality of her marriage than Shamai's loving acceptance of that decision. Not that he didn't try hard to get her to change her mind. He pleaded with her to wait until they could all go together and said that she had chosen the worst possible time for her to take the two children, because on May 1, 1921, following a series of attacks on the Jewish settlements in the north of the country, full-scale Arab riots against the Jews had broken out in Palestine. More than forty people, many of them new immigrants, had been murdered and mutilated. Only a year earlier, Jews had been murdered and raped by Arab gangs in the Old City of Jerusalem, and although it was hoped that the British civil administration (which had just taken over from the military) would deal sternly with those responsible for the riots and thus restore calm, violence had just erupted again. Within a few years, Shamai argued, Palestine might be at peace; the Arab nationalists might no longer be able to incite Arab villagers to bloodshed; it might become a reasonably safe country in which to live! But having made her decision, Sheyna was adamant, and even after we learned that a Jew from Milwaukee had been killed in those riots, she serenely continued to pack.

In Milwaukee we parted from my parents and Clara. It wasn't an easy parting, although we took it for granted that eventually, when Clara finished her studies at the University of Wisconsin, they all would follow us to Palestine.

Still, I felt terribly sorry for my parents—especially for my father—when I kissed them good-bye at the station. My father was a strong man and able to bear pain, but that morning he just stood there, tears rolling down his cheeks. And my mother—perhaps remembering her own voyage across the ocean—looked so small and withdrawn.

The American chapter of my life was closing. I was to return to the United States often, in good times and bad and even to remain there for many months at a time. But it was never to be my home again. I took a great deal with me from America to Palestine, more perhaps than I can express: an understanding of the meaning of freedom, and awareness of the opportunities offered to the individual in a true democracy and a permanent nostalgia for the great beauty of the American countryside. I loved America and was always glad to come back to it. But never in all the years that followed have I known one moment of homesickness or ever once regretted leaving it for Palestine. Nor, I am sure, did Sheyna. Of course, at the station that morning I thought I would never be back, and I parted from the friends of my youth very sorrowfully, promising to write and keep in touch.

About our voyage to Palestine aboard the wretched SS *Pocahontas*, one could write a whole book. It was doomed from the outset; whatever could possibly go wrong did, and the miracle was that we managed to live through it all. Because the vessel was known to be absolutely unseaworthy, the crew went on strike even before we embarked. The next day, May 23, 1921, we got under way—but not for long. The moment we put out to sea, supposedly repaired, the crew mutinied, expressing its resentment of the shipping company by tormenting the poor passengers. Not only did the sailors mix sea water with our drinking water and sprinkle salt on our food, but they managed to damage the engines so severely that the ship listed alarmingly and even had to stop altogether now and then. It took a full week to get from New York to Boston, and then we had to wait for another nine days before we could continue the uneasy journey. In Boston, a delegation of Labor Zionists came to visit us aboard ship; they brought refreshments, made speeches and cheered us up by referring to us as their heroic comrades. Three of our group (it numbered twenty-two at the start) proved, understandably enough, not to be so heroic; one old couple and a young bride left the ship in Boston. Sheyna received a pathetic cable from Shamai, begging her to disembark, too, but of course, she refused to budge.

At last we set off again. The voyage across the Atlantic was a nightmare. The mutiny had only subsided somewhat, not ended, and every day there were power cuts, salty water to drink and indescribably bad food. At Ponta Delgada in the Azores, the *Pocahontas* was discovered to be in such bad shape that it required another week for repairs. Four crew members went ashore boasting that they would sink the ship before it got to Naples, and when the captain found out about their talk, he clapped them into irons. In the meantime, we spent the week trying to relax, which was not easy. I remember touring the pretty port town, enjoying the mild climate and the lovely, unfamiliar scenery. One curious aspect of our enforced stopover was that we discovered a tiny Sephardic Jewish community (some thirty people in all) which was extremely observant. The rabbi had died several years earlier, and the community—like my grandfather—was so worried about the possibility of violating the Jewish dietary laws that it decided to forgo eating meat permanently. By the time we left the Azores we had been en route for one month, but we still had to face the horror of the rest of the voyage. During the last lap of our trip—the semimutiny still in force—the ship's refrigerator was smashed, so we had to make do with rice and salty tea three times a day, but we were kept from being bored by a succession of incredible dramas. First of all, one of the passengers died, and since the *Pocahontas'* cooling facilities no longer functioned, the body was simply thrown overboard. Then the captain's brother, who was also on board, went stark raving mad and had to be chained and locked up in his cabin. Finally, in a state of justified depression, just before we reached Naples, the captain killed himself, although some people said he was murdered.

The state of affairs aboard the *Pocahontas* had not escaped attention abroad, and a rumor spread among our friends in New York and Boston that we had all gone down with the ship. But in Naples we were able to write home that we were more or less all right. We stayed in Naples for five days, ironing out the inevitable complications over our passports, buying oil lamps and some food and looking for our baggage, which had disappeared. Finally, we boarded a train for Brindisi.

There we met up with a group of Labor Zionists from Lithuania who had actually reached Palestine twice before but had been turned away. Now they were going to try to enter the country again. We had never met "real" pioneers of our own age before, and we were very impressed by them. They reminded me of people like Ben-Zvi and Ben-Gurion, although they were much younger. Compared to us, they were so experienced and hardy, and they seemed so sure of themselves. In Europe they had worked on training farms established by the Zionist movement, and they obviously regarded themselves, not without reason, as being infinitely superior to us. They made it quite clear that we were "soft," spoiled immigrants from the United States, members of the bourgeoisie, in fact, who would probably run away from Palestine after a few weeks. Although we were all bound for the same destination on the same ship, they were going to travel as deck passengers and wanted nothing to do with us. I could hardly take my eyes off them; they were everything I wanted and hoped to be myself—dedicated, austere and determined. I admired and envied them enormously and wanted them to accept us as comrades, but they were very aloof.

In a letter written to Shamai from Brindisi, Yossel described the Lithuanians as they appeared to us. "Real Hercules," he wrote, "who are ready to build a land on just foundations with their backs. And not only a land but a new language . . . splendid human material which would be the pride of any people."

When we boarded the ship that was to take us to Alexandria, I suggested to my companions that we give up our "luxurious" cabins and join the young Lithuanians on deck. No one was very keen about the idea, particularly since deck passengers were not entitled to any hot meals and by now we were all looking forward to some decent food. But I pressed the point; I argued that in fact, it was our duty as potential pioneers ourselves to start sharing the life of our fellow Zionists as soon as possible and that our behavior, even on board ship, would be indicative of our sincerity and ability to take hardships in our stride. "Let's organize our own 'kitchen' on deck," I proposed, adding that we could probably make some sort of arrangements so that the children in the group wouldn't have to sleep in the open. Gradually, despite their reluctance, I succeeded in wearing my friends down, and the Lithuanians thawed out a bit. For a few dollars we got the head waiter in the dining room to agree to let the children eat there—after everyone else was through—and we found them empty cabins for the night (except for Sheyna's daughter; I persuaded the chief steward to let her sleep on a couch in the lounge but she had to vacate it at 5 A.M.!). On deck the barriers between the two groups finally collapsed. We told the Lithuanians about life in America, they told us how they had lived in Eastern Europe, and as the stars came out, we sang Hebrew and Yiddish songs together and danced the hora.

But bad luck still dogged us. In Alexandria Egyptian police boarded the ship looking for a couple called Rapaport—"miserable Communists" they called them. There were a pair of Rapaports traveling in our group, but of course, they were the wrong ones. Nonetheless, they were hauled off the ship and questioned for hours. The incident frightened and depressed us all. When the Rapaports finally came back to the ship, we decided to continue on by rail, so we said good-bye to our Lithuanian friends and set off for the station to take the train to El Qantara. On the way to the station we got our first taste of the Middle East at its worst: crowds of beggars—men, women and children wrapped in filthy rags and covered with flies. They made me think of the beggars who had so terrified me in Pinsk, and I knew that if one of them actually touched me, I would scream—pioneer or not. Somehow we pushed and shoved our way through them and got to the train. By now we were so resigned to minor disasters that we weren't really surprised to find it unspeakably dirty. The heat was close to unbearable, and there was no water to be had anywhere; but at least we knew that we were nearly at our journey's end. At last the train moved out of Alexandria, and we were on our way again, a bit more travel-stained and a bit tired, but still able to sing, quite rousingly, about our "Return to Zion."

In El Qantara, covered with dust, we changed trains in the middle of the night. The procedure took hours; the immigration officials, when we finally found them, were in no hurry at all to attend to the necessary formalities and seemed unable to understand why we were all so despondent. I re-

member standing on that dark platform and losing my temper with one of them, to very little avail. But before dawn we
climbed wearily on to our last train, the one that was to
bring us, jolting and jogging, through a blinding sandstorm,
across the Sinai Peninsula to Palestine. Sitting there, on a
hard, dirt-encrusted bench, with one of Sheyna's children
asleep in my arms, I wondered for the first time since we
left Milwaukee whether we would ever really reach Tel
Aviv.

4. The Start of a New Life

Although Tel Aviv looked to me like a large and not very attractive village on that scorching July morning when I first saw it through the filthy windows of the train from El Qantara, it was, in fact, already well on its way to becoming the world's youngest city and the pride of the *yishuv*. I don't know what I had expected it to look like, but I certainly was not at all prepared for what I saw.

Actually all that I (or any of us, for that matter) knew about Tel Aviv at that point was that it had been founded in 1909 by sixty optimistic Jewish families. Some of them had even dared predict that one day their new garden suburb (built on the outskirts of Arab Jaffa) might achieve a population of 25,000. But none of them dreamed in their wildest dreams that within only fifty years Tel Aviv would be a major metropolis, with barely enough housing for its more than 400,000 inhabitants, or that in 1948 it would be the first provisional capital of a Jewish state.

During the war Tel Aviv's entire population had been expelled by the Turks. But by the time we arrived 15,000 people were living there again, and a real building boom was on. Some parts of the town, as I was to discover later, were really very pretty; row upon row of neat little houses, each with its own garden, was set out on paved streets lined with casuarina and pepper trees, through which caravans of donkeys and camels passed, laden with bags of coarse sand that was taken from the seashore for building. But other sections looked—and were—unplanned, unfinished and frightfully untidy. The May Day riots of 1921 had flooded Tel Aviv with Jewish refugees from Jaffa, and when we came, only a few weeks afterward, several hundred of these refugees were still living in ramshackle huts and even in tents.

The population of Tel Aviv in 1921 was made up in part

of Jews who had come to Palestine (mostly from Lithuania, Poland and Russia) in what was known as the Third
Aliyah (or wave) of Zionist immigration and in part of
"old-timers" who had been there from the beginning. Although some of the new immigrants were self-defined "cap-
italists"—merchants and tradesmen who set up small factories and shops—the vast majority were laborers. Just a year
earlier a General Federation of Jewish Labor (the Histadrut) had been established, and within twelve months it already had a membership of more than 4,000.

Although it was only twelve years old, Tel Aviv was rapidly becoming self-governing. It had just been permitted by
the British mandatory government to levy its own taxes on
buildings and workshops and to run its own water system.
Also, although it had no prison—and was not to have one
for many years—it had its own twenty-five-man, all-Jewish
police force, of which everyone was very proud. The main
street (named for Theodor Herzl) was adorned at one end
by the Herzlia High School, which was the town's first and
most imposing building. There were a few other streets, a
small "business district" and a water tower that served as a
gathering place for the young people. Public transportation
was either by small buses or horse-drawn carriages, while
Tel Aviv's mayor, Meier Dizengoff, periodically rode
through town on a splendid white horse.

By 1921 Tel Aviv already had a thriving cultural life; a
number of writers were settling there, among them the
great Jewish philosopher and writer Ahad Ha-Am and the
poet Chaim Nachman Bialik. A workers' theatrical group
called the Ohel (Tent) was already functioning, and so
were a few cafés where lively debates on political and cultural problems went on every afternoon and evening. But
none of this activity or any of Tel Aviv's remarkable potential was at all apparent to us as we pulled into the town's
tiny railway station. We could hardly have arrived at a
worse time; everything—the air, the sand, the white stucco
houses—blazed in the midday sun, and as we stood wilting
on the empty platform, we realized with sinking hearts that
no one was coming to meet us, although we had carefully
written to tell friends of ours in Tel Aviv (who had emigrated to Palestine two years before) when we were due.
Later on we learned that on that very day they had gone to
Jerusalem to complete arrangements for *leaving* the coun-

try, news that added to our mood of confusion and uncertainty.

Anyhow, there we were—after that terrible journey—in Tel Aviv at last. Our dream had come true. The railway station, the houses we could see in the distance, even the deep sand that surrounded us all were part of the Jewish national home. But as we waited there in the glaring sun, not knowing where to go or even where to turn, it was hard to remember just why we had come. Someone in our group (it may have been Yossel) even put our feeling of anticlimax into words. He turned to me and said, only half-jokingly, "Well, Goldie, you wanted to come to *Eretz Yisroel*. Here we are. Now we can all go back—it's enough." I don't remember who said it, but I do remember that I didn't smile.

Suddenly a man came up to us and introduced himself, in Yiddish, as Mr. Barash, the owner of a nearby hotel. Perhaps he could help us. He hailed a carriage for us, and we gratefully piled our luggage into it. Then, as it led the way, we trudged wearily behind it, wondering how far we could manage to walk in the dreadful heat. Just outside the station I caught sight of a tree. It wasn't a very large tree, by American standards, but it was the first one I had seen that day. And I thought that it was like a symbol of the young town itself, growing miraculously out of the sand.

In the hotel we ate, drank and bathed. The rooms were large and light, and Mr. and Mrs. Barash were very hospitable. We cheered up considerably and decided not to unpack or make any plans until we had rested. Then, to our horror, we discovered that the beds bore traces of bedbugs. Mr. Barash denied the accusation very indignantly; maybe there were fleas, he said, but bedbugs? Never! By the time the linen had been changed Sheyna, Regina and I had lost any desire to sleep and we spent the remainder of our first day in Tel Aviv assuring each other that problems more serious than bedbugs probably lay ahead of us.

Early the next morning Sheyna volunteered to go to the market to buy some fruit for the children. In a little while she was back, filled with gloom. Everything was covered with flies, she said; no wrapping paper or paper bags were available; it was all so primitive; and the sun was so strong that she could hardly stand it. I don't think I had ever heard Sheyna complain about anything before, and now I began to wonder how she and I would ever get used to our new life. It was all very well to talk in Milwaukee about pioneering, but was it, after all, possible that we weren't up to facing these minor inconveniences and that those Lithuanians on the trip were right when they thought we were too soft for the country? My sense of uneasiness and guilt about my own failings—to say nothing of my nervousness about Morris' reaction to these unfortunate experiences—lasted throughout our first week in Tel Aviv. Perhaps if we had arrived in the autumn, rather than in the middle of the summer, or stayed closer to the sea and its breezes, it would have been easier. But as it was, we were hot, tired and dispirited most of the time.

On top of everything else, our friends came back from Jerusalem and invited us for Saturday dinner. Not only did they go on at great length about all the difficulties we would encounter, but they fed us hamburgers that tasted of soap, and we couldn't make ourselves swallow them. After some embarrassment all around—and telling the children that they must stop choking and crying—it turned out that a piece of soap had fallen into the precious ground meat. But the explanation didn't make the meat more palatable, and we went back to Mr. Barash's hotel feeling sick as well as dejected.

After a few days there seemed no point in staying at Mr. Barash's hotel any longer. Like that tree near the station, we had to strike roots sooner or later, and besides, our money was running out. True, we had come from America, but we nonetheless had only very limited funds—though no one seemed to believe this. That summer I met a woman in Tel Aviv who threw her arms around me, kissed me and said with tears in her eyes, "Thank God you millionaires have come to us from America. *Now* everything will be all right here!"

Our original plan had been to stay in Tel Aviv for a week or two and then to join a kibbutz. In Milwaukee we had even picked out the kibbutz to which we would apply for membership. But when we made inquiries in Tel Aviv, we were told to wait until the summer was over and then submit formal applications. So instead of starting our conquest of the land at once, we embarked on a far less heroic mission: the conquest of landlords. That wasn't a simple matter either. Housing was very scarce, prices were sky high, and we needed room for at least seven beds. We split up into teams and began to house-hunt feverishly. Within a few days we found a two-room apartment at the end of a still-unpaved street in the oldest part of Tel Aviv, Neveh Zedek, a quarter that was actually founded even before Tel Aviv itself. The apartment had no electricity and no bathroom or toilets; these amenities, shared with some forty other people, were located in the yard. But there was a little kitchen, and we were asked to pay only three months' rent in advance, despite the fact that we were from the States.

We moved in—without much enthusiasm but with great relief—and began to get organized. We borrowed sheets, pots and pans and some cutlery, and Sheyna undertook to housekeep for all of us, cooking on a Primus stove (fueled by kerosene), which periodically and noisily exploded. Regina got a job as a typist in an office; Yossel went to work in a barbershop; Morris was taken on as a sort of bookkeeper in a British public works installation at Lydda, and I began to give private English lessons. Actually, I was asked to teach at the high school, but since we were going to join a kibbutz as soon as possible, I thought it would be better not to commit myself to a steady job. Teaching, however, was regarded by most of the people we met in Tel Aviv then as being too intellectual an occupation for a would-be pioneer, and I had to keep explaining that it was only temporary and that I had not come to Palestine in order to spread American culture.

On the whole, we managed pretty well, although it took a long time for our neighbors to accept the strange American way in which we did things, like putting screens on our windows against flies. Everybody else had big mesh screens to protect them against the stray cats that roamed the city, but against *flies?* What was wrong with flies? Surely they were inevitable in this part of the world? Nonetheless, we persisted in trying to make the apartment livable, and on the whole we succeeded. When our trunks came from Naples, we turned them into sofas and tables. Morris decorated the bare walls for us, and we improvised bedspreads and curtains. Our most cherished possessions, needless to say, were our record player and records, and slowly people began to drop by in the evenings to drink tea and listen to music with us.

I have often been tempted to explain to new immigrants to Israel just how well I understand the difficulties of adjustment and to tell them something of what it was like when I myself first came to Palestine, but I have learned, through bitter experience, that people tend to regard such stories as propaganda or, even worse, as preaching and generally would much rather not listen to them. Still, the fact remains that we had to make our way alone in the land in which we had chosen to live. There was no State of Israel then, no Ministry of Absorption, no Jewish Agency. No one helped us settle or learn Hebrew or find a place to live. We had to do everything for ourselves, by ourselves, and it never occurred to us that anyone else was morally obligated to assist us. Not that we were in any way superior to the immigrants who come to Israel today, nor am I in the least sentimental about the greater discomforts (many of them quite unnecessary) that we faced sixty years ago and for which we were so woefully unprepared. But I am quite convinced, in retrospect, that having always to bear in mind the purpose for which we had come to Palestine and knowing that nobody had asked us to come or had promised us anything did, in the end, make our acclimatization fairly rapid. We knew that it was up to each one of us personally to make our life in Palestine easier or better or more meaningful and that we had no alternative other than to settle in and settle down as quickly as we possibly could.

At all events, though admittedly that first summer was no treat—to add to everything else, Sheyna's son, Chaim, developed badly infected eyes and Judith came down with an attack of boils that persisted for weeks—as far as I know, none of us ever seriously contemplated leaving the country, and gradually as the weeks went by, we began to feel ourselves part of it. Of course, we wrote very cautious letters to our parents and friends, glossing over the more unpleasant aspects of the way we lived. But one letter which I wrote to Shamai after we had been in Palestine for about six weeks expresses something of our feelings about the great adventure:

> Those who talk about returning are the recent arrivals. An old worker is full of inspiration and faith. I say that as long as those who created the little that is here are still here, I cannot leave and you must come.

I would not say this if I did not know that you are
ready to work hard. True, even hard work is hard to
find, but I have no doubt you will find something. Of
course, this is no America, and one may have to suffer
a lot economically. There may even be riots again. But
if one wants one's own land and if one wants it with
one's whole heart, one must be ready for this. When
you come, I am sure we will be able to plan. . . .
There is nothing to wait for.

It was, I suppose, natural that I should feel that way;
after all, I was in my very early twenties, doing exactly
what I wanted to do, physically fit, full of energy and together with the people who meant most to me—my husband, my sister, my best friend. I had no children to worry
about and I didn't really care whether we had an ice box
or not, or if the butcher wrapped our meat in pieces of
newspaper he picked up off the floor. There were all kinds
of compensations for these small hardships, like walking
down the street on our first Friday evening in Tel Aviv
and feeling that life could hold no greater joy for me than
to be where I was—in the only all-Jewish town in the
world, where everyone from the bus driver to our landlady
shared, in the deepest sense, not only a common past, but
also common goals for the future. These people hurrying
home for the Sabbath, each one carrying a few flowers for
the table, were really brothers and sisters of mine, and I
knew we would remain bound to each other for all our
lives. Although we had come to Palestine from different
countries and from different cultures and often spoke different languages, we were alike in our belief that only here
could Jews live as of right, rather than sufferance, and only
here Jews could be masters, not victims, of their fate. So it
was not surprising that for all the petty irritations and
problems, I was profoundly happy.

But when I remember how Sheyna managed to cope
with everything and everybody without ever once suggesting that perhaps it was all too much for her—despite the
fact that both her small children were sick and Shamai was
so far away and the postal service so inefficient that she
only got letters from him months after they were written—
or how determined Morris was to stick it out—despite his
hesitations about coming to Palestine at all or the fact, for

instance, that the books which meant so much to him arrived in Palestine torn and waterlogged—I am filled again with admiration for them and can only wonder whether in their place I myself would have been as adamant about staying. Of course, like those friends who were supposed to meet us when we first arrived, there were newcomers in Palestine even then who couldn't take it and who left—just as there are some who can't take it today and leave. I have always felt sorry for those people because, to my mind, the loss has always been theirs.

In September we applied for membership to Kibbutz Merhavia in the Plain of Jezreel, which we call the Emek. We had chosen this particular kibbutz (as so often happens) for a not very important reason; a friend of Morris' and mine, who had come to Palestine with the Jewish Legion, was already there. We knew very little about Merhavia itself; in fact, we knew very little about kibbutzim in general, other than that they were communal farming settlements in which there was no personal property, no hired labor and no private trading and that the group as such was responsible for all production, all services and the supplying of all individual needs. But we both believed—I with complete faith, Morris less so—that the kibbutz way of life was more likely than any other to offer us a channel for expressing ourselves as Zionists, as Jews and as human beings.

Perhaps at this point, I should say something briefly about the Emek, because the story of the struggle to develop it is so integral a part of the story of the whole Zionist effort. When World War I ended and the Mandate over Palestine was awarded by the League of Nations to Great Britain, the new hopes raised by the Balfour Declaration for the establishment of a full-fledged Jewish national home seemed to be on the way toward fulfillment. Years earlier, however, in 1901, the Jewish National Fund had already been formed by the Zionist movement for the exclusive purpose of buying and developing land in Palestine in the name of the entire Jewish people. And a great deal of the Jewish-owned land in Palestine was bought by the "people"—the bakers, tailors and carpenters of Pinsk, Berlin and Milwaukee. As a matter of fact, ever since I was a little girl, I can remember the small tin blue collection box that stood next to the Sabbath candles in our living room and into which not only we but our guests dropped coins every week, and this blue box was likewise a feature in every Jewish home we visited. The truth is, from 1904 on it was with these coins that the Jewish people began to buy extensive tracts of land in Palestine.

Come to think of it, I am more than a little tired of hearing about how the Jews "stole" land from Arabs in Palestine. The facts are quite different. A lot of good money changed hands, and a lot of Arabs became very rich indeed. Of course, there were other organizations and countless individuals who also bought tracts. But by 1947 the JNF alone—millions of filled blue boxes—owned more than half of all the Jewish holdings in the country. So let that libel, at least, be done with.

About the time that we came to Palestine a number of such purchases were carried out in the Emek—despite the fact that much of the area consisted of the kind of deadly black swamps that inevitably brought malaria and blackwater fever in their wake. Still, what mattered most was that this pestilential land could be bought, though not cheaply; much of it, incidentally, was sold to the Jewish National Fund by a single well-to-do Arab family that lived in Beirut.

The next step was to make this land arable. In the nature of things, private farmers did not and could not interest themselves in a backbreaking and dangerous project which would obviously take years before it showed any profit. The only people who could possibly undertake the job of draining the Emek swamps were the highly motivated pioneers of the Labor Zionist movement, who were prepared to reclaim the land, however difficult the circumstances and regardless of the human cost. What's more, they were prepared to do it themselves, rather than have the work done by hired Arab laborers under the supervision of Jewish farm managers. The early settlers of Merhavia were such people, and many of them lived to see the Emek become Israel's most fertile and loveliest valley, dotted by flourishing villages and collective settlements.

Merhavia (its name means God's wide spaces) was one of the first kibbutzim to be founded in the Emek. In 1911 a group of young people from Europe had set up a farm there, but they barely managed to keep it going. When war broke out in 1914, the combination of malaria, the hostility

of their Arab neighbors and the attempts of the Turkish
authorities to dissuade them from staying finally proved too
strong, and the original group pulled up stakes and dispersed. After the war another group of European pioneers
founded a settlement in the same place, joined by British
and American veterans of the Jewish Legion (and eventually by Morris and me), but later on it, too, dispersed. A
third and final group of Labor Zionist settlers took over
the site in 1929, and this time the group made it—and remained there.

Since we were so anxious to join Merhavia and had applied for membership so quickly, we were very much taken
aback when our application was turned down flat, for reasons that seemed to me to be quite inadequate. As a matter
of fact, at first no one even wanted to explain to us why we
had been rejected; but I insisted on being told the truth,
and we were rather reluctantly informed that there were
two basic objections to us. One was that the kibbutz didn't
want any married people yet; babies were a luxury that the
young settlement couldn't afford. The other reason—and
this was really unacceptable to me—was that the group,
which was made up at that time of about seven women and
thirty men, couldn't imagine that an "American" girl either
could or would do the extremely tough physical work that
was required. Since many of the members had come from
the States, they regarded themselves, understandably I suppose, as experts on everything American, including the
character and capabilities of an "American" girl like myself. And some of the single girls at Merhavia, who were
already veterans in Palestine and who had heard a lot
about American girls from these expert males, objected
even more strenuously to us. I felt as though I were back
again with the Lithuanians, having to prove that even though
I had lived in the States, I was still perfectly capable of doing
a hard day's work. I argued fiercely that no one had the
right to make such assumptions and that it was only fair to
give us a chance to show what we could do. One of the
specific points against me, I remember, was that in Tel
Aviv I had chosen to give English lessons rather than do
physical work; a decision that apparently indicated how
"spoiled" I was.

We won the battle. We were invited to come to Merhavia for a few days so that the members could look us

over and make their minds up about us on the spot. I was sure that in the end they would let us stay—which was, in fact, what happened. Our Tel Aviv "commune" began to disintegrate; Regina left for a new job, and Yossel also moved. Only Sheyna and the children remained in the apartment. I remember happily packing for Merhavia one hot evening in late September and suddenly realizing that in a way Morris and I were walking out on Sheyna, leaving her alone with an apartment she couldn't afford to maintain by herself, with Shamai still thousands of miles away and both the children still ill. I asked her if she thought we should stay in Tel Aviv a little longer, but she wouldn't hear of any change in our plans. "I am going to rent one of the two rooms," she said crisply, "and look for work. Don't worry about me." She would try, she said, to get taken on as a volunteer nurse at the Hadassah Hospital, which had just opened in Tel Aviv, and perhaps eventually she would be put on the payroll. As for Shamai, she was sure that he would be able to come to Palestine soon. In the interim she could manage. Human nature being what it is, I pretended to believe her, although in my heart of hearts I knew that however hard life in Merhavia might be for us, it would be easier than whatever faced Sheyna on her own in Tel Aviv.

Today Merhavia is a big, bustling settlement with a regional high school to which children come from all over the Emek. Like many of the other great kibbutzim, it has successfully combined industry with agriculture and now houses a factory for plastic pipes and a printing press. The men and women of modern Merhavia live well, although they still work hard. Their rooms are attractive and comfortable, the collective dining room is spacious and air-conditioned, and the kitchen is fully mechanized, all without having to sacrifice or even radically to change any of the principles on which life in kibbutzim was based back in 1921. Today kibbutz members still work an eight-hour day at whatever jobs are assigned to them by the work committee, although nowadays they are usually able to do the work they do best, have been trained to do and enjoy. Everyone still takes turns with chores—serving in the dining room, working in the kitchen, doing guard duty and so on—and everyone participates in all major decisions affecting the settlement, which are discussed and voted on at the weekly general meeting. As was true in 1921, the kibbutz children are still brought up together; they eat together, sleep in dormitories and study together—although, of course, their parents' room is still home to them, the place reserved for the family, and in some kibbutzim children even sleep in an adjoining room.

I myself have always believed that the kibbutz is the one place in the world where people are judged, accepted and given a chance to participate fully in the community to which they belong not in accordance with the kind of work they do or how well they do it, but for their intrinsic value as human beings. Not that kibbutz life is never flawed by envy, dishonesty or laziness. Kibbutz members are not angels, but they are the only people, as far as I know, who truly share almost everything—problems, rewards, responsibilities and satisfactions. And because of the way in which they live, they have certainly been able to contribute to Israel's development far in excess of their numbers. Today there are only some 230 kibbutzim in Israel, but it is impossible (at least for me) to imagine what the country would be like without them. My daughter, Sarah, has been a member of Kibbutz Revivim in the Negev for the past thirty years, and whenever I visit her and her family there—which in the past was only as often as circumstances permitted and therefore never often enough—I always recall with what mingled hopes and fears her father and I set out for Merhavia so long ago, fully expecting to remain there all our lives—if they would only have us.

For many years I hoped that one day I would be able to return to life on a kibbutz, and one of my great disappointments in myself has been that I never did so. Of course, there were always reasons why this seemed impossible, mostly the accumulating obligations of public life and my involvement with it. But to this day I deeply regret that I failed to find the strength within myself to ignore those pressures and persuasions, and when the time finally came, I was too old to make the change. There are a great many things about which I am unsure, but of this I am certain: Had I spent my life as a member of kibbutz—a real member of a kibbutz, not just a weekend visitor—the inner rewards and satisfactions would have been at least as great as those I derived from publice office.

The kibbutz to which we came in the autumn of 1921 consisted of a few houses and a cluster of trees left over

from the original settlement. There were no orchards, no
meadows, no flowers, nothing, in fact, except wind, rocks
and some sun-scorched fields. In the spring the entire
Emek would bloom. The mountains that framed the valley,
even the black swamps, would be covered with wild flowers, and for a few weeks Merhavia would turn into the
most beautiful place I had ever seen. But my first sight of it
was before the reviving winter rains fell, and it looked not
at all as I had imagined it. The first and most important
obstacle to be overcome, however, had nothing to do with
scenery. I was determined to prove that I was at least as
rugged as any of the other women in the settlement and
that I could carry out whatever mission was assigned to
me. I can't remember all the jobs that I was given during
that crucial "trial period," but I know that I picked al-
monds for days on end in a grove near the kibbutz and that
I helped plant a little forest in the rocks on the road leading to Merhavia. Today it is quite an impressive forest, and
whenever I pass it, I remember how we dug endless holes
in the soil between the rocks and then carefully planted
each sapling, wondering whether it would ever grow to ma-
turity there and thinking how lovely the roadside, the
whole country in fact, would be if only those trees of ours
managed to survive. I will never forget the first days I
worked at that job. When I returned to my room in the
evening, I couldn't as much as move a finger, but I knew
that if I didn't show up for supper everyone would jeer,
"What did we tell you? That's American girls for you!" I
would gladly have forgone my supper, for the chick-pea
mush we ate wasn't worth the effort of lifting the fork to
my mouth, but I went. In the end the trees survived, and so
did I. After a few months Morris and I were accepted as
members, and Merhavia became our home.

Life on a kibbutz in the twenties was very far from luxurious. To begin with, there was very little to eat, and what
was available tasted dreadful. The staples of our diet were
sour cereals, unrefined oil (which we bought from the Arabs in goatskin bags, making it as bitter as death), a few
vegetables from the kibbutz's own precious vegetable patch,
canned bully beef that came from British military supplies
left over from the war and an incredible dish made up of
herring preserved in tomato sauce, which, ironically
enough, was known as "fresh" (I suppose from the mis-

leading "fresh herring" printed on the label). We ate "fresh" every morning for breakfast! When my turn came to work in the kitchen, to everyone's astonishment I was delighted. Now I could really do something about the frightful food.

Let me explain that in those days kibbutz women hated kitchen duty, not because it was hard (compared to other work on the settlement, it was rather easy), but because they felt it to be demeaning. Their struggle wasn't for equal "civic" rights, which they had in abundance, but for equal burdens. They wanted to be given whatever work their male comrades were given—paving roads, hoeing fields, building houses or standing guard duty—not to be treated as though they were different and automatically relegated to the kitchen. All this was at least half a century before anyone invented the unfortunate term "women's lib," but the fact is that kibbutz women were among the world's first and most successful fighters for true equality. But I didn't feel that way about working in the kitchen. I couldn't for the life of me understand what all the fuss was about and said so. "Why is it so much better," I asked the girls who were moping (or storming) about kitchen duty, "to work in the barn and feed the cows, rather than in the kitchen and feed your comrades?" No one ever answered this question convincingly, and I remained more concerned with the quality of our diet than with feminine emancipation.

I began energetically to reorganize the kitchen. First of all, I did away with the dreadful oil. Then I eliminated "fresh" from the breakfast menu and substituted oatmeal, so that when people came in from work on cold, damp winter mornings, they could at least have something hot and nutritious to eat with their compulsory dose of quinine. No one objected to the disappearance of the oil, but there was an immediate outcry about the oatmeal. "It's food for babies," everyone said. "One of her American ideas." But I persisted, and gradually Merhavia became accustomed to the novelty. Next, I decided that something had to be done about the way we ate; our enamel tea mugs—which looked so white and clean when they were brand-new—became chipped and rusted after just a few weeks, and it depressed me even to look at them. So before my turn came again to work in the kitchen, encouraged by the success of the oatmeal, I went off and bought glasses for everyone. They were much prettier and much more pleasant to drink from, although I must confess that almost all of them broke within a week and the whole kibbutz was reduced to drinking in shifts from the two or three glasses that were still intact.

The herring—eliminated for breakfast but now served in the middle of the day—also presented a problem. Not everyone had a knife, fork *and* spoon; mostly each person had one utensil, either a knife, a fork or a spoon. The girls who worked in the kitchen used to wash the herring and cut it into small pieces, but they didn't peel off the skin, so that when the herring was brought to the table, everyone had to peel his own. And since there was nothing on which one could wipe one's hands, they were wiped on our work clothes. When I came to work in the kitchen, I decided to peel the herring. The other girls complained. "You'll see, she'll get them used to that, too." But I had an answer for this as well. "What would you have done in your own home? How would you have served herring at your own family table? This is your home! They are your family!"

Saturday mornings we used to make coffee. Because we couldn't ship our milk to Haifa on the Sabbath, our Saturday menu was based on milk. We had coffee, and we made *leben* (cultured milk similar to yogurt) and *lebeniya* (a slightly enriched version of *leben*). The girl in charge of the cookies, who was on the Saturday-morning kitchen shift, guarded them as if her life depended on it, because breakfast consisted of coffee and cookies. Friday nights, after supper, some of the young men used to start hunting for the cookies and sometimes managed to lay their hands on them, so that on Saturday mornings there would be a tragedy. When my turn came to work on Saturday morning, I figured as follows: We have no more oil, sugar or eggs (we started off with a few scrawny chickens that laid a solitary egg now and again), so let's add more water and a little flour and make a lot of cookies, enough for Friday night and Saturday breakfast, too. At first this was regarded as being "counterrevolutionary," but after a while everyone liked the idea of cookies twice a week—for the same money.

My most celebrated "bourgeois" contribution, however—about which settlers all over the Emek talked disparagingly for months—was the "tablecloth" (made from a sheet) that I spread on the table for Friday night suppers—with a centerpiece of wild flowers yet! The members of Merhavia sighed, grumbled and warned me that I was giving the kibbutz a bad name, but they let me have my way.

We had much the same arguments about other things—clothes, for instance. The girls all wore the same kind of dresses then, made of a rough material woven by the Arabs into which we cut three holes: one for the head and two for the arms. Then we tied a piece of rope around the waist, and that was that. On Friday evenings it was customary for the kibbutzniks to change: The men put on clean shirts, and the girls wore skirts and blouses instead of work dresses or pants. But I couldn't see the logic of once-a-week neatness. I didn't care what I wore every day, but it *had* to be ironed. Every night, using a heavy iron heated by coal, I religiously pressed my "sack," knowing that the kibbutzniks not only thought I was mad, but also suspected me of not being a true pioneer at heart. There was similar disapproval about the flower designs that Morris painted on the walls of our room so that it would look nicer, to say nothing of the fuss about the crates he painted and turned into cupboards for us. It took quite a while, in fact, for the kibbutz to accept our strange "American" ways and us. It is more than probable that the one most important factor in this acceptance was our famous record player. I had left it behind in Tel Aviv for Sheyna; but after a few months I felt that the kibbutz needed it more than she did, and I ruthlessly hauled it off to the Emek, where it drew almost as many people to the kibbutz as it had done in Tel Aviv. I even wonder sometimes whether it might not have been a relief for Merhavia to accept the dowry without the bride!

That winter I was assigned to work in the kibbutz poultry yard and was sent to an agricultural school for a few weeks to study the finer points of poultry breeding. Years later, when I told my parents about this period of my life, they were very amused at my having become such an expert on poultry, since until we came to Merhavia, I was known in the family for my marked lack of affection for any animals, including birds. I can't say that I ever grew really fond of the inhabitants of the poultry yard; but I did become very involved with them, and I was very proud when poultrymen throughout the Emek came to see Merhavia's chicken coops in order to learn how we succeeded in running them so efficiently. For a while I talked poultry, poultry breeding and poultry feeding morning, noon and night, and when a jackal once raided the coops, I dreamed of the hen-house slaughter for weeks afterward. There was also one significant by-product of the energy and time I invested in the poultry yard. Although God knows we could never afford to be lavish with them, eventually eggs and even chickens and geese appeared on the dining-room table. Sometimes, when Sheyna came to visit us with Judith and Chaim, we made a Merhavia "specialty": fried onions and bits of our own hard-boiled eggs washed down with tepid tea. It doesn't sound so good nowadays, but we thought it was marvelous then.

The months passed very quickly. We were always short of working hands, and sometimes it seemed as if all the people who weren't down with malaria had dysentery or were sick with pappataci, a very unpleasant local form of sand-fly fever. All winter the kibbutz swam in a sea of mud, through which we waded for meals, to the outhouse and to work. The summers were no easier; they were very long and terribly hot. From spring to autumn we were tormented by clouds of gnats, sand flies and mosquitoes. By 4 A.M. we were usually at work, since one had to come in from the fields by the time the merciless sun was up. Our only defenses against the insects were Vaseline (when it was available)—which we smeared on the exposed parts of our bodies and onto which the gnats and flies resolutely stuck—and the high collars, long skirts, sleeves and kerchiefs—which we wore miserably throughout the summer, despite the great heat. Once or twice I fell ill myself, and to this day I remember how grateful I was when one of the boys brought me a lump of ice and a tiny lemon from a nearby village so I could make myself lemonade. Perhaps if we had been able to boil a cup of hot tea when it was cold or make a cold drink when we were exhausted by the summer heat, it wouldn't have been so physically grueling. But kibbutz discipline included not taking anything unless it was shared by everyone.

I understood and approved of the underlying reason for this seemingly exaggerated attitude, but Morris, for whom kibbutz life was holding less and less charm as time passed, thought it was absurd for the group to be so rigid and for a difficult life to be made more difficult for doctrinaire reasons. He suffered greatly from the lack of privacy and from what he felt to be the intellectual limitations of our way of life. No one in Merhavia at that time was interested in talking about the kinds of things that mattered to Morris—books and music and paintings. Not that the kibbutzniks were uneducated. Far from it. But their priorities were different. They were as concerned with whether the kibbutz could afford to buy a "giant" 500-egg incubator or with thrashing out the ideological implications of something that someone had said at last Tuesday's general meeting as they were with books, music or paintings. Nonetheless, Morris felt that people in Merhavia had one-track minds—and even that track was too narrow. Also, he said, they were much too earnest about everything and seemed to think that a sense of humor was somehow out of place.

He was not entirely wrong, of course. Now I can see that if the kibbutzim of that time had had the means and the ideological flexibility, for instance, to accept two things which today are commonplace—private showers and toilets and private tea-making facilities in members' rooms—thousands of people like Morris who later left the kibbutzim might have stayed. But these were the kinds of things which no kibbutz could possibly afford in the 1920s, and I wasn't especially bothered by their absence.

I enjoyed being with people who were my kind of people, who shared my political and social views, who debated everything so thoroughly and with such intensity and who took social problems so seriously. I enjoyed everything about the kibbutz—whether it was working in the chicken coops, learning the mysteries of kneading dough for bread in the little shack we used as a bakery or sharing a midnight snack with the boys coming back from guard duty and staying on in the kitchen for hours to hear their stories. After a very short time I felt completely at home, as though I had never lived anywhere else, and it was just those aspects of communal life which Morris regarded as impossible barriers to happiness that pleased me most. Of course, there were people in Merhavia to whom I found it difficult to adjust, particularly some of the "veteran" women, who regarded themselves as entitled to lay down the law on how one should or should not behave on the kibbutz. But in the main I felt absolutely fulfilled.

Naturally there were penalties to be paid for the hard

work out of doors all year round and in all kinds of
weather and for the primitive conditions in which we lived.
The wind and sun battered and burned my skin, and in
those days there were no beauty parlors or cosmeticians on
kibbutzim, as there are now, so kibbutz women aged much
more rapidly than women in the towns. But they weren't
any the less feminine, despite their wrinkles. I remember a
friend from Merhavia, a girl from New York who had
come to the kibbutz about half a year before we did, telling
me that she once went to say good-bye to a young poet
who had served in Palestine with the Jewish Legion but
was going back to the States. When she held her work-
worn hand out to shake his, he said, "In America, it was a
pleasure to hold your hand. Now, it is an honor." She was
very impressed with this gallantry, but I thought it was
nonsense. Men enjoyed holding women's hands on the kibbutz then—and still do—just as much as anywhere else. In
those days—and now, too—kibbutz romances and marriages were like romances and marriages everywhere, some
better, some worse. Of course, young people then were
much more discreet about their love lives and talked about
them less openly than they do now, but that was because
people were universally more puritanical in 1921, not because people didn't fall in love in Merhavia or Degania.

For all the hardship, though, I was very happy in those
years. I liked the kibbutz, and the kibbutz liked me and
showed it. To begin with, I was elected to the settlement's
"steering" committee—the committee that was responsible
for setting overall policy—which was a great honor for a
relative newcomer. Then I was elected to be Merhavia's
delegate to a convention of the kibbutz movement that took
place in 1922, and this was really an accolade. Even now,
writing about it, I have a sense of pride in the fact that the
kibbutz trusted me enough to let me represent it at such an
important gathering and even gave me special permission
to make my remarks in Yiddish, since my Hebrew was still
so halting.

The convention was held in Degania, "mother of the kibbutzim," the settlement which Gordon had helped build
and where, within the year, he would be buried. The sessions I attended dealt mostly with issues that directly concerned the future of the kibbutz as such. To an outsider, I
suppose, it might have seemed strange—even unrealistic,

considering the times—for people to be spending several days in such intense discussion of the optimum size a kibbutz should attain, or how often during the day mothers should visit their infants in the communal baby house, or how applicants for membership could best be screened. After all, there were only a handful of kibbutzim in Palestine then, and their total membership was only a few hundred. The country had just suffered serious anti-Jewish riots, and in any case, the status of its by now 83,000-odd Jews (they made up about 11 percent of the population in 1922) was very unclear. One might well have asked what was the point of those long, detailed debates that went on and on, far into the night, all that week. I can see us now, sitting around a smoky kerosene lamp, our entire beings concentrated on some still theoretical aspect of kibbutz life, trying to solve knotty problems, many of which had not even arisen yet.

On the other hand, in the final analysis, what is realistic and what is not realistic depends very much on who makes the definition. The fact is that none of the people at that meeting—who worked all day in what now would be considered intolerable conditions and divided the nights between standing guard duty and constructing complicated ideological arguments—had any doubt at all that they were laying the foundations for an ideal society in the very dawn of a great experiment in Jewish history. And of course, they were right.

At Degania that week I met many of the major personalities of the *yishuv*'s labor movement—not only Ben-Gurion and Ben-Zvi, whom I had already met in Milwaukee, but also other remarkable people who were later to become close friends and colleagues of mine, men like Avraham Hartzfeld, Yitzhak Tabenkin, Levi Eshkol, Berl Katznelson, Zalman Rubashov (Shazar) and David Remez, to name just a few. I was to be intimately associated with all of them in the stormy years that lay ahead, but then, in Degania, I just listened to their speeches and drank in their words, hardly daring to talk to any of them. I came back to Merhavia stimulated, inspired and barely able to wait to tell Morris about everything that had been said and done.

I also started to see some of the country in those years. When Mrs. Philip Snowden—married to one of the foremost leaders of the British Labour Party and a prominent political figure in her own right—visited Palestine, she needed an English-speaking guide to accompany her, and the labor movement called me to Tel Aviv and asked me to volunteer. "I should waste my time traveling around the country with someone?" I asked furiously. But in the end party discipline won out, and I agreed, though not meekly. Afterward I was glad I had gone. I saw a Bedouin encampment for the first time on that trip, and Mrs. Snowden and I, sitting on the floor, consumed an immense meal of lamb, rice and pitta (flat bread), for which our Arab hosts thoughfully provided us with spoons because I looked so aghast at the idea of eating with my hands, as everyone else was doing. Mrs. Snowden must also have enjoyed herself because I was often to be asked to show VIPs around—although I never got used to doing it during work hours!

But life has a way of becoming complicated just when it seems to be at its smoothest. Morris not only was ill at ease in Merhavia, but was now actually physically ill. The climate, recurrent bouts of malaria, the food, the backbreaking work in thē fields all were too hard for him. Although he was making an enormous effort for my sake, it was becoming increasingly clear now that one day we would have to leave the kibbutz, at least until he recovered his strength. That day came much sooner than I expected. We had been at Merhavia for about two and a half years then, and Morris had been sick for several weeks in a row. One afternoon the doctor informed me gravely that it was absolutely out of the question for us to remain there any longer unless I wanted Morris to be chronically ill. We should leave Merhavia as soon as we could.

I have often wondered in the years that have passed whether Morris would have made a better adjustment to the kibbutz, physically and emotionally, had I been more attentive, spent more time with him and generally been less involved with the group as a whole. But it had never occurred to me that by sitting up in the kitchen until all hours making snacks for the boys when they came off guard duty, or taking that poultry course, or spending so much time talking to and singing with other people, I was depriving Morris of anything. If I had ever thought deeply enough about our marriage or worried enough about it, I would have realized, of course, that Morris was struggling all alone to get used to a way of life that was really immensely hard for him.

There was also one important and specific ongoing disagreement between us. I wanted very much to have a baby, but Morris was tremendously opposed to the collective child-rearing methods of the kibbutz. Just as he wanted his wife for himself, so he wanted us to bring up our own children as he and I saw fit, not to subject each and every detail of their lives to the scrutiny and approval (or disapproval) of a committee and eventually of the entire kibbutz. And he refused to have children at all unless we left Merhavia. He might have changed his mind about this in time, but his health was so poor that we obviously had to leave in any case.

So we packed up again—for the third time in three years—and made our farewells. It was a great wrench for me to leave the kibbutz, but I consoled myself tearfully by hoping that we would both be back soon, that Morris would regain his health quickly, that we would have a baby and that the relationship between us—which had so deteriorated in Merhavia—would improve. If all this happened, I told myself, then leaving the kibbutz for a while was a very small price to pay. Unfortunately, it didn't work out that way.

For a few weeks we stayed in Tel Aviv. Shamai had arrived in Palestine by then, and the family had moved to a new house (with a bathroom). Sheyna was earning a fairly good salary and Shamai eventually joined a not very successful shoe-manufacturing cooperative as its "business manager." Still, they had a home and were making enough money to live on. All in all, their situation was enviable compared to ours. Somehow or other, we couldn't fine a place for ourselves in Tel Aviv. I got a job as a cashier in the Histadrut's Public Works and Building Office (later to be renamed Solel Boneh), which had recently been established, and Morris tried to regain his health. But we couldn't settle down properly. I missed the kibbutz even more than I thought I would, and Morris was being bombarded by letters from his mother and sisters imploring him to return to the States and offering to pay for his fare. I knew he wouldn't leave me or the country, but we both were very restless and depressed.

Compared with "God's wide spaces" in the Emek, Tel

Aviv seemed unbearably small, noisy and crowded. It took Morris a long time to get back on his feet and to shake off the aftereffects of months of sickness, and I felt lost and directionless away from Merhavia and as though we were now doomed to being transients forever. I missed the warmth of the friendships I had made on the kibbutz and the sense of accomplishment that my work there had given me. I couldn't help wondering whether my usual drive and optimism had gone for good and, if so, what would happen to us. Although neither of us ever said anything aloud, I think we probably blamed each other for the situation we were in now. After all, it was because of me that Morris had gone to Merhavia in the first place, and now it was because of Morris' "failure" there that I had to tear myself away from it. Maybe if we had reproached each other openly, it would have been much better for us, but we didn't. Instead, we both felt very much at loose ends and were irritable most of the time.

Under the circumstances it was natural that when I bumped one day into David Remez, whom I had met at Degania, and he asked me if Morris and I would be willing to work in the Jerusalem office of Solel Boneh, we both jumped at the opportunity to leave Tel Aviv. Perhaps, we thought, in the crisp mountain air of Jerusalem we would come alive again and everything would be all right. It seemed like a spectacularly good omen to me when, on the very eve of our departure from Tel Aviv, I learned I was pregnant.

That autumn, in Jerusalem, on November 23, our son, Menachem, was born. He was a lovely, healthy baby, and Morris and I were overcome by being parents. We spent hours looking at the baby we had produced and talking about his future. But I had still not got over my hankerings for Merhavia, and when Menachem was six months old, I returned to the kibbutz with him for a while. I thought that if I went back, I could find myself again, but of course, things are never so simple. I couldn't settle down there without Morris, and by now I had no illusions; it was clear that he neither could nor would ever go back to Merhavia. A binding decision one way or the other had to be made, and it was up to me to make it. To put it very bluntly, I had to decide which came first: my duty to my husband, my home and my child or the kind of life I myself really wanted. Not for the first time—and certainly not for the last—I realized that in a conflict between my duty and my innermost desires, it was my duty that had the prior claim. There was really no alternative other than to stop pining for a way of life that couldn't be mine, so I returned to Jerusalem—not without some forebodings, but determined to make a fresh start. After all, I was a very lucky woman indeed. I was married to a man I loved. True, he was not a man who was cut out for communal life or manual work, but I wanted to remain his wife and to make him happy, if only I possibly could. And I thought that if I tried very hard I would succeed—particularly now that we shared a son.

5. Pioneers and Problems

All these hopes and good intentions notwithstanding, instead of the placid domestic life that I now told myself I was ready to accept, the four years that we lived in Jerusalem were the most miserable I ever experienced—and when you have lived as long as I have, that's saying a lot! Almost everything went wrong; sometimes I even felt that I was reliving the worst part of my mother's life, and I used to remember—with a heart like a stone—the stories she told us about the years when she and Father were so terribly poor in Russia. It wasn't that money, as such, really mattered to me then, or has ever mattered since, or that physical comfort was particularly important. To begin with, I had never had much of either, and anyhow we had not come to Palestine to improve our material circumstances. Both Morris and I had known poverty before only too well, and we both were used to a very modest standard of living, to say the least. We were also committed to a way of life that was based on wanting and having very little. Enough to eat, a clean place to sleep, a new book or record now and again were all that either of us hoped for in material terms. The so-called better things of life not only were beyond our reach, but, for the most part, unknown to us, and if times had been a little easier, we would have managed perfectly well on Morris' small salary.

But times were not easier, and there were basic needs that had to be filled: our own needs and, above all, those of our children. They had to be decently fed and housed somehow. Freedom from the fear that you may not be able to give even these essentials to your children, however hard you try, is, I believe, the fundamental human right of all parents. I knew this in theory long before I experienced such anxiety myself, but having once experienced it, I never forgot it. One of the great built-in strengths of kibbutz life, of course, is that no one ever has to cope with this kind of anxiety alone. Even if a kibbutz is still very young or has had a poor year and the adults have to tighten their belts, kibbutz children always have enough to eat. I thought often and unhappily about Merhavia during that difficult time in Jerusalem, and twenty years later, in the early stages of World War II, remembering how I had felt then, I once suggested publicly that the entire *yishuv* turn itself into a kind of kibbutz for the duration of the emergency by establishing a network of cooperative kitchens among other things, so that whatever else happened, the children would at least be guaranteed sufficient food. The suggestion was turned down or anyhow never taken up, although I still think it made a lot of sense.

But it wasn't only our actual poverty—or even my constant fear that my children would be hungry—that made me so wretched. There was also my loneliness, the sense of isolation to which I was so unaccustomed and the constant feeling that I was being deprived of just those things for which I had come to Palestine in the first place. Instead of actively helping build the Jewish national home and working hard and productively for it, I found myself cooped up in a tiny apartment in Jerusalem, all my thoughts and energy concentrated on making do with Morris' wages. To make things worse, his salary was more often than not paid by Solel Boneh in credit slips that no one—neither the landlord, milkman nor Menachem's nursery-school teacher—wanted to accept in lieu of cash.

On "payday" I used to dash to the little grocery store on the corner to try to talk the grocer into taking a chit worth one pound (100 piasters) for 80 piasters, which I knew was all he would give me for it. But even those 80 piasters were given not, God forbid, in cash, but in a handful of more credit slips. With these I would then run to the woman who sold chickens, argue with her for twenty minutes or so and finally, on a good day, persuade her to take my slips (after she had deducted 10 or 15 percent of their value) in exchange for a small piece of chicken with which I could make soup for the children.

Sometimes Shamai came up to Jerusalem for a day or two with some cheese or a box of fruit or vegetables that Sheyna sent with him. We would have a real "banquet," and I would feel less tense about the family diet for a while. But most of the time I was eaten up with worry.

Until Sarah was born, in the spring of 1926, we made a little extra money by renting out one of our two rooms, though they lacked gas and electricity. But when Sarah arrived, we decided that we would have to forgo the rent, regardless of how difficult it would be to manage without it, so that the children might have a small room of their own. The only way we could possibly make up the difference would be for me to get some sort of work that I could do without leaving the baby alone. So I suggested to Menachem's nursery-school teacher that I do the laundry for the entire nursery school in exchange for the school fees. So, standing in the yard, for hours, I grimly scrubbed piles of little towels, aprons and bibs, heating pail after pail of water on the Primus stove and wondering what I would do if the washboard broke.

It wasn't the work I minded. In Merhavia I had worked much harder—and liked it. But in Merhavia I had been part of a group, a member of a dynamic society whose success mattered to me more than almost anything else in the world. In Jerusalem I was a sort of prisoner, sentenced—as are millions of women by circumstances beyond their control—to battling over bills that I couldn't pay, trying to keep shoes from falling apart because it was impossible to buy another pair, worrying whenever a child coughed or ran a fever that our inadequate diet and inability to keep the apartment warm in winter might be permanently damaging their health.

Of course, some days were better than others. When the sun shone and the sky was blue (and in Jerusalem the summer sky is bluer, I think, than anywhere else), I sat on the steps, watching the children play, and counted my blessings. But when it was windy and cold and the children weren't well (particularly Sarah, who seemed to be sick much of the time), I was filled if not with despair then with a bitter resentment against my lot in life. Was this what it was all about—poverty, drudgery and worry? The worst of it was that I couldn't even tell Morris how I felt. He desperately needed rest, proper food and peace of mind; but none of these were available, and I couldn't see how anything would change in the immediate future.

Solel Boneh was doing very badly, too, and we were terrified that it might close down altogether. It was one thing to set out enthusiastically to create an unofficial public works department and undertake to train and employ Jewish workers in the building trades, but an altogether different thing to acquire the necessary capital and the experience needed for building roads and houses. The only way Solel Boneh could pay anyone in those days was in promissory notes for 100 or 200 pounds, which were covered by larger promissory notes that Solel Boneh received as payment for work completed. One of the many stories people used to tell then about building in Palestine had to do with the Jew who said that if he only had a good feather pillow to start off with, he could build himself a house. How? Very simple, he said. "Look, a good pillow you can sell for a pound. With this pound you can pay the membership fee of a loan society, which will entitle you to borrow up to ten pounds. With ten pounds in hand you can begin looking around for a nice little plot of land. Once you've found a plot, you can approach the owner with your ten pounds in cash and naturally, he will agree to take the rest in promissory notes. Now you are a landowner, and you can look for a contractor. To him you say, 'The land I have—now you build a house on it. All I want is a flat for myself and the family.'"

But there was nothing funny about the way I felt. Sometimes Regina, who was working in the office of the Zionist Executive in Jerusalem then, came to see me, and while I glumly cleaned house, she listened to all my grievances and tried to cheer me up. Of course, when I wrote to my parents, I painted a very different picture of our life, and I even tried to keep Sheyna from knowing how bad it really was—though I don't think I fooled her at all.

Strangely enough, when I look back to that time, I realize that I wasn't really aware of any but my most immediate surroundings, even though Jerusalem was the seat of the mandatory government then, the place from which the British high commissioners—first Sir Herbert Samuel, who was replaced in 1925 by Lord Plumer—governed the country. As it has always been throughout history, Jerusalem was a fascinating city. In part it was then, as it still is, a mosaic of shrines and holy places, in part it was the headquarters of a colonial administration. But above all, it was the living symbol of the continuity of Jewish history and the tie that bound, and binds, the Jewish people to this land. Its population was unlike that of any other place in Palestine. Even our neighborhood was exotic, located on the frontier of Mea Shearim, the section of Jerusalem that is still inhabited by ultra-Orthodox Jews, whose bearing, dress and religious practices have been carried over, almost intact, from sixteenth-century Eastern Europe and who thought that Jews like Morris and myself were only a step away from being pagan. But somehow the city's landmarks and landscapes, the colorful procession of people of all faiths and races who walked Jerusalem's streets even on the most ordinary days didn't make much of an impression on me. I was too tired, too dispirited and too concerned with myself and my family to look about me as I should have.

One evening, however, I went to the Western Wall—not for the first time. Morris and I had gone there a week or two after our arrival in Palestine. I had grown up in a Jewish home, a good traditional Jewish home, but I wasn't at all pious, and the truth is that I went to the Wall without much emotion, just as something that I knew I ought to do. Then, all of a sudden, at the end of those narrow, winding alleys in the Old City, I saw it. The Wall itself looked much smaller than it does today, after all the excavations. But for the first time I saw the Jews, men and women, praying and weeping before it and putting *kvitlach*—their scribbled petitions to the Almighty—into its crannies. So this was what was left of a past glory, I thought, all that has remained of Solomon's Temple. But at least it was still there. And in those Orthodox Jews with their *kvitlach,* I saw a nation's refusal to accept that only these stones were left to it and an expression of confidence in what was to come in the future. I left the Wall changed in feeling—uplifted is perhaps the word. And on that evening, years later, when I was so dissatisfied with everything, the Wall still had a message for me.

In 1971 I was awarded the Freedom of Jerusalem— probably the greatest tribute ever paid me—and at that ceremony I told of yet another memorable visit I had made to the Wall, this time in 1967, after the Six-Day War. For nineteen years, from 1948 to 1967, we were banned by the Arabs from going to the Old City or praying at the Wall. But on the third day of the Six-Day War—Wednesday,

June 7—all Israel was electrified by the news that our soldiers had liberated the Old City and that it was open to us
again. I had to fly to the United States three days later, but
I couldn't bring myself to leave Israel without going to the
Wall again. So that Friday morning—although civilians
were not yet allowed to enter the Old City because shooting was still going on there—I received permission to go to
the Wall, despite the fact that I wasn't in the government
then but just an ordinary citizen, like any other.

I went to the Wall together with some soldiers. There in
front of it stood a plain wooden table with some submachine guns on it. Uniformed paratroopers wrapped in
prayer shawls clung so tightly to the wall that it seemed
impossible to separate them from it. They and the Wall
were one. Only a few hours earlier they had fought furiously for the liberation of Jerusalem and had seen their
comrades fall for its sake. Now, standing before the Wall,
they wrapped themselves in prayer shawls and wept, and I,
too, took a sheet of paper, wrote the word *"shalom"*
(peace) on it and pushed it into a cranny of the Wall, as I
had seen the Jews do so long ago. As I stood there, one of
the soldiers (I doubt that he knew who I was) suddenly
put his arms around me, laid his head on my shoulder, and
we cried together. I suppose he needed the release and the
comfort of an old woman's warmth, and for me it was one
of the most moving moments of my life. But all that, of
course, belongs to a much later era.

The late 1920s were depressing years throughout Jewish
Palestine, not just for me. By 1927 there were 7,000
men and women without work in the *yishuv*—a sobering 5 percent of Palestine's total Jewish population. It
was almost as though Zionism, in its great zeal, had overreached itself. Many more immigrants were entering the
country than the *yishuv* could possibly employ. Of the
13,000 Jews who arrived in Palestine in 1926, for instance,
more than half left, and in 1927, for the first time, emigration was ominously higher than immigration. Some of the
emigrants went to the United States, others to various parts
of the British Empire. There was also a group that included
members of the "Labor Battalion" (which had been
founded in 1920 to employ immigrants in cooperative road
building and quarrying projects financed by the mandatory
government) who returned for ideological reasons to Rus-

sia, where many of them subsequently were sent to Siberia or executed, also for "ideological" reasons.

There were various reasons for the severe crisis. The *yishuv*'s economy was still almost totally undeveloped. Other than in the building trades (which employed almost half of all the Jewish workers in Palestine) and the orange groves, there simply weren't enough job opportunities or capital to go around. You could count the Jewish industrial enterprises on the fingers of one hand. There were the Dead Sea Works, a salt factory and quarries at Athlit, the Palestine Electric Corporation (which had built a power station in the banks of the Jordan River), the Shemen soap and edible oils factory and the Nesher cement factory in Haifa. There were also a few other smaller enterprises, including printing plants and wine cellars, but that was all.

There was also another very serious problem: The wages of Jewish workers were very low then; but Arab laborers were willing to work for even less, and many Jewish orange growers yielded to the temptation of hiring the cheaper Arab labor. As for the mandatory government, other than the network of roads it constructed, it did virtually nothing to develop the economy of the country and had already begun to give way to the anti-Jewish pressure of Arab extremists, such as the mufti of Jerusalem, Haj Amin el-Husseini, and others. Although only a few years had passed since the mandate over Palestine was granted to Britain, the government was already displaying considerable hostility to the Jews. Even worse, it had moved to curb the rate of Jewish immigration into Palestine and in 1930 threatened to stop it altogether for a while. In short, the Jewish national home was not flourishing.

I hardly went to Tel Aviv during the years I lived in Jerusalem, and when I did go it was usually only to see Sheyna and her family or to visit my parents, who had come to Palestine in 1926. In between the family visits, I did my best to see old friends, catch up on what was happening in the labor movement, hear some gossip from or about Merhavia and feel myself again—if only for a few hours—part of what was going on in the country. My father, now that I come to think of it, was in a way typical of the immigrants of 1926 and 1927, even though he had come from the States and not from Europe. In Milwaukee he had managed to save up a little money, with which he

proudly brought two plots of land in Palestine—partly because as a Zionist he wanted to live there, partly because
he wanted to reunite the family. Both his plots were in
places that were little more than sand. One was in Herzlia,
a few miles north of Tel Aviv. The other was in Afula (not
far from Merhavia), where he intended to build a house.
When I asked him why he wanted to live in Afula, of all
places, which was near neither to Sheyna nor to me, he
told me that Afula was to be the site of Palestine's first
opera house and that he would be living in a great center
of music. I knew Afula very well and had gone there often on errands when we lived in the kibbutz. It was a dusty
little village, and I was pretty sure that an opera house
wouldn't be built there—at least not in the foreseeable future. But my father was adamant. For a long time he refused to listen to any argument and accused Sheyna and me
of having little faith. "Tel Aviv was built on sand dunes,
wasn't it?" he said reproachfully. In the end my mother
joined forces with us, and with a sigh, my father gave up
the idea of living in the Emek and agreed to make his
home in Herzlia—without arias.

He built that home largely with his own hands, as befitted a good carpenter. It was one of the first real houses in
the area, and my parents settled down there as quickly as
they had once settled in Milwaukee. My father joined the
local synagogue, discovered that it had no cantor and
promptly volunteered for the position himself. He also
joined a carpenters' cooperative, but since work was scarce,
that didn't help much. But my enterprising mother had an
idea. She would cook and serve midday meals, and he
would help her. There were very few restaurants anywhere
in Palestine and none at all in Herzlia, so my mother's idea
was very successful. For a few piasters she provided the
laborers in the vicinity with cheap, nourishing food.

But even so, for all their determination to make a life for
themselves in Palestine—although by now they were both
well past their prime—my parents suffered greatly from the
economic situation. I remember, for example, that once I
took the children to Herzlia a week before Passover so I
could help my mother prepare for the holiday. Morris was
to join us on the eve of the holiday, and Sheyna and her
family were also coming. But we all were so poor that there
wasn't anything to prepare. My father walked around look-

ing as though someone had beaten him over the head. Imagine, here he was in Palestine with almost his entire family (Clara was still in college then at Wisconsin University but planned to come to Palestine as soon as she got her degree), and there wasn't even a package of matzo or a bottle of wine in the house, let alone food for the Seder. I couldn't bear to see him look so miserable, and I even thought that he might be driven to do something desperate. He was so humiliated, although poverty had never crushed him before.

Then a wonderful thing happened. I was bitten by a dog! For someone else it would have been terrible, but for me it was a miracle. I had to go to Tel Aviv for antirabies injections, and while I was there, I could scour the town for someone who would lend me money. I managed to find a bank that was willing to lend me 10 pounds (which was a lot of money in those days), provided I had guarantors. So I ran around town again; but no one I found was good enough for the bank, and whenever the bank suggested a name to me, it was someone who wasn't about to run any risks. At last I found a man who had the necessary capital, a fine reputation and a good Jewish heart, and I came back to Herzlia with 10 whole pounds in my pocket for my father—and a warmer feeling than I had ever had in my life for dogs.

On those rare visits to Tel Aviv I was always depressed and shocked by the sight of unemployed men on the street corners and the desolate look of half-finished building all over town. It was as though a huge burst of energy had worn itself out. Of course, outsiders might have seen it all differently. Despite the economic crisis, thousands of Jews were living in Palestine, raising their children there, developing their own leadership, creating agricultural and urban settlements and doing all this aided—in the final analysis—only by a Zionist movement abroad, which was in itself a remarkable achievement. Seen as historians would one day see it, even that bleak period would take on a brighter hue. But I wasn't an outsider or a historian, and I longed to take an active part in helping improve the situation, to do something about it myself.

My great good fortune was that the Histadrut (the General Federation of Jewish Labor), that organization in which and for which I was to work for so many years, was interested in the services of someone like myself. I had already worked in Tel Aviv for Solel Boneh and had gone on working for it—though only briefly—in Jerusalem, and I knew many of the people in the labor movement. They were the kind of men and women I most admired and liked. I wanted to learn from them and work with them, and I felt completely at home with them. They saw the basic aims of the Histadrut as I did—not so much the protection of the immediate bread-and-butter interests of the workers as the creation of a labor community committed to the future of the Jews of Palestine, those who were already there and those who were still to come.

In many ways, the Histadrut was unique. It could model itself on no other existing labor organization because the position of the Jewish worker in Palestine then was totally unlike that of the worker in Britain, France, or America. As elsewhere, the economic rights of the Jewish worker, as well as the Arab worker, in Palestine had to be guarded, including the right to strike, the right to a decent wage, the right to paid annual holidays, to sick leaves, and so forth. But even though its official title was the General Federation of Jewish Labor, it would be an oversimplification to describe the Histadrut only as a trade union, because it was much more than that, in concept as well as practice. First of all, the Histadrut based itself on unity of *all* the workers in the *yishuv*—whether they were wage earners, members of kibbutzim, blue- or white-collar workers, manual laborers or intellectuals, and from the start it was in the forefront of the struggle to bring Jews to Palestine, even though the burden of increased immigration inevitably fell on its own shoulders.

Secondly, Palestine didn't have a "ready-made" economy that could absorb the steady flow of Jewish immigrants into the country. There was the smattering of small industry, of course, and the agricultural settlements. But these enterprises couldn't sustain a country with a growing population, and we who had come to Palestine to build the Jewish national home knew that we had to create what today is so casually referred to as a "national economy"! If you stop to think about what this involves—industry, transportation, construction, finance, not to speak of tools for dealing with welfare, unemployment and so forth—the job ahead of us was actually the creation of something almost out of nothing. Even at the time of which I write, when the workers of Palestine were still few in number and very isolated, through the Histadrut they unhesitatingly undertook the responsibility of being the vanguard of a state in the making, although certainly no one imposed this mission on them.

Because it was so highly motivated from the very beginning by the Zionist ideal, the Histadrut regarded every facet of life in the Jewish national home as of equal importance. There were (and there still are) two standards by which all Histadrut projects were judged: Did they answer an urgent national need and were they acceptable (or necessary) from the socialist point of view?

One good example is the Histadrut's determination to develop its own econimic enterprises, control of which would be vested in the labor community *as a whole*. As early as 1924 a legal body called Hevrat Ha-Ovdim (its clumsy English name was the General Cooperative Association of Jewish Labor in Palestine), representing every member of the Histadrut, become the "owner" of all of the Histadrut's "assets," of which there were not very many then. Solel Boneh was one of these "assets," and when it overexpanded and collapsed in 1927, nobody outside the labor movement imagined that it could ever be reestablished. But the Histadrut knew that there was, and would always be, a great need for a building and public works company that could serve the national requirement in a way that no private company ever could or would. So, eventually, Solel Boneh was reborn. Today—having undergone various processes of reorganization, including, its 1958 reconstruction on the basis of three companies (a building company, an overseas and harbor works company and an industrial holding company with its subsidiaries), it is one of the largest and most successful firms in the entire Middle East. When I recall the gloom and tension that existed in Solel Boneh's dingy little office in Jerusalem in 1927, when there wasn't enough cash to pay the bookkeeper even once a month, and then think of the 50,000 men and women employed last year by these three components of the original Solel Boneh, with their combined turnover of about 2.5 billion Israeli pounds, I defy anyone to argue that Zionism is not utterly incompatible with pessimism— or that socialism is, of necessity, inefficient unless combined with ruthlessness.

To those critics of the Jewish labor movement who said fifty years ago that the Histadrut's concept of its role was romantic, grandiose and doomed to failure, let me point out that Solel Boneh not only weathered five remarkably difficult decades, but lived to play a most decisive role in the building of thousands of homes, roads, schools and hospitals in Israel, as well as to pioneer in extensive Israeli projects carried out in Africa, parts of Asia and the Middle East itself. But Solel Boneh was only one of the Histadrut's creations. There are dozens of others—agricultural, industrial, educational, cultural and even medical—and all of them are rooted in the enduring conviction that the real strength of the workers in Israel expresses itself in the priority given to the upbuilding of what is now the Jewish state.

At all events, I was delighted (and very flattered) when one rainy day, as I stood talking to someone outside the Histadrut offices in Tel Aviv, David Remez (who had suggested four years earlier that Morris and I work for Solel Boneh in Jerusalem) asked me if I was interested in returning to work and whether I would like to become the secretary of the Moetzet Hapoalot (Women's Labor Council) of the Histadrut. On the way back to Jerusalem I made up my mind. It wasn't an easy decision to take. I knew that if I took the job, it would involve considerable traveling both in Palestine and abroad and that we would have to find a place to live in Tel Aviv—which was difficult. But, hardest and most serious of all, I had to face up to the fact that going back to work would spell the end to my attempts to devote myself entirely to the family. Although I wasn't yet prepared to concede total defeat, even to myself, I had already realized in the course of those four years in Jerusalem that my marriage was a failure. Taking on a full-time job, under the circumstances, meant reconciling myself to this, and the thought frightened me. On the other hand, I told myself that perhaps if I were happier and more fulfilled, it would be better for everyone—for Morris, for the children and for me. Perhaps I would be able to cope with everything: save what was left of my marriage from going farther downhill, be a good mother to Sarah and Menachem and even have the kind of purposeful, interesting life for which I so yearned.

It didn't work out quite that way, of course. Nothing

ever works out exactly as one expects it to. But I can't honestly say that I have ever regretted that decision or that in retrospect I think I was wrong to have made it. What I do regret—and bitterly so—is that although Morris and I remained married to each other and loving each other until the day he died in my house in 1951 (when symbolically enough, I was away), I was not able to make a success of our marriage after all. The decision I took in 1928 actually marked the start of our separation, although it didn't become final for almost ten years.

The tragedy was not that Morris didn't understand me, but, on the contrary, that he understood me only too well and felt that he couldn't make me over or change me. I had to be what I was, and what I was made it impossible for him to have the sort of wife he wanted and needed. So he didn't discourage me from going back to work, although he knew what it really meant.

He remained part of my life always and, of course, of the children's. The bond between Sarah and Menachem and Morris never weakened. They adored him and saw him very often. He had a great deal to give them, just as he had given a great deal to me, and he was a wonderful father to them even after we began to live apart. He read to them, bought them books and talked to them for hours about music, always with the tenderness and warmth that characterized him. He had always been quiet and reserved. To the outside world he may have appeared ineffectual or unsuccessful; but the truth is that his inner life was very rich— richer than mine, for all my activity and drive—and he shared it generously with his close friends, his family and, particularly, his children.

So in 1928 I left Jerusalem with Sarah and Menachem and returned to Tel Aviv; Morris came home to us only for weekends. The children went to a school—one of several run by the labor movement—and I went back to work.

The Women's Labor Council and its sister organization abroad, the Pioneer Women, were the first and last women's organizations for which I ever worked. I was attracted to them not so much because they concerned women as such, but because I was very interested in the work they were doing, particularly in the agricultural training farms they set up for immigrant girls. Today the Labor Council (which is part of the Histadrut) is occupied mainly with

social services and with labor legislation for women (maternity benefits, retirement, and so on), but in the 1930s its
emphasis was almost entirely on vocational training for the
hundreds of young girls who came to Palestine to work on
the land but who had no farming background at all, or any
trade. The council's training farms gave those girls a lot
more than just vocational know-how. They helped speed up
the girls' integration in the country, to teach them Hebrew
and to give them a sense of stability in a new land, to
which most of them came without families and some even
without the consent of their parents. These "workingwom-
en's farms" were set up at a time when the idea that
women should be trained for anything, let alone agriculture, was still considered absurd by most people.

I am not a great admirer of the kind of feminism that
gives rise to bra burning, hatred of men or a campaign
against motherhood, but I have had very great regard for
those energetic hard-working women within the ranks of
the labor movement—Ada Maimon, Beba Idelson, Rachel
Yanait-Ben-Zvi, to name just a few—who succeeded in
equipping dozens of city-bred girls with the sort of theoretical knowledge and a sound practical training that made it
possible for them to do their share (and often much more
than their share) of the work going on in agricultural settlements throughout Palestine. That kind of constructive
feminism really does women credit and matters much more
than who sweeps the house or who sets the table.

About the position of women generally, of course, there
is very much to say (and much, perhaps too much, has
already been said), but I can put my own thoughts on the
subject into a nutshell. Naturally women should be treated
as the equals of men in all respects, but, as is true also of
the Jewish people, they shouldn't have to be better than
everyone else in order to live like human beings or feel that
they must accomplish wonders all the time to be accepted
at all. On the other hand, a story—which, as far as I know,
is all it was—once went the rounds of Israel to the effect
that Ben-Gurion described me as the "only man" in his
cabinet. What amused me about it was that obviously he
(or whoever invented the story) thought that this was the
greatest possible compliment that could be paid to a
woman. I very much doubt that any man would have been

flattered if I had said about him that he was the only woman in the government!

The fact is that I have lived and worked with men all my life, but being a woman has never hindered me in any way at all. It has never caused me unease or given me an inferiority complex or made me think that men are better than women—or that it is a disaster to give birth to children. Not at all. Nor have men ever given me preferential treatment. But what is true, I think, is that women who want and need a life outside as well as inside the home have a much, much harder time than men because they carry such a heavy double burden (with the notable exception of women who live in kibbutzim, where life is organized to enable them to work and rear children at the same time). And the life of a working mother who lives without the constant presence and support of the father of her children is three times harder than that of any man I have ever met.

To some extent my own life in Tel Aviv after we moved from Jerusalem is an illustration of these dilemmas and difficulties. I was always rushing from one place to another—to work, home, to a meeting, to take Menachem to a music lesson, to keep a doctor's appointment with Sarah, to shop, to cook, to work and back home again. And still to this day I am not sure that I didn't harm the children or neglect them, despite the efforts I made not to be away from them even an hour more than was strictly necessary. They grew up to be healthy, productive, talented and good people, and they both are wonderful parents to their own children and wonderful companions to me. But when they were growing up, I knew that they deeply resented my activities outside our home.

I stayed up at night to cook for them. I mended their clothes. I went to concerts and films with them. We always talked and laughed a lot together. But were Sheyna and my mother right when they charged me for years with depriving the children of their due? I suppose that I shall never be able to answer this question to my own satisfaction and that I will never stop asking it. Were they proud of me, then or later? I like to think so, of course, but I am not really sure that being proud of one's mother makes up for her frequent absences. I remember that once when I was the chairwoman of a public meeting and asked "all those in favor" of whatever the issue was to raise their hands, to my utter astonishment I saw Sarah and Menachem (who had stolen into the hall to fetch me) loyally raise their hands to indicate their approval. It was the most reassuring vote of confidence I ever got, but it didn't keep me from feeling that being able to vote for your mother is not nearly as good or as important as having her at home when you get back from school.

And of course, later on I was abroad often. When I traveled, my guilt was overwhelming. I wrote to them all the time, even made records for them, which seemed more intimate and I never came back without presents; but I was also never free of the feeling that I was injuring them in some way. Years later I put some of these feelings in an article written anonymously for a collection of memoirs (it was called "The Ploughwoman") by some of the women who were active in the *yishuv* in those days. A few paragraphs from that article written in 1930 may possibly be of interest to many women even today because the problems that so preoccupied me then are not affected very much by today's washing machines, dishwashers or dryers—although they all would certainly have been a great help to me:

> Taken as a whole, the inner struggles and despairs of a mother who goes to work have few parallels. But within that whole there are many shades and variations. There are mothers who work only when they are forced to, when the husband is sick or unemployed or when the family has, in some other way, gone off the track of a normal life. In such cases the mother feels her course of action justified by necessity—her children would not be fed otherwise. But there is a type of woman who cannot remain home for other reasons. In spite of the place which her children and her family take up in her life, her nature and being demand something more; she cannot divorce herself from a larger social life. She cannot let her children narrow her horizon. And for such a woman, there is no rest.
>
> Theoretically it looks straightforward enough. The woman who takes her place with the children is devoted, loves the children, is reliable and suited to the work; the children are fully looked after. But there are even pedagogic theorists who claim that it is actually

better for the children not to have their mother hovering over them constantly, and a mother who is occupied and who has given up all the external world for her husband and her children has done it not out of a sense of duty, out of devotion and love, but out of incapacity, because her soul is not able to take into itself the many-sidedness of life, with its sufferings but also with its joys. And if a woman does remain with her children and gives herself to nothing else, does that really prove that she is more devoted than the other kind of mother? And if a wife has no intimate friends, does that prove that she has a greater love for her husband?

But the mother also suffers in the very work she has taken up. Always she has the feeling that her work is not as productive as that of a man or even of an unmarried woman. The children, too, always demand her, in health and even more in sickness. And this eternal inner division, this double pull, this alternating feeling of unfulfilled duty—today toward her family, the next day toward her work—this is the burden of the working mother.

It wasn't a very elegantly written article, and read today, it seems a bit stiff to me; but I wrote it then in real anguish.

Apart from everything else, for several years Sarah wasn't at all well. We had been told that the trouble was with her kidneys, and there was hardly a month without an anxious visit to the doctor. She was a pretty, gay, very alert little girl and very good about the strict diet she had to keep, the medicines she had to swallow and having to be in bed for weeks at a time. On the days when she had to stay in bed, leaving her with someone else was not simple, and when she was up and around, she had to be watched all the time. Sheyna and my mother were of great assistance, but I always felt I had to explain and apologize to them for going to work in the morning and not coming back till the afternoon.

Not long ago I came across one of the letters I wrote to Sheyna around this time. I had been sent to the States for several weeks on a mission to the Pioneer Women. It was the first time I had been back in the States in seven years, and on my way I attended the Socialist International, which was then taking place in Brussels. Brussels overwhelmed me. I had completely forgotten what the world was like outside Palestine, and I could hardly believe the trees, the trams, the flower and fruit stands, the cool, gray weather. It was all so unlike Tel Aviv. I was entranced by everything. Since I was the most junior member of our delegation (which included Ben-Gurion and Ben-Zvi), I had time to sightsee and to listen for hours to the speeches of famous socialists whom I had, of course, never seen before—men like Arthur Henderson, the British Labour Party leader, who was the president of the Socialist International, or Léon Blum, who became France's first socialist and first Jewish Premier. Henderson had just agreed to organize a League for Labour Palestine, for which he came under bitter attack from the Jewish non-Zionist socialists— of all people—and as far as we were concerned, the atmosphere was very charged. Nonetheless, despite everything that was happening around me, I took an hour off one day to try—aided by distance—to win Sheyna over and to convince her that I was not just a selfish and bad mother. I wrote to her from Brussels:

> I ask only one thing, that I be understood and believed. My social activities are not accidental; they are an absolute necessity for me. . . . Before I left, the doctor assured me that Sarah's health permits my going, and I have made adequate arrangements for Menachem. . . . But in our present situation I could not refuse to do what was asked of me. Believe me, I know it will not bring the Messiah, but I think we must miss no opportunity to explain to influential people what we want and what we are. . . .

But though Sheyna herself was to go back to America shortly to study to become a dietitian, leaving her two older children in Palestine, she continued to accuse me of turning, as she put it, "into a public person, not a homebody." And my mother went on chastising me, too. I suppose that what really upset them so much was that I was away from home so often and that the children had to eat their midday meal without me in the rather Spartan but good communal dining room that was part of the workers' housing estate in which we lived on Hayarkon Street, facing the sea in the north of Tel Aviv.

Actually we all managed quite well. I always let one of our three rooms so that the children were never alone (for years I slept—and very well—on a couch in what was our combined dining-living room), and whenever I had to go abroad, I got someone to come in and take care of them. But of course, they saw less of me than they should have, and I was constantly pressed for time and preoccupied by the conflicting demands made on me by home and work.

Today the head offices of the Histadrut occupy an immense building on one of Tel Aviv's main streets and are like a great beehive that hums with the sound of hundreds of voices, typewriters and telephones, but in those days things were very different. We had just a few rooms, a couple of typists, only one telephone, and everybody knew everybody else. We were, in the most literal sense of the word, *chaverim* (comrades), and although we argued among ourselves all the time about details and techniques, we shared the same basic outlook on life and the same values. Most of the relationships I made then have lasted—in one way or another—till today (although, of course, over the past few years I have had to attend a great many funerals of colleagues who were young when I and the Histadrut were also young).

Of that group, three or four were to become well known outside the *Yishuv*. About Ben-Gurion, who became—and with good reason—the very personification of Israel throughout the world and who will almost certainly be remembered as one of the truly great Jews of the twentieth century, I shall write later. Of all of us he was the only one of whom it could be said that he was literally indispensable to the Jewish people in its struggle for independence. But I hardly knew him at this point. Among the people I was getting to know well were Shneur Zalman Shazar, who was to become third president of Israel; Levi Eshkol, who became its third prime minister; David Remez and Berl Katznelson; and Yosef Shprinzak, who was to become the first Speaker of the Knesset.

I met Shazar (whose name before he hebraized it was Rubashov) for the first time just after we left Merhavia and returned to Tel Aviv. It was on May 1, the workers' holiday, and Morris and I went to a rally sponsored by the

Histadrut in the yard of the Herzlia High School. I have never particularly enjoyed listening to long speeches—even if they are about the labor movement—and my mind was wandering a bit when a young man got up to speak. I can see him now, a vigorous young man in a *rubashka* (the Russian type of blouse that workers wore in Palestine then), a sash fixed around his waist and khaki trousers. He spoke with such fervor and enthusiasm and in such marvelous Hebrew that I immediately asked who he was. "That is Rubashov," I was told reproachfully, as though I should have known. "A poet and a writer. A *most* important man." When I came to know him, I was also very impressed by him, and we eventually became extremely close friends.

Unlike some of us who were lent stature by the great challenge of Zionism and who might never have amounted to much under other circumstances and in other situations, Shazar had remarkable personal gifts. He was a true scholar, steeped in Jewish learning—as was only proper for a son of the famous Hasidic family of the Lubavitchers (his first names are those of the first Lubavitcher rabbi)—and a most talented journalist, essayist and editor. He died in 1974 at the age of eighty-five, about a year after he left the presidency of the state. When he was already a very old man, the young people in Israel tended to smile (though I think rather affectionately) at his emotion-charged, long and flowery speeches, which had changed very little in style since the 1920s.

But Shazar always had something relevant to say, even if it took him some time to say it. As president of the state he unfailingly stressed the essential unity of what he called the "family of Israel," by which he meant all the Jews in the country, those of European (his own) origin and those thousands upon thousands who came from Arabic-speaking countries and to whom Hasidism and Yiddish culture meant nothing at all. For many years Shazar edited *Davar*, the daily newspaper of the labor movement, and I remember someone saying to me once, "Zalman finds it much more enjoyable to correct mistakes in what others write than to write himself. He should really have been a teacher."

He never did teach, but he did become Israel's first minister of education in 1948, a job that he undertook with enormous zest. I always liked the story of his first day at the ministry because I think it makes clear what a warm, unpretentious, and dedicated man he was. When he arrived at the ministry, he discovered that one room and one male secretary had been set aside for him, but no typewriter. This didn't bother Shazar much. He hung up his hat, sat down and said briskly to his new secretary, "Please take a note. No typewriter? It doesn't matter. Take it in longhand. Ready? All Israeli children between the ages of four and eighteen are to receive free education of the highest quality." When the secretary commented that this might have to wait a few days before it could be carried out since the state was only one day old, Shazar said fiercely, "When it comes to education, I want no arguments. This is my first order as the minister responsible for it." He did, in fact, promulgate Israel's Education Act very soon afterward.

When Shazar was president and I was prime minister, I used to see him as often as I could. He hated the relative isolation of the presidency, and I was always calling him up or visiting him to keep him from involving himself in some explosive political situation, especially those concerning the labor movement. "Don't forget you are the president now, Zalman," I used to say. "You mustn't interfere." Most of the time Shazar would shake his head unhappily at my advice but take it nonetheless.

Levi Eshkol (his original name was Shkolnik) was another of the promising young men with whom I became friendly in the 1920s. He was quite different from Shazar, although he also came from a Hasidic family in Russia. But he was much more a man of action and much less a man of words. He had come to Palestine when he was only nineteen, and after working as an agricultural laborer in various parts of the country, he joined the Jewish Legion together with Ben-Gurion and Ben-Zvi (for years, he boasted that he had been made a lance corporal before Ben-Gurion). When the war ended, he became a member of Degania, from which he was coopted by the Histadrut, although his ties with the kibbutz remained strong all his life. Eshkol was typical of the practical idealists of that era: His great interests were land, water and defense, though not necessarily in that order, and he was happiest dealing with such down-to-earth and crucial problems. Politics in the abstract didn't particularly attract him, and he hated bureaucratic procedures; but give him a specific challenge, and he met it with an extraordinary continuation of doggedness, ingenuity and shrewdness. If you wanted a Jewish national home, you had to settle Jews on the land—never mind how much the land cost or what obstacles the mandatory government put in the way of the Jewish institutions that wanted to buy it. "Not enough room to swing a cat in Palestine," said the British Colonial Office in 1929, by way of trying to excuse its inexcusable policy of limiting Jewish immigration and land purchase. So Eshkol spent the next thirty years looking for places in which new settlements could indeed be established, and as head of the Jewish Agency's land settlement department he supervised the founding of nearly 400 new Jewish villages. You couldn't have settlements without irrigation or irrigate without water, so Eshkol proceeded to organize an intensive search for water. It was a very expensive search, so he also looked for money and managed to find both—though not, needless to say, in quantities that would last forever. If you had land and water and the misfortune of having extremely hostile neighbors, you also had to acquire arms and train an army, and the story of Eshkol's contribution to Israel's armed strength from 1921 (when he joined the Histradrut's first defense committee) all the way through his tenure as prime minister and minister of defense which began in 1963) is a story in its own right. As Israel's prime minister during the Six-Day War he was much (and most unfairly) abused for what his critics called his hesitancy—although surely a leader who is not hesitant about sending young men into battle is a national disaster—and all kinds of malicious jokes were circulated about his supposed inability to make up his mind. The great drama and pain of Eshkol's last years, however (he died of a heart attack—a polite name, I think, for a broken heart—in 1969), was his rift with Ben-Gurion, whose absolutely loyal follower he had been for decades and at whose request he reluctantly took over as prime minister in 1963. That bitter conflict involved the entire labor movement and almost tore Israel apart, but it belongs to a much later period, so I postpone writing about it for the moment.

Eshkol was not, to use the fashionable word, "charismatic." He had no "glamor," but he was an unusually creative person, a man who got things done when they really needed doing, however hard the job was, and a man to whom the people and their feelings mattered a great deal. From the start, I liked and trusted him although who would have dreamed when we worked together in Tel Aviv then that he would eventually be a prime minister or that I would follow him in that office? In the 1950s, when Eshkol was Israel's minister of finance and I was minister of labor, we had a great many clashes—though they were never in any way personal. Those were the years when the young state was flooded with hundreds of thousands of poverty-stricken, undernourished, homeless Jews from the DP camps of Europe and the ghettos of the Arabic-speaking states, and the only way that we could house this torrent of people was by setting up camps of our own for them.

One day Eshkol burst into my office. "We've got to get them out of these camps," he shouted. "We've got to spread them all over the country. I don't know how we'll do it or what we'll use for money or what they'll do for a living, but we've got to get them out of the camps." I told him that it was impossible to do now, out of the question, it would take time, but he was adamant—and he was quite right. Looking back, I don't think Israel would have survived those first chaotic years after 1948 if Eshkol hadn't insisted on taking close to 700,000 immigrants out of the reception centers at once and distributing them throughout the country in the tent cities which covered the state like toadstools within a few weeks, but which, in the end, made it possible for them to be absorbed.

As minister of labor it was my job to find these people work and get them out of those miserable tents, and I was forever plaguing Eshkol for money to finance special projects and housing. But he had other priorities and one slogan. "Look," he used to say to me, "you can't milk a house. But you can milk a cow. Right now if you want money you can have it—but only for cows!" Once I got so angry that I went to Ben-Gurion and told him I was resigning. I had undertaken to be minister of labor and development (which included housing), not minister of unemployment and tents! In the end, of course, I didn't resign, and Eshkol found some more money from somewhere or other for housing.

Another dear friend made in those first years after I went back to work was David Remez, whom I have already mentioned. He had Eshkol's warmth and sense of humor, and like Eshkol, he was drawn to the solving of the practical problems of Zionism, in particular to Solel Boneh and later to Histadrut projects that concerned transportation—roads, shipping and even attempts to encourage local aviation. Remez belonged to the tail end of what we call the Second Aliyah (the 35,000-odd Jews who made their way to Palestine from about 1909 until the outbreak of World War I), and to some extent he was typical of that generation of pioneers. In his youth he wrote poetry, read and talked about socialism, acquired a lifelong interest in Hebrew and studied law (for a while he attended the University of Constantinople, where he met Ben-Gurion, Ben-Zvi and the young Moshe Sharett). But when he arrived in Palestine, he put theory and book learning behind him, picked up the hoe and the spade and for five tough years practiced what he preached as a laborer in the Jewish orange groves and vineyards of the country.

All his life (he died in 1951) Remez combined a passionate concern for the content of the movement—the unity of the workers and the future of socialism in the Jewish national home—with an equally passionate concern for its form. He was as involved with the revival of the Hebrew language as he was with Jewish shipping, and one of his methods of relaxing was to create useful new Hebrew words from ancient Hebrew roots. Even the words that Remez invented (probably the three most important were the Hebrew for bulldozer, road sign and seniority) had to do characteristically with real life—rather than with ideology—although he was extremely active in the leadership of the labor movement and served for many years as secretary-general of the Histadrut. Incidentally, in 1948 Remez was among the drafters of Israel's Declaration of Independence. When the state was established, he became its first minister of transport and then minister of education. We saw a great deal of each other, and we had much in common in terms of our approach to things. Remez was one of the very few of my comrades with whom I even discussed any personal, non-political matters, and I relied a great deal on his advice and guidance—and miss them to this day.

Above all, there was Berl Katznelson. He died in 1944 and so never saw the State of Israel, though I have often wondered what he would have thought of it—and of us. I

have no doubt that many things would have been different—and better—had Berl been with us over the past thirty
years. The labor movement, whose undisputed spiritual
leader and guide he was, would have remained, I am sure,
more loyal to itself and its stated principles than it has,
and maybe we would have achieved a society blessed by
greater equality. Berl played a unique role in the movement, although he held few official posts in it, and I am
ashamed of the fact that despite the twelve volumes of his
essays and speeches that have been published, no one has
yet written a real biography of him. I am certainly no historian, and I cannot (and will not) presume to try to ana-
lyze or assess the extent of Berl's influence on all of us. But
at least I can do something to introduce his name to the
world outside Israel's borders, for he was the one man
whom all of us, including Ben-Gurion, deeply revered and
who served us all as an unquestioned and much loved
moral authority.

Berl was not at all physically impressive. He was small;
his hair was always untidy; his clothes always looked rumpled. But his lovely smile lit up his face, and his eyes—
always a little sad—looked right through you, so that no
one who ever talked to Berl forgot him. I think of him as I
saw him, hundreds of times, buried in a shabby old armchair in one of the two book-lined rooms in which he lived
in the heart of Tel Aviv, where everyone came to see him
and where he worked (because he hated going to an office). "Berl would like you to stop by" was like a command that no one disobeyed. Not that he held court or ever
gave orders, but nothing was done, no decision of any importance to the labor movement in particular, or the *yishuv*
in general, taken without Berl's opinion being sought first.

He sat in that chair, chin in hand, and talked and listened for hours, and his views were almost always decisive,
although the only administrative offices he held in the labor establishment were as editor of *Davar* and director of
the Am Oved publishing house. I am sure that had he lived
until 1948, he would have refused to serve in the cabinet
and that all of us would still have come to him for guidance
and encouragement. It was nothing as cheap as false modesty that kept Berl from seeking power. It was his real dis-
interest in the machinery of politics, which he regarded as
trivial, and his intense, almost burning preoccupation with

the kernel of every issue. He was like an archaeologist digging for the truth, and most of the time he arrived at it—with no concern at all for what was fashionable or likely to make him popular. So throughout the twenties, thirties, and early forties, until he died, no one in the labor movement made up his mind about anything that mattered without first asking, "But what does Berl think?"

He had at least two other outstanding attributes in addition to this unquenchable thirst for the truth. Berl was a man of penetrating intelligence and tremendous charm. It was impossible not to be impressed by his wisdom or deeply attracted by his personality. I remember that at party conferences he used to spend most of the time standing in the corridors talking to "unimportant" people about important things, instead of sitting with the party's leaders at the high table, and when his turn would come to speak, everyone would rush around looking for him. He was no orator. He never made formal speeches. He never spoke *at* anyone. He just stood on the platform and conversed—sometimes for hours—taking little sips of water now and then and weighing the pros and cons of everything with marvelous simplicity. He used that magnificent intellect to clarify and cut through confusion and examine. And no one ever wrote notes, whispered or left the room when Berl spoke, although often he talked for two or three hours at a single stretch.

What did he believe in? Like most of us—though we might have forgotten had Berl not reminded us so often—he believed that our kind of socialism had to be different, that we were creating a society, not just a trade union, and that the class struggle had no significance in a community that had no classes yet. He believed that Zionism was one of the world's greatest revolutionary movements, and he described it as the "plot on which contemporary Jewish history hinges." It meant, he said, "a total rebellion against the bondage of the Diaspora—in any form," and the "creation of a working Jewish population versed in all branches of agriculture and industry." He became the intellectual parent of many of the Histadrut's most important bodies. It was Berl who formulated the need for a workers' bank, for a cooperative wholesale society, and for a workers' sick fund.

This concern with essentials led him also to father first

the concept of a large *unselective* immigration of Jews to Palestine (at a time when there was a tendency in the labor movement to advocate the support primarily of pioneers who had already received some prior training in agriculture abroad) and then the so-called illegal immigration of Jews into Palestine. "From now on," he said, "not the pioneer but the refugee will lead us," and what he was talking about was the destiny of the *yishuv* working itself out through heroic acts undertaken in small stages, step by step—as indeed happened, although Berl didn't live long enough to know it. One of those small stages for which he was also responsible was the dropping of Palestinian Jews behind the Nazi lines (within the framework of the Allied armies) in a desperate attempt to reach the Jews of Europe during World War II, and he was the first of us to formulate the urgent claim to statehood, though it was Ben-Gurion who brought it before the world at a meeting in a New York City hotel in 1942.

Considering how truly erudite Berl was, it is interesting, I think, that he had practically no formal schooling. He had been a rather sickly child and was tutored at home, which gave him time to read. "I read everything I could lay my hands on," he told me once, "the Talmud in Hebrew and Aramaic, Pushkin and Gorky in Russian, Mendele Mocher Sforim in Yiddish and Goethe and Heine in German." By the time he was bar mitzvah at thirteen his father was dead and he was helping support the family by giving private lessons.

Since it took him so long to come to a conclusion about anything, Berl was always a great admirer of people like Ben-Gurion, who could make up their minds quickly and take action. He considered Ben-Gurion the greatest statesman that the movement—and the Jewish people—had "in our time," and to his dying day Ben-Gurion kept Berl's photograph on his desk. (It is also the only photograph in my living room now.) On at least one occasion, however, Berl's obvious lack of enthusiasm for policies favored by Ben-Gurion led to a vote in the Labor Party against Ben-Gurion. Not that Berl canvassed against him or tried to sway anyone in the opposite direction. It was enough for the Labor leadership to know that Berl was not in favor of something for that something to be reviewed very carefully, even if its proponent was B-G. In 1937, when Ben-

Gurion favored the Royal (Peel) Commission proposal to
partition Palestine, Berl opposed our giving our consent to
the Peel plan on the grounds (which turned out to be correct) that the British would never go through with it,
whereas our agreement would forever be on the record and
would certainly be held against us.

He was a very loving man, quite without cynicism, and
he gave a great deal of time and attention to young people—perhaps because he had no children of his own.
Whenever I needed to talk to him, he took me for long
walks. We would march back and forth on Rothschild Bou-
levard for half the night and thrash things out—what was
happening in Russia (he hated the Bolsheviks), the place
Hebrew had to occupy in the Zionist revolution, the importance of publishing good entertaining books in Hebrew
and the need to maintain the unity of the Jewish people by
observing the Sabbath and the dietary laws of Judaism
(kashrut) in all the public institutions of the Jewish national home. He abhorred having to keep a schedule, so he
gave me all the time I wanted without once looking at his
watch, and I loved him for that, too. He used to meet with
groups of youngsters all over the country and listen to what
they had to say. I remember a Saturday not long before he
died, when I took a bunch of young people (including
Sarah) to a kibbutz where Berl was staying for the weekend and they sat on the lawn all afternoon—Berl and fifteen boys and girls—and talked and listened to one another. He organized a month's study course in Rehovot in
1943 with youngsters from all over Palestine, and I can see
him now on the porch with them, his old gray cap pushed
down on his head, concentrating on the not very original
points some boy was making about the Histadrut.

And of course, I shall never forget the dreadful night
that Berl died, in Jerusalem, of a stroke. Years later, when
President Kennedy was assassinated and the United States
stood still in its shock and bereavement, I thought at once
about that night thirty years before when Berl died and we
couldn't, any of us, imagine how anything would go on
without him. I was in Tel Aviv. I had been to a play given
by the Habimah Theater, and on the bus going home I
heard people whispering to each other as though something
awful had happened. Awful things happened all the time in
1944, and I was a bit worried when I saw a knot of friends

standing outside the house I lived in on Hayarkon Street. They were waiting for me. "Berl is dead," they said. There was nothing else to say. I left for Jerusalem at once. Ben-Gurion was in Haifa that night, but after he heard the news, no one dared to talk to him. He just lay on his bed all night, shivering and crying. He had lost the only man whose opinion he ever really valued, perhaps his only real friend.

6. "We Shall Fight Hitler"

I was away from Palestine often in 1929 and 1930. Once I returned to the United States on behalf of the Women's Labor Council, and twice I visited England, also as a representative of the labor movement. In those days, of course, one didn't just hop across the ocean in a plane (although I flew for the first time in 1929—in the United States—and sat bolt upright all the way, frozen with fear but hoping that I looked more confident than I felt), and each trip abroad lasted for several weeks. I knew that Menachem and Sarah dreaded my long absences. On the rare occasions that I had to stay home from work in Tel Aviv because I had a headache, they were overjoyed and used to dance around me, singing a little song: "Mommy's staying at home today! Mommy has a headache! Mommy's staying at home today!" It didn't help the headache any, 'and it hurt the heart a lot; but I was learning that you can get used to anything if you have to, even to feeling perpetually guilty.

It was very strange to be back in the States after seven years. It was like visiting a foreign country, and it took me some time to get my bearings, to find my way around New York, to cope with railway timetables and day coaches and even to get used to the sound of English all around me again, though, in fact, most of the women with whom I actually worked spoke Yiddish. The organization to which I was sent in the States, the Pioneer Women, had been founded by Rachel Yanait-Ben-Zvi only three or four years earlier by women whose husbands were active in the American Labor Zionist movement. Almost all these women were European born. They spoke Yiddish at home, and to people who didn't know them, I suppose they appeared very much like their own mothers, like typical working-class *yiddishe mamas* whose main concern was feeding the family and maintaining the home. But of course, they were different. These were idealistic, politically committed, liberal young women to whom what was happening in Palestine really mattered. They found time to involve themselves in organizational activities and fund raising for farms that were training girls in agricultural work in Petach Tikva, Nachlat Yehuda and Hadera, places that they had never seen and never expected to see. What's more, the ideals of Labor Zionism were not particularly popular anywhere in 1929, least of all perhaps in the States, and the Pioneer Women's campaign for the Women's Labor Council was an uphill road, to put it mildly.

I did what I could to help and encourage them. I made speeches, answered hundreds of questions, explained the urgency of the workingwomen's farms and talked for hours about the new society that was being created in Jewish Palestine by the labor movement, with its guarantees of full emancipation for women. I talked also about the internal Zionist political scene in Palestine and was amazed by and found heartwarming the interest these women showed in the various shades of political belief that were represented in the labor factions of the *yishuv* at that point. Within the year two major labor parties were to merge: Hapoel Hatzair (the Young Worker), which was greatly influenced by A. D. Gordon, and Achdut Ha Avodah (to which I and they belonged), which was based on socialist ideology and considered itself part of the Socialist International. Despite the differences between them, they united into one party called Mapai (which stood for the Labor Party of the Land of Israel), while Hashomer Hatzair (the Young Guard), made up mostly of members of kibbutzim with a Marxist ideology, was on the rise.

Much later, in the 1940s, a group split off from Mapai and eventually joined up with Hashomer Hatzair to form a new party called Mapam (the United Workers Party). Later again, at the end of the 1960s, there were to be other fateful combinations and changes. But Mapai remained dominant throughout the years. Its history has been that of the country itself, and the State of Israel has never yet had a government without at least a Mapai plurality, however small it has been sometimes. As for myself, Mapai was my party from the start, and I have never wavered in my loyalty to it or in my conviction that the only firm foundation for Labor Zionism is the rule of one unified labor party representing the various shades of opinion. In the years to come, I was lucky enough to be able to put this conviction to work, more than once.

At all events, the Pioneer Women were immensely concerned with whatever was going on in Palestine, and it gave me a great deal of satisfaction to know that I was playing a role in their work, although I was worried about the extent to which they seemed determined to remain a Yiddish-speaking group in a country in which the Jewish immigration from Europe was dwindling yearly. It was all very well for them to assure me that all their children spoke Yiddish and that the Yiddish newspapers and theater were still flourishing in America. I came from a country of immigration, too, and just as I was sure that in Palestine Yiddish would eventually be replaced altogether by Hebrew, so I was sure that if it were to survive the next decade, the Pioneer Women would have to broaden its base and attract younger, more Americanized, English-speaking women to its ranks. And I talked about this, too, for days on end with my American comrades.

I also went to Cleveland to see Clara. She was married by then to a young man called Fred Stern and had a bright, handsome little boy, Daniel David. I hadn't seen Clara since she was a teenager, and although we sometimes wrote to each other (and, of course, my parents corresponded regularly with her) it took me a while to get used to her. We seemed—and were—worlds apart. Everything I cared for was in Palestine. Everything that Clara cared for was in the United States. I was totally committed to Zionism and to the extent that I had embarked on a career (though I never thought in those terms) it was obviously within the ranks of the labor movement of the *yishuv;* Clara and Fred were both sociologists, and by the time I met him Fred already had a graduate degree. He was a very intelligent man, very well read and very cultured. He had grown up more or less on the streets of Milwaukee, selling newspapers from the time he was six, and he was entirely "self-made." They were just as involved with Jewish life as I was, but on the community and social-work level, rather than politically or nationally, and we spoke entirely different languages. I knew that Clara would stay in the States, not because life was easier for her there (I was appalled by their poverty in Cleveland), but because that was where she felt she belonged. Although she was interested in Palestine, it was an academic interest, while Fred made it clear to me within a few hours that he disapproved of all nationalism and regarded Zionism as an extremely reactionary movement.

Clara and Fred planned to have only one child so they could give him everything, but as my mother used to say, *"Mensch tracht und Gott lacht"* (Man proposes and God disposes), and Daniel David died when he was eighteen as the result of a severe illness while serving in the U.S. army. After that, Fred became terribly ill. He lost a leg and was bedridden for years. But Clara never felt sorry for herself, never stopped working hard and managed—despite all the tragedies—to make a great success of her professional life. They moved to Bridgeport, Connecticut, prior to David's death and Fred's illness and she became executive director of the United Jewish Council there. But of course, in 1929 all I knew was that my baby sister was not going to join the rest of us in Palestine, and it upset me.

In 1930 I was away again. I attended the Conference of Socialist Women in England. There were more than 1,000 other delegates, and I think it was the first time that I understood how interested people outside Palestine, non-Jews, could become in what was already being called the "Palestine problem." I addressed the conference for only a few minutes; but afterward I was asked to speak to smaller groups in various parts of England, and I met the British in their own country for the first time. The socialist women who bombarded me with questions about the Histadrut, the kibbutz, the Women's Labor Council, the way we lived and how we treated the Arabs were quite different from the one or two British women I had met in Palestine itself. There the British regarded us as a singularly complicated breed of native, less charming than the humble and picturesque Arabs and much more pretentious and demanding. But in England itself, in London, Manchester and Hull, I talked to women who were genuinely fascinated by the Zionist "experiment" and who, if not always sympathetic, were at least eager to learn the facts.

I didn't think that Zionist rhetoric would impress them much, and I decided that a few home truths would be more useful. There had been another wave of Arab riots in 1929,

directed by the mufti of Jerusalem, Haj Amin el-Husseini
(who was to become notorious for his pro-Fascist and Nazi
agitation among the Arabs during World War II), and although the British had eventually restored peace, they did
so in a manner calculated to impress on the Arabs that no
one would be punished very severely for murdering Jews or
for looting Jewish property. I was only too glad, therefore,
to have a chance to explain the real sequence of events to
my socialist sisters in England.

On that same visit I met—also for the first time—women
members of British cooperative societies and heard their
glowing reports about the wonders of Soviet Russia. I remember thinking that perhaps if we brought them to Palestine and showed them what we had accomplished there,
they might talk about us in that same breathless way. I
have never changed my mind about that either, and to this
day I believe that one visit to Israel is worth a hundred
speeches.

I returned to London again that year for a week or two
as a delegate to the Imperial Labour Conference. Ramsay
MacDonald was then prime minister. Although he himself
was sympathetic to, even concerned with, the *yishuv's*
progress, it was his government that issued the notorious
White Paper of 1930 (known as the Passfield Paper) whit-
tling down Jewish immigration and settlement in Palestine.
Thirteen years after the Balfour Declaration, the British
seemed to be more concerned with appeasing the Arabs
than fulfilling their promise to the Jews. Someone in London said to me cynically, "You Jews wanted to own a national home, but all you are getting is a rented flat!" The
truth was even harsher, however. It was beginning to look
as though our landlord now wanted to break the lease altogether, although in 1930, of course, no one imagined that it
would take only eighteen more years for the British to declare that the mandate was absolutely unworkable.

Perhaps it was because I had lived in America for so
long that I didn't fall quite as thoroughly under the spell of
the British as many of my colleagues did. I admired and
liked the British people, including the leadership of the Labour Party, but I can't honestly say that I was really taken
by surprise when we were let down so badly by them, then
or later. Many, if not most, Palestinian Jews were afflicted
in those years by what turned out to be the pathetic be-

lief—all evidence to the contrary notwithstanding—that Britain would keep faith with us after all, regardless of increasing Arab pressure and the traditionally pro-Arab stand of the Colonial Office. I think that much of this reluctance to face up to the fact that the British government was in the process of changing its mind about its responsibility to the Zionists stemmed from the tremendous respect in which British democracy was held by Jews who had been brought up in nineteenth-century Eastern Europe.

On the whole, for many years, most of my colleagues tended to regard British parliamentary and civic institutions and procedures as only a little short of miraculous, while I, who had actually lived in a democracy, was rather less dazzled. Incidentally, it is remarkable that despite the long, stormy and often terrible conflict between us and the British and the way in which that conflict ended in 1948, we Israelis still hold the British people in great and truly affectionate esteem and are more hurt by being let down by the British than by any other nation. There are various reasons for this. One is, of course, that it was Britain that gave us the Balfour Declaration. Another is that the Jews have never forgotten the lonely British stand against the Nazis, and yet another may be, I think, the inborn Jewish respect for tradition. At all events, throughout the thirty-odd years of the mandate, the *yishuv* always made a clear-cut distinction between the Palestine mandatory government and the British people, between the man in the street in England and the officials of the Colonial and Foreign offices, and went on hoping to win unqualified British support. But on the political level, at least, it remained mostly an unrequited love.

I probably would have been sent back to the States sooner or later in any case; but in 1932 Sarah became very ill indeed, and it was I who suggested that I return to America with the children so that she could get expert medical treatment there—although the doctors at home weren't even sure that she would survive the trip. She looked dreadful. Her little face was so swollen that sometimes I could hardly see her eyes, and she was running a fever. "You'll kill her if you take her to the States," our doctor said. "You mustn't cross the ocean with her," and the specialists backed him up. She was virtually fasting by now; there were days when she could have only six or seven glasses of very sweet tea and no food at all. "This is soup," she would pretend. "This is meat, this is bread, this is carrots, and *this* is pudding." One night, while Menachem and Sarah were asleep, Morris and I sat up on the balcony till morning trying to decide what should be done, and by the morning we had made up our minds. I went to the Women's Labor Council and asked if I could be sent as a *shlichah* (an emissary) to the Pioneer Women.

"If we don't take her, she may die here and we'll all know, for the rest of our lives, that we didn't do absolutely everything possible," I explained to my parents, who thought it was madness to travel so far with such a terribly sick child. But I knew that we had no real alternative and that I couldn't sit by her bed with folded hands and watch her grow weaker, paler and more swollen every day until she just faded away.

It wasn't a simple trip to plan. Morris was going to stay and work in Haifa, and I was going to travel alone with the children, first by train to Port Said, then on a French liner to Marseilles, then by train to Cherbourg and finally on the SS *Bremen* to New York. It would take at least two weeks, and who knew what would happen to Sarah during those two weeks? But I felt there was no alternative, and we set out on our dangerous voyage.

I don't think I relaxed for one minute during those two weeks. Menachem was very good and kept himself busy, and Sarah—considering that she was only six and extremely ill—was amazing. It was almost as though she knew how frightened I was and felt that she had to reassure me. We had a cabin with two bunks on the *Bremen*, and at night I brought in a deck chair for myself and lay near Sarah, watching her and, I suppose, in my own way praying.

Fanny and Jacob Goodman, dear and old friends, put us up in their apartment in Brooklyn, and I began at once to arrange for Sarah to be admitted to the Beth Israel Hospital on Manhattan's Lower East Side. No one who has ever hospitalized a child needs to be told what it is like to leave a small son or daughter in a hospital ward. Not only was the hospital strange; but Sarah, of course, knew no English at all, and for the first two weeks she sobbed her heart out and begged me not to leave her.

It didn't take the Beth Israel doctors long to arrive at a

diagnosis. Sarah was indeed suffering from a kidney disease, but not the one for which she had been treated in Palestine. There was no need for a strict diet, no need for her to stay in bed. As soon as she regained her strength, she could go to school, roller-skate and swim, walk down stairs and run up them. She was given treatment, fattened up and, after six weeks, released from the hospital "in perfect health," as I wrote to Morris, tears of relief streaming down my face.

Now I had time for my work and for Menachem, who hadn't been allowed to visit Sarah in the hospital and who had therefore seen very little of me since we arrived in New York. He was furious that she had already learned some English from the nurses at Beth Israel, while he was still having to make himself understood in a mixture of Hebrew and Yiddish. The children missed Morris very much and hated my traveling from city to city for the Pioneer Women, often not coming "home" at all for a month at a time. But I took them to meet Clara and Fred and Morris' mother, to children's concerts, movies and the opera and hoped that their exposure to a richer world than Tel Aviv would make up for their having been uprooted again. Anyhow, they both flourished, and Sarah was literally not to be recognized. This is not to say that either of them ever admitted out loud that anything in the States was better or more imposing than in Palestine or that they weren't confused by being abroad. I remember, for instance, that for weeks Menachem couldn't understand why all our friends in New York said that they were going to vote for Roosevelt. "Why not for Ben-Zvi or Ben-Gurion?" he asked.

As for myself, I worked very hard indeed during those two years. When I left, a rather exaggerated tribute was paid to me in the magazine of the Pioneer Women, which I edited for a while. Headlined "Goldie Meyerson's Tour," it read:

> Goldie brought us a waft of fragrant orange blossoms, sprouting vegetables, budding trees, well-cared-for cows and chickens, stubborn territory conquered, dangerous natural elements vanquished, all the result of work, work, work. Work, not under pressure or for personal gain, but sweat and blood, field and plow, road and cement, barrenness and endurance, swamps

and disease, dangers, deprivations, obstacles, tribulations, inspiration and work, just for work's own sake, just for the ecstasy of creation. . . . Her eloquence and sincerity, her poise and simplicity have instilled in her hearers a reverence for our cause and respect for our organization. We will endeavor to enlist her admirers on behalf of our work and hope to be successful.

But what I recall most vividly of those months of touring (once I traveled for nearly eight weeks at a stretch, talking about Palestine and trying to raise money and bring in recruits for the organization) was the smell of railway stations and the sound of my own voice. The sums of money that were raised in those days bore no resemblance to the millions of dollars that are raised on similar tours nowadays, and the quotas set by each community were very rarely met. But each penny mattered as much then as it does now. If the Pioneer Women of Newark, New Jersey, had hoped to raise $165 from October, 1933, to July, 1934, and had, in fact only raised $17.40 or the Chicago West Side Club had undertaken to raise $425 and had scraped together only $76, it just meant that an extra effort had to be made by the membership. Yet another raffle or bazaar had to be scheduled, another masquerade dance (for which twenty-five cents could be charged) had to be planned, or another lecture delivered on "The Role of the Woman in the Kibbutz" or "The Life of Labor in Palestine."

A typical letter (this one from Winnipeg) sent to me at the Pioneer Women headquarters in New York read:

We have chairmen in charge of the various branches of the work, helped by committees. We meet every week and at every alternate meeting, we have some prominent lectures. Last week we were addressed by Dr. Hennell, who gave a very interesting talk on his visit to Palestine. Our first financial venture this year was a Silver Tea at which we raised $45. We are now planning a Hanukkah celebration, but are not certain as to which form it will take as yet. At present all our members are working enthusiastically on the $5 luncheon and are eagerly looking forward to your visit here.

In the same mail Cleveland asked for my help in organizing an outing with a treasure hunt and a meal cooked out of doors as well as a cultural program tracing "The Beginning and Development of Political Groups in Zionism," while from Kansas City came a request that I speak at a meeting and attend a Friday night social with a lecture "on some Jewish topic." I must have stayed overnight in dozens of homes throughout the United States and Canada and mapped out hundreds of programs in Yiddish and English for study groups. Very often I was exhausted; but I was never bored, and more important, I never doubted for a minute the significance or urgency of the work that the Pioneer Women were doing.

There are also lighter memories of the incessant traveling. Once, on a blustery winter morning, I arrived in Winnipeg on a train that came in early. Since I couldn't see any of the women who were supposed to meet me, I decided to go to a nearby hotel rather than wake any of the women at such an early hour. But no sooner had I unpacked than the telephone rang. A despairing voice said to me, "Mrs. Meyerson, we are all at the station. A large delegation has come to greet you. How can I tell them that we missed you? How can I deprive them of the excitement and the enthusiasm, of the special privilege of being among the first to press your hand in welcome? They will be so disappointed!"

So I said, "Don't worry. I'll be there in a few minutes." I packed again, called a cab and within fifteen minutes was back at the station, meeting the delegation, which happily escorted me to my hostess' home.

And I remember going to a big meeting in some Eastern city where I was to speak three times, once on Saturday evening, again on Sunday morning and a third time on Sunday evening. On Sunday afternoon I was lying down in someone's home to rest for an hour when the president of the local Pioneer Women club came in, sat herself down on my bed and began a harangue. "Look, Golda," she said firmly, "you speak very well, but you don't speak like a woman. When Rachel Yanait-Ben-Zvi was here, she wept and we all wept with her. But you talk like a man, and no one weeps."

All I could say lamely was: "I'm sorry, but I really can't talk any other way." Although she could see that I was dead tired, she felt she had a mission, and she sat there for that precious hour, repeating over and over that I *must* learn to talk like a woman. What upset her, she explained, was that I spoke to the Pioneer Women not only about the Women's Labor Council, but about the Histadrut in general, about the problems of immigration and the political situation, and she didn't think *that* would bring in any money!

On the other hand, I certainly didn't know all there was to know about fund raising either. On one trip I came to a small town in the Midwest to find all the members very excited. They had raised more money that year than ever before, although they were only a very small group. I said, "How did you do it?"

They said, "Oh, by playing cards." I hit the ceiling.

"For Palestine you play cards! *That's* the kind of money we need? If you want to play cards, play as long as you like, but not in our name."

No one said anything, except for one woman who said very quietly, *"Chavera Goldie*, in Palestine you don't play cards?"

"Certainly not," I answered furiously. "What sort of people do you think we are?"

Then, when I came back to my apartment in Tel Aviv a year later, I noticed that some of the members of the Histadrut sat on their verandas in the evening playing cards, though not for money, thank God. I wanted to write to that woman and apologize, but I didn't know her name.

Between tours of the country, I wrote editorials for the magazine and inaugurated the sale of products made or grown in Palestine. One project I started in the Bronx was the sale of matzos baked in Palestine for Passover. I set up headquarters in an enormous warehouse, where we first packed and then delivered the matzos ourselves to the entire neighborhood. I have always been a great believer in not wasting time, so while we packed, I taught the women the latest songs from the *yishuv*.

My editorials always dealt with the political issues that most closely concerned Labor Zionism, and I can now see why that talkative lady accused me of not being sentimental enough—although, as Ben-Gurion once wrote to a colleague of his with whom he was quarreling, "Sentimentality is not a sin, either from the socialist or from the Zionist point of view." I believed, and I still believe, that people who are involved in a cause deserve to be spoken to about it as seriously and as intelligently as possible, and tears don't have to be elicited from anyone in the Zionist movement. God knows, there is always enough to cry about!

One article that I wrote in the spring of 1933 was in answer to a charge made by a leader of Hadassah to the effect that the success of Labor Zionism depended on the financial support of "bourgeois-capitalist Jews":

> We have always maintained that the success of the Zionist work depends mainly on two inner Jewish factors—workers to do the work and money to make this work possible. We did not know that the money coming from large Jewish masses must be labeled as "class money." . . . We consider the money for the Jewish National Fund and the Keren Hayesod [which was responsible for financing Jewish immigration and settlement in Palestine] as well as the manpower, the Halutz [pioneering] movement, to be a manifestation of the will and determination of the nation at large . . . Does this mean that we are opposed to private capital and private initiative? Indeed not. Labor Zionists are primarily interested in mass immigration into Palestine. If we cannot achieve this end through national capital, we welcome private capital. It is true that we say that even private capital must serve the ends of Zionism. Private capital that does not employ Jewish labor does not help our cause. . . . To our sorrow, it is only too often that we have witnessed private enterprise in Palestine used exclusively for private benefit, forgetting that Jewish immigration in Palestine depends primarily on possibilities of work created in the country. And we wish to state here again very emphatically: private capital that does not employ Jewish labor is *not* welcome in Palestine because private capital of such a character will not make possible the mass immigration which we—and the Hadassah—desire. . . .

In the summer of 1934 we got ready to return home. I made a final round of the States, to part from the Pioneer Women clubs and chapters I had come to know so well. I was filled with respect for those hardworking, unfashionable, devoted women who had given me so much affection, and I wanted them to know how grateful I was. I knew that whatever happened in Palestine, they would always support and aid us—and of course, time was to prove me right.

I had arrived in New York in 1932 with two small children, neither of whom spoke one word of English. I arrived back in Palestine in 1934 with two small children who now spoke both English and Hebrew—and who were beside themselves with joy at seeing Morris again. There were many disappointments in Morris' life, but it was a source of constant delight to him that Menachem was profoundly interested in music and obviously talented. Although, later on, it was usually I who had to carry the cello to and from Menachem's music lessons (until he was big enough to haul it around himself), it was Morris who, throughout the years, listened on weekends to Menachem practice, played records for him and strengthened and deepened his growing love for music.

But I had come back to Palestine to face an even greater challenge than serving as national secretary for the Pioneer Women in the United States. Within a few weeks of our homecoming I was asked to join the Va'ad Hapoel (the Executive Committee of the Histadrut).

To the extent that the Histadrut represented what was, on the whole, an extremely advanced form of Jewish self-government in Palestine, the Va'ad Hapoel was its "cabinet"—within which, for the next very stormy fourteen years, I was assigned various portfolios and responsibilities. None of these, as I look back, were either easy to carry out or likely to make me particularly popular inside the Histadrut itself. But they did have one great asset. They all had to do with what in fact most concerned and interested me—the translation of socialist principles into the down-to-earth terminology of everyday life.

I suppose that if times had been good economically and politically—or at least better—in the Palestine of the mid-1930s and 1940s, it would have been relatively easy to ensure a just sharing of burdens within the labor community. After all, other than what they did for a living, there really were no differences at all—either economic or social—between the so-called rank and file of the membership and the so-called Histadrut leadership. We all were paid a fixed basic living wage, which varied only according to actual seniority and the number of dependents in each family, and there were no exceptions to this rule. I know that today people in Israel and elsewhere regard this kind of egalitarianism not only as old-fashioned but as downright unworkable. Perhaps it is, but I myself approved it and have always approved of it. I still think that it made good sound socialist sense—which usually means good sound common sense—for the janitor of the Histadrut building in Tel Aviv who had nine children to support to get a considerably fatter pay envelope than I, who had only two children to support.

Socialism in practice involved much more than my calling this janitor Shmuel and than his calling me Golda. It meant also that his obligations to the other members of the Histadrut were the same as mine, and the economic situation in Palestine, as well as everywhere else, being as difficult as it was then, this aspect of trade unionism became the focal point of most of my battles within the Histadrut.

Payment of Histadrut dues was fixed according to a sliding scale, like income tax. It was paid every month in a lump sum that covered trade union funds, pension funds and the Kupat Holim (the Workers' Sick Fund) and was known as the single tax. I was convinced that this single tax should be assessed not according to basic wages or average earnings or some theoretical sum, but on the full pay that each worker actually received. Otherwise, where was the "equality" we talked about so much? Was sharing to be the sole property of the kibbutzim, or could give-and-take be made the way of life among the workers of Tel Aviv, too? And what about the Histadrut membership's collective responsibility for comrades who were unemployed? Was it conceivable that the Histadrut should make its voice heard (and its presence felt) on each and every issue that vitally concerned the *yishuv*—immigration, settlement, self-defense—but avert its gaze from the men and women who were without jobs and whose children were barely getting enough to eat? If nothing else, mutual aid—one of the bases of the Histadrut—was certainly a prerequisite of socialism, however hard up an *employed* member of the Histadrut might be and regardless of how painful it was to turn over a day's salary each month to a special unemployment fund. But I felt very strongly about these fundamental matters and persisted in setting up an unemployment fund, despite the very vocal opposition to it. We called it Mifdeh, which means redemption, and when the number of unemployed increased (at one point during the 1930s reaching about 10,000 Histadrut members), I pressed for an increase in the unemployment tax, and we established Mifdeh B.

Some of my friends charged me with "destroying the Histadrut" and "demanding the impossible," but Ben-Gurion, Berl Katznelson and David Remez all backed me, and the Histadrut nonetheless managed to remain intact. As a matter of fact, it turned out that the Mifdeh campaign served as a very important precedent for much heavier voluntary taxation that came not very long afterward in the form of the *Kofer Hayishuv* (ransom of the yishuv), established when the toll in life and property of the Arab disturbances of 1936 became so high that we were forced to levy a defense tax on virtually the entire Jewish population. And even later, during World War II, when we set up a War Needs and Rescue Fund, we relied again on experience gained in the days of those loathed Mifdeh drives.

I was also involved in the bitter aftermath (it lasted many years) of a terrible tragedy that overtook the labor movement when I was in the States. One of the brightest and best of the rising stars of Mapai, young Chaim Arlosoroff, who had just returned from what today would be called a fact-finding mission to the Germany in which Hitler had just come to power, was shot to death as he walked along the Tel Aviv beach with his wife. A member of the right-wing Revisionist Party, Abraham Stavasky, was accused and convicted of Arlosoroff's murder, though he was acquitted afterward by the court of appeals for lack of evidence. The identity of the assassin will probably never be known, but at the time virtually the entire leadership of the shocked and bereaved labor movement was convinced of Stavasky's guilt, as I myself was. Arlosoroff represented moderation, caution, a balanced approach to world problems and, of course, to our own, and his tragic death seemed the inevitable consequence of the kind of antisocialist right-wing militarism and violent chauvinism that was being advocated by the Revisionists. I hadn't got to know

Arlosoroff very well yet; but like everyone who knew him at all, I was greatly impressed by his intellectual powers and his political acumen, and I was deeply shaken by his murder, news of which had reached me in New York.

But even more, I was horrified by the very notion that in Palestine one Jew might be capable of killing another and that political extremism within the *yishuv* could lead to bloodshed. At all events, with Arlosoroff's murder, what had been for years a growing friction between the left and right wings of the Zionist movement turned into a breach that in some respects has not healed to this day—and perhaps will never heal entirely.

At the end of 1933 and the beginning of 1934 it looked as though battle lines had been drawn up within the *yishuv*—particularly on the labor front. The Revisionists accused the Histadrut of a "blood libel" and of maintaining a stranglehold on the *yishuv* by keeping nonsocialists out of work and thus literally starving out its political opponents, and there were constant, sometimes bloody clashes between workers all over the country. Ben-Gurion thought that unity within the Jewish community of Palestine must be preserved at all costs, and many of us (myself included) agreed with him. He proposed a "cease-fire" in the form of a labor agreement between left and right that would, he believed, help put an end to the dissension. We spent weeks and weeks discussing the "treaty" heatedly, sometimes even hysterically; but Arlosoroff's murder dominated all the discussions, and Ben-Gurion's proposal was turned down— most unfortunately, I think.

But unemployment, on the one hand, and internal conflict, on the other, were only two of the problems we faced. There were even more serious issues at stake. Both in Palestine and abroad, storm clouds had gathered. Hitler had come to power in 1933, and however absurd his loudly proclaimed program for world domination by the Aryan race had seemed at first, the violent anti-Semitism which he had preached from the start was obviously not just a rhetorical device. One of Hitler's very first acts, in fact, was the passage of savage anti-Jewish legislation that stripped Germany's Jews of all usual civil and human rights. Of course, no one, myself included, dreamed then that Hitler's vow to destroy the Jews would ever be literally carried out. In a way, I suppose, it should be chalked up to the credit of normal decent men and women that we couldn't believe that such a monstrously evil thing would ever actually happen—or that the world would permit it to happen. It wasn't that we were gullible. It was simply that we couldn't conceive of what was then still inconceivable. Today, however, no horror is inconceivable to me anymore.

But even before Hitler's "Final Solution," the first results of Nazi persecution—legally enacted—were terrible enough, and I again felt that there was only one place on the face of the globe to which the Jews could come as a right, no matter what restrictions the British sought to impose on their immigration to Palestine. By 1934 thousands of uprooted homeless refugees from Nazism were making their way to Palestine. Some of them brought with them what few possessions they could rescue, but most of them came with nothing at all. They were highly educated, industrious, energetic people, and their contribution to the *yishuv* was immense. But it meant that 60,000 men, women and children had to be absorbed at once by a population of fewer than 400,000 that was barely able to make ends meet in any case, and they all had somehow to survive not only growing Arab terror, but also the indifference—not to say hostility—of the mandatory government.

Absorbing immigrants, particularly if they are refugees, is quite different from merely welcoming them. The thousands of men, women and children who came to us then from Germany and Austria had to be housed, given jobs, taught Hebrew and helped acclimatize. The lawyer from Berlin, the musician from Frankfurt, the research chemist from Vienna had to be turned, overnight, into a chicken farmer, a waiter and a bricklayer; otherwise they wouldn't have work at all. They also had to get used—again overnight—to a new and harder way of life and to new dangers and deprivations. It was not easy for them or for us, and to this day I think it was remarkable that the *yishuv* weathered those years and emerged from them stronger than it had been before. But I suppose there are only two reasonable or even possible responses to national adversity. One is to collapse, to give in and to say, "It just can't be done." The other is to grit your teeth and to fight on as many fronts as necessary for as long as necessary—which is exactly what we did and, as it turns out, exactly what we are still doing now.

In fact, today I often think of how it was in Palestine in the 1930s and the 1940s and derive considerable encouragement from these memories, although certainly not all of them are pleasant. But when people say to me in 1975, "How can Israel possibly cope with everything—with the Arab determination to liquidate the state, with the overwhelming Arab superiority of money, men and arms, with the influx of thousands of immigrants from Russia, with the relative indifference, at best, of most of the world to these problems and with a critical economic situation that seems impossible to remedy?" I can only answer, and with perfect honesty, "It was all much more difficult forty years ago, and we did manage somehow—though the price was always very high." Sometimes, in fact, I think that only those of us who were active forty years ago can really understand how much was accomplished since then or how great our victories have really been, and maybe that is why the greatest optimists in Israel today tend to be the old people like myself, who take it for granted that nothing as tremendous as the rebirth of a nation can be accomplished rapidly, painlessly or effortlessly!

Anyhow, we sorted out our priorities. The daily job had to be done, however acute the emergency. As far as I personally was concerned, this meant serving as chairman of the board of directors of the Workers' Sick Fund, supervising the working conditions of Histadrut members employed on building British army camps all over the country, conducting a variety of other labor negotiations—and getting the housework done and helping Menachem and Sarah with their homework. Those were the routine preoccupations.

But at the same time we had to formulate and implement a series of major decisions about the overall situation of the *yishuv*. The first question that required an immediate reply was what were we going to do about the constant outbreaks of Arab terror? In 1936 alone they had resulted in the wanton destruction of hundreds of thousands of trees planted by the Jews with so much love, care and hope; the derailing of countless trains and buses; the burning of hundreds of fields; and, most dreadful of all, in some 2,000 armed attacks on Jews—eighty of whom were killed (and many more gravely wounded).

The riots started in April, 1936. By the summer it was

no longer safe for Jews to travel from one city to another. Whenever I had to go from Tel Aviv to Jerusalem for a meeting—which was frequently—I kissed the children good-bye in the morning knowing that I might well never come home again, that my bus might be ambushed, that I might be shot by an Arab sniper at the entrance to Jerusalem or stoned to death by an Arab mob on the outskirts of Tel Aviv. The Haganah (the underground Jewish self-defense organization) was much better equipped and larger than it had been at the time of the Arab riots of 1929, but we had no intention either of turning it into an instrument of counterterror against the Arabs just because they were Arabs or of providing the British with any excuse for further clamping down on Jewish immigration and settlement, as they tended to do whenever we visibly played too active a role in our own defense. Although it is always much harder to exercise self-restraint than it is to hit back, we had one paramount consideration: Nothing must be done— even in the face of constant danger and harassment—that might provoke the British into slashing the number of Jews allowed to enter Palestine. The policy of self-restraint (*havlagah* in Hebrew) was rigidly enforced. Whenever and wherever possible, Jews defended themselves from attack, but there were virtually no acts of retaliation by the Haganah throughout the three years of what the British, with splendid understatement, chose to call "the disturbances."

This determination of ours to defend ourselves but not to retaliate was not, however, universally applauded in the *yishuv*. A minority clamored for counterterror and denounced the policy of *havlagah* as cowardly. I was always among the majority that was absolutely convinced that *havlagah* was the one and only ethical course we could follow. The notion of attacking Arabs indiscriminately, regardless of whether or not they were the particular perpetrators of an outrage, was morally abhorrent to me. A specific attack had to be repelled, and a specific criminal had to be punished. Well and good. But we were not going to kill Arabs just because they were Arabs or engaged in the kind of wanton violence that typified the Arab method of fighting us.

Let me at this juncture deal also—even if very briefly— with the ridiculous accusation that I have heard for so many years to the effect that we ignored the Arabs of Palestine and set about developing the country as though it had no Arab population at all. When the instigators of the Arab disturbances of the late 1930s claimed, as they did, that the Arabs were attacking us because they had been "disposed," I did not have to look up British census figures to know that the Arab population of Palestine had doubled since the start of Jewish settlements there. I had seen for myself the rate of growth of the Arab population ever since I had first come to Palestine. Not only did the living standard of the Arabs of Palestine far exceed that of the Arabs anywhere else in the Middle East, but attracted by the new opportunities, hordes of Arabs were emigrating to Palestine from Syria and other neighboring countries all through those years. Whenever some kindly representative of the British government sought to shut off Jewish immigration by declaring that there was not enough room in Palestine, I remember making speeches about Palestine's larger absorptive capacity, complete with statistical references which I dutifully took from British sources, but which were based on what I had actually witnessed with my own eyes.

And let me add, there was no time during the thirties that I did not hope that eventually the Arabs of Palestine would live with us in peace and equality as citizens of a Jewish homeland—just as I kept on hoping that Jews who lived in Arab countries would be allowed to live there in peace and equality. This was another reason why our policy of self-restraint in the face of the Arab attack seemed so important to me. Nothing, I felt, must be allowed to complicate or embitter the future. It didn't work out that way, but it took us all a long time to accept the fact that the reconciliation we expected was not going to take place.

Then we decided to step into the economic vacuum that was created when the Arab Higher Committee, headed by the mufti, declared a general strike in the hope of paralyzing the *yishuv* altogether. No Arab anywhere in Palestine was to go to work, the mufti ordered, until all Jewish immigration ended and all land purchases by Jews came to a stop. To this we had a simple reply. If the port in Jaffa no longer operated, we would open a port of our own in Tel Aviv. If Arab farmers no longer marketed their crops, then Jewish farmers would double and triple their efforts. If all Arab transport ceased on the roads of Palestine, then Jewish trucks and bus drivers would work extra shifts and

armor-plate their vehicles. Whatever the Arabs refused to
do, we would get done—somehow or other.

There were, of course, many people whose judgment,
opinions and personalities affected these decisions—
including, to a very small extent, my own—but there was
one man, above all others, on whose remarkable qualities
of leadership and stunning political intuition we all relied
and were to continue to rely in the years that lay ahead.
That man was David Ben-Gurion, the only one among us
whose name, I profoundly believe, will be known to Jews
and non-Jews alike even in a hundred years. Not long ago,
I visited Ben-Gurion's grave in the Negev kibbutz of Sdeh
Boker, where he spent the last years of his life and where
he wished to be buried. Standing there alone, I suddenly
recalled a conversation I had with him in 1963, when he
resigned (for the second and last time) as prime minister
of Israel and several of us begged him to change his mind.

"Of course no one man is ever really indispensable," I
said to him. "You know that, and we know that. But
I'll tell you one thing, Ben-Gurion. If we were to go
to Times Square today, stop people in the street and ask
them the names of the presidents and prime ministers of
most of the important countries in the world, they wouldn't
be able to answer us. But if we asked them, 'Who is the
prime minister of Israel?' they would all know." It didn't
make much of an impression on Ben-Gurion; but I think it
was true, and what's more, I am sure that the names Israel
and Ben-Gurion will be linked in men's minds for a very long
time, maybe forever. No one, of course, can tell what or
who the future may bring, but I very much doubt that the
Jewish people will ever produce a greater leader or a more
astute and courageous statesman.

What was he like as a person? It is a hard question for
me to answer because it is so difficult to describe someone
whom you have both admired and followed for so long and
have also opposed as strongly as I was eventually to oppose
Ben-Gurion. But I will try—not that the way I saw him is
necessarily the only way he can be seen or that my own
perceptions are necessarily so sharp.

The first thing that occurs to me about Ben-Gurion
when I sit down to write about him now is that he was not
a man to whom one could be close. Not only to whom I
was never really close, but to whom I don't think anyone

was ever close, except perhaps his wife, Paula, and maybe
his daughter, Renana. The rest of us—Berl, Shazar, Remez,
Eshkol—not only were comrades-in-arms, but also liked
each other's company, and we used to drop in on one
another and talk about all sorts of things—not just the big
political or economic issues, but about people, about ourselves and our families. But not Ben-Gurion. It never entered my mind, for instance, to call up Ben-Gurion and
say, "Look, suppose I come over tonight?" Either you had
something specific to talk about, some business to conduct
with him, or you didn't go to him. He didn't need people
the way the rest of us did. He was much more self-
sufficient than we were, but of course he also didn't know
much about people, though he used to get very angry with
me indeed whenever I told him this.

I think part of his not needing anyone was due to the
fact that he found it so difficult to talk to people. He had
no small talk at all. I remember his telling me that when he
first came to Palestine in 1906, he once walked the streets
of Jerusalem for almost an entire night with Rachel Yanait
without saying a single word to her. I could only compare
it to a story that Marc Chagall once told me about himself
years ago. Chagall's father had been a poor water carrier in
Vitebsk. He carried pails of water all day and only came
home late at night. "He would come in, sit down, and my
mother would give him something to eat," Chagall said. "I
never remember his talking to me or our having a single
conversation together. My father would just sit at the table
and tap on it with his fingers all evening. So I grew up
without knowing how to talk to anyone." Then Chagall fell
in love with a girl, and they went together for years, but he
couldn't ever talk to her. When he left Vitebsk, she waited
for him, and he wanted to write to her and ask her to
marry him; but he couldn't write a letter, just as he
couldn't converse with anyone. So she stopped waiting and
married someone else. Ben-Gurion was like that, although
he could write, but I can't imagine his ever talking to anyone about his marriage or his children or anything like
that. It would have been a waste of time for him.

On the other hand, whatever interested him or mattered
to him he did with complete and total concentration—
something that not everyone always appreciated or understood. Once—I think it was in 1946—he asked for a few

months' leave from the Jewish Agency, which he headed at that time, so that he could learn exactly what the Haganah had at its disposal and what it was likely to need for the struggle he was so sure lay ahead. Everyone laughed at the idea of what they called Ben-Gurion's "seminar." Who took time off, in those days of incessant crisis "to study"? The answer, of course, is that Ben-Gurion did, and when he came back to work, he knew more about the real strength of the Haganah than all of us put together. After he had been back at work for a few days, he called me up. "Golda," he said, "come over. I want to talk to you." He was walking back and forth in his big study upstairs, pacing the floor. "I tell you," he said to me, "I feel as though I were going mad. What's going to happen to us? I'm sure the Arabs will attack us, and we're not prepared for it. We have nothing. What's going to happen to us?" He was literally beside himself with anxiety. Then we sat down and talked, and I told him how frightened of the future one of our colleagues in the labor movement was, a man who had always been opposed to Ben-Gurion's activism and now, in the dark years of what we called the *ma'avak* (our full-fledged struggle) against the British, was all the more so. Ben-Gurion listened to me very attentively. Then he said, "You know, it takes a lot of courage to be afraid—and still more courage to say so. But even Y. doesn't know how much there is to be afraid of." Fortunately, Ben-Gurion knew. He combined his fantastic intuition with as much information as he could acquire, and then he did something about it. He went to the Jews of the United States— almost three years before the War of Independence broke out in 1948—and enlisted their help in what he called the "probable eventuality" of war with the Arabs. He wasn't always right, but he was more often right than wrong—and he was absolutely right about that.

Ben-Gurion wasn't a callous or a heartless man at all, but he knew that sometimes it is necessary to make decisions that cost lives. At a time when many people in the *yishuv* thought it was impossible for us to establish the State of Israel and defend it successfully, Ben-Gurion saw no real alternative—and I, for one, agreed with him. Even people like Remez had grave doubts. I remember we sat on my balcony overlooking the sea one night early in 1948, talking about what the future might bring, and Remez said to me solemnly, "You and Ben-Gurion will smash the last hope of the Jewish people." Nevertheless, Ben-Gurion brought the Jewish state into being. Not alone, of course, but I doubt that without his leadership it would have been established.

From the start we worked together very well. Ben-Gurion trusted me and, I think, liked me. For years he never let anyone criticize me in his presence, although there were times when I disagreed with him on significant issues—such as the Peel Commission's proposal to partition Palestine in 1931 or the importance of the "illegal" immigration to Palestine, which Ben-Gurion didn't take very seriously at first.

Was he dictatorial? Not really. It is a vulgarization to say that people were frightened of him, but he was certainly not a man with whom anyone disagreed lightly. Among the people who fell out of favor with Ben-Gurion—and for whom he made life difficult—were two of the prime ministers of Israel, Moshe Sharett and Levi Eshkol. But there were also others.

He hated to be accused of running the party, and later the government, in an autocratic way. At one party meeting when this charge was leveled at him, he appealed to a minister whom he regarded as being beyond reproach from the point of view of intellectual honesty and who, Ben-Gurion knew only too well, was not in the least scared of him. "Tell me, Naphtali," he asked. *"Do* I conduct party meetings undemocratically?"

Peretz Naphtali looked at him for a minute, smiled his charming smile and answered thoughtfully, "No, I wouldn't say that. I would say rather that in the most democratic fashion possible, the party always decides to vote the way you want it to." Since Ben-Gurion had no sense of humor at all (I can't remember his ever having cracked a joke), he was quite satisfied with Naphtali's reply—and, by the way, it was not inaccurate.

The subject of government meetings and votes reminds me of a conversation I had a few years ago at a party held during a meeting of the Socialist International. I was sitting with Willy Brandt, Bruno Kreisky, one of the prime ministers of a Scandinavian country and Harold Wilson, who was not prime minister then. We were chatting about the processes of government when one of them turned to me and asked, "How do you conduct cabinet meetings?"

I said, "We vote."

They were all horrified. "You *vote* at cabinet meetings?"

"Well, of course," I answered. "What do you do?"

Brandt explained that in Bonn he presented an issue, it was discussed, he gave a résumé of the discussion and then his decision. Kreisky nodded his head in agreement and added, "Any minister who dared say that he was opposed to the prime minister's summary and decision—well, he'd have to go home." But that's not the way it is or ever was in Israel, even in Ben-Gurion's day. We always have long discussions and when necessary take a real vote. I don't think that I was ever in the minority when I was prime minister, but since we have coalition governments and therefore large cabinets—and most members of an Israeli cabinet think that they aren't performing their duty properly if they don't ask for the floor on each and every question—cabinet meetings often last for hours, even when the subjects discussed could be decided on in half an hour. I shall never forget the astonishment on Brandt and Kreisky's faces when I patiently explained all this to them.

But to get back to Ben-Gurion, the really uncanny thing about him for most of his political life was that even when in theory he was quite wrong, he would usually be proved right in practice, and that, after all, is the difference between a statesman and a politician. Although I never forgave him the wounds he inflicted upon us over the Lavon Affair, the abuse he heaped on his former comrades or the damage he did to the labor movement in the last ten years or so of his life, I still feel the way I felt once when I sent him a cable on his birthday from one of my missions abroad. "Dear Ben-Gurion," I wrote. "We have had many arguments in the past and doubtless will have many more, but no one, regardless of what the future may hold, will ever be able to take away from me my sense of the enormous privilege I have had in working side by side, for tens of years, with the one man who, more than any other single person, was responsible for the establishment of the Jewish state." I believed it then, and I still believe it.

In 1937 I was sent back to the United States, this time to raise funds for a Histadrut project that held tremendous appeal for me (and, as a fringe benefit, also fascinated my

children). It was a campaign to launch a shipping enterprise called Nachshon (after the first of the Children of
Israel to obey Moses' command and jump into the Red Sea
during the Exodus from Egypt), and I liked everything
about it. It was a brainchild of David Remez's, born in the
wake of the Arab general strike. The ancient Jews in Palestine had been a seafaring people, of course; but the art was
lost in the course of the 2,000 years of landlocked exile,
and it was only just being revived. Then the strike of the
Jaffa port workers in 1936 served as the starting signal for
a major effort on the part of the *yishuv* to train people, as I
told audiences throughout the States, "to work on the sea
as we had trained them for so many years to work on the
soil." This meant opening a port of our own, buying ships,
training seamen and generally becoming a seafaring nation
again.

The day the port of Tel Aviv opened for business was, in
every sense of the words, a national holiday for the Jews of
Palestine. It still moves me to remember how the waiting
crowds on the shore rushed into the sea to help the long-
shoremen—all of them Jews from Salonika—to unload the
sacks of cement from the Yugoslav ship that was the first
to anchor in Tel Aviv. We all knew that a wooden jetty
was not really a harbor yet, certainly no Rotterdam or
Hamburg; but it was ours, and we were very proud of it
and very excited. Later it was replaced by an iron jetty,
and every evening (if the British didn't slap a curfew on
Tel Aviv), the whole town came to see how work was
progressing. Poets wrote poems about the port, songs were
composed in its honor, and more important, ships actually
used it!

There was something about the idea of the return of the
Jews to the sea that had always attracted me, and I sailed
whenever I could on "Jewish" ships, of which the first was
the SS *Tel Aviv*, on whose decks the details of Nachshon
were first worked out when Remez, Berl Katznelson and I
once traveled together to a Zionist congress in Switzerland.
Of course, there were skeptics who couldn't understand
what difference it made that almost all of Palestine's sea-
borne traffic was in non-Jewish hands; but I saw Nachshon
as one more stage toward Jewish independence, and for a
while I ate, drank, slept and talked shipping and fishing—
and made yet another fund-raising trip to the United States

on their behalf. But in a sense, that was just a romantic interlude. Sometimes in the evenings, when I was finished with cooking for the next day and whatever mending I had to do, if there were no meetings of theVa'ad Hapoel and nobody needed to see me for anything, I used to sit on my veranda, cool off in the breeze and look out at the sea, wondering what it would be like if we had a navy of our own, a flourishing merchant fleet and passenger liners, flying the Star of David, going to Europe, Asia and Africa. It was a form of relaxation for me, just as Ben-Gurion secretly went to the movies and devoured detective stories or other people collected stamps. I knew all the time that for us the real meaning of the sea was much grimmer, for it was only by sea that Jewish refugees from Nazi Europe could make their way to Palestine, provided that the British would let them in. And by 1939, with a world war looming, it was clear that the British Colonial Office was going to give way completely to Arab pressure and virtually stop all immigration of Jews to Palestine.

The Peel Commission, which had toured Palestine in 1936, had recommended that the country be partitioned into two states, a Jewish state to occupy all of 2,000 square miles and an Arab state occupying the rest of the country, with the exception of an international enclave for Jerusalem and a corridor from it to the coast. The proposed Jewish state was not my idea of a viable national home for the Jewish people. It was far too small and far too cramped. I thought it was a grotesque proposal, and I said so, although most of my colleagues, led by Ben-Gurion, reluctantly decided to accept it in the end. "Someday my son will ask me by what right I gave up most of the country, and I won't know how to answer him," I said at one of the many party meetings at which the Peel proposal was debated. I was not entirely alone in my party, of course. Berl, as I have already mentioned, and a few other ranking members of the labor movement agreed with me. But we were wrong, and Ben-Gurion, in his greater wisdom, arguing that any state was better than none, was right.

Thank God it was not because of me that we didn't get that state in 1937, but because of the Arabs, who flatly turned down the partition plan—although had they accepted it, they could have had a "Palestinian" state forty years ago. The guiding principle behind the attitude of the

Arabs in 1936 and 1937, however, was exactly what it has been ever since: Decisions are made not on the basis of what is good for them, but on the basis of what is bad for us. And in retrospect, it is clear that the British themselves never intended to implement the Peel plan. At all events, I certainly couldn't have lived with myself all these years if I had thought—in the light of what happened afterward—that it was I who was to blame for its collapse. If we had had even a tiny little mockery of a state only a year before the war broke out, hundreds of thousands of Jews—perhaps many more—might have been saved from the ovens and gas chambers of the Nazis.

Although the question of immigration was quickly turning into a matter of life or death for the Jews of Europe, we seemed to be the only people in the world who understood this—and who was going to listen to us? What were we? A few hundred thousand Jews who were very far from being masters of their own fate, stuck away in some small corner of the Middle East, not even an integral part of the British Commonwealth and lacking so much as the elementary right to say to the threatened Jews of Europe, "Come to us now before it is too late." It was the British who held the keys to the gates of the Jewish homeland, and they were clearly about to lock them—regardless of what was already happening.

But if Palestine was to be out of bounds for the Jews of Europe, then what about other countries? In the summer of 1938 I was sent to the International Conference on Refugees that was called by Franklin Delano Roosevelt in Evian-les-Bains. I was there in the ludicrous capacity of the "Jewish observer from Palestine," not even seated with the delegates but with the audience, although the refugees under discussion were my own people, members of my own family, not just inconvenient numbers to be squeezed into official quotas, if at all possible. Sitting there in that magnificent hall, listening to the delegates of thirty-two countries rise, each in turn, to explain how much they would have liked to take in substantial numbers of refugees and how unfortunate it was that they were not able to do so, was a terrible experience. I don't think that anyone who didn't live through it can understand what I felt at Evian—a mixture of sorrow, rage, frustration and horror. I wanted to get up and scream at them all, "Don't you know that these 'numbers' are human beings, people who may spend the rest of their lives in concentration camps, or wandering around the world like lepers, if you don't let them in?" Of course, I didn't know then that not concentration camps but death camps awaited the refugees whom no one wanted. If I had known that, I couldn't have gone on sitting there silently hour after hour being disciplined and polite.

I remember at one point thinking back to the Socialist International I had attended the year before, when I had watched the Spanish delegation, weeping and imploring for help so Madrid might be saved. All that Ernest Bevin could find it in his heart to say to them was: "British labor is not prepared to go to war for you." Much later I was to learn lessons of my own about socialist brotherhood, but at Evian I realized—perhaps for the first time since I was a little girl in Russia listening in terror to the hooves of Cossack horses thundering through town—that it is not enough for a weak people to demonstrate the justice of its demands.

To the question "To be or not to be?" each nation must make its own reply in its own way, and Jews neither can nor should ever depend on anyone else for permission to stay alive. A great deal has happened to the world, to the *yishuv* and to me personally since 1938, and much of what has happened has been terrible. But at least the words "Jewish refugees" are no longer heard anywhere because now there is a Jewish state that is prepared and able to take in every Jew—skilled worker or not, old or young, sick or healthy—who wants to live there.

Nothing was accomplished at Evian except phraseology, but before I left, I held a press conference. At least the journalists wanted to hear what I had to say, and through them we could reach the rest of the world and try again to get its attention. "There is only one thing I hope to see before I die," I told the press, "and that is that my people should not need expressions of sympathy anymore."

But in May, 1939, despite the escalating persecution and murder of Jews in Austria and Germany, the British decided that the time was ripe, after all, for finally slamming Palestine's gates shut. The Chamberlain government gave way to Arab blackmail in much the same fashion that it was giving way to the Nazis. If appeasement was the solution to the "problem" of Czechoslovakia, then it could certainly serve the same purpose in Palestine—about which no one seemed to care very much in any case. The 1939 White Paper on Palestine, in effect, ended the British mandate, although the death throes were to go on for another nine years. A Palestinian state was to be created within a decade based on a constitution that guaranteed the "rights of minorities" and a canton system. Jewish land purchases in Palestine were to end altogether—except in some 5 percent of the country—and Jewish immigration into Palestine was first to be restricted to a maximum of 75,000 Jews over the forthcoming five years and then stopped forever "unless the Arabs of Palestine are prepared to acquiesce in it."

A day or two before the White Paper was published, I had written an article for the magazine put out by the Women's Labor Council. I had stayed up almost all night to write it, and I remember telling Menachem that even if no one read it, it had given me some relief to do it. Today, reading it again, I am struck by the irony of the timing.

> Every day brings forth new edicts that engulf hundreds of thousands of people. We know, we mothers, that Jewish children are scattered everywhere in the world and that Jewish mothers in many countries ask for only one thing: "Take our children away. Take them wherever you choose. Only save them from this hell!"
>
> Children cross from Germany to Austria, from Austria to Czechoslovakia, from Czechoslovakia to England—and who can assure their mothers that by getting them out of one hell, they have not got them into another?
>
> Here, however, our children will be safe for the Jewish people. And I cannot conceive that we shall fail in our work here, in our defense of every single settlement, even the smallest, if we keep before us the picture of the thousands of Jews in the concentration camps of Europe. Therein lies our strength . . . our fundamental faith is alive. What has been done to other peoples and to other countries will not be done to us.

Little did I know that what would be done to the Jews would be indescribably worse.

Obviously, the White Paper was unacceptable. We held protest meetings and strikes and signed manifestos. But also decisions had to be taken. It was not enough to bemoan our betrayal at the hands of the British or to march, sick at heart and with bowed heads, down the main streets of Tel Aviv, Jerusalem and Haifa. What were we going to do? Were we going to defy the British, and if so, how? Toward what goal was the Zionist movement going to direct its activities now that the British had chosen—in the hour of our greatest need—to wipe their hands of the national aspirations of the Jews?

In August I wearily explained to the children that I had to go abroad again, this time to the Zionist congress in Geneva, where monumental issues that concerned the life of the *yishuv* were going to be thrashed out. They were terribly disappointed, I could see, but although sometimes they argued and asked if it was really necessary, this time they didn't argue at all. Actually, by the time I left for Geneva, Mapai policy had already been formulated. Whatever position Zionist delegates from abroad would take, we were clear about our own. Immigration would go on, even if it came to armed clashes with the British, and we would also continue to settle and defend the land. This meant, in fact, that we were committing ourselves to waging war against the British—if we had to. We, who were not even important enough to be represented fully and formally at an International Conference on Refugees? But there seemed to be no alternative, unless we, too, adopted a quota system and thus joined the society of nations that "deeply regretted" their inability to participate in the rescue of Jews.

By the time war broke out in September, 1939, Ben-Gurion had defined our position, tersely but very lucidly: "We shall fight Hitler as if there were no White Paper, and fight the White Paper as if there were no Hitler."

7. The Struggle Against the British

I suppose I must have tried a thousand times since 1939 to explain to myself—let alone to others—just how and why it happened that during the very years that the British stood with so much courage and determination against the Nazis, they were also able (and willing) to find the time, energy and resources to fight so long and as bitter a war against the admittance of Jewish refugees from the Nazis to Palestine. But I have still not found any rational explanation—and perhaps there is none. All I know is that the State of Israel might not have come into being for many years if that British war within a war had not been waged so ferociously and with such insane persistence.

As a matter of fact, it was only when the British government decided—in the face of all reason or humanity—to place itself like an iron wall between us and whatever chance we had of rescuing Jews from the hands of the Nazis that we realized that political independence was not something that we could go on regarding as a distant aim: The need to control immigration because human lives depended on such control was the one thing that pushed us into making the sort of decision which might otherwise have waited for much better (if not ideal) conditions. But the 1939 White Paper—those rules and regulations laid down for us by strangers to whom the lives of Jews were obviously of secondary importance—turned the entire subject of the right of the *yishuv* to govern itself into the most pressing and immediate need that any of us had ever known. And it was out of the depth of this need, essentially, that the State of Israel was founded, only three years after the end of the war.

What was it that we demanded of the British and that they so stubbornly refused to give us? Today the answer seems incredible, even to me. The truth is that all that the *yishuv* wanted from 1939 to 1945 was to take as many Jews as could be saved from the Nazis. That was all. Just to be allowed to share the little that we had with men, women and children who were fortunate enough not to have been shot, gassed or buried alive yet by the very people to whose downfall the entire British Empire was in any case totally committed.

We didn't ask for anything else: not for privileges of any kind, not for power, not for promises relating to the future. We just begged—in view of the death sentence that had been passed on millions of European Jews by Hitler and was being carried out—to be permitted to try to rescue as many of them as possible before they all perished and bring them to the one place where they were wanted. When the British first turned a deaf ear to this request and then answered that they couldn't "cope" with it, for all sorts of technical and absolutely invalid reasons (for instance, a "lack of ships," although ships were produced in abundance when, in 1940, it became "necessary" to haul "illegal" immigrants from Palestine to Mauritius), we stopped making requests and began to insist.

But nothing—no pleas, no tears, no demonstrations, no intervention by friends, however influential—did any good. The British White Paper remained in force, and the gates of Palestine opened only long enough and wide enough to let in the exact number of Jews stipulated in that shameful document, and not one more. It was then that we all knew what many of us had always suspected: No foreign government could or would ever feel our agonies as we felt them, and no foreign government would ever put the same value on Jewish lives that we did. It wasn't a very complicated lesson to learn, but once it was learned, it wasn't likely that any of us would forget it, although, just as incredibly, the rest of the world, with very few exceptions, seems by now to have done so. It was not, mind you, as though any real choices were involved or as though a long line of other nations were queuing up in front of the British Colonial Office and clamoring to receive refugees, and shelter, feed and rehabilitate them. A few countries were prepared—to their eternal credit—to take in some of the Jews if and when they managed to escape the Holocaust. But nowhere on the face of the earth except in Palestine was there a single country that was anxious to receive the Jews, prepared to pay any price for them, to do anything and take any risks required to save them.

The British remained adamant. They went on fighting like lions against the Germans, the Italians and the Japanese, but they couldn't or wouldn't stand up to the Arabs at all—although much of the Arab world was openly pro-Nazi. For the life of me, I cannot understand to this day, in the light of what was happening to the Jewish people, why the British found it impossible to say to the Arabs, "You have nothing at all to worry about. Once the war is over, we will see to it that each and every clause of the White Paper is fully enforced, and if they defy us, we will send the British army, navy and air force to subdue the Jews of Palestine. But right now what is at stake is not the future of the Middle East or of the mandate or of national aspirations of any kind. It is the lives of millions of human beings, and we, the British, will not stand in the way of the rescue of Hitler's victims. The White Paper will have to wait until after the war."

After all, what would have happened if the British had issued a declaration of this sort? A few Arab leaders might have made threatening speeches. Perhaps there would have been a protest march or two. Maybe there would even have been an additional act of pro-Nazi sabotage somewhere in the Middle East. And maybe it would have been too late to save most of the Jews of Europe anyway. But thousands more of the 6,000,000 might have survived. Thousands more of the ghetto fighters and Jewish partisans might have been armed. And the civilized world might then have been freed of the terrible accusation that not a finger was lifted to help the Jews in their torment.

As it was, in all those long, tragic years of the war and its immediate aftermath, I did not once encounter—or even hear of—a single Palestinian Jew who hesitated for one moment to offer whatever personal or national sacrifices might be needed in order to reach out to the Jews of Europe and bring them into safety. Not that there was always unanimity among us as to how this could best be done, but to the best of my knowledge, the question of whether it should be done or not never once arose. If no one else was going to help us, then we were going to have to try to go it alone—which is just what we did.

In Geneva, at that Zionist Congress of 1939, I had spent

most of my time closeted with the delegates of the labor movement's European youth organizations, planning the ways in which we could stay in touch with each other when and if war broke out. Of course, neither I nor they knew then about Hitler's "Final Solution," but I remember looking into their eyes as we shook hands and said *shalom* to each other and wondering what awaited each of them when they returned to their homes.

I have often replayed in my mind those relatively optimistic conversations we had in my room in Geneva toward the end of August, 1939. All but a few of those dedicated young people perished later in Auschwitz, Maidanek and Sobibor, but among them were the leaders of the Jewish resistance movements of Eastern Europe who fought the Nazis inside the ghettos, outside them with the partisans and finally behind the electrified barbed wire of the death camps. I can hardly bear to think of them now, but I believe with all my heart that one of the things that made it possible for them to go on fighting against such odds to the very end was the knowledge that we were with them all the time and so they were never really alone. I am not particularly given to mysticism, but I hope I will be pardoned for saying that in our darkest hours it was the memory of their spirit that gave us heart, inspired us to go on and, above all, lent validity to our own refusal to be wiped out to make life easier for the rest of the world. In the final analysis, it was the Jews of Europe, trapped, doomed and destroyed, who taught us once and for all that we must become the masters of our own undertaking, and I think it can be said that we have kept faith with them.

"We shall fight Hitler as if there were no White Paper and fight the White Paper as if there were no Hitler" was a ringing slogan, but not simple to implement. Actually, not one but three closely linked (though still separate) struggles were under way in Palestine during the first years of the war, and as a member of the Va'ad Hapoel I participated in each of them: There was the desperate struggle to get as many Jews as possible into Palestine, the humiliating and inexplicable battle we were forced to fight in order to persuade the British to let us take part in military action against the Nazis, and finally the struggle—in the face of almost total British indifference—to preserve the *yishuv*'s economy so that we could somehow emerge from the war strong enough and healthy enough to absorb a large immigration—provided there were any Jews left to immigrate.

Since then, I have sometimes wondered how we got through those years without going to pieces; but perhaps physical and emotional stamina is mostly a matter of habit, and whatever else we lacked, we did not lack opportunities for testing ourselves in times of crisis. People, especially my own family, have charged me for almost as long as I can remember with driving myself too hard, whatever that means. Even now, when my life is relatively easy, the children are forever at me because I don't "rest" enough. But during those war years I learned a very important lesson: One can always push oneself a little bit beyond what only yesterday was thought to be the absolute limit of one's endurance. Anyhow, I don't recall ever having felt "tired" then, so I must have gotten used to fatigue. Like everyone else, I was so driven by anxiety and anguish that no day (or night, for that matter) was long enough for everything that had to be done. The main reason, of course, was that regardless of how difficult others found it to believe that the Nazis were in the process of liquidating the Jews of Europe, most of us believed it at once, and when you know that the clock is ticking away the lives of your people, there is no such thing as too much to do.

I remember distinctly the day that those first awful reports reached us about the gas chambers and the soap and lamp shades that were being made from Jewish bodies. We held an emergency meeting in the offices of the Histadrut and decided on the spot to send someone to Ankara to try to make contact with the Jews from there. The curious and terrible thing was that none of us questioned the information we had received. We all believed the reports immediately and in their entirety. The next day I had an appointment on some minor, routine matter with a British official whom I had always liked, and naturally I told him what we had just learned about the Nazi atrocities. After a few minutes he looked at me with an odd expression and said, "But, Mrs. Meyerson, surely you don't believe all that, do you?" Then he went on to explain to me about the atrocity propaganda of World War I and how utterly outlandish it had been. I couldn't explain to him how or why I knew that this was different, but I could see in his worried, rather kind blue eyes that he thought I had gone quite mad. "You mustn't believe everything you hear," he said to me gently before I left.

Anyhow, we did our regular jobs during the day, and in between and at night we did whatever we could about the war against the Jews. Since I had worked in the field of labor negotiations before, I went on with this work, although now I dealt almost exclusively with the British military authorities. The British, as I have mentioned, were dead set against letting the Jews of Palestine volunteer for the army (although 130,000 did so) and invented a series of complicated schemes (most of which failed) for keeping enlistment in the *yishuv* down to the bare minimum, including insistence on equal numbers of Jewish and Arab recruits. But when the war spread to the Middle East, the Allies found themselves increasingly dependent on the one source of highly skilled (and, of course, politically completely reliable) manpower in the area. Tens of thousands of young Palestinian Jews who were barred from serving in British combat units worked throughout the war as army drivers, in the ordnance service corps and with the medical corps. They were known, needless to say, as "Palestinians," not as Jews, and they were treated as "natives," but at least they were part of the army. The *yishuv*'s civilian labor force, however—both skilled and unskilled—was not only treated as "natives" but also paid at Egyptian rates of pay. Since this was not acceptable to the Histadrut, I spent months and months arguing and negotiating with GHQ Middle East. A great many Palestinian Arabs eventually joined us in those stormy representations, although one of them, a charming man from Haifa, was to pay with his life for that united front when he was assassinated by Arab terrorists in 1947.

Among the typical episodes of that period were the talks I conducted for weeks with a firm that had operated in Burma and was then appointed as transport agents for the Palestine mandatory government. I don't think it had ever occurred to these gentlemen before that they couldn't just hire and fire individual drivers when and as they saw fit, but I was determined to get them to acknowledge the existence of trade unions and the importance of collective bargaining. "In Burma," they told me airily when we first met, "we didn't need any workers' cooperatives. We had our own 'cooperative' of eighty thousand laborers." But in the end they agreed to negotiate with the Histadrut, and I think they also may have learned something concerning the *yishuv* and what it was all about.

As the military situation in the Middle East went from bad to worse, more and more Palestinian Jews were absorbed in the war effort, and the mandatory government began to feel itself obliged to create some kind of public body with which it could consult on economic matters. It set up a War Econimic Advisory Council, of which I was a member until the war ended.

These were things that had to be done and that were important, but they were very far indeed from being central. My real preoccupations were different. The man we had sent to Ankara (Mellech Neustadt, today Noy) came back to the Va'ad Hapoel one day with news that made us tremble. It was as though he had returned with a message from another planet. He had found people in Turkey who could establish contact with the Jewish underground in Poland. He warned us that they were not angels, of course. In addition to asking a great deal of money for their services, he thought they would probably take for themselves huge cuts out of anything they undertook to deliver to the ghettos, and some of them were almost certainly Nazis. But we weren't hiring office workers. We were looking for emissaries who could move more or less freely in Nazi-occupied Europe, and their *cirricula vitae* didn't matter. That very day we began to organize a secret fund. We set what was then a staggering goal for ourselves—75,000 pounds sterling—although we already knew that only a fraction of this sum—if we ever raised it—would get to its destination. But with that fraction Jews might be able to secure arms and food, not much of either under any circumstances, but enough, perhaps, to keep the Jewish resistance movements going, however briefly.

That was the real beginning of our desperate attempts to batter our way into Nazi-occupied Europe and throw a lifeline to the Jews. By the time the war ended there was no route we hadn't explored, no opening we hadn't pursued, no possibility we hadn't investigated at once. For years we beseeched the Allies to help us send our young men into the very heart of Europe—on foot, by submarine and finally by air. In the summer of 1943, with great reservations, the British at last agreed. They consented to let us drop, not hundreds, as we had asked, but thirty-two Palestinian Jews into Axis-held territory, where they would be able to perform a twofold task: aid Allied prisoners of war (mostly captured fliers) to escape and go to the aid and encouragement of the Jewish partisans.

As I write these lines, I see before me the faces of two men, neither of whom is alive today. They were very different from each other in background, personality and manner; but both were dear to me, and I think of them now—with a piercing pain—as typifying those dark and agonizing times. One was Eliahu Golomb, the other was Enzo Sereni, and since it must be left to writers and historians to tell the detailed story of what the Jews of Palestine tried to do—and did—during the Holocaust, I shall write only about them, although there were many many others, men and women alike, who gave to their people as much as Eliahu and Enzo did.

I knew Eliahu better and for longer than Enzo. He was part of a remarkable family—four brothers-in-law who played a major role in the upbuilding of the *yishuv* and its labor movement. About one of them, Moshe Sharett, I shall tell even more later, because our lives and work were to become closely intertwined, but the other three were no less important at the time of the war. Each of the four (or all of them together) could well be the subject of a book that would, I think, then inevitably become a saga of the entire *yishuv*—and I very much hope that one day someone will write it.

Moshe Sharett was then the head of the Political Department of the Jewish Agency. He had inherited Chaim Arlosoroff's mantle in 1933 and always thought of himself (even then, I suspect) as the obvious candidate for foreign minister—if a Jewish state should ever come into being. He was the most "man of the world" of the four brothers-in-law, intelligent, able and a brilliant linguist. But he was also formalistic and very pedantic. Despite his considerable talents, he was no Ben-Gurion or Berl Katznelson. But he served for years, with great distinction, as Israel's foreign minister and even, for a short, bitterly unhappy period between the first and second of Ben-Gurion's resignations, as prime minister. During the war it was Sharett, more than anyone else, who threw himself heart and soul into the maddening battle for the establishment of the Jewish Brigade, which was finally created in the last years of the war, just in time to see action in Italy.

One of Sharett's sisters was married to Dov Hos, who for years served the Histadrut as its "man in London" and had developed extremely warm personal ties with many of the leaders of the British Labor Party. He was not a particularly imposing figure physically; but he had tremendous charm, and he understood and liked the British. So we often chose Dov to represent us with the mandatory authorities. His pet project was the development of aviation in Palestine, and he was a pilot himself, which the rest of us thought was very dashing. In 1940 he was killed in Palestine, together with Rivkah, his wife, and daughter, in a traffic accident, and when he died, we lost one of our real pillars of strength. I used to spend a lot of time with Dov whenever I was in London before the war, and afterward we had much to do together concerning the recruiting of volunteers for the British army.

Service in the British army was not, by the way, something about which everyone in the *yishuv* felt as we did. There were people—and not a few—who argued that by putting all our eggs into one basket, so to speak, we were endangering the actual security of Jewish towns and settlements in the event of a British defeat in the Middle East. "It is all very well to campagin for volunteers for the army to fight the Nazis abroad, but what will happen to the *yishuv*," they asked, "if the Axis is victorious? Who will be left to defend Tel Aviv, or Degania or Rehovot? A handful of poorly equipped members of the Haganah?" They had a point, of course, but not a good one in my opinion. The idea of waiting to fight Hitler until the Germans approached the borders of Palestine was absurd. We wanted to help overthrow the Nazis wherever they were, and we spent days upon days trying to persuade our opponents both inside and outside the Histadrut and Mapai that they were wrong.

Another of Sharett's in-laws (Zipporah Sharett's brother) was that fantastic man Shaul Avigur, who is still alive, thank God. No one passing Shaul today, or even then, on the streets of Tel Aviv or working in the garden of Kibbutz Kinneret (of which he is still a member) would ever guess from his rather rumpled and very ordinary appearance that for all the years preceding the establishment of the State of Israel he was, in effect, our underground minister of defense. Shaul was the man who set up the Haganah's legendary intelligence service and who, when the war ended, stood at the head of what we called the Mossad (the Institution), organizing and directing the intricate and dangerous "illegal" immigration to Palestine of the remnants of European Jewry. Nothing about Shaul's exterior or manner of speech reveals the fact that unlike Sharett, Dov, Eliahu, or myself, for that matter, he was a born conspirator. I have never known Shaul to write an unnecessary note or say an unnecessary word. Whatever he did or ordered to have done was carried out with maximum secrecy, and everyone was suspect, in his eyes, of possible indiscretion. Sometimes we laughed at him for what we thought was his exaggeratedly cautious attitude. I remember that when his daughter was in England for a while, she asked him to send her a bundle of Hebrew newspapers and wasn't at all surprised when her father automatically wrote "Strictly Confidential" on the wrapper! But we all respected him immensely and still do. His authority on any matter that had to do with the underground—the secret purchase of arms in Europe in 1947, the bringing in to Palestine of Jewish refugees from Arab countries at the height of the war, the essential compilation of dossiers about the British CID—was unquestioned. Typically, Shaul was the first of us to devote himself, years and years ago, to the cause of Jewish emigration from Russia.

But it was the fourth brother-in-law, Eliahu Golomb, who was at the heart of everything in those days. It was his house in Tel Aviv and his office (Room 17) in the Histadrut building that were our real nerve centers. I don't think the light was ever turned off in Eliahu's home during the entire war or that the house was ever empty. If we had any kind of headquarters of our own then, that was it. Whatever time of the day or night you turned up to consult Eliahu (and we always walked through the kitchen, for some reason), you found his mother-in-law (Sharett's mother, whom we all called Mamochka) calmly ironing away, even at midnight, and Ada Golomb unfailingly ready with a glass of tea. Ben-Gurion, Sharett, Dov Hos and others were the policy makers, the negotiators, the spokesmen of the *yishuv* to the world outside, while Eliahu Golomb— not unlike Berl in the sphere of pure ideology—was our commander in chief, the effective head of the Haganah from 1931 until he died in 1945. Like Berl, he never saw the State of Israel for himself, and also like Berl, his absence from the scene during Israel's first years was a great, I would even say constant, deprivation for all of us, because in many ways Eliahu was one of its real founders.

What did our "commander in chief" look like? Well, what did any of us look like? Other than Ben-Gurion with his flying white hair, I can't think of a single one of the "founding fathers" of the State of Israel who cut much of a figure, and Eliahu was certainly no exception. He was a small, short man with a very high forehead that was always wrinkled and deepset, rather beautiful eyes. Like Berl, he wore a sort of uniform—a *rubashka* that buttoned down the side and a pair of creased khaki trousers. I don't remember ever having seen him in a suit. He spoke very quietly, very slowly and very persuasively and was astonishingly well read. Actually, he was probably the least military-looking man I knew and had none of the mannerisms or affectations that leaders of underground movements often develop in order to impress their followers. In fact, there was nothing at all distinctive about him, except for his strong personality, and even that was not revealed except to the people with whom he worked most closely. But the Haganah, its philosophy and its strength were very largely Eliahu's creation. He had come to Palestine from Russia in 1909 and, together with Sharett, was among the first graduates of Tel Aviv's Herzlia High School. In the Jewish Legion, during World War I, he had made friends with Berl, and under Berl's influence he began to develop his concept of Jewish self-defense in Palestine.

From the start, Eliahu conceived of the Haganah not as a guerrilla movement or as any kind of elite force, but as the most broadly based possible national response to the need of the *yishuv* to protect itself and as integral part of the Zionist movement. Self-defense, he believed, was neither less nor more important than the conquest of the desert or the ingathering of the exiles. This being so, the Haganah had both to grow out of and to belong to the entire Jewish population, and therefore, it had to function under the supreme authority of the *yishuv*'s national institutions, regardless of how secret its specific functions might have to be. From this concept stemmed also Eliahu's attitude toward the two dissident military organizations that eventually came into being: the Irgun Zvai Le'umi and Lehi (the Stern Group), which evolved primarily because they disapproved of the Haganah's policy of self-restraint, nonretaliation and avoidance, not to say abhorrence, of Jewish terrorism. But from the very beginning Eliahu understood the need to prepare the Haganah for its ultimate role in the struggle for independence, and he always regarded it as the nucleus of a Jewish army able and entitled to defend the right of the Jews to come to Palestine, to settle in it and to lead a free life in it.

Defined in these terms, the Haganah had a unique role to play. Self-defense, in Eliahu's eyes, meant that the *yishuv* used its always-meager resources wherever and whenever they were needed most. The same young men and women who "illegally" brought Jews to Palestine also guarded settlers putting up stockades and water towers in areas forbidden to Jewish settlement under the White Paper, manufactured and tried to stockpile arms against future attacks and even parachuted into Nazi-occupied Europe. He molded the Haganah into a true instrument of national redemption, always keeping its component parts interchangeable and readying it so that in 1948, when it proved necessary, it could become *the* instrument of national redemption. He guarded and cherished this ultimate purpose so that it never became contaminated. But of course, he could do this because he was basically a pioneer, an idealist, a socialist and a good Jew, as well as an underground leader.

It is bitter to write about Eliahu now, in a world that has chosen to endow Arab terrorism with glamor and to admit to the so-called council of nations a man like Yasir Arafat, who has not one constructive thought or action to his credit and who, to put it plainly, is only a costumed multiple murderer heading a movement dedicated solely to the destruction of the State of Israel. But it is my most profound conviction—and consolation—that the seeds of the inevitable failure of Arab terrorism lie in the very concept of terrorism itself. No movement, regardless of the money available to it or the appeasement upon which it feeds—and in this case it is the sort of appeasement that has always brought disaster upon the world—can succeed for long if the caliber of its leadership is shoddy and if its only commitments are to blackmail and bloodshed. It is not by killing and maiming children, hijacking aircraft or murdering diplomats that real movements of national liberation accomplish their aims. They must also have content, goals that will serve them long after the immediate crisis has passed, and they must—to use an old-fashioned word—have some claim to intellectual and moral purity.

In the end Eliahu's greatest gift to the *yishuv* was not the skill with which the Haganah carried out its operations, but its fundamental purpose, which, when the time came, was taken over almost intact into the ranks of Israel's army. Of course, there were mistakes (sometimes costly ones) and breakdowns and many disappointments; but from its first day, the mission of the Haganah was to serve the Jewish people, not to terriorize or to dominate others, and because it gave equal weight to development and to self-determination, it prevailed and its spirit endured.

Although I myself had nothing to do with the selection of the Haganah volunteers who parachuted into Europe, I met all of them because each came to the Histadrut to take their leave of us. It was on one of these occasions that I even tried to argue Enzo Sereni out of going at all. One afternoon I was working in my room at the Va'ad Hapoel when the door opened and Enzo came in. Behind his glasses, his eyes looked brighter than usual. "I've come to say good-bye," he said. "I'm off."

"Don't go," I told him. "First of all, you are really much too old and much too valuable here. Please be reasonable, for everyone's sake, and stay." I knew I would never persuade him, although I tried very hard for about a quarter of an hour.

But when I was through, he took my hand and said, "Golda, you must understand. I can't possibly stay behind when it is I who sent so many of the others. Just don't worry. I give you my word of honor that we'll meet again."

But we never did. In 1945 I stood on a beach in Palestine one windy night and watched a Haganah ship called the *Enzo Sereni* spill 1,000 or more survivors of the death camps onto the sand, having brought them safely through the British blockade. I remember thinking then that each nation honors its heroes as best it can, in its own way, and that this was ours—and Enzo would have liked it.

Enzo came from a background that was strikingly different from that of most of my colleagues. He had been born and reared in Italy, where his father had been a personal physician to the king. His was a well-to-do, very assimilated, highly cultured family. One of his uncles was a famous lawyer, and a brother became a leading communist senator. There was nothing that connected Enzo with Zionism, except for his great interest in socialism and his fascination with the kibbutz movement, about which he read and thought a great deal. In the late 1920s, after a major clash with the Fascists, he came to Palestine, helped found a kibbutz (Givat Brenner, not far from Tel Aviv, which is where I met him) and became very active in the labor movement. He believed in a special brand of socialism that was mixed with a strong feeling for religion, and typically, he was a confirmed pacifist. We got along very well, although we always argued a lot, particularly during the 1936-39 riots, when Enzo insisted on moving around Arab villages at night, unarmed, because he said it was his duty to try to calm the Arab population. But no one could ever get him to change his mind about anything that involved principles. If something was worth doing, then he himself had to do it. So we weren't very surprised when, almost at once after the outbreak of war, he volunteered for the army.

Volunteering was one thing, but parachuting behind enemy lines was something else. He was already forty years old, had a family, was badly needed in Palestine itself and had no chance whatsoever of surviving Fascist imprisonment if he were captured. It wasn't as though he were not already participating fully in the war effort. He broadcast regularly to Italy on behalf of the Allies and edited an anti-Fascist newspaper that was read by thousands of Italian POWs. Nor did he lack adventure. The real story of Enzo's exploits in Iraq in 1941 has still to be told, but one of the things he did was lead young Jews out of the ghettos of Iraq, across the desert into Palestine at tremendous personal risk. All the time, however, he was haunted by the suffering of Italian Jewry and determined to go to its rescue, or at least be with it in its misery. So, having helped Eliahu to choose the parachutists, he insisted on training with them and being dropped into Italy. He was caught almost immediately, shipped in a transport of Jews to Dachau and killed there by the Nazis. He was only one of the thirty-two parachutists—the most famous of whom was the young poet Hanna Senesh—but somehow for me he symbolized all of them and the basic helplessness of our situation.

Interviewers have sometimes asked me what I feel about the Germans, and perhaps this is the time and place to answer that question. Postwar Germany was something with which the State of Israel had to deal, make contact, and work. That was one of the facts of life after World War II, and facts of life had to be faced, however painful they are. It should go without saying that nothing will ever diminish the impact of the Holocaust. Six million murdered Jews are also a fact of life, a fact that must never be erased from the memory of man and certainly that no Jew—or German—should ever forget. But although it took years before I forced myself—in 1967—to set foot on German soil again, I was always in favor of reparations, of taking money from the Germans so that we could build up the State of Israel, for I believe that they owed us at least that much, so that we could absorb the Jews who had remained alive. I also believed that Israel itself is the strongest guarantee against another Holocaust.

And when the time was ripe, I was also in favor of diplomatic relations with Germany's government, although I violently opposed that government's choice of an ambassador and was outraged when I learned that Rolf Pauls had fought and even been wounded (he lost an arm) in the war. "Never mind that he is a brilliant career diplomat," I said, "and never mind that he was not a member of the Nazi Party. Let the Germans at least send an ambassador who has no war record at all." But the German Government refused to change its mind. Rolf Pauls came to Isreal, and there were demonstrations against him, and I was sure he would have to be recalled. Fortunately, I was wrong. Today he is Bonn's ambassador to Peking, but he is still one of Israel's staunchest and best friends.

When Pauls first presented his credentials in Jerusalem, I was Israel's foreign minister. Since I assumed that he had been told and thus knew exactly how I felt about his appointment, it was not an easy moment, but at least, I thought, it was a moment for truth. "You have a most difficult task before you," I said to him. "This is a country made up, to a large extent, of the victims of the Holocaust. There is hardly a family that does not live with nightmare recol-

lections of the crematoria, of babies used as targets for
Nazi bullets, of Nazi 'scientific' experiments. You cannot
expect a warm reception. Even the women who will wait at
table, if you ever come to me for a meal, have Nazi numbers tattooed on their arms."

"I know," Pauls answered. "I have come to you now
from Yad Vashem [Israel's memorial to the 6,000,000],
and there is already one thing I can promise you. For as
long as I serve here, I shall make it my business to see that
any German who comes to this country goes first—as I did
today—to that memorial." And he kept his word.

Once I told Pauls about my twenty-four-hour visit to
Germany, and I remember how white his face was as he
listened to me. I had gone to Germany right after the Six-
Day War, when I was out of government. I had been at-
tending a socialist conference in Paris with an old comrade
of mine, Reuven Barkatt. One morning the phone rang, and
it was Abba Eban, our foreign minister, calling from New
York. He was at the United Nations, fighting what looked
at that point like a losing battle against a so-called Yugoslav (really Russian) resolution, one of those standard resolutions that condemned us as "aggressors" and demanded
our immediate unconditional withdrawal from the "occupied territories." The French, who supported this resolution, were putting tremendous pressure on the representatives of the French-speaking African states, Eban said, in
an attempt to get them to vote for it, too. The leading
French-speaking African delegation was that of the Ivory
Coast, whose foreign minister was most sympathetic to Israel and whose president, Felix Houphouët-Boigny, was and
is a dear personal friend of mine. Would I go, Eban asked,
to see Houphouët-Boigny, who was somewhere in Europe
at the time—he didn't know exactly where—and talk to
him at once about that resolution?

It turned out that Houphouët-Boigny was resting
at a German resort before starting an official visit to
Germany. I would have given my right arm not to go
there, but Eban kept pressing, and of course, I fully understood why. So I went and I talked to the president, but I
barely ate or drank, and I left as soon as I could. When I
returned to Paris, Barkatt, who knew how hard it had been
for me to go to Germany, said to me, "Nothing else you
have ever done for Israel was quite as difficult as that trip,

was it?" But I didn't answer him. I couldn't even put into words for Barkatt then or Pauls later the horror and revulsion I had felt during those twenty-four hours. All I could think of were the faces of the people I had seen at the Eichmann trial, Adolf Eichmann himself and the eyes of the men, women and children whom we had brought out of that hell in the 1940s.

Although nothing ever can or will bring the slaughtered back to life, the trial of Adolf Eichmann in Jerusalem in 1961 was, I believe, a great, necessary act of historic justice. It took place two decades after those desperate years in which we tried in every way possible to deny him his prey, but it is part of the record of the Holocaust nonetheless. I was (and I am) absolutely convinced that only the Israelis were entitled to try Eichmann on behalf of world Jewry, and I am deeply proud that we did so. It was not, in any sense, a question of revenge. As the Hebrew poet Biolik once wrote, not even the devil himself could dream up an adequate revenge for the death of a single child, but those who remained alive—and generations still unborn—deserve, if nothing else, that the world know, in all its dreadful detail, what was done to the Jews of Europe and by whom.

For as long as I live, I shall never forget sitting huddled in that courtroom with Sheyna, hearing the evidence of the survivors. Many of my friends had the strength to attend the trial day after day, but I must confess that I went only twice. There are not many things in life that I have knowingly dodged; but those living testimonies of torture, degradation and death—given in the chill presence of Eichmann himself—were literally unbearable for me, and instead, I listened to the trial on the radio, as did most people in Israel. But that, too, made it impossible to go on normally with life. I worked, of course, went to the office every day, ate my meals, brushed my hair; but my inner attention was always fixed on what was happening in the courtroom, and the radio was always on, so that the trial dominated everything for weeks, for me and for everyone else. I remember listening to the people who gave evidence and wondering how and where they had found the will to live, to rear new families, to become human beings once more. I suppose the answer is that all of us, finally, crave life—regardless of what the past has held—but just as I cannot really know what it was like in the death camps, so I cannot really ever

know what it was like to start all over again. That knowledge belongs to the survivors.

In 1960, standing before the Security Council to answer
the charges of illegality brought against Israel by the government of Argentina (from which country Eichmann had
been plucked by Irsraeli volunteers), I tried to explain at
least what the trial meant to the Jews. Of all the public
addresses I have made, that was the one that most drained
me because I felt I was speaking for millions who could no
longer speak for themselves and I wanted each word to
have meaning—not just to be moving or horrifying for a
minute or two. It is always much easier, I have discovered,
to make people cry or gasp than to make them think.

It wasn't a long statement, but I shall quote only part of
it here. I do so not in order to see my own words in print,
but because to my sorrow there are still people who do not
understand that we are committed to live and act so that
those Jews who were killed in the gas chambers will have
been the last Jews ever to die without defending themselves. And because they do not or cannot understand
this, such people have also never understood what is called
our "obstinacy."

In the record of the Nürnberg trial, we read what
Dieter Wisliceny, Eichmann's aide, said about the
process of the "Final Solution":
Until 1940 the general policy within the section was
to settle the Jewish question in Germany and in areas
occupied by Germany by means of a planned emigration. The second phase, after that date, was the concentration of all Jews, in Poland and in other territories occupied by Germany in the East, in ghettos. This
period lasted approximately until the beginning of
1942. The third period was the so-called "Final Solution" of the Jewish question—that is, the planned extermination and destruction of the Jewish race; this period lasted until October, 1944, when Himmler gave
the order to stop their destruction.
Further, in answer to a question whether in his official connection with Section IV A 4 he learned of any
order which directed the annihilation of all Jews, he
said: "Yes, I learned of such an order for the first
time from Eichmann in the summer of 1942."

Hitler did not solve the Jewish question according to his plans. But he annihilated six million Jews—Jews of Germany, France, Belgium, Holland, Luxembourg, Poland, the USSR, Hungary, Yugoslavia, Greece, Italy, Czechoslovakia, Austria, Rumania, Bulgaria. With these Jews were destroyed over thirty thousand Jewish communities which for centuries had been the center of Jewish faith, learning and scholarship. From this Jewry stemmed some of the giants in the field of arts, literature and science. Was it only this generation of Jews of Europe that was gassed? One million children—the future generation—were annihilated. Who can encompass this picture in all its horror and its consequences for the Jewish people for many generations to come and for Israel? Here was destroyed the natural reservoir for all that is needed for a new country—learning, skill, devotion, idealism, a pioneering spirit.

I spoke also of Eichmann himself and of his direct personal responsibility and went on:

I am convinced that many in the world were anxious to bring Eichmann to trial, but the fact remains that for fifteen years nobody found him. And he could break laws of who knows how many countries, by entering them under a false name and forged passport and abuse the hospitality of countries which, I am sure, recoil in horror from his deeds. But Jews, some of whom personally were the victims of his brutality, found no rest until they located him and brought him to Israel—to the country to whose shores hundreds of thousands of the survivors of the Eichmann horror have come home; to the country that existed in the hearts and minds of the six million, as on the way to the crematoria they chanted the great article of our faith: *Ani ma'amin be'emuna shelma beviat ha-Mashiah* (I believe with perfect faith in the coming of the Messiah).

And then, I ended with a question:

Is this a problem for the Security Council to deal with? This is a body that deals with threats to the peace. Is this a threat to peace—Eichmann brought to trial by the very people to whose total physical annihilation he dedicated all his energies, even if the manner of his apprehension violated the laws of Argentina? Or did the threat to peace lie in Eichmann at large, Eichmann unpunished, Eichmann free to spread the poison of his twisted soul to a new generation?

My hands shook for hours afterward, but I hoped I had partly explained why we had brought Eichmann to trial.

That was fifteen years after the Holocaust ended. But in the early 1940s no one knew how or when it would end—or even whether it would end at all. Despite the tightening of the British blockade, one Haganah ship after another (there were more than sixty in all) was purchased, filled with Jews and sent on its way to Palestine. Each time the British patrols were more alert, and the voyage in those barely seaworthy, crowded, filthy ships became more dangerous. It was not, however, only Jews escaping the European camps that the British hunted down so obsessively. It was also the Haganah and whatever arms it managed to accumulate, although now and then there was a lull in the British pursuit until some new restriction or anti-Jewish measure forced the Haganah deeper underground.

Two years stand out particularly in my memory, for both personal and political reasons. In 1943 Sarah informed me that she was leaving high school and going to help found a new kibbutz in the Negev, although she still had one more year at school. She had grown up to be a sweet, very shy, very serious girl and a better student than Menachem, who was absorbed in his music and had already decided to be a professional cellist. Both the children, like nearly all the teenagers in the *yishuv,* were involved in Haganah activities, although the subject was never openly discussed at home. But even if they said nothing, parents and schoolteachers knew that youngsters had often been up late serving as couriers for the underground or circulating Haganah posters and leaflets. I remember actually writing one of those posters myself at home, although of course I took great care not to let the children see what I was doing. A day or two afterward Sarah said, "Ima, I'll be back late tonight, maybe even very late." Naturally I wanted to know why. "I can't tell you," she said, and walked off with a parcel under her arm. I knew perfectly well what was in that parcel, and I also knew that pasting up "illegal" posters was a very risky business in those days. I stayed awake till dawn that night waiting for her to come home; but we observed all the rules, and I didn't as much as touch on the subject next morning, although I was dying to say something.

Like Menachem, Sarah had belonged for years to one of the labor movement's pioneer youth organizations, so I wasn't really taken aback when she made her announcement about the kibbutz. To begin with, I had wanted to live permanently on a kibbutz, and I thought it was a wonderful way of life. Secondly, I could quite understand her desire to participate more directly in what was happening in the country. The British had dismissed 85 percent of the Negev as "entirely uncultivable," although it accounted in area for almost one-half of Palestine. But the Jewish Agency had worked out a detailed long-range plan for trying to irrigate at least part of those 2,000,000 acres of scorched sand in the belief that hundreds of thousands of immigrants could be settled there, and Sarah and her friends in the youth movement had decided to take part in the great experiment. The plan called for the establishment of three settlements—observation posts really—south of Beersheba, which was then just a dusty little Arab town. "If we manage to prove now that people can live and raise crops in the Negev, we will be doing much more for the country than if we just finish school," Sarah proclaimed, and in my heart of hearts, I thought she might be right. But perhaps it could wait one year? Graduating from high school was such an important step, and very few people, having once left school, ever went back to it, I argued. Besides, was she absolutely sure that the whole scheme wasn't a method of avoiding the last difficult year of high school and final exams? Because if it was, then I certainly disapproved.

We talked on and on. Morris was furious at the very idea of her leaving school. Eliahu Golomb, whose orphaned niece had come home with a similar announcement, begged me to join him in a collective stand against the youngsters. Sheyna told me that if I gave in, I would regret it all my life, and so would Sarah. But although this may come as a surprise to some people, I have never believed in inflexibility—except when Israel is concerned. On matters that have to do with my country, I have never conceded an inch, but people are something else. Anyhow, I thought it was unlikely that Sarah would surrender, so *I* did, though not light-heartedly.

The first time I went to visit her in Revivim, I really thought I would die. For miles around there was nothing, not a tree, not a blade of grass, not a bird, nothing but sand and glaring sun. There was practically nothing to eat either, and the precious water which the settlers drilled from the ground was so salty that I couldn't drink it—although they had managed to raise some vegetables, which, mercifully, were less fussy about the water than I was! The "settlement" consisted of a protective wall, a watchtower and a few tents. It was intolerably hot during most of the year but freezing cold in the winter, and I thought it was the last place in the universe for a girl who had once almost died of a kidney disease. But I said nothing about that either. Whenever I could, I drove down and spent a few hours with Sarah listening to reports on the kibbutz's progress, looking at the sluiceways and reservoir they were building to catch the winter rains and sometimes talking to a very nice young man, Zechariah Rehabi, a Yemenite boy from Jerusalem, of whom Sarah seemed extremely fond. To myself, I often thought that life in Revivim (which means dewdrops in Hebrew) might have been made more comfortable with only a little effort—despite its surroundings. But then I recalled how irritated everyone in Merhavia had been with me for such advice, and I held my tongue.

In September, 1943, I appeared as a witness in an arms trial that became something of a *cause célèbre* in Palestine. Two young Jews were accused by the British of stealing arms from the army in order to turn them over to the Haganah, and as a member of the Va'ad Hapoel I was called upon to testify in the military court. The prosecutor was a disagreeable gentleman called Major Baxter, who was obviously not nearly as interested in the two boys as he was in portraying the Jewish self-defense organization as a widespread movement of terrorists who menaced public security in Palestine. He also permitted himself to slander the *yishuv* by saying that one of the reasons for the rate of Jewish enlistment was that the Jews could thus lay their hands on weapons. It was more than merely an unjust charge; it was wicked. (Nobody could have been as astonished as I was in 1975 when I got a letter from Major Baxter, written from Ireland, congratulating me on having been named Woman of the Year in an American poll. "If you are ever looking for a job," he wrote, "I can get you one here in Ulster, where your talents would be valuable"!)

To tell the truth, I was rather glad of the chance to show Major Baxter what I thought of him, although I had to watch my step carefully. I knew that Baxter wanted more than anything else to prove that the Jewish Agency, an official institution, and the Haganah, which was illegal, were working hand in glove. I swore to myself that Baxter would get nothing from me except what he deserved, and I took as my motto one of my mother's favorite sayings: "When you say no, you never regret it." I think that excerpts of that cross-examination by Major Baxter tell more about the British attitude and behavior toward us in 1943 than anything I could write about it now. Here is part of the report that appeared in the English-language Palestine *Post* (now the Jerusalem *Post*) on September 7, 1943. (One word of explanation: Ben Shemen is a youth village that was turned upside down by the British in their frenzied search for arms there.)

Major B. Q: You are a nice, peaceful, law-abiding lady, are you not?

G.M. A: I think I am.

Major B. Q: And you have always been so?

G.M. A: I have never been accused of anything.

Major B. Q: Well, listen to this from a speech of yours on May 2, 1940 (reading out of a file): "For twenty years we were led to trust the British government but we have been betrayed. The Ben Shemen case is an example of this. We have never taught our youth the use of firearms for offense but for defensive purposes only. And if they are criminals, then all the Jews in Palestine are criminals." What about that?

G.M. A: If it is a question of defense, then I, like every Jew in Palestine, am for defense.

Major B.   Q: Were you yourself trained in the use of arms?

G.M.   A: I do not know whether I am required to answer to that question. In any case I have never used firearms.

Major B.   Q: Have you trained the Jewish youth in the use of firearms?

G.M.   A: Jewish youth will defend Jewish life and property in the events of riots and the necessity to defend life and property. I, as well as other Jews, would defend myself.

President
of the Court: Please reply only to the questions.

Major B.   Q: Do you have an intelligence service in the Histadrut?

G.M.   A: No.

Major B.   Q: What?

G.M.   A: You heard me: No!

Major B.   Q: Have you heard of "Haganah"?

G.M.   A: Yes.

Major B.   Q: Do they have arms?

G.M.   A: I don't know, but I suppose so.

Major B.   Q: Have you heard of "Palmach"?

G.M.   A: Yes.

Major B.   Q: What is it?

G.M.   A: I first heard of the Palmach as groups of young people, organized with the knowledge of the authorities, who were specially trained at the time that the German army was drawing near to Palestine. Its function was to help the British army in any way necessary should the enemy invade the country.

Major B.   Q: And are these groups still in existence?

G.M.   A: I don't know.

Major B.   Q: Is this a legal organization?

G.M.   A: All I know is that these groups were organized to help the British army and with the knowledge of the authorities. (After witness stated that a member of the Histadrut might be a member of the Haganah and Palmach, Major Baxter asked if they were prepared to do what she had said in her speech [in 1940].)

G.M. A: They are prepared to defend themselves when attacked. We have had very bad experiences in this country. When I say we are ready to defend, I want to make myself clear. This defense is not theoretical. We still remember the riots of 1921, 1922, and 1929 and the four years of disturbances from 1936 to 1939. Everybody in Palestine knows, as do the authorities, that not only would there have been nothing left, but Jewish honor would have been blemished had there not been people ready for defense, and if brave Jewish youths had not defended the Jewish settlements.

Major B. Q: Don't you know that government has provided 30,000 Jewish armed special constables?

G.M. A: Yes, I know, and I know that before 1936 government was also providing for us. But no one in government can deny the fact that if the Jews had not been prepared to defend themselves, terrible things would have happened to us. Furthermore, we are proud of the Jews of the Warsaw Ghetto who stood up against their persecutors, practically unarmed, and we are certain that they took their example from the Jewish self-defense in Palestine.

Major B. Q: What about this business of stealing 300 rifles and ammunition from the army?

G.M. A: We are interested in this war and in the victory of the British forces, and stealing from the army is a crime in our eyes.

Major B. Q: But these arms might be useful for the Haganah?

G.M. A: There is not a Jew who is not interested in this war and in the victory of the British forces.

Major B.   Q: You wouldn't say, would you, that the
                  rifles walked off by themselves?
                  (showing the witness the exemption card
                  of one of the defendants): This exemp-
                  tion card seems to indicate that you had
                  conscription?
                  (The witness stated that it was no secret
                  that the Jewish Agency had for some
                  time been conducting a campaign for en-
                  listment and that every able-bodied Jew
                  was ordered to place himself in the
                  armed forces. "We have been at war with
                  Hitler since 1933," she said.)

President
of the Court: Don't you think that the government is
                  the best judge of whether there should
                  be conscription or not? Would it not have
                  been wiser to follow loyally the govern-
                  ment decision not to have conscription
                  in this country?

G.M.   A: We are not in a position to impose con-
                  scription in Palestine, but on the other
                  hand both the government and the army
                  asked for Jews to go into the forces and
                  asked the Agency to help, and we
                  thought it right to tell the Jews that
                  this was their war.

Major B.   Q: Do you call it volunteering when a man
                  is dismissed from his job on account of
                  his refusal to enlist?

G.M.   A: It is only moral pressure. This war means
                  more to the Jews than to anybody else.
                  (Reexamined by the defense counsel, Dr.
                  Joseph, Mrs. Meyerson said that even
                  high British army officers had taken part
                  in the Jewish Agency recruiting cam-
                  paign and that some of them had come
                  to the Histadrut to ask for its advice
                  and help in recruiting Jews to the British
                  army.)

Dr. Joseph Q: Is it true that there was a terrible massa-
                  cre and almost all the Jewish population

		killed in Hebron only because there was no Jewish self-defense there?
G.M.	A:	Yes, that was in 1929, and the same thing happened that year in Safad; in 1936 there was a night of terrible slaughter in the Jewish quarter of Tiberias, and all this only because there was no Haganah in those places.
Major B.	Q:	Did Haganah also have arms before the outbreak of war?
G.M.	A:	I do not know, but I suppose so. There were also riots before the war.
President:		I ask you to limit yourself only to what concerns this case and not to go backwards, or otherwise we'll soon be back two thousand years ago.
G.M.	A:	If the Jewish question had been solved two thousand years ago. . . .
President:		Keep quiet!
G.M.	A:	I object to being addressed in that manner.
President:		You should know how to conduct yourself in court.
G.M.	A:	I beg your pardon if I interrupted you, but you should not address me in that manner.

The next day I went to visit my parents in Herzlia. My mother opened the door and said, "Your father has been out all morning showing the newspapers to the neighbors and saying, 'You see, my Golda!' to everyone."

Still, it seemed probable to most of us that when the war ended in an Allied victory, as it obviously would, the British would rethink their catastrophic Palestine policy. At the very least we were sure in 1945 that whatever Jews had stayed alive in Europe would be let into Palestine. In the dawn of a new postwar era the White Paper would certainly be abrogated, particularly since there was now a Labour government in Britain. For thirty years the British Labourites had condemned the restrictions on Jewish immigration to Palestine and issued one pro-Zionist statement after another. It may have been extremely naïve of us to have believed that now everything would change, but it was certainly not unreasonable—especially in the light of the horrifying spectacle of hundreds of thousands of emaciated survivors tottering out of the death camps into the arms of the liberating British forces.

Of course, we were wrong. British policy certainly did change but it changed for the worse. Not only did Mr. Attlee's government not revoke the White Paper, but it announced that it saw no need to honor any of the pledges it had made about Palestine—pledges made, even worse, not only to us, but to millions of British workers and soldiers. Ernest Bevin, the new British foreign secretary, had a "Final Solution" of his own for the problem of the Jews of Europe, who were now becoming known conveniently as displaced persons. If they pulled themselves together and made a real effort, they could settle down quietly in Europe again. Never mind that the Continent was one great cemetery for millions of murdered Jews or that there was only one place in the whole world to which the wretched DPs wanted to go—Palestine.

It was hard, almost impossible for me to believe that instead of helping us—as it had solemnly promised to do for so long—lay the foundations for Jewish independence in Palestine, a British Labour government, come to power in the wake of a world war, was now prepared to send British soldiers to wage war against innocent people who asked only one thing: that they be allowed to live out their days among other Jews in Palestine. All things considered, it was not much of a request, but Bevin turned it down with unprecedented harshness and with a lunatic stubbornness, as though the fate and future of the entire British Empire depended on keeping those few hundred thousand half-dead Jews from entering Palestine. I couldn't account then—and even today I cannot account—for the blind fury with which the British government pursued those Jews—and us. But it was that fury which left us with no alternative at all other than to take up the challenge, although we certainly weren't equipped to do so. Between the summer of 1945 and the winter of 1947 we transported some 70,000 Jews from the DP camps of Europe on those thoroughly inadequate ships of ours and got them through a blockade ferociously maintained by a government made up of men to whose stirring proclamations of Zionism I myself had listened at countless Labour Party conferences.

The real struggle—the *ma'avak* itself—should be dated from 1945, but 1946 was, I think, the year of decision. The immediate background was the British government's astonishing refusal to agree to an appeal made by no less a person than President Truman, who asked that 100,000 Jewish refugees from Germany and Austria be allowed to enter Palestine—exclusive of the White Paper—in a onetime gesture of mercy and humanity. But Mr. Attlee and Mr. Bevin, who apparently thought that the "problem" of European Jews was created only in order to embarrass the British government, said no to President Truman, too. They added, however, that if the U.S. government was so worried about the Jews, perhaps it would help find some solution for the Palestine question. An Anglo-American Committee of Inquiry was duly formed. It visited the DP camps, heard the Jews there declare that they wanted to go only to Palestine, talked to the leaders of British and American Jewry and then came to Palestine in the early spring of 1946 to hold hearings there.

On March 25, 1946 I appeared before the committee as a representative of the Histadrut. Once again, the facts (which one might have been forgiven for supposing that everyone already knew by now) had to be restated, including a capsule history of the Jews and their effort in Palestine. I tried to explain what it was like to have watched from Palestine the slaughter of millions of Jews and to have been able to do nothing about it. I also tried to warn the committee that we were determined to put an end to what the great Hebrew poet Chaim Nachman Bialik had called "the senseless living and senseless dying" of our people.

"I am authorized," I said, "on behalf of the close to one hundred and sixty thousand members of the Histadrut to state here in the clearest terms that there is nothing that Jewish labor is not prepared to do in this country in order to receive large masses of Jewish immigrants, with no limitations and with no conditions whatsoever. . . ." But did the honorable members of the committee really understand what I meant? I wanted to be very sure that the issue was not confused, so I decided to tell them how it actually felt to stand in a courtroom and have to "testify" on such matters. It couldn't hurt, and it might even help. After all, they were civilized and learned men. I told them:

I don't know, gentlemen, whether you who have the good fortune to belong to the two great democratic nations, the British and the American, can, even with the best of will to understand our problems, *realize what it means to be the member of a people whose very right to exist is constantly being questioned:* our right to be Jews such as we are, no better, but no worse, than others in this world, with our own language, our culture, with the right of self-determination and with a readiness to dwell in friendship and cooperation with those near us and those far away. Together with the young and the old survivors in the DP camps, the Jewish workers in this country have decided to do away with this helplessness and dependence upon others within our generation. We want only that which is given naturally to all peoples of the world, to be masters of our own fate—*only* of our fate, not of the destiny of others; to live as of right and not on sufferance, to have the chance to bring the surviving Jewish children, of whom not so many are left in the world now, to this country so that they may grow up like our youngsters who were born here, free of fear, with heads high. Our children here don't understand why the very existence of the Jewish people as such is questioned. For *them,* it is natural to be a Jew.

But I couldn't guess from the expression on their faces whether they had, after all, understood or not, At least three members of the committee, however, were to become fast friends of ours—Bartley Crum, Richard Crossman and James G. McDonald, who served as the first U.S. ambassador to the State of Israel.

By now Palestine was in a state of great unrest. Ship after ship brought refugees to its shores only to have the British subtract the number of "illegal" immigrants from that month's quota of certificates of entry, and when the Haganah refused to halt this immigration, the British issued emergency regulations that amounted to martial law.

In April, while the committee was preparing its report, the British took one more step in their war against the refugees. It wasn't enough that the Royal Navy, the Royal Air Force and thousands of British soldiers were engaged in patrolling the coast of Palestine and trying to trap the

"dangerous political offenders" who were helping bring the
DPs out of Europe. Now the battle spread to another country. Two Haganah ships (one, the *Fede,* renamed the *Dov
Hos,* and the second named the *Eliahu Golomb*) were
caught at La Spezia, on the Italian Riviera, just before they
were due to leave for Palestine with 1,014 refugees on
board. Under British pressure the Italians refused to let the
ships sail, while the refugees, for their part, refused to disembark. They declared a hunger strike and said that if
force were used against them, they would kill themselves
and sink the ships.

I had no doubt at all that they were desperate enough to
do it, and I couldn't bear the thought of those poor, exhausted people, jammed together like sardines, depriving
themselves of even the little food we managed to give them.
If we couldn't bring the boats in ourselves, at least we
could show the immigrants—and the rest of the world—
how profoundly outraged we were. I went first to the Va'ad
Hapoel and then to the Va'ad Le'umi (the Jewish National
Council, which represented the entire *yishuv* and of which
Remez was then chairman) and suggested that we declare
a hunger strike to relieve the refugees in La Spezia. We
made two conditions: that each major group in the *yishuv*
send not more than one representative to the Va'ad Le'umi
in Jerusalem, where the strike was to take place, and that
only fifteen persons in good health would be allowed to
participate.

I was on rather shaky ground here because I had just
been rather ill, and I wasn't really surprised when my doctor told me that it was out of the question for me to join
the strikers. "OK," I said to him. "You can choose. Either
I sit with them in the Va'ad Le'umi or I'll sit at home and
fast. You can't expect me not be in on the strike at all." He
wasn't pleased, but he eventually gave in and handed me
the precious medical certificate. I wasn't the only person to
have trouble with doctors. Shazar had been ill too, but he
went to a gynecologist friend of his in Rehovot and got a
certificate from him without any trouble (although after
the strike, by the way, he was taken straight to hospital,
where he stayed for nearly a month).

We set up beds in the Va'ad Le'umi offices, drank tea
without sugar when we were parched but ate nothing for
101 hours, though I had decided, thank God, that smoking

was permissible. One difficulty that presented itself was that the third day of the hunger strike coincided with the beginning of Passover, and Chief Rabbi Herzog informed us that we must end our strike since, according to Jewish law, all Jews must eat at the Seder. So we had a consultation, the experts among us said that we need not eat more than a piece of matzo (no larger than an olive), and we went on with the strike. The Seder that night was very moving. Then, and for the duration of our hunger strike, Jews filled the courtyard below us, praying and chanting, and delegations came from all over the country to wish us well. One day, to my delight, Menachem and Sarah appeared, and Ben-Gurion was with us often, although he had been against the strike for some reason. In theory people were only allowed to visit us once a day between 12 and 1 P.M., but in fact we were very rarely alone.

I remember that a few minutes before we began the strike, we decided to visit the chief secretary of the Palestine government and make one last plea that the people at La Spezia be allowed in. He listened; then he turned to me and said, "Mrs. Meyerson, do you think for a moment that His Majesty's government will change its policy because *you* are not going to eat?" I said, "No, I have no such illusions. If the death of six million didn't change government policy, I don't expect that my not eating will do so. But it will at least be a mark of solidarity."

Nonetheless, the hunger strike *did* make an impression. On May 8 the *Dov Hos* and the *Eliahu Golomb*, under heavy British escort, sailed for Palestine—1,014 certificates having been duly deducted from the May quota. That month the Anglo-American Committee published its report. It proposed that 100,000 immigrants be admitted to Palestine at once and the land-sale regulations of the White Paper be abolished. There was also a long-term suggestion that the mandate be extended into a UN trusteeship. But Mr. Bevin said no again. If 100,000 refugees entered in the face of Arab opposition, it would take an entire British division to restore order in Palestine, he said. "In that case," I told a party conference in Haifa that week, "we shall have to prove to Mr. Bevin that unless his policy is altered, he will have to send an army division to fight *us*." Mr. Bevin was, in fact, quite anxious to do just that—and did.

On Saturday, June 29, 1946, the British government in

effect declared war on the *yishuv*. One hundred thousand British soldiers and nearly 2,000 policemen broke into dozens of kibbutzim and villages; raided the national institutions, such as the Jewish Agency, the Va'ad Le'umi and the Va'ad Hapoel; slapped a curfew on all the cities in the country that had a Jewish population; and imprisoned more than 3,000 Jews, including most of the *yishuv*'s leaders. The purpose of this was at least threefold: It was intended to demoralize and punish the *yishuv*, to destroy the Haganah and to put a stop—once and for all—to "illegal" immigration by jailing the people who were responsible. It failed on all three counts, but from that "Black Saturday" (as it is known today in Israel) on, Palestine became literally a police state.

Luckily, we had been tipped off that an operation of this kind was in the making. Dozens of Haganah commanders went into hiding, arms were moved to new caches, and new codes were invented. Ben-Gurion was abroad in any case, but Remez, Sharett and virtually all the members of the Jewish Agency and the Va'ad Le'umi were rounded up and sent to a detention camp in Latrun. I wasn't arrested, however, although there were people who said unkindly that this was the worst thing the mandatory government ever did to me! Perhaps I really wasn't important enough—or perhaps they couldn't accommodate women in Latrun. At all events, it was considered by many to be a mark of honor to have been rounded up that day, and one of my colleagues was so anxious to be jailed with everyone else that instead of hiding, he walked around the streets all day until a policeman finally told him to go home. I remember Paula Ben-Gurion (a woman not known for her tact) phoning me every few hours: "Golda, you are still at home? They didn't come to take you?" I'd say no and hang up. Then she'd call again: "Golda, they haven't come yet?" All this on the phone as though nobody else could listen in.

The British didn't only arrest people and search for arms and documents, but caused enormous wanton damage. One of the big kibbutzim, Yugar, was occupied for a whole week. The British had found a Haganah arsenal there, and they tore the kibbutz apart. The settlers, assumed by the British to be members of the Haganah, refused to identify themselves by name, only as "Jews in Palestine," and the men were all dragged off to detention camps so that only the women and children were left in Yugar when the troops took over. As soon as the soldiers left, I went there to see the damage, and I shall never forget picking up snapshots of kibbutz children with the eyes poked out of the photographs.

Since Sharett was in Latrun, I became acting head of the Jewish Agency's Political Department, and in that capacity I suggested that the *yishuv*'s reponse to the mass arrest of thousands of people could only be civil resistance. Not only was it impossible to take what had happened lying down, but unless we did something effective, I was sure that the Irgun Zvai Le'umi and the Stern Group would take the matter into their own hands.

There is a time and place for everything, and this book is not the place, nor the time, for going into the full, detailed and on the whole tragic story of the two dissident underground organizations that existed in the *yishuv* then or of their relationship with the Haganah. I leave that to others and the future. But I feel that it would be dishonest for me not to make crystal clear my own attitude to the methods (and philosophy) of the Irgun Zvai Le'umi and the Sternists. I was and always have been unalterably opposed—both on moral grounds and tactically—to terror of any kinds, whether waged against Arabs because they are Arabs or against the British because they were British. It was, and has remained, my firm conviction that although many individual members of these dissident groups were certainly extremely brave and extremely dedicated, they were wrong (and thus dangerous to the *yishuv*) from start to finish. And I was positive in the summer of 1946 that if we did not react effectively to the events of "Black Saturday," they would do so and bring even greater disasters upon us. As soon as I could, I went to see Dr. Chaim Weizmann in Rehovot in the hope of persuading him to call for this kind of massive demonstration. At that time, Dr. Weizmann was president of the World Zionist Organization and chairman of the Jewish Agency. He was, without question, the leader and the premier spokesman of world Jewry.

A noted scientist, he was Russian-born, but he had lived and worked in England for many years and had played a major role in the securing of the Balfour Declaration. He was a majestic man, tall, good-looking and regal in bearing.

Jews throughout the world thought and spoke of him as "king of the Jews," and although he belonged to no one political party, he was always deeply involved with the kibbutz movement in particular and close to the labor movement in general—although inevitably there was friction between Weizmann the gradualist and Ben-Gurion the activist. Their relationship worsened during the war, when Ben-Gurion felt that Dr. Weizmann was not doing enough to press for the creation of a Jewish Brigade and even proposed to the party that we ask Weizmann to resign from office. We didn't go along with Ben-Gurion, of course, but later, at the Zionist Congress of 1946 in Basel, Weizmann received a vote of no-confidence.

Despite stories that are told in Israel today regarding the real relationship between these two men, so entirely different from each other in temperament and approach, Ben-Gurion, like the rest of us, admired and loved Weizmann, although he never shared Weizmann's trusting and optimistic attitude toward the British. Weizmann believed—even after 1946—that the British would come to their senses one day, and he found it impossible to accept the extent of their betrayal of us. But whether in or out of office, he was, for the thirty years of the mandate, the one man who embodied Zionism for the world outside Palestine, and his influence was immense.

It was only Weizmann who could have persuaded President Truman, at zero hour in 1948, to recognize a Jewish state of which the Negev was a part. He was old and frail then and nearly blind, but when Truman did authorize the recognition of Israel by the United States on the afternoon of May 14, 1948, it was of Dr. Weizmann that he thought and spoke. "The old doctor will believe me now," he said. And there was never any doubt in Ben-Gurion's mind that when we had a state of our own, Chaim Weizmann would be its first president.

I used to visit Weizmann often in Rehobt, where he and his wife, Vera, had built a house in the 1930s (it was to serve as the presidential residence from 1948 to 1952, when Dr. Weizmann died). Every now and then he would call me up and say, "Come and have a meal with us," and I would spend an evenng with him, gossiping and talking politics. He grew very bitter toward the end of his life. He spoke of himself as the "prisoner of Rehobot" and felt that he was being deliberately excluded from policymaking. I remember once I had lunch with him and he spoke very sadly about De Gaulle and the fact that when De Gaulle wanted to, he could attend cabinet meetings and even preside over them, whereas our parliamentary system was different. I think that perhaps it was a mistake that Weizmann went on living in Rehobot although he wanted, of course, to be near the Weizmann Institute of Science, that wonderful center of scientific research that grew out of the Daniel Sieff Research Institute, which he had founded in 1934. If Weizmann had lived in Jerusalem and opened his house to the people of Israel—as Ben-Zvi and Shazar did when they were presidents—he would have been less and felt less isolated. And if Mrs. Weizmann had been less elegant and aloof, that might have helped, too. At any rate, he was a very great man, and I was deeply honored when the chancellor of the Weizmann Institute, my friend Meyer Weisgal, asked me to serve as honorary world chairman of the Weizmann Centenary Celebrations in 1974.

But when I went to see him that day in 1946, he was still in his prime and very powerful. "If you call upon the *yishuv* to adopt a policy of civil disobedience toward the government of Palestine," I said, "it will show the world that we cannot acquiesce in what has happened. Only you have the necessary authority to make this proclamation effective."

"All right," he said. "But I must be assured by the Haganah that nothing will be done—no actions taken—until the Jewish Agency meets in Paris in August." I promised him to make every effort to secure such an assurance from the five people (I was not yet one of them) who decided these matters, and I went to Eshkol at once to find out whether this could be done. In actual fact, action had already been decided on by a vote of three to two, but when Eshkol heard what Weizmann wanted, he immediately said that he would change his vote. He, too, realized that if the national institutions failed to react, the Irgun Zvai Le'umi would certainly do something. Then Weizmann backed down. I think probably his friends in England talked him out of leading a civil disobedience campaign, but whatever his reason, I was very upset and angry.

In August the Jewish Agency meeting took place in Paris as scheduled. We didn't want Ben-Gurion, who was still abroad, to return to Palestine because he probably would have been arrested, so we went to France and heard the details of a new proposal made by Mr. Bevin. This time Bevin suggested that cantonization of Palestine with one Jewish canton. At this point, the British were already deporting "illegal" immigrants from Palestine to camps on Cyprus and pouring more and more troops into the country. There seemed no point at all to any proposal except one that would result in the creation of a Jewish state, but Weizmann was carrying on conversations with the British which were not exactly along these lines.

Ben-Gurion was ready to tear the world apart, but I suggested that we fly to London and talk to Weizmann ourselves. Poor man, he had lost a son in the war, his eyesight was going, and his heart was being broken by the British and by his anxiety lest in our rejection of a British cantonization plan we plunge the *yishuv* into total war. But I couldn't stand the charge that we were being "irresponsible," and I lost my temper—which is something I very rarely do. I got up and walked out of the room, and it took years before Dr. Weizmann forgave my opposition to him—then and later that year in Basel.

Incidentally, it was not the only time I walked out of a room in that period. Only a few months earlier I had gone to see the government's chief secretary about something and was astounded to hear him say pleasantly, "Mrs. Meyerson, you must agree that if the Nazis persecuted the Jews, they must have had some reason for it." I got up and walked out without a word and refused to see him again. Afterward I was told that he couldn't imagine why I was so enraged.

The Twenty-second Zionist Congress in Basel was the first to be convened after the war. It was like the gathering of a terribly bereaved family mourning the death of multitudes, but rallying itself—despite its great grief—to save the remnants and to face the problems of the present. Now we talked openly to the world about a Jewish state. Speaking in Yiddsh, I recalled the dark days of the war and the events that had followed it, and I talked about our youth, the young sabras born in Palestine, about whom we had once asked each other, "What is to bind these children of ours to the Jewish people throughout the world?" I wanted the Zionist delegates to know that these youngsters who had not long ago been so unfamiliar with the Diaspora were no less committed to the free immigration of Jews than we were.

The time came when the sabras themselves gave us the answer. They are strangers to casuistry and abstract precepts. They are plain and pure as the sun of Palestine. For them, matters are simple, clear and uncomplicated. When the catastrophe descended upon the Jews of the world, and Jews began coming to Palestine in "illegal" ships, as they still do, we saw these children of ours go down to the seas and risk their lives—this is no rhetoric, but literally so—to ford the waves and reach the boats and bear the Jews ashore on their shoulders. This, too, is no rhetoric, no flowery speech, but the literal truth: sixteen- and eighteen-year-old Palestinian girls and boys carried the survivors on their backs. From the mouths of Jews borne on those shoulders I have heard how they shed tears for the first time—after all they had been through in Europe for seven years—when they saw Palestinian youngsters bearing grown men and women to the soil of the homeland. We have been blessed in this youth, which sets out to offer its life not on behalf of its own particular kibbutz, or of the *yishuv* in Palestine in general, but for the sake of every Jewish child, or old man, seeking entry.

One miracle was that the Jews still came, in the face of British gas bombs and truncheons, knowing that some might be killed and that all would be shipped off to detention in Cyprus. But the other miracle was that our own children were with us in the struggle.

As to the future, these blows have strengthened our determination to demand that full measure of political independence which can only be attained through the establishment of a Jewish state.

What I did not say to congress, because I did not yet know it myself, was that the blows awaiting us in the twenty-one months that were to pass before Israel was born were to be crueler by far than any that we had experienced in Palestine before.

8. We Have Our State

If 1946 was difficult, then I can only describe 1947 as the year in which the situation in Palestine got completely out of hand as far as the British were concerned. In the course of that year the battle against Jewish immigration turned into open warfare, not only against the entire *yishuv* as such, but also against the refugees themselves. It was as though Ernest Bevin had nothing else whatsoever on his mind except how to keep Jewish refugees out of the Jewish homeland. The fact that we refused to solve this problem for him apparently infuriated him so that he eventually lost control altogether, and I honestly believe that some of the decisions he made regarding Palestine could only have been the result of his intense personal rage against the Jews because they could not and would not accept the judgment of the British foreign secretary as to how or where they should live.

I don't know (nor does it really matter anymore) whether Bevin was a little insane, or just anti-Semitic, or both. What I do know is that he insisted on pitting the strength of the British Empire against the will of the Jews to live and that by so doing he not only brought great suffering to people who had already suffered enormously, but also forced upon thousands of British soldiers and sailors a role that must have filled them with horror. I remember staring at some of the young Englishmen who guarded the DP detention camps on Cyprus—when I went there myself in 1947—and wondering how on earth they managed to reconcile themselves to the fact that not so long ago they were liberating from Nazi camps the very same people whom they now kept penned behind barbed wire on Cyprus only because these people found it impossible to go on living anywhere except Palestine. I looked at those nice young English boys and was filled with pity for them. I couldn't help thinking that they were no less victims of Bevin's obsession than the men, women and children on whom their guns were now trained night and day.

I had gone to Cyprus to see what, if anything, could be done about the hundreds of children who were being kept there. At that point about 40,000 Jews were living in the Cyprus camps. Each month, with great precision, the British allowed exactly 1,500 Jews to enter Palestine: 750 from the camps of Europe and 750 from Cyprus. The principle under which this policy operated in Cyprus was "first in, first out," which meant that, inevitably, many small children were doomed to live under very difficult conditions for months. Our doctors in the Cyprus camps were very concerned about this, and one day a delegation of physicians appeared in my office in Jerusalem.

"We can take no further responsibility for the health of the infants if they stay in the camps for one more winter," they informed me. So I began to negotiate with the Palestine government. What we suggested was some scheme that would permit DP families with a child under the age of one year to leave Cyprus "out of turn" and then subtract their number from the DPs who left "in turn." This meant persuading the Palestine government to be both flexible and reasonable—at a time when it was neither—and also persuading the DPs themselves to set up a special system of priorities. It took quite a time for me to work something out with the government, but in the end I managed to do so and even get permission for orphaned children to leave as soon as possible.

The next step was obviously for me to go to Cyprus and talk to the DPs. "They'll never listen to you," my friends warned me. "You will only be sticking your neck out and asking for trouble. The one thing that these people are waiting for is to get out of Cyprus, and now you want to ask them to agree to let some people who may have only been there for a week or two jump to the head of the queue. It won't work!" But I couldn't see it that way. I thought that at least it had to be tried, so I went.

When I got to Cyprus, I immediately reported to the office of the British commandant of the camp, an elderly, tall, thin Englishman who had served for years with the army in India. It was what you might call a courtesy call. I told him briefly who I was and what I wanted and asked whether he had any objection to my touring the camps the next day.

He listened to me very stiffly and then said, "I know all about the families with babies, but I haven't received any instructions about orphans."

"But that was part of the agreement I made with the chief secretary," I said.

"Well, I'll have to check it," he answered rather unpleasantly. Nonetheless, we went on talking, and after a while he said suddenly, "Oh, very well then. Include the orphans." I couldn't understand why he had surrendered so quickly, but in the morning I discovered that he had received a telegram from the chief secretariat in Jerusalem that read: BEWARE OF MRS. MEYERSON. SHE IS A FORMIDABLE PERSON! And, I suppose, he decided on the spot to take the advice seriously.

The camps themselves were even more depressing than I had expected, in a way worse than the camps for DPs that were being run in Germany by the U.S. authorities. They looked like prison camps, ugly clusters of huts and tents—with a watchtower at each end—set down on the sand, with nothing green or growing anywhere in sight. There wasn't nearly enough water for drinking and even less for bathing, despite the heat. Although the camps were right on the shore, none of the refugees was allowed to go swimming, and they spent their time, for the most part, sitting in those filthy, stifling tents, which, if nothing else, protected them from the glaring sun. As I walked through the camps, the DPs pressed up against the barbed-wire fences that surrounded them to welcome me, and at one camp two tiny little children came up with a bouquet of paper flowers for me. I have been given a great many bouquets of flowers since then, but I have never been as moved by any of them as I was by those flowers presented to me in Cyprus by children who had probably forgotten—if they ever knew—what real flowers looked like and who had been helped in making those pathetic bouquets by nursery-school teachers whom we had sent to the camps. Incidentally, one of the Palestinian Jews in Cyprus then—though she later escaped—was a girl named Ayan, an attractive young radio operator from a captured Haganah ship who is today a child psychiatrist in Tel Aviv and my daughter-in-law.

At any rate, the first item on the agenda was a meeting

at which I explained my mission to the committee representing all the detainees. This was followed by an open-air meeting with most of the detainees themselves. I told them that I was sure that they would not have to remain on Cyprus for long and that eventually everyone would be released; but until this time came, I needed their cooperation in order to save the children. The Irgun Zvai Le'umi sympathizers in the camps objected violently to the agreement I had made with the British. It was all or nothing, they shouted, and there was even an attempt to attack me physically. But finally they calmed down, and we made the necessary arrangements.

There was still one problem bothering me. We had asked that "orphans" be allowed to enter Palestine "out of turn," but what about the children on Cyprus who had only one surviving parent? When I got back to Jerusalem, I went to see the high commissioner, Sir Alan Cunningham, and thanked him for what he had done. Then I said, "But there is one very tragic aspect of our agreement. It seems terribly unfair that a child whose mother or father was killed in Europe should have to stay on Cyprus when a friend who may have been 'lucky' enough to have lost both parents is able to leave. Is there anything at all that we can do about this?"

Cunningham—who was to be the last British high commissioner to Palestine and who was an extremely kind and decent man—shook his head rather unhappily. Then he heaved a resigned sigh, smiled and said, "Don't worry. I'll take care of that at once, Mrs. Meyerson."

I used to see him from time to time, and however tense or chaotic the situation in Palestine was, he and I were always able to talk to each other like friends. After Cunnigham left Palestine on May 14, 1948, I didn't expect to hear from him ever again. But one day several months after I became prime minister, I got a letter from him. It was written by hand from the country place in England to which he had retired, and its essence was that however great the pressures on us, Israel should not budge from any of the territories we had taken in the Six-Day War, unless and until we were guaranteed secure and defensible borders. I was very touched indeed by his letter.

A less pleasant reminder of those days was the ceremony I attended in Haifa in 1970, when the bodies of 100 chil-

dren who had died in those dreadful camps were brought
to Haifa for reburial in the lovely foothills of Mount Carmel. I tried to shake off the thought, but I couldn't help
wondering if the two little girls who had so solemnly
handed me those flowers in 1947 were not among them.
On the other hand, I often bumped into people who had
attended that meeting in Cyprus and remembered it well.
About five years ago, for instance, I was visiting a kibbutz
in the Negev when a middle-aged woman came up to me
very hesitantly. "Excuse me for bothering you," she said,
"but this is the first opportunity I have had in all these
years to thank you."

"For what?" I asked.

"I was on Cyprus with a baby in 1947," she replied,
"and you saved us. Now, I'd like you to meet the 'baby'."
The "baby" was a sturdy, pretty girl of twenty who had just
finished her military service and obviously thought I had
taken leave of my senses when I gave her a great big kiss in
front of everybody—without a word of explanation.

At the Zionist Congress in Basel in 1946 it had been
decided that Moshe Sharett should head the Political Department of the Jewish Agency from Washington and that I
should remain its head in Jerusalem. But by 1947 living in
Jerusalem was like living in a city occupied by an extremely hostile foreign power. The British shut themselves
up in what was actually an improvised fortress—a heavily
guarded compound (we called it Bevingrad) right in the
middle of town—sent their tanks rumbling through the
streets at the slightest provocation and forbade their troops
to have anything to do with the Jews. Whenever the Irgun
Zvai Le'u-mi and the Stern Group took the law into their
own hands—which, most unfortunately, they did fairly regularly—the British responded with retaliatory actions that
were aimed at the entire *yishuv*, particularly at the Haganah, and hardly a week went by without some sort of
crisis—arms searches, mass arrests, curfews that lasted for
days and paralyzed everyday life and, finally, the deportation of Jews without even a charge, let alone a trial. When
the British began flogging members of the Irgun or Sternists whom they caught, the two dissident organizations responded by kidnapping and even executing two British soldiers—and all this while our battle for free immigration
and land settlement was in full force.

Looking back at that period, I can see, of course, that almost any other colonial power imposing itself on a rebellious native population (which is how the British saw us) would probably have behaved in an even harsher manner. But the British were harsh enough. It wasn't only their often very cruel punitive measures that made the situation so intolerable; it was also our knowledge that whenever possible, they aided and abetted the Arabs, not to speak of inciting them against us. On the other hand, the idea of a perpetual bloodbath in Palestine was also not very appealing to Britain—least of all in its postwar mood—and in February, 1947, Mr. Bevin himself decided that his government was tired of the whole thing and said so in the House of Commons. Let the United Nations deal with the Palestine problem. The British had had enough. I can't imagine that the United Nations was overjoyed at having this responsibility dumped on it, but it couldn't very well refuse to accept it.

The UN Special Committee on Palestine (UNSCOP) arrived in the country in June. According to its terms of reference, it was to report back to the UN General Assembly by September 1, 1947, with some sort of concrete proposal for a solution. The Palestinian Arabs, as usual, refused to cooperate with it in any way, but everyone else did, though a little wearily: the leaders of the *yishuv*, the Palestine government and later even the leaders of some of the Arab states. I spent a lot of time with the eleven members of the committee and was horrified to discover how little they knew of the history of Palestine or of Zionism, for that matter. But since it was essential that they learn—and as quickly as possible—we began to explain and expound as we had done so often before, and eventually they started to grasp what all the fuss was about and why we were not prepared to give up our right to bring the survivors of the Holocaust to Palestine.

Then, for reasons which will never be understood by me—nor, I suspect, by anyone else—just before UNSCOP was scheduled to leave Palestine, the British chose to demonstrate in the most unmistakable way just how brutally and tyrannically they were dealing with us and with the question of Jewish immigration. Before the shocked eyes of the members of UNSCOP they forcibly caged and returned to Germany the 4,500 refugees who had come to Palestine aboard the Haganah ship *Exodus* 1947, and I think that by so doing, they actually contributed considerably to UN-SCOP's final recommendations. If I live to be a hundred, I shall never erase from my mind the gruesome picture of hundreds of British soldiers in full combat dress, bearing and using clubs, pistols and grenades against the wretched refugees on the *Exodus*, 400 of whom were pregnant women determined to give birth to their babies in Palestine. Nor will I ever be able to forget the revulsion with which I heard that these people were actually going to be shipped back, like animals in their wire cages, to DP camps in the one country that symbolized the graveyard of European Jewry.

Speaking at a meeting of the Va'ad Le'umi only a few days before the passengers of the *Exodus* left on their grim journey to Hamburg, I tried to express the disgust and grief of the *yishuv*, as well as its flickering hope that somehow, someone, somewhere would intervene to save the refugees from this new torment:

> The British hope that through deportation of the *Exodus* 1947 they will succeed in frightening the Jews of the DP camps and terrify us. There can be only one answer on our part: this flow of boats will not cease. I am aware that the Jews seeking to immigrate to Palestine and those assisting them now face terrible difficulties, with all the forces of the British Empire concentrated for one purpose: to attack these creaking boats laden with human suffering. Nevertheless, I believe that there can be only one effective answer: the uninterrupted flow of the "illegal" ships. I have no doubts about the stand of the Jews of the camps; they are ready for all perils in order to leave the camps. The Jewish survivors of many European countries cannot remain where they are.
>
> If we in Palestine, together with American, South African and British Jewry, do not let ourselves be frightened, the boats will continue to come. With much travail, greater than in the past—but come they will. I do not, for one moment, disregard what the thousands of these boats will face in the coming days. I know that each one of us would deem himself happy if he could be with them. Each one of us worries over

what may happen when the Jews on the *Exodus* are brought to Germany . . . with the British forces completely free to teach these lawbreakers a lesson. There can be no doubt that they will be steadfast, as they have been until now. The question is only whether there is no hope for some last-minute change of heart on the part of the British.

Since we are incapable of despair, we wish at this moment, from this place, once more to address our call to the world, to the nations—to the many who suffered so much during the war, to those on many of whose fronts Jews fought and helped in their liberation. To these nations we issue this last-minute appeal. Is it possible that no voice will be raised, that the British government will not be told: Remove the whip and the rifle from over the heads of the Jews on the *Exodus?* And to Britain we must say: it is a great illusion to believe us to be weak. Let Great Britain with her mighty fleet and her many guns and planes know that this people is not so weak and that its strength will yet stand in good stead. . . .

But the fate of the *Exodus* had already been sealed, and the ship returned to Germany.

The summer of 1947 dragged on and on. Despite the fact that the Tel Aviv-Jerusalem road was increasingly coming under the control of armed Arab bands, who shot at all Jewish transport from the hills above it, there was no alternative other than for me to ferry back and forth between the two cities and rely on the young Haganah guards who accompanied me. What was really at stake was not whether I would be killed or wounded traveling to Tel Aviv and back, but whether the Arabs would succeed in their proclaimed intention of cutting the road altogether and thus starving out the Jews of Jerusalem. And I was certainly not about to help them achieve this aim by refraining from using the one road that connected Jerusalem to the Jewish centers of the country. Once or twice a bullet whizzed through the window of the Jewish Agency car in which I used to travel, and once we took a wrong turn and arrived in an Arab village that I knew to be a nest of cutthroats; but we escaped without a scratch.

Sometimes there were also "adventures" of a different

nature. For instance, one time British soldiers searched my car for arms just after I had been promised by the chief secretary himself that these searches would end, in view of the growing danger to Jewish traffic on the roads. My protests did no good at all. A gun was found on one of the Haganah escorts and she was promptly arrested.

"Where are you dragging her to?" I asked the officer in charge of this great operation.

"To Majdal," he said.

Majdal, an Arab town, was certainly no place for a young girl to spend the night, and I told the captain that if she were taken there, I would insist on going with her. By then he knew who I was, and I don't think he looked forward at all to explaining to his superiors why a member of the Jewish Agency Executive had gone to sleep in Majdal, so he changed his mind, and we all went off to a police station in a nearby Jewish town. By then it was midnight, but I still had to get to Tel Aviv—which I duly did, royally escorted by British policemen and the Haganah girl, who was hastily released. Others, however, were not so lucky. The death toll on the roads rose weekly, and by November, 1947, the Arabs—in full view of the British—had begun to lay siege to Jerusalem.

On August 31—only a minute or two before their deadline expired—the eleven gentlemen of UNSCOP, convened in Geneva, turned in their report on Palestine. Eight members of the committee recommended—as the Peel Commission had—that the country be partitioned into an Arab state and a Jewish state, plus an international enclave that would take in Jerusalem and its immediate vicinity. The minority (consisting, among others, of the representatives of India, Iran and Yugoslavia—all of which had large Moslem populations) suggested a federal Arab-Jewish state. It was now up to the UN General Assembly to decide. In the meantime, all the parties concerned made their responses known, and I can't say that any surprises awaited the United Nations in this respect. We accepted the plan, of course—without much elation but with great relief—and demanded that the mandate come to an end at once. All the Arabs said that they would have nothing to do with either set of recommendations and threatened war unless all Palestine was made an Arab state. The British made clear that they would not cooperate with the implementa-

tion of any partition plan unless both the Jews and the Arabs were enthusiastic about it, and we all knew what that
meant. And the Americans and the Russians each published statements in favor of the majority recommendation.

The next day I held a press conference in Jerusalem. In
addition to thanking the committee for having worked so
rapidly, I stressed that "we could hardly imagine a Jewish
state without Jerusalem" and that "we still hoped that this
wrong would be rectified by the UN Assembly." We were
also very unhappy, I said, about the exclusion of western
Galilee from the Jewish state and assumed that this would
be taken up at the Assembly, too. But the most important
point I wanted to make was that we were extremely anxious to establish a new and different relationship with the
Arabs—of whom, I thought, there would be some 500,000
in the Jewish state. "A Jewish state in this part of the
world," I told the press, "is not only a solution for us. It
should and can be a great aid for everyone in the Middle
East." It is heart-rending now to think that we were using
those words—to no avail—as long ago as 1947!

The voting took place at Lake Success in New York on
November 29. Like everyone else in the *yishuv,* I was
glued to the radio, with pencil and paper, writing down the
votes as they came through. Finally, at about midnight our
time, the results were announced: Thirty-three nations (including the United States and the Soviet Union) were in
favor of the partition plan; thirteen, including all the Arab
states, opposed it; ten, including Great Britain, abstained. I
immediately went to the compound of the Jewish Agency
building, which was already jammed with people. It was an
incredible sight: hundreds of people, British soldiers among
them, holding hands, singing and dancing, with truckloads
of more people arriving at the compound all the time. I
remember walking up to my office alone, unable to share
in the general festivity. The Arabs had turned the plan
down and talked only of war. The crowd, drunk with happiness, wanted a speech, and I thought it would be wicked
to dampen the mood by refusing. So from the balcony of
my office I spoke for a few minutes. But it was not really to
the mass of people below me that I talked; it was, once
again, to the Arabs.

"You have fought your battle against us in the United
Nations," I said. "The United Nations—the majority of

countries in the world—have had their say. The partition plan is a compromise: not what you wanted, not what we wanted. But let us now live in friendship and peace together." That speech was hardly the solution for our situation. Arab riots broke out all over Palestine the next day (seven Jews were killed in an Arab ambush on a bus) and on December 2 an Arab mob set the Jewish commercial center in Jerusalem on fire, while British police stood by, interfering only when the Haganah tried to take action.

We were of course, totally unprepared for war. That we had managed for so long to hold the local Arabs at bay, more or less, didn't mean that we could cope with regular armies. We needed weapons urgently, if we could find anyone willing to sell them to us; but before we could buy anything, we needed money—not the sort of money which had helped us to afforest the country or bring in refugees, but millions of dollars. And there was only one group of people in the whole world that we had any chance of getting these dollars from: the Jews of America. There was simply nowhere else to go and no one else to go to.

It was, of course, out of the question for Ben-Gurion to leave Palestine then. His role was absolutely central. I think that he himself felt that no one else could possibly raise the kind of money that was being discussed in the series of secret meetings we held in Tel Aviv in December, 1947, and the early part of January, 1948, and I certainly agreed with him. But he had to stay in the country. So who would go? At one of these meetings, I looked around the table at my colleagues, so tired and harassed, and wondered for the first time whether I ought not to volunteer for the mission. After all, I had done some fund raising in the States before, and I spoke English fluently. My services in Palestine could certainly be dispensed with for a few weeks, and though I wasn't used to proposing myself, I began to feel that I should suggest this to Ben-Gurion. At first, he wouldn't hear of it. He was going, he said, and was taking with him Eliezer Kaplan, the treasurer of the Jewish Agency.

"But no one can take your place here," I argued, "while I may be able to do what you can do in the United States."

He was adamant.

"No. I need you here."

"Then let's put it to the vote," I said. He looked at me

for a second, then nodded. The vote was in favor of my going.

"But at once," Ben-Gurion said. "Don't even try to get back to Jerusalem." So I flew to the States that day—without any luggage, wearing the dress I had worn to the meeting with a winter coat over it.

The first appearance I made in 1948 before American Jewry was unscheduled, unrehearsed and, of course, unannounced. Also, I was quite unknown to the people I addressed. It was in Chicago on January 21, at the General Assembly of the Council of Jewish Federations and Welfare Funds, which were non-Zionist organizations. Palestine, in fact, was not on the agenda at all. But this was a meeting of professional fund raisers, of the tough experienced men who controlled the Jewish fund-raising machinery in the United States and I knew that if I could get through to them, there was some chance of getting the money that was the key to our ability to defend ourselves. I didn't speak for long, but I said everything that was in my heart. I described the situation as it had been the day I left Palestine, and then I said:

The Jewish community in Palestine is going to fight to the very end. If we have arms to fight with, we will fight with them. If not, we will fight with stones in our hands.

I want you to believe me when I say that I came on this special mission to the United States today not to save seven hundred thousand Jews. During the last few years the Jewish people lost six million Jews, and it would be audacity on our part to worry Jews throughout the world because a few hundred thousand more Jews are in danger.

That is not the issue. The issue is that if these seven hundred thousand Jews in Palestine can remain alive, then the Jewish people as such is alive and Jewish independence assured. If these seven hundred thousand people are killed off, then for centuries we are through with the dream of a Jewish people and a Jewish homeland.

My friends, we are at war. There is no Jew in Palestine who does not believe that finally we will be victorious. That is the spirit of the country. . . . But this valiant spirit alone cannot face rifles and machine guns. Rifles and machine guns without spirit are not worth very much, but spirit without arms can, in time, be broken together with the body.

Our problem is time. . . . The question is what can we get immediately. And, when I say immediately, I do not mean next month. I do not mean two months from now. I mean now.

I have come here to try to impress Jews in the United States with the fact that within a very short period, a couple of weeks, we must have in cash between twenty-five and thirty million dollars. In the next two or three weeks we can establish ourselves. Of that we are convinced.

The Egyptian government can vote a budget to aid our antagonists. The Syrian government can do the same. We have no governments. But we have millions of Jews in the Diaspora, and exactly as we have faith in our youngsters in Palestine so I have faith in the Jews of the United States; I believe that they will realize the peril of our situation and do what they have to do.

I know that we are not asking for something easy. I myself have sometimes been active in various campaigns and fund collections, and I know that collecting at once a sum such as I ask is not simple. But I have seen our people at home. I have seen them come from the offices to the clinics when we called the community to give their blood for a blood bank to treat the wounded. I have seen them lined up for hours, waiting so that some of their blood can be added to this bank. It is blood plus money that is being given in Palestine. . . .

We are not a better breed; we are not the best Jews of the Jewish people. It so happened that we are there and you are here. I am certain that if you were in Palestine and we were in the United States, you would be doing what we are doing there, and you would ask us here to do what you will have to do.

I want to close by paraphrasing one of the greatest speeches that was made during the Second World War—the words of Churchill. I am not exaggerating when I say that the *yishuv* in Palestine will fight in the

Negev and will fight in Galilee and will fight on the outskirts of Jerusalem until the very end.

You cannot decide whether we should fight or not. We will. The Jewish community in Palestine will raise no white flag for the mufti. That decision is taken. Nobody can change it. You can only decide one thing: whether we shall be victorious in this fight or whether the mufti will be victorious. That decision American Jews can make. It has to be made quickly, within hours, within days.

And I beg of you—don't be too late. Don't be bitterly sorry three months from now for what you failed to do today. The time is now.

They listened, and they wept, and they pledged money in amounts that no community had ever given before. I stayed in the United States for as long as I could bear to be away from home, for about six weeks, and the Jews all over the country listened, wept and gave money—and, when they had to, took loans from banks in order to cover their pledges. By the time I came back to Palestine in March I had raised $50,000,000, which was turned over at once for the Haganah's secret purchase of arms in Europe. But I never deceived myself—not even when upon my return Ben-Gurion said to me, "Someday when history will be written, it will be said that there was a Jewish woman who got the money which made the state possible." I always knew that these dollars were given not to me, but to Israel.

That journey to the States, however, was only one of the journeys I made that year. In the six months that preceded the establishment of the state, I met twice with King Abdullah of Transjordan, who was King Hussein's grandfather. Although both those talks remained closely guarded secrets for many years—long after Abdullah's assassination by his Arab enemies (probably the mufti's henchmen) in Jerusalem in 1951—no one knows to this day to what extent rumors about them were responsible for his death. Assassination is an endemic disease in the Arab world, and one of the first lessons that most Arab rulers learn is the connection between secrecy and longevity. Abdullah's murder made a lasting impression on all subsequent Arab leaders, and I remember that Nasser once said to an intermediary whom we dispatched to Cairo, "If Ben-Gurion came to

Egypt to talk to me, he would return home as a conquering hero. But if I went to him, I would be shot when I came back." And I am afraid that is still the situation.

The first time I met King Abdullah was early in November, 1947. He had agreed to meet me—in my capacity as head of the Political Department of the Jewish Agency—in a house at Naharayim (on the Jordan), where the Palestine Electric Corporation ran a hydroelectric power station. I came to Naharayim with one of our Arab experts— Eliahu Sasson. We drank the usual ceremonial cups of coffee, and then we began to talk. Abdullah was a small, very poised man with great charm. He soon made the heart of the matter clear: He would not join in any Arab attack on us. He would always remain our friend, he said, and like us, he wanted peace more than anything else. After all, we had a common foe, the mufti of Jerusalem, Haj Amin el-Husseini. Not only that, but he suggested that we meet again, after the United Nations vote.

On the way back to Tel Aviv, Ezra Danin, who had met with Abdullah often before, filled me in on the king's general concept of the role of the Jews. It was that Providence had scattered the Jews throughout the Western world in order that they might absorb European culture and bring it back to the Middle East with them, thus reviving the area. As for his reliability, Danin was dubious. It was not, he told me, that Abdullah was a liar, but that he was a Bedouin, and that the Bedouin had their own ideas about truth—which they saw as something much less absolute than we did. At any rate, he said, Abdullah was certainly sincere in his expressions of friendship, although they would not necessarily be at all binding on him.

Throughout January and February we maintained contact with Abdullah, as a rule through the good offices of a mutual friend, through whom I was able to send direct messages to the king. As the weeks passed, my messages became more worried. The air was thick with conjecture, and there were reports that despite his promise to me, Abdullah was about to join the Arab League. Was this indeed so? I asked. The reply from Amman was prompt and negative. King Abdullah was astonished and hurt by my question. He asked me to remember three things: that he was a Bedouin and therefore a man of honor; that he was a king and therefore doubly an honorable man; and finally, that he would never break a promise made to a woman. So there could not possibly be any justification for my concern.

But we knew differently. By the first week of May there was no doubt that for all his assurances, Abdullah had, in fact, thrown his lot in with the Arab League. We debated the pros and cons of requesting another meeting before it was too late. Perhaps he could be persuaded to change his mind at the last minute. If not, perhaps we could at least find out from him just how deeply he had committed himself and his British-trained and officered Arab Legion to the war against us. A great deal hung in the balance: Not only was the legion by far the best Arab army in the area, but there was also another vital consideration. If, by some miracle, Transjordan stayed out of the war, it would be much harder for the Iraqi army to cross over into Palestine and join in the attack on us. Ben-Gurion was of the opinion that we could lose nothing by trying again, so I requested a second meeting, and asked Ezra Danin to accompany me.

This time, however, Abdullah refused to come to Naharayim. It was too dangerous, he told us through his emissary. If I wanted to see him, I would have to come to Amman, and the risk would have to be entirely mine. He could not be expected, he informed us, to alert the legion to the fact that he awaited Jewish guests from Palestine, and he would take no responsibility for anything that might happen to us en route. The first problem was to get to Tel Aviv, which at that point was almost as difficult as getting to Amman itself. I waited in Jerusalem from early in the morning until 7 P.M. for a plane to arrive from Tel Aviv, and when it finally turned up, it was so windy that we could hardly take off. Under normal conditions I would have tried to postpone the trip for another day, but there were no days left. It was already May 10 and the Jewish state would be proclaimed on May 14. This was our very last chance to talk to Abdullah. So I insisted that we try to reach Tel Aviv—even in that Piper Cub, which looked as though it would collapse even in a strong breeze, let alone a gale. After we left, a message arrived at the airstrip in Jerusalem to say that the weather was far too bad for us to attempt the flight, but we were already on our way by then.

The next morning I set out by car for Haifa, where Ezra and I were to meet. It had already been decided that he would not disguise himself other than by wearing traditional Arab headgear. He spoke fluent Arabic, was familiar with Arab customs and could easily be taken for an Arab. As for me, I would travel in the traditional dark and voluminous robes of an Arab woman. I spoke no Arabic at all, but as a Moslem wife accompanying her husband, it was most unlikely that I would be called on to say anything to anyone. The Arab dress and veils I needed had already been ordered and Ezra explained the route to me. We would change several times, he said, in order to be sure that we were not followed, and at a given point that night someone would turn up not far from the king's palace to lead us to Abdullah. The major problem was to avoid arousing the suspicions of the Arab legionnaires at the various checkposts we had to pass before we got to the place, where our guide was to meet us.

It was a long, long series of rides through the night. First into one car, then out of it, and into another for a few more miles and then, at Naharayim into a third car. We didn't talk to each other at all during the journey. I had perfect faith in Ezra's ability to get us through the enemy lines safely, and I was much too concerned with the outcome of our mission to think about what would happen if, God forbid, we were caught. Luckily, although we had to identify ourselves several times, we got to our appointed meeting place on time and undetected. The man who was to take us to Abdullah was one of his most trusted associates, a Bedouin whom the king had adopted and reared since childhood and who was used to running perilous errands for his master.

In his car, its windows covered with heavy black material, he drove Ezra and myself to his house. While we waited for Abdullah to appear, I talked to our guide's attractive and intelligent wife, who came from a well-to-do Turkish family and complained to me bitterly about the terrible monotony of her life in Transjordan. I remember thinking that I could have done with some monotony myself at that point, but I only nodded my head sympathetically.

Then Abdullah entered the room. He was very pale and seemed under great strain. Ezra interpreted for us, and we talked for about an hour. I started the conversation by coming to the point at once. "Have you broken your promise to me, after all?" I asked him.

He didn't answer my question directly. Instead he said, "When I made that promise, I thought I was in control of my own destiny and could do what I thought right, but since then I have learned otherwise." Then he went on to say that before he had been alone, but now, "I am one of five," the other four, we gathered, being Egypt, Syria, Lebanon and Iraq. Still, he thought war could be averted.

"Why are you in such a hurry to proclaim your state?" he asked me. "What is the rush? You are so impatient!" I told him that I didn't think that a people who had waited 2,000 years should be described as being "in a hurry," and he seemed to accept that.

"Don't you understand," I said, "that we are your only allies in this region? The others are all your enemies."

"Yes," he said. "I know that. But what can I do? It is not up to me."

So then I said to him, "You must know that if war is forced upon us, we will fight and we will win."

He sighed and again said, "Yes. I know that. It is your duty to fight. But why don't you wait a few years? Drop your demands for free immigration. I will take over the whole country and you will be represented in my parliament. I will treat you very well, and there will be no war."

I tried to explain to him that this plan was impossible. "You know all that we have done and how hard we have worked," I said. "Do you think we did all that just to be represented in a foreign parliament? You know what we want and to what we aspire. If you can offer us nothing more than you have just done, then there will be a war and we will win it. But perhaps we can meet again—after the war and after there is a Jewish state."

"You place much too much reliance on your tanks," Danin said. "You have no real friends in the Arab world, and we will smash your tanks as the Maginot Line was smashed." They were very brave words, particularly since Danin knew exactly what the state of our armor was. But Abdullah looked even graver and said again that he knew that we had to do our duty. He also added, unhappily I thought, that events would just have to run their course. All of us would know eventually what fate had in store for us.

There was obviously no more to say. I wanted to leave, but Danin and Abdullah had begun a new conversation.

"I hope we will stay in touch even after the war starts," Danin said.

"Of course," Abdullah answered. "You must come to see me."

"But how will I be able to get to you?" asked Danin.

"Oh, I trust you to find a way," Abdullah said with a smile.

Then Danin chided him for not taking adequate precautions. "You worship at the mosque," he said to Abdullah, "and permit your subjects to kiss the hem of your garments. One day some evildoer will harm you. The time has come for you to forbid the custom, for safety's sake."

Abdullah was visibly shocked. "I shall never become the prisoner of my own guards," he said very sternly to Danin. "I was born a Bedouin, a free man, and I shall remain free. Let those who wish to kill me try to do so. I will not put myself in chains." Then he bid us farewell and left.

Our host's wife invited us to eat. At one end of the room there was an enormous table laden with food. I wasn't at all hungry, but Danin told me that I must fill my plate—whether I ate or not—because otherwise it would appear that I was abstaining from accepting Arab hospitality. So I heaped the plate but only toyed with the food. There was no doubt left in my mind that Abdullah would wage war against us. And for all of Danin's bravado, I knew that the legion's tanks were no joke, and my heart sank at the thought of the news I would have to bring back to Tel Aviv. It was now nearly midnight. We still had a long and dangerous trip ahead of us—and this time we wouldn't be bolstered by any false hopes.

After a few minutes we took our leave and departed. It was a very dark night, and the Arab driver who was to take us back to Naharayim (from there we would drive to Haifa) was terrified each time the car was stopped at a legion check post. In the end he made us get out some distance before we reached the power station. By now it was two or three o'clock in the morning, and we were faced with having to find our way back alone. Neither of us was armed, and I must admit that I was very frightened, as well as very depressed. From the windows of the car, we had seen the Iraqi forces massing at Camp Mafraq and

had talked in whispers of what would happen on May 14. I
remember my heart pounding when Danin said, "If we are
lucky—and victorious—we will only lose ten thousand
men. If we are unlucky, we may have up to fifty thousand
casualties." I was so upset by this that by common consent
we changed the subject, and for the rest of the trip we
talked about Moslem tradition and Arab cuisine. But stum-
bling around in the dark, we couldn't talk at all. In fact, we
didn't even dare breathe too loudly. I was badly hampered
by the clothes I was wearing, not at all sure that we were
going in the right direction and unable to shake off my
depression and sense of failure about the talk with Abdullah.

I suppose Danin and I must have been walking for about
half an hour when the young Haganah member from Naharayim—who had been waiting for us in a fever of anxiety
all night—suddenly spotted us. I couldn't see his face in the
dark, but I don't think I ever held onto anyone's hand so
tightly or with such relief. Anyhow, he led us effortlessly
over the hills and across the wadis to Naharayim. I saw
him again only a few years ago when a middle-aged man
came up to me in the lobby of a Jerusalem hotel. "Mrs.
Meir," he said, "don't you recognize me?" I searched my
mind but couldn't place him at all until he grinned at me
very sweetly and said, "It was I who showed you the way
back to Naharayim that night."

But I never saw Abdullah again, although after the War
of Independence there were prolonged negotiations with
him. Later I was told that he said about me, "If any one
person was responsible for the war, it was she, because she
was too proud to accept the offer I made her." I must say
that when I think of what would have befallen us as a "protected" minority in the kingdom of an Arab ruler who was
himself murdered by Arabs within just over two years, I
can't bring myself to regret the fact that I disappointed Abdullah so much that night. But I wish that he had been
brave enough to stay out of the war. It would have been so
much better for him—and for us—if he had been a little
prouder.

At all events, from Naharayim, I was driven straight
back to Tel Aviv. The next morning there was to be a
meeting at the headquarters of the Mapai—almost incessant
rounds of meetings were going on, of course, all that

week—and I knew that Ben-Gurion would be there. When I entered the room, he lifted his head, looked at me and said, *"Nu?"* I sat down and scribbled a note. "It didn't work," I wrote. "There will be war. From Mafraq Ezra and I saw the troop concentrations and the lights." I could hardly bear to watch Ben-Gurion's face as he read the note, but thank God, he didn't change his mind—or ours.

Within two days the final decision had to be taken: Should a Jewish state be proclaimed or not? After I had reported on my conversation with Abdullah, a number of people on the Minhelet Ha'am (literally the People's Administration), made up of members of the Jewish Agency, the Va'ad Le'umi and various small parties and groups which later became the provisional government of Israel, pressed Ben-Gurion for one last evaluation of the situation. They wanted to know what the Haganah's assessment was at zero hour. So Ben-Gurion called in two men: Yigael Yadin, who was the Haganah's chief of operations, and Yisrael Galili, who was its *de facto* commander in chief. Their answers were virtually identical—and terrifying. We could be sure of only two things, they said: The British would pull out, and the Arabs would invade. And then? They were both silent. But after a minute Yadin said, "The best we can tell you is that we have a fifty-fifty chance. We are as likely to win as we are to be defeated."

So it was on that bright note that the final decision was made. On Friday, May 14, 1948 (the fifth of Iyar, 5708, according to the Hebrew calendar), the Jewish state would come into being, its population numbering 650,000, its chance of surviving its birth depending on whether or not the *yishuv* could possibly meet the assault of five regular Arab armies actively aided by Palestine's 1,000,000 Arabs.

According to the original plan, I was to return to Jerusalem on Thursday and remain there for the duration. Needless to say, I very much wanted to stay in Tel Aviv, at least for long enough to attend the proclamation ceremony—the time and place of which were being kept secret (except for the 200-odd invitees) until about an hour before the event. All day Wednesday I hoped against hope that Ben-Gurion would relent, but he was adamant. "You must go back to Jerusalem," he said. So on Thursday, May 13, I was back in that little Piper Cub again. The pilot's orders were to take me to Jerusalem and return to Tel Aviv at once with

Yitzhak Gruenbaum, who was to be the minister of interior in the provisional government. But as soon as we got past the coastal plain and reached the Judean Hills, the engine began to act up in the most alarming way. I was sitting next to the pilot (those tiny planes, which we affectionately called Primuses, boasted only two seats), and I could see that even he was very nervous. The engine began to sound as though it were about to break away from the plane altogether, and I wasn't really surprised when the pilot said, apologetically, "I'm awfully sorry, but I don't think I can clear the hills. I'll have to go back." He turned the plane around; but the engine went on making dreadful sounds, and I noticed that the pilot was looking around below. I didn't say a word, yet after a while the engine picked up a bit and he asked me, "Do you know what is happening?"

"Yes," I replied.

"I was looking," he said, "for the most likely Arab village where we could land." This was on May 13, mind you. Then he added, "But now I think I can put down in Ben Shemen." At that point the engine improved a bit more. "No," he said, "I think we can make it back to Tel Aviv."

So I was able to attend the ceremony after all, and poor Yitzhak Gruenbaum had to stay in Jerusalem and couldn't sign the Declaration of Independence until after the first cease-fire.

On the morning of May 14, I participated in a meeting of the People's Council at which we were to decide on the name of the state and on the final formulation of the declaration. The name was less of a problem than the declaration because there was a last-minute argument about the inclusion of a reference to God. Actually the issue had been brought up the day before. The very last sentence, as finally submitted to the small subcommittee charged with producing the final version of the proclamation, began with the words "With trust in the Rock of Israel, we set our hands in witness to this Proclamation. . . ." Ben-Gurion had hoped that the phrase "Rock of Israel" was sufficiently ambiguous to satisfy those Jews for whom it was inconceivable that the document which established the Jewish state should not contain any reference to God, as well as those who were certain to object strenuously to even the least hint of clericalism in the proclamation.

But the compromise was not so easily accepted. The

spokesman of the religious parties, Rabbi Fishman-Maimon, demanded that the reference to God be unequivocal and said that he would approve of the "Rock of Israel" only if the words "and its Redeemer" were added, while Aaron Zisling of the left wing of the Labor Party was just as determined in the opposite direction. "I cannot sign a document referring in any way to a God in whom I do not believe," he said. It took Ben-Gurion most of the morning to persuade Maimon and Zisling that the meaning of the "Rock of Israel" was actually twofold: While it signified "God" for a great many Jews, perhaps for most, it could also be considered a symbolic and secular reference to the "strength of the Jewish people." In the end Maimon agreed that the word "Redeemer" should be left out of the text, though, funnily enough, the first English-language translation of the proclamation, released for publication abroad that day, contained no reference at all to the "Rock of Israel" since the military censor had struck out the entire last paragraph as a security precaution because it mentioned the time and place of the ceremony.

The argument itself, however, although it was perhaps not exactly what one would have expected a prime minister-designate to be spending his time on only a few hours before proclaiming the independence of a new state—particularly one threatened by immediate invasion—was far from being just an argument about terminology. We were all deeply aware of the fact that the proclamation not only spelled the formal end to 2,000 years of Jewish homelessness, but also gave expression to the most fundamental principles of the State of Israel. For this reason, each and every word mattered greatly. Incidentally, my good friend Zeev Sharef, the first secretary of the government-to-be (who laid the foundations for the machinery of government), even found time to see to it that the scroll we were about to sign that afternoon should be rushed to the vaults of the Anglo-Palestine Bank after the ceremony, so that it could at least be preserved for posterity—even if the state and we ourselves did not survive for very long.

At about 2 P.M. I went back to my hotel on the seashore, washed my hair and changed into my best black dress. Then I sat down for a few minutes, partly to catch my breath, partly to think—for the first time in the past

two or three days—about the children. Menachem was in
the United States then—a student at the Manhattan School
of Music. I knew that he would come back now that war
was inevitable, and I wondered when and how we would
meet again. Sarah was in Revivim, and although not so
very far away, as the crow flies, we were quite cut off from
each other. Months ago, gangs of Palestinian Arabs and
armed infiltrators from Egypt had blocked the road that
connected the Negev to the rest of the country and were
still systematically blowing up or cutting most of the pipe-
lines that brought water to the twenty-seven Jewish settlements that then dotted the Negev. The Haganah had done
its best to break the siege. It had opened a dirt track, paral-
lel to the main road, on which convoys managed, now and
then, to bring food and water to the 1,000-odd settlers in
the south. But who knew what would happen to Revivim
or any other of the small, ill-armed ill-equipped Negev settlements when the full-scale Egyptian invasion of Israel began, as it almost certainly would, within only a few hours?
Both Sarah and her Zechariah were wireless operators in
Revivim, and I had been able to keep in touch with them
up till then. But I hadn't heard about or from either of
them for several days, and I was extremely worried. It
was on youngsters like them, their spirit and their courage,
that the future of the Negev and, therefore, of Israel depended, and I shuddered at the thought of their having to
face the invading troops of the Egyptian army.

I was so lost in my thoughts about the children that I can
remember being momentarily surprised when the phone
rang in my room and I was told that a car was waiting to
take me to the museum. It had been decided to hold the
ceremony at the Tel Aviv museum on Rothschild Boule-
vard, not because it was such an imposing building (which it
wasn't), but because it was small enough to be easily
guarded. One of the oldest buildings in Tel Aviv, it had
originally belonged to the city's first mayor, who had willed
it to the citizens of Tel Aviv for use as an art museum.
The grand total of about $200 had been allocated for
decorating it suitably for the ceremony; the floors
had been scrubbed, the nude paintings on the walls mod-
estly draped, the windows blacked out in case of an air raid
and a large picture of Theodor Herzl hung behind the table
at which the thirteen members of the provisional govern-

ment were to sit. Although supposedly only the 200-odd
people who had been invited to participate knew the details, a large crowd was already waiting outside the museum by the time I arrived there.

A few minutes later, at exactly 4 P.M., the ceremony
began. Ben-Gurion, wearing a dark suit and tie, stood up
and rapped a gavel. According to the plan, this was to be
the signal for the orchestra, tucked away in a second floor
gallery, to play "Hatikvah." But something went wrong,
and there was no music. Spontaneously, we rose to our feet
and sang our national anthem. Then Ben-Gurion cleared
his throat and said quietly, "I shall now read the Scroll of
Independence." It took him only a quarter of an hour to
read the entire proclamation. He read it slowly and very
clearly, and I remember his voice changing and rising a
little as he came to the eleventh paragraph:

> Accordingly we, the members of the National
> Council, representing the Jewish people in the Land of
> Israel and the Zionist movement, have assembled on
> the day of the termination of the British mandate for
> Palestine, and, by virtue of our natural and historic
> right and of the resolution of the General Assembly of
> the United Nations, do hereby proclaim the establish-
> ment of a Jewish state in the Land of Israel—the State
> of Israel.

The State of Israel! My eyes filled with tears, and my
hands shook. We had done it. We had brought the Jewish
state into existence—and I, Golda Mabovitch Meyerson,
had lived to see the day. Whatever happened now, whatever price any of us would have to pay for it, we had re-
created the Jewish national home. The long exile was over.
From this day on we would no longer live on sufferance in
the land of our forefathers. Now we were a nation like
other nations, master—for the first time in twenty centuries—of our own destiny. The dream had come true—too
late to save those who had perished in the Holocaust, but
not too late for the generations to come. Almost exactly
fifty years ago, at the close of the First Zionist Congress in
Basel, Theodor Herzl had written in his diary: "At Basel, I
founded the Jewish state. If I were to say this today, I
would be greeted with laughter. In five years perhaps, and

certainly in fifty, everyone will see it." And so it had come
to pass.

As Ben-Gurion read, I thought again about my children
and the children that they would have, how different their
lives would be from mine and how different my own life
would be from what it had been in the past, and I thought
about my colleagues in besieged Jerusalem, gathered in the
offices of the Jewish Agency, listening to the ceremony
through static on the radio, while I, by sheer accident, was
in the museum itself. It seemed to me that no Jew on earth
had ever been more privileged than I was that Friday afternoon.

Then, as though a signal had been given, we rose to our
feet, crying and clapping, while Ben-Gurion, his voice
breaking for the only time, read: "The State of Israel will
be open to Jewish immigration and the ingathering of exiles." This was the very heart of the proclamation, the reason for the state and the point of it all. I remember sobbing
out loud when I heard those words spoken in that hot,
packed little hall. But Ben-Gurion just rapped his gavel
again for order and went on reading:

"Even amidst the violent attacks launched against us for
months past, we call upon the sons of the Arab people
dwelling in Israel to keep the peace and to play their part
in building the state on the basis of full and equal citizenship and due representation in all its institutions, provisional and permanent."

And: "We extend the hand of peace and good neighbor-
liness to all the states around us and to their peoples, and
we call upon them to cooperate in mutual helpfulness with
the independent Jewish nation in its land. The State of Israel is prepared to make its contribution in a concerted
effort for the advancement of the entire Middle East."

When he finished reading the 979 Hebrew words of the
proclamation, he asked us to stand and "adopt the scroll
establishing the Jewish state," so once again we rose to our
feet. Then, something quite unscheduled and very moving
happened. All of a sudden Rabbi Fishman-Maimon stood
up, and, in a trembling voice, pronounced the traditional
Hebrew prayer of thanksgiving. "Blessed be Thou, O Lord
our God, King of the Universe, who has kept us alive and
made us endure and brought us to this day. Amen." It was

a prayer that I had heard often, but it had never held such meaning for me as it did that day.

Before we came up, each in turn, in alphabetical order, to sign the proclamation, there was one other point of "business" that required our attention. Ben-Gurion read the first decrees of the new state. The White Paper was declared null and void, while, to avoid a legal vacuum, all the other mandatory rules and regulations were declared valid and in temporary effect. Then the signing began. As I got up from my seat to sign my name to the scroll, I caught sight of Ada Golomb, standing not far away. I wanted to go over to her, take her in my arms and tell her that I knew that Eliahu and Dov should have been there in my place, but I couldn't hold up the line of the signatories, so I walked straight to the middle of the table, where Ben-Gurion and Sharett sat with the scroll between them. All I recall about my actual signing of the proclamation is that I was crying openly, not able even to wipe the tears from my face, and I remember that as Sharett held the scroll in place for me, a man called David Zvi Pincus, who belonged to the religious Mizrachi Party, came over to try and calm me. "Why do you weep so much, Golda?" he asked me.

"Because it breaks my heart to think of all those who should have been here today and are not," I replied, but I still couldn't stop crying.

Only twenty-five members of the People's Council signed the proclamation on May 14. Eleven others were in Jerusalem, and one was in the States. The last to sign was Moshe Sharett. He looked very controlled and calm compared to me—as though he were merely performing a standard duty. Later, when once we talked about that day, he told me that when he wrote his name on the scroll, he felt as though he were standing on a cliff with a gale blowing up all around him and nothing to hold on to except his determination not to be blown over into the raging sea below—but none of this showed at the time.

After the Palestine Philharmonic Orchestra played "Hatikvah," Ben-Gurion rapped his gavel for the third time. "The State of Israel is established. This meeting is ended." We all shook hands and embraced each other. The ceremony was over. Israel was a reality.

Not unexpectedly, the evening was filled with suspense. I stayed in the hotel, talking to friends. Someone opened a bottle of wine, and we drank a toast to the state. A few of the guests and their young Haganah escorts sang and danced, and we heard people laughing and singing in the street. But we knew that at midnight the mandate would terminate, the British high commissioner would sail away, the last British soldier would leave Palestine, and we were certain that the Arab armies would march across the borders of the state we had just founded. We were independent now, but in a few hours we would be at war. Not only was I not gay, but I was very frightened—and with good reason. Still, there is a great difference between being frightened and lacking faith, and although the entire Jewish population of the reborn state numbered only 650,000, I knew for certain that night that we had dug in and that no one would be able to disperse or displace us ever again.

But I think it was only on the following day that I really grasped what had happened in the Tel Aviv Museum. Three separate but very closely linked events brought the truth home to me as nothing else could have done, and I realized, perhaps for the first time, that nothing would ever be the same again. Not for me, not for the Jewish people, not for the Middle East. To begin with, just before dawn on Saturday, I saw for myself through the windows of my room what might be called the formal start of the War of Independence: four Egyptian Spitfires zooming across the city on their way to bomb Tel Aviv's power station and airport in what was the first air raid of the war. Then, a little later, I watched the first boatload of Jewish immigrants—no longer "illegals"—enter the port of Tel Aviv, freely and proudly. No one hunted them down anymore or chased them or punished them for coming home. The shameful era of the "certificates" and the human arithmetic had ended, and as I stood there in the sun, my eyes fixed on that ship (an old Greek vessel called the SS *Teti*), I felt that no price demanded of us for this gift could possibly be too high. The first legal immigrant to land in the State of Israel was a tired, shabby old man called Samuel Brand, a survivor of Buchenwald. In his hand he clutched a crumpled slip of paper. It said only, "The right to settle in Israel is hereby given"; but it was signed by the "Immigration Department" of the state, and it was the first visa we ever issued.

And then, of course, there was the wonderful moment of

our formal entry into the family of nations. A few minutes after midnight on the night of May 14, my phone rang. It had been ringing all evening, and as I ran to answer it, I wondered what bad news I would hear now. But the voice at the other end of the phone sounded jubilant. "Golda? Are you listening? Truman has recognized us!" I can't remember what I said or did, but I remember how I felt. It was like a miracle coming at the time of our greatest vulnerability, on the eve of the invasion, and I was filled with joy and relief. In a way, although all Israel rejoiced and gave thanks, I think that what President Truman did that night may have meant more to me than to most of my colleagues because I was the "American" among us, the one who knew most about the United States, its history and its people, the only one who had grown up in that great democracy. And although I was as astonished as everyone else by the speed of the recognition, I was not at all surprised by the generous and good impulse that had brought it about. In retrospect, I think that like most miracles, this one was probably triggered by two very simple things: the fact that Harry Truman understood and respected our drive for independence because he was the sort of man who, under different circumstances, might well have been one of us himself, and the profound impression made on him by Chaim Weizmann, whom he had received in Washington and who had pleaded our cause and explained our situation in a way that no one had ever done in the White House before. Weizmann's work was of incalculable value. American recognition was the greatest thing that could have happened to us that night.

As for the Soviet recognition of Israel, which followed the American recognition, that had other roots. There is now no doubt in my mind that the primary Soviet consideration was to get the British out of the Middle East. But all through the debates that had taken place at the United Nations in the autumn of 1947, it had seemed to me that the Soviet bloc was supporting us also because of the terrible toll that the Russians themselves had paid in the world war and their resultantly deep feeling that the Jews, who had also suffered so bitterly at the hands of the Nazis, deserved to have their state. However radically the Soviet attitude has changed in the intervening two and a half decades, I cannot now falsify the picture as I saw it then. Had

My Life

it not been for the arms and ammunition that we were able to buy in Czechoslovakia and transport through Yugoslavia and other Balkan countries in those dark days at the start of the war, I do not know whether we actually could have held out until the tide changed, as it did by June, 1948. For the first six weeks of the War of Independence, we relied largely (though not, of course, entirely) on the shells, machine guns, bullets—and even planes—that the Haganah had been able to purchase in Eastern Europe at a time when even the United States had declared an embargo on the sale or shipment of arms to the Middle East. One cannot and must not try to erase the past merely because it does not fit the present, and the fact remains that although the Soviet Union was to turn so savagely against and upon us in the years to come, the Soviet recognition of the State of Israel on May 18 was of immense significance for us. It meant that the two greatest powers in the world had come together, for the first time since World War II, to back the Jewish state, and although we were still in deadly danger, we knew, at last, that we were not alone. It was in that knowledge—combined with sheer necessity—that we found the spiritual, if not the material, strength that was to lead us to victory.

Also, while I am on this subject, let me say—for the record—that the second state to offer recognition to Israel on the day of its birth was little Guatemala, whose ambassador to the United Nations, Jorge García Granados, had been one of the most active members of UNSCOP.

So now we were an accepted fact. The only question that remained—and, incredibly enough, remains to this very day—was how we would stay alive. Not "if," but "how." By the morning of May 15 Israel was already under armed attack by the Egyptians from the south, the Syrians and Lebanese from the north and the northeast, the Jordanians and the Iraqis from the east. On paper it seemed that week as though there might be some grounds for the Arab boast that within ten days Israel would be crushed.

The most relentless advance was that of the Egyptians—though of all the invading armies, the Egyptians certainly had least to gain. Abdullah had a reason. It was a bad one; but it was there, and he was able to define it: He wanted the whole country and especially Jerusalem. Lebanon and Syria also had a reason: They hoped to be able to divide up the Galilee between themselves. Iraq wanted to participate in the bloodletting and—as a fringe benefit—acquire an outlet to the Mediterranean, through Jordan if necessary. But Egypt had no real war aim at all—except to loot and destroy whatever the Jews had built. As a matter of fact, it has never ceased to astonish me that the Arab states have been so eager to go to war against us. Almost from the very beginning of Zionist settlement until today they have been consumed by hatred for us. The only possible explanation—and it is a ridiculous one—is that they simply cannot bear our presence or forgive us for existing, and I find it hard to believe that the leaders of *all* the Arab states are and always have been so hopelessly primitive in their thinking.

On the other hand, what have we ever done to threaten the Arab states? True, we have not stood in line to return territory we won in wars they started, but territory, after all, has never ever been what Arab aggression is all about—and in 1948 it was certainly not a need for more land that drove the Egyptians northward in the hope of reaching and destroying Tel Aviv and Jewish Jerusalem. So what was it? An overpowering irrational urge to eliminate us physically? Fear of the progress we might introduce in the Middle East? A distaste for Western civilization? Who knows? Whatever it was, it has lasted—but then so have we—and the solution will probably not be found for many years, although I have no doubt at all that the time will come when the Arab states will accept us—as we are and for what we are. In a nutshell, peace is—and always has been—dependent entirely on only one thing: The Arab leaders must acquiesce in our being here.

In 1948, however, it was understandable that the Arab states—given in any case to chronic flights of fancy—saw themselves as racing through what was now Israel in a matter of days. To begin with, they had begun the war which gave them great tactical superiority. Secondly, they had easy, not to say effortless, overland access to Palestine, with its Arab population, which had been incited against the Jews for years. Thirdly, the Arabs could move without any problems from one part of the country to the other. Fourthly, the Arabs controlled most of the hilly regions of Palestine from which our lowland settlements could be attacked without much difficulty. Finally, the Arabs had an absolute superiority of manpower and arms and had been given considerable help by the British in various ways, both direct and indirect.

And what did we have? Not much of anything—and even that is an exaggeration. A few thousand rifles, a few hundred machine guns, an assortment of other firearms, but on May 14, 1948, not a single cannon or tank, although we had all of nine planes (never mind that only one had two engines!). The machinery for making arms had been bought abroad—thanks to Ben-Gurion's amazing foresight—but couldn't be brought into Israel until the British had left, and then it had to be assembled and run in. Our trained manpower situation was also very unimpressive, as far as statistics were concerned. There were about 45,000 men, women and teenagers in the Haganah, a few thousand members of the two dissident underground organizations and a few hundred recent arrivals who had been given some training—with wooden rifles and dummy bullets—in the DP camps of Germany and the detention camps of Cyprus and after independence, another few thousand Jewish and non-Jewish volunteers from abroad. That was all. But we couldn't afford the luxury of pessimism either, so we made an altogether different kind of calculation based on the fact that the 650,000 of us were more highly motivated to stay alive than anyone outside Israel could be expected to understand and that the only option available to us, if we didn't want to be pushed into the sea, was to win the war. So we won it. But it wasn't easy, it wasn't quick, and it wasn't cheap. From the day that the UN resolution to partition Palestine was passed (November 29, 1947) until the day that the first armistice agreement was signed by Israel and Egypt (February 24, 1949) 6,000 young Israelis were killed, 1 percent of our entire population, and although we couldn't have known it then, we hadn't even bought peace with all those lives.

For me to have had to leave Israel the moment the state was established was more difficult than I can say. The very last thing I wanted to do was to go abroad, but on Sunday, May 16, a cable came from Henry Montor, vice-president of the United Jewish Appeal. American Jewry had been profoundly moved by what had happened. There were no limits to its excitement or its pride. If I came back, even for a short tour, he thought we might raise another $50,000,-

000. No one knew better than I what that kind of money would mean to Israel, how desperately we needed the arms it would buy or how much it would cost to move and settle the 30,000 Jews penned up in Cyprus, who had waited so long to come to Israel. My heart sank at the thought of tearing myself away from the country, but there was no real choice at all. After discussing the matter with Ben-Gurion, I cabled back at once that I would leave on the first plane. Luckily, there were no preparations to make for the trip. My clothes, such as they were, were all in Jerusalem, as out of reach as though they were on the moon, so all I had to "pack" was a hairbrush, a toothbrush and a clean blouse, though when I got to New York, I discovered that the veil I had worn to Amman was still in my bag! I managed to speak to Sarah briefly and tell her that I would be back in a month at the very most and to receive a hastily produced laissez-passer, which was, in fact, the first travel document to be given any citizen of the State of Israel. Then I left on the very first plane that was available.

In the States I was greeted as though I were the personification of Israel. Over and over again I told the story of the proclamation, of the beginning of the war, of the continuing siege of Jerusalem, and over and over again I assured the Jews of America that with their help Israel would prevail. I spoke in city after city throughout the States, at UJA lunches, dinners and teas and at parlor meetings in people's homes. Whenever I felt overwhelmed by fatigue—which was often—all I had to do was to remind myself that I was now talking as an emissary of a Jewish state, and my tiredness simply drained away. It even took me weeks to accustom myself to the sound of the word "Israel" and to the fact that I now had a new nationality. But the purpose of my journey was not in the least sentimental. I had come to raise money, as much money as possible, as quickly as possible, and my message was as blunt in May as it had been in January. The State of Israel, I told Jews all over America, could not survive on applause. The war would not be won by speeches or declarations or even tears of happiness. And time was of the essence, or there would be nothing to applaud.

"We cannot go on without your help," I said in dozens of public and private appearances. "What we ask of you is that you share in our responsibility, with everything that this implies—difficulties, problems, hardships and joys. Surely what is happening in the Jewish world today is so important, so vital that you, too, can change your way of life for a year, or two, or three until together we have put Israel on its feet. Make up your minds and give me your answers."

They answered me with unprecedented generosity and speed, with their whole hearts and souls. Nothing was too much or too good, and by their response they reaffirmed their sense of partnership with us, as I had hoped they would. Although there was as yet no separate drive for Israel, and although less than 50 percent of the $150,000,000 raised for the UJA in 1948 actually went to Israel (the rest was turned over to the Joint Distribution Committee for aid to Jews in European countries), that 50 percent unquestionably helped us win the war. It also taught us that the involvement of American Jewry in the State of Israel was a factor on which we could count.

As I traveled, I met many people who were themselves later to become "spokesmen" of the state, men who had not been intimately involved in the Zionist effort before 1948, but who now were moved to make Israel their life's work—and who were to be my close associates in the founding of the Israel Bond Organization in 1950. In the past, whenever I had come to the United States, it had been on missions for the Histadrut, and I had spent my time almost entirely with Labor Zionts. But in 1948 I met a new kind of American Jew—well-to-do, super efficient and totally committed. In the first instance there was, of course, Henry Montor himself, brusque, gifted and deeply concerned with Israel, a slave driver who mercilessly drove himself as well as others in the attempt to raise ever larger sums of money. But there were also businessmen, hard headed, experienced industrialists like Bill Rosenwald, Sam Rothberg, Lou Boyar and Harold Goldenberg, to name just a few of the men with whom I found time to talk hurriedly on that whirlwind tour about the possibility of selling bonds for Israel, as well as making appeals for philanthropy.

But all the time I waited anxiously for the moment when I could return home, although I already knew that the newly created Foreign Office, particularly the new foreign minister, Moshe Sharett, had other plans for me. The day before I left for the States, Sharett and I had met in my hotel, and he had spoken to me of the problems of manning the embassies and consulates that Israel would have to establish in those countries that had either already recognized it or were likely to do so within a few weeks.

"I have no one for Moscow," he said in a very worried voice.

"Well, thank God, you can't offer it to me," I replied. "My Russian is almost nonexistent."

"As a matter of fact, that isn't what matters," he answered. But he didn't pursue the topic and I tried to dismiss it as a good joke. Although I sometimes thought about that conversation when I was flying from one place to another in the States, I fervently hoped that Sharett himself had forgotten all about it.

One day, however, a cable came from Tel Aviv. I glanced at the signature before I read the text to make sure that it wasn't about Sarah or Menachem (already with his brigade and in combat). But when I saw the name Moshe, I knew that it was about Moscow, and I had to steel myself to read the message. The state was not even a month old. The war was not over. The children were not yet safe. I had a family and dear friends in Israel, and it seemed to me that it was grossly unfair to ask me to pack my bags again so soon and take off for such a remote and essentially unknown post. "Why is it always me?" I thought, in a burst of self-pity. There were plenty of other people who could do the job as well, better in fact. And Russia of all places, the country I had left as a little girl and of which I had not a single pleasant memory. At least in America I was doing something real, concrete and practical, but what did I know or care about diplomacy? Of all my comrades, I thought, I was surely the least suited to diplomatic life. But I also knew that Sharett must have secured Ben-Gurion's consent to the appointment, and Ben-Gurion was certainly not likely to be swayed by any personal appeals. And then there was the matter of discipline. Who was I to disobey or even demur at a time when each day brought news of fresh casualties? One's duty was one's duty—and it had nothing to do with justice. So what if I longed to be in Israel? Other people longed for their children to be alive or whole again. So after a few more cables and telephone calls, I answered Sharett's cable, not very enthusiastically but affirmatively. "When I get back to Israel, I will try to persuade Moshe and Ben-Gurion that they have made a mistake," I promised myself. At the end of the first week of June, however, my appointment as Israel's minister to Moscow was made public.

I took a day off to see old friends in New York and say good-bye to new ones. I was determined to visit Fanny and Jacob Goodman before I left. Neither the children nor I had ever lost touch with them, and I thought it would cheer me up to spend an hour or two with them, telling them about Sarah and Zechariah and Sheyna's children, whom they hadn't seen for so long. But I never got to their house. On the way to Brooklyn a car crashed into my cab, and the next thing I knew I had a badly fractured leg enveloped in a gigantic plaster cast and my address for the next few weeks was neither Moscow nor Tel Aviv, but the New York Hospital for Joint Diseases! Looking back at the times and at my mood, I think that nothing (including the blessing of the phlebitis and blood clots I developed) could have kept me in that hospital had it not been for the fact that on June 11, the fighting had temporarily ended in Israel.

By June 11 the progress of the Arab invasion had been halted. The Egyptian attempt to conquer Tel Aviv and Jerusalem had failed, although the Jordanians were still battering away at Jerusalem from the east and the north, and the Jewish Quarter of the Old City had fallen to Abdullah's Arab Legion. The Syrians, although their advance in the north had been stopped, still held a bridgehead on the Jordan River, and the Iraqis were still poised against the narrowest part of the country in Samaria. The United Nations had been trying for weeks to impose a truce, but as long as they had some hope of defeating Israel, the Arabs were not at all interested. However, as soon as it became quite clear to them, as well as to us, that this was not about to happen, they agreed to a cease-fire—to the first truce, which was to last for twenty-eight days and gave us a chance to rest, rally and plan the major offensives that in July removed the last threats to Tel Aviv and the coastal plain, lifted the siege on Jerusalem and destroyed all the major Arab bases in the Galilee.

So in theory, pain or no pain, I might have caught my breath a bit in the hospital—both physically and emotionally—but actually I was under enormous pressure there all the time. To begin with, there were the television cameras and the newspapermen. A woman minister to Moscow would have been a novelty in any case in 1948, but a woman minister to Moscow who represented the tiny embattled State of Israel and who was totally immobilized in New York must have been a real bargain. I suppose I could have refused to be interviewed—and today, of course, that is just what I would do under such circumstances. But at that time I thought it would be good for Israel if we got a lot of publicity, and I felt that I mustn't turn down a single request from the press—although the various members of the family, especially Clara, were absolutely appalled by the three-ring circus going on in my room.

What was much worse, though, was the pressure I was under to get to Moscow. I was literally bombarded with cables from Israel. WHEN CAN YOU LEAVE NEW YORK? WHEN CAN YOU TAKE OVER? HOW DO YOU FEEL? Rumors had spread in Israel that this was a "diplomatic" illness and that nothing was really wrong with me except that I didn't want to go to Russia. But as if this disgusting whispering campaign was not bad enough, there were also indications that the Soviet government was offended by my supposed "malingering," which was "actually" a tactic designed to delay the exchange of ministers so that the U.S. ambassador to Israel could arrive first and thus become dean of the diplomatic corps. All this was something I had to take very seriously, regardless of my state of health. So there was nothing I could do except start tormenting my doctors for permission to leave the hospital. It was, need I say, the wrong thing to have done. I should have remained in New York until I was completely well. Both our Foreign Office and the Soviet Ministry of Foreign Affairs would have survived without me for a few more weeks and I would have spared myself a great deal of misery and at least one operation later on. But one of the penalties of public office is that one loses one's sense of proportion in certain respects, and I was convinced that there would be some kind of terrible crisis unless I turned up in Moscow as soon as possible.

I did make one attempt, when I got back to Israel, to talk Sharett out of the whole thing, but by then it wasn't a very wholehearted attempt. One day I heard an interesting story that cheered me up: Ehud Avriel, one of the Haganah men who had done most to secure arms for us in Czechoslovakia and who later became Israel's first minister to Prague, had been invited for a talk with the Soviet ambassador in that city. In the course of the conversation the Russian said to Avriel, "I suppose your people are looking around for someone to send to Moscow. Don't feel that it has to be a person whose Russian is fluent or who is an expert on Marxism and Leninism. Neither of these qualifications is important." Then, after a while, as though a propos of nothing, he said to Avriel, "By the way, what is happening to Mrs. Meyerson? Is she going to stay in Israel or does she have other plans?" From this my friends—including Sharett—gathered that the Russians had more or less asked for me, in their own way, and I began to feel differently about going.

Also, one of the few pleasant things that had occurred while I was in the hospital was that one morning I got a cable from Tel Aviv: DO YOU HAVE ANY OBJECTION TO APPOINTMENT OF SARAH AND ZECHARIAH AS RADIO OPERATORS IN MOSCOW EMBASSY? I was very touched—and grateful. To have Sarah and Zechariah with me in Russia was almost worth the exile from Israel. One of my first projects when I came back to Tel Aviv was to ask Sheyna if Sarah and Zechariah could be married in the small house which Shamai and she had bought years ago. We decided it would be a real family wedding, with only a few "outside" guests. My father had died in 1946—another of the people who were most dear to me and who had not lived to see the state—and my mother, poor soul, had been incapacitated for several years, her memory gone, her eyesight bad, her personality quite faded away, leaving almost no trace of the critical, energetic, peppery woman she had been. But Morris was there, as gentle as ever and beaming with pride, and so were Zechariah's parents. His father had come to Palestine from Yemen when the Turks still ruled the country. He was very poor, very religious and not formally educated, except in the Torah, but he had brought up a wonderful and loving family—though Zechariah himself by now was quite removed from Yemenite customs and traditions.

I settled in again at the hotel on the seashore. Sarah flew

from Revivim to Tel Aviv and moved in with me for a few days, and Zechariah, who had been very ill and in a hospital near Tel Aviv for weeks, was finally discharged. Of our immediate family, only Clara and Menachem were missing at the wedding in Sheyna's garden. I couldn't help thinking how different my own wedding had been—under what different circumstances it had taken place and how differently Morris and I had started out on life together. There was no point to wondering now who had been to blame or why our marriage had fallen apart, but I felt (and rightly it turned out) that Sarah and Zechariah, although they were the same age that we had been when we stood under that bridal canopy in Milwaukee, were more mature and better suited to each other and that they would succeed where Morris and I had failed.

In between rushing around to party meetings, being briefed on the Soviet Union and making plans for our departure, I concentrated on thinking about the kind of representation that Israel should have in the Soviet Union. How did we want to show ourselves abroad? What did we want the world in general and the USSR in particular to think about Israel? What sort of state were we in the process of creating, and how could we best reflect its quality? The more I thought about it, the less I thought that our legations should mimic those of other countries. Israel was small, poor and still at war. Its government was still a provisional government (the first elections to the Knesset took place only in January 1949), but the majority of its members would certainly represent the labor movement. The face we turned to the world, I was convinced, needed no make up at all. We had established a pioneering state in a sorely beleaguered country, devoid of natural resources or any wealth, a state to which hundreds of thousands of DPs—who also had nothing—were already streaming in the hope of making a new life for themselves. If we wanted to be understood and respected by other states, we would have to be abroad what we were at home. Lavish entertaining, grand apartments, conspicuous consumption of any kind were not for us. Austerity, modesty and a sense of our own worth and purpose were what we had to offer, and anything else would be false.

There was something at the back of my mind all the

time that I was thinking along these lines, and then one day I found it. The legation in Moscow would be run in the most typically Israeli style I knew: like a kibbutz. We would work together, eat together, get the same amount of pocket money and take turns doing whatever chores had to be done. As in Merhavia or Revivim, people would do the work that they were trained for and suited to in the opinion of our Foreign Office but the spirit of the legation, its atmosphere and flavor would be that of a collective settlement—which, apart from any other consideration, ought, I believed, to be especially attractive to the Russians (not that their own brand of collectivism was or is anything to write home about). We were to be twenty-six people in all, including Sarah, Zechariah and myself, and the legation's counselor, Mordechai Namir, a widower who brought his fifteen-year-old daughter, Yael, with him. (Namir afterward served as Israel's ambassador to the USSR, then as minister of labor and, for ten years, as mayor of Tel Aviv.) As my personal assistant I chose a most charming woman, Eiga Shapiro, who not only spoke Russian, but also knew much more about the niceties of life than I did and who could be entrusted, I was sure, with such (to me terrifying) missions as deciding what furniture and clothing legation personnel and the minister would need.

Even before I returned to Tel Aviv, I wrote to Eiga to ask her to join me, if and when I indeed went to Moscow—and to my delight she agreed at once. One of the notes she sent to New York at the end of June is before me now, and it tells something, I think, of what was involved in sending a woman to a top diplomatic post—particularly a woman like myself who was so determined to live in Russia in much the same way she lived at home. She wrote:

> I have had a talk with Ehud. He tells me that we shall have to be very *comme il faut*. So please, Golda, what about a fur coat for yourself? It is very cold in the place to which you are traveling, and most people there wear fur coats in the winter. You need not buy yourself mink, but a good Persian lamb will be very serviceable. . . . You will also need a few evening dresses, and buy yourself woollies—warm nightgowns, woolen stockings and woolen underwear. And please get yourself a pair of good snow shoes.

The question of dress was obviously not uppermost in
my mind, but for a while I regretted that we had no national costume—which would have solved at least one
problem for me, as it did for Mrs. Pandit, the only other
woman diplomat in Moscow, who wore her sari, of course,
on all ceremonial occasions. In the end Eiga and I agreed
that when I presented my credentials, I would wear a long
black dress sewn for me in Tel Aviv and that, when necessary, I would wear a small black velvet turban with it. As
far as furnishing the legation was concerned, Eiga undertook to do that in Scandinavia as soon as we found permanent accommodation in Moscow. In the interim, we would
establish our "kibbutz" in a hotel. There was also the question of finding and taking with us to Russia someone whose
French was absolutely perfect, since it had been decided
that French would be Israel's diplomatic language. Eiga introduced me to a bright, amusing, painfully thin young
woman called Lou Kaddar, who was born in Paris, whose
French was beyond reproach and who had lived in Jerusalem all through the siege and had been badly wounded. I
liked her the moment I set eyes on her—and it was just as
well that I did, because for the better part of the next
twenty-seven years Lou was my close friend, my indispensable assistant and, more often that not, my travel compan-
ion. At all events, she agreed to go with us to Russia.

I stayed in Israel long enough that summer to welcome
the first U.S. ambassador to Israel, that delightfully frank
and warm gentleman James G. McDonald, whom I had
met before, and to meet the Russian minister, Pavel I. Yershov. It was typical of the newness of the state—and of its
lack of proper housing—that the American and Soviet missions in Tel Aviv made their first home in the same hotel,
not far from mine, and I never quite got used to seeing the
stars and stripes fly from one end of the hotel roof and the
hammer and sickle from the other. There were all sorts of
"incidents" during the first weeks of this "coexistence." I
remember, for instance, a gala performance of the Israel
National Opera at which the orchestra opened with first
"Hatikvah" and then, in McDonald's honor, "The Star-
Spangled Banner," but not the "Internationale," though
Yershov's counselor was present—at least until the inter-
mission, when he and his party rather noisily walked out.
Everyone in our Foreign Office was reduced to trembling

in his boots until Yershov himself agreed to accept our explanation that had he been there, the Soviet anthem would
have certainly been played. Today these minor disasters
seem funny, but at the time we all took them very seriously. Nothing ever appeared unimportant to us, and Sharett, by nature, was both exacting and sensitive to a remarkable degree and felt—as did the Russians themselves, by
the way—that protocol was of the utmost importance, although I could never see why it mattered so much.

A second truce began on July 19, signaling the start of
a long, painful round of negotiations over the Negev, which
Count Folke Bernadotte, the Swedish UN mediator, recommended be handed over to the Arabs. Considering the
fact that he was really a referee, his position was amazingly
lacking in neutrality, and he became extremely unpopular—particularly when he added insult to injury by advocating also that Jerusalem be torn away from the Jewish
state and that the UN supervise Israel's air- and seaports.
God knows that these recommendations were unacceptable
and that they proved only that Bernadotte really never understood what the State of Israel was all about. But it is
certainly no crime to be obtuse, and I was horrified when,
on September 17, only two weeks after I arrived in Moscow, I learned that Bernadotte had been shot to death on a
quiet street in Jerusalem. Although his assailants were
never identified, we knew it would be assumed that they
were Jews. I thought the end of the world had come, and I
would have given anything to have been able to fly home
and be there during the ensuing crisis, but by then I was
already deeply involved in a totally new and very demanding way of life.

9. Minister to Moscow

We arrived in Moscow (via Prague) on the gray rainy afternoon of September 3, 1948. The first thing I was told by the officials of the Soviet Ministry of Foreign Affairs who welcomed me at the airport was that we might have some difficulty getting to the hotel because at that very moment, the funeral of Andrea Zhdanov, one of Stalin's closest associates, was taking place in the city. My first impressions of the Soviet Union, therefore, were the length and solemnity of that funeral and the hundreds of thousands—perhaps millions—of people whom we saw in the streets on our way to the Hotel Metropole. The hotel, which was reserved for the use of foreigners, looked like something from another era. The rooms were huge with great cut-glass chandeliers, long velvet curtains, overstuffed plush armchairs and, in one room, even a grand piano. On each landing sat a stern old lady to whom one handed one's keys when leaving the hotel, but whose job obviously was to report to the KGB on the guests, although it was very unlikely that she was the sole source of information. We never found any microphones in our rooms, although we conducted regular searches for them, and more veteran members of the diplomatic corps in Moscow took it for granted that every word I said in the two-bedroom suite I shared with Sarah and Zechariah was being recorded.

By the time we had been in the hotel for a week I realized that we would have to start our kibbutz style of life as soon as possible or else we would run out of money. The cost of living was unbelievably high, and the first hotel bill we got staggered me. "There is only one way we can manage on our very modest budget," I told my staff, "and that is if we all eat only one meal a day in the hotel dining room. I will provide food for breakfasts and suppers, and on Fridays we'll have our main meal together in the evening." The very next day Lou Kaddar and I went out to buy electric plates, which I then distributed to each of our rooms, together with crockery and cutlery that I borrowed from the hotel—since there was still none to be had in any shop in postwar Moscow. As for food, once or twice a week Lou and I loaded up our baskets with cheeses, sausages, bread, butter and eggs (which we bought at a market that was slightly cheaper than any shop in town) and placed them between the big double windows of our rooms to keep from spoiling. On Saturdays I prepared a sort of brunch for my own family (and the "bachelors" of the staff, including Eiga and Lou), cooked on a hot plate in the dining room of my suite.

I think those trips to market so early on frosty winter mornings were perhaps the most pleasant single thing I did during my seven months in the Soviet Union. Neither Lou nor I could speak Russian but the peasants at the market were very nice to us and waited patiently, smiling and gesturing that we needn't hurry while we nibbled and made up our minds about what to buy. Like most people, I was charmed by the politeness, sincerity and warmth of the ordinary Russian although, of course, as a socialist I was constantly shocked by what I saw of the supposedly classless Soviet society. I couldn't believe my eyes when I used to drive through the streets of Moscow and see middle-aged women digging ditches and sweeping the roads with only rags bound around their feet when it was 40 degrees below zero, while other women in furs and high heels stepped into enormous shiny cars.

From the beginning, we had open house in my rooms on Friday evenings. I had hoped that local people would drop in—as people do in Israel—for a piece of cake and a cup of tea with us, but it was a very naïve hope, although the Friday night tradition was to continue long after I left Moscow. Newspapermen came, Jews and non-Jews from other embassies came, visiting Jewish businessmen (such as furriers from the States) came, but never any Russians, and never, never any Russian Jews, but of that more later.

My first official job was to write a formal letter of condolence to Mr. Molotov, the Soviet foreign minister, on Zhdanov's death and then to present my credentials. The president of the USSR, Nikolai Shvernik, was away, so the ceremony took place in the presence of the deputy president. I won't deny that I was very nervous. Suppose I did or said the wrong thing? The consequences for Israel might be critical. Or suppose I disappointed the Russians? I had never done anything remotely like this before, and I was filled with a sense of responsibility. But Eiga soothed me, persuaded me to wear her string of pearls and, accompanied by Namir, Arieh Levavi (our first secretary) and Yohanan Rattner (our military attaché), I went off more or less calmly to participate in the brief ritual that actually marked the start of the official existence of the Israeli mission to the USSR. After my credentials were read, I delivered a little speech in Hebrew (we had sent it earlier to the Soviet chief of protocol so he could prepare a translation), and then there was a modest, rather pleasant reception in my honor.

Now that the major formality was over, I desperately wanted to make contact with the Jews. I had already told my staff that just as soon as I presented my credentials, we all would visit the synagogue. There, if nowhere else, I was sure we would meet the Jews of Russia, from whom we had been separated for thirty years since the Revolution—and about whom we knew almost nothing. What were they like? What had remained of their Jewishness after so many years of life under a regime that had proclaimed war not only against all religions as such, but also specifically against Judaism and that regarded Zionism as a crime for which the only appropriate punishments were penal servitude in a forced-labor camp or exile to Soviet Asia. Although Hebrew was banned, Yiddish had been tolerated for a while, and there had even been official sponsorship of a Yiddish-speaking Jewish autonomous region, Birobidzhan, on the Chinese border. But it had never really got off the ground, and after World War II (in which millions of Russian Jews perished), the Soviet authorities saw to it that most Yiddish schools and newspapers never reopened. By the time we arrived in the USSR there was not only overt repression, but also a vicious brand of government-directed anti-Semitism, which was to "blossom" within a few years into the wholesale and ruthless persecution of Jews and the imprisonment of Jewish intellectuals—actors, doctors, writers—accused of "cosmopolitanism" and "Zionist imperialism." The situation was already so tragic that those members of the legation who had close relatives in Russia—brothers, sisters, even parents—were in an agony of doubt throughout my stay in Moscow as to whether or not they should contact people whom they longed to see, but who they knew might be condemned to deportation if their relationship with any Israeli were to be revealed.

It was an excruciating dilemma, and we often spent days trying to decide the pros and cons of getting in touch with X's sister or sending food and money to Y's aged and ill mother and usually came to the conclusion that whatever we did would harm their relatives, so for their sake it would be better to do nothing at all. Of course, there were exceptions, but even now I dare not write freely about this, because to do so might place Jews who are still in Russia in terrible danger. Today the entire civilized world is aware of what happens to Soviet citizens who ignore the perverted rules and regulations by which their leaders seek to control them. But 1948 was still a "honeymoon" year, and it was very hard for us either to understand or to accept a system of things in which it was an offense against the state for an old woman to meet the son she had not seen for three decades—particularly when that son was a recognized member of the diplomatic corps and his presence presumably welcome in the Soviet Union.

At all events, on the first Saturday following the presentation of credentials, we set off on foot for the Great Synagogue (Moscow's other two synagogues were only small wooden structures), each of the legation's men carrying a prayer shawl and a siddur (prayer book). In the synagogue we found only about 100 or perhaps 150 elderly Jews, who, of course, had no idea that we were coming, although we had notified Rabbi Schliefer that we hoped to attend the Sabbath services. As was customary, toward the end of the service, a blessing was recited for the good health of the heads of the state—and then, to my surprise, a blessing for me. I was sitting in the women's gallery (in Orthodox synagogues men and women are separated), and when my name was mentioned, the whole congregation turned to stare at me as though it were memorizing my face. No one said anything. They just looked and looked at me.

After the service was over, I introduced myself to the rabbi, and we chatted for a few minutes. Meanwhile, the rest of the legation staff had gone on ahead, and I began to walk to the hotel alone, my head filled with thoughts about the service and the few weary-looking, shabby men and women who still went to the synagogue every week in Moscow. I hadn't gone very far when an elderly man brushed up against me in a way that I knew at once was not accidental. "Don't say anything," he whispered to me in Yiddish. "I'll walk on, and you follow me." When we were near the hotel, he suddenly stopped, turned around to face me, and standing there on that windy Moscow street, he recited the thanksgiving prayer, *Shehehiyanu,* that I had last heard intoned by Rabbi Fishman-Maimon in Tel Aviv on May 14. Before I could say or do anything, the old Jew had slipped away, and I entered the hotel alone, my eyes brimming, wondering if that strange pathetic encounter had really taken place or whether I had dreamed it.

A few weeks later it was Rosh Hashanah, the Jewish New Year. I had been told that on the High Holidays many more people came to the synagogue than on Saturdays, and I decided, once again, that the entire legation would attend the Rosh Hashanah service. Then, a day or two before the holiday, a long article appeared in *Pravda,* written by Ilya Ehrenburg, the well-known Soviet journalist and apologist who was himself a Jew. Were it not for Stalin, Ehrenburg wrote piously, there would be no such thing as a Jewish state. "Nonetheless, let there be no mistake about it," he explained, "the State of Israel has nothing to do with the Jews of the Soviet Union, where there is no Jewish problem and therefore no need for Israel. That is for the Jews of the capitalist countries, in which, inevitably, anti-Semitism flourishes. And in any case there is no such entity as the Jewish people. That is as ridiculous a concept as if one claimed that everybody who had red hair or a certain shape of nose belongs to one people." Not only I but the Jews of Moscow read this article. And like me, because they were used to reading between the lines, they understood what it was all about and knew that they were being warned to keep away from us! The response which thousands upon thousands of these Jews deliberately and courageously chose to make to that sinister warning was something which shattered and overwhelmed me at the time I witnessed it and which has inspired me ever since. There is not a detail about what happened on that New Year's Day that I do not remember as vividly—and with as much emotion—as if it had taken place only a few hours ago.

As we had planned, we went to the synagogue on Rosh Hashanah. All of us—the men, women and children of the legation—dressed in our best clothes, as befitted Jews on a Jewish holiday. But the street in front of the synagogue had changed. Now it was filled with people, packed together like sardines, hundreds and hundreds of them, of all ages, including Red Army officers, soldiers, teenagers and babies carried in their parents' arms. Instead of the 2,000-odd Jews who usually came to the synagogue on the holidays, a crowd of close to 50,000 people was waiting for us. For a minute I couldn't grasp what had happened—or even who they were. And then it dawned on me. They had come— those good, brave Jews—in order to be with us, to demonstrate their sense of kinship and to celebrate the establishment of the State of Israel. Within seconds they had surrounded me, almost lifting me bodily, almost crushing me, saying my name over and over again. Eventually, they parted ranks and let me enter the synagogue, but there, too, the demonstration went on. Every now and then, in the women's gallery, someone would come to me, touch my hand, stroke or even kiss my dress. Without speeches or parades, without any words at all really, the Jews of Moscow were proving their profound desire—and their need—to participate in the miracle of the establishment of the Jewish state, and I was the symbol of the state for them.

I couldn't talk, or smile, or wave my hand. I sat in that gallery like a stone, without moving, with those thousands of eyes fixed on me. No such entity as the Jewish people, Ehrenburg had written. The State of Israel meant nothing to the Jews of the USSR! But his warning had fallen on deaf ears. For thirty years we and they had been separated. Now we were together again, and as I watched them, I knew that no threat, however awful, could possibly have stopped the ecstatic people I saw in the synagogue that day from telling us, in their own way, what Israel meant to them. The service ended, and I got up to leave; but I could hardly walk. I felt as though I had been caught up in a torrent of love so strong that it had literally taken my breath away and slowed down my heart. I was on the verge of fainting, I think. But the crowd still surged around me, stretching out its hands and saying *Nasha Golda* (our Golda) and *Shalom, shalom,* and crying.

Out of that ocean of people, I can still see two figures clearly: a little man who kept popping up in front of me and saying, *"Goldele, leben zolst du. Shana Tova!"* (Goldele, a long life to you and a Happy New Year), and a woman who just kept repeating, "Goldele! Goldele!" and smiling and blowing kisses at me.

It was impossible for me to walk back to the hotel, so although there is an injunction against riding on the Sabbath or on Jewish holidays, someone pushed me into a cab. But the cab couldn't move either because the crowd of cheering, laughing, weeping Jews had engulfed it. I wanted to say something, anything, to those people, to let them know that I begged their forgiveness for not having wanted to come to Moscow and for not having known the strength of their ties to us. For having wondered, in fact, whether there was still a link between them and us. But I couldn't find the words. All I could say, clumsily, and in a voice that didn't even sound like my own, was one sentence in Yiddish. I stuck my head out of the window of the cab and said, *"A dank eich vos ihr seit geblieben Yidden"* (Thank you for having remained Jews), and I heard that miserable, inadequate sentence being passed on through the enormous crowd as though it were some wonderful prophetic saying.

Finally, after a few more minutes, they let the cab move forward and leave. In the hotel everyone gathered in my room. We had been shaken to our very depths. Nobody talked. We just sat there. It had been far too great a revelation for us to discuss it, but we needed to be together. Eiga, Lou and Sarah were sobbing as though their hearts would break, and several of the men held their faces in their hands. But I couldn't even cry. I just sat, my face drained of color, staring in front of me. And that was how we stayed, for hours, flooded with emotions so powerful that we couldn't even communicate them to each other. I can't pretend that I knew for certain then that within twenty years I would see many of those Jews in Israel. But I did know one thing: I knew that the Soviet Union had not succeeded in breaking their spirit, that Russia, with all its power, had failed. The Jews had remained Jews.

Someone took a photograph of that Rosh Hashanah crowd, and I suppose that thousands of copies were made of it because later people passing me in the street would whisper to me, so quietly that at first I didn't understand what they were saying, "We have the picture." Of course, I knew that they would have showered the same love and pride on a broomstick, if it had been sent to them to represent Israel. But all the same, I was very touched when years later Russian immigrants to Israel brought me either yellowing twenty-year-old prints of that photograph or of a photograph showing me presenting my credentials in the Kremlin, which appeared in 1948 in a Soviet periodical and had also been lovingly saved for two decades.

On Yom Kippur (the Day of Atonement), which comes ten days after the Jewish New Year, thousands of Jews once again crowded the synagogue, and this time I stayed there with them all day. I remember that when the rabbi recited the closing sentence of the service, *"Leshanah ha-ba'ah b'yerushalayim"* (Next year in Jerusalem), a tremor went through the entire synagogue, and I said a little prayer of my own: "God, let it happen. If not next year, then let the Jews of Russia come to us soon." But even then I didn't really expect that it would happen within my lifetime.

Not long afterward I was also given the privilege of meeting Mr. Ehrenburg. One of the foreign correspondents stationed in Moscow, an Englishman, who used to drop in on Friday nights, asked me once if I wanted to meet Ehrenburg. "As a matter of fact, I do," I said. "There are one or two things I'd very much like to talk to him about."

"I'll arrange it," promised the Englishman, but he never did. Then, a few weeks later, there was an Independence Day party in the Czech embassy, and the same journalist came up to me. "Mr. Ehrenburg is here," he said. "Shall I bring him over to you?" Ehrenburg was quite drunk—not an unusual condition for him, I was told—and, from the start, very aggressive. He began speaking to me in Russian.

"I'm sorry, but I can't speak Russian," I said. "Do you speak English?"

He looked at me nastily and replied, "I hate Russian-born Jews who speak English."

"And I am sorry for Jews who don't speak Hebrew or at least Yiddish!" I answered. Of course, lots of people milling around overheard this exchange, and I don't think it increased anyone's respect for Mr. Ehrenburg.

I had a much more interesting and rewarding encounter

with another Soviet citizen at the reception given by Mr. Molotov on the anniversary of the Russian Revolution, to which all diplomats in Moscow are invited each year. The heads of legations were received by the foreign minister in a special room. After I had shaken hands with Molotov, his wife, Ivy Molotov, came up to me. "I am so pleased to meet you, at last," she said with real warmth and even excitement. Then she added, "I speak Yiddish, you know."

"Are you Jewish?" I asked in some surprise.

"Yes," she said, answering me in Yiddish, *"Ich bin a yiddishe tochter."* (I am a daughter of the Jewish people.) We talked together for quite a long time. She knew all about the events at the synagogue and told me how good it was that we had gone. "The Jews wanted so much to see you," she said. Then we touched on the question of the Negev, which was being debated at the United Nations. I made some remark about not being able to give it up because my daughter lived there and added that Sarah was with me in Moscow. "I must meet her," said Mrs. Molotov. So I introduced Sarah and Yael Namir to her, and she talked to them about Israel and asked Sarah dozens of questions about the kibbutzim, who lived in them and how they were run. She spoke Yiddish to the girls and was overjoyed when Sarah answered in the same language. When Sarah explained that everything in Revivim was owned collectively and that there was no private property, Mrs. Molotov looked troubled. "That's not a good idea," she said. "People don't like sharing everything. Even Stalin is against that. You should acquaint yourself with Stalin's thoughts and writings on the subject." Before she returned to her other guests, she put her arm around Sarah and, with tears in her eyes, said, "be well. If everything goes well with you, it will go well for all Jews everywhere."

I never saw or heard from Mrs. Molotov again. Many years later, in New York, Henry Shapiro, the veteran United Press correspondent in Moscow, told me that after her conversation with us, Ivy Molotov had been arrested, and I remembered that anniversary celebration and how, earlier that day, we had watched the military parade in Red Square. I had so envied the Russians all those weapons on display—the tiniest fraction of which was beyond our means—and, as if he had read my thoughts, Molotov had raised a glass of vodka to me later and said, "Don't think we got it in a single day. The time will come when you, too, will have these things. It will all be all right."

But by January, 1949, it was apparent that Russian Jewry was going to pay a heavy price for the welcome it had given us, for the "treachery" to communist ideals that was—in the eyes of the Soviet government—implicit in the joy with which we had been greeted. The Yiddish theater in Moscow was closed. The Yiddish newspaper *Enigkeit* was closed. The Yiddish publishing house Emes was closed. It didn't matter that all these had faithfully followed the communist line. The fact remained that Russian Jewry had shown far too great an interest in Israel and the Israelis to please the Kremlin. Within five months there was practically no single Jewish organization left in Russia, and the Jews kept their distance from us.

In the meantime, I dutifully went on the necessary rounds of courtesy calls to the heads of other Moscow legations and embassies and waited for permanent quarters. At last, we were given a house, a two-story villa that boasted a large courtyard containing a few small buildings which could be used for housing. It was very hard for me to keep my mind off what was happening in Israel and on the dinner parties and teas I had to attend—not to speak of the matter of furnishing the new house. But the sooner we moved, the better, so I asked Eiga to go to Sweden to buy the furniture, curtains and lamps we needed for it. It took her several weeks to find the things we wanted at the prices we could afford, but she did a wonderful job and furnished our seven bedrooms, reception hall, dining room, kitchen and all the offices both inexpensively and attractively. Incidentally, when she left for Stockholm, she stuck all the mail we wanted to send to Europe with her into her suitcase; but on the way she decided that Israel really needed a diplomatic pouch and she had one designed for us in a Stockholm department store. She also bought warm clothing for everyone and canned food.

I went back to Israel twice during my seven months in Moscow, and each time I felt as though I had come from another planet, from a vast, cold land of suspicion, hostility and silence into the warmth of a small country—still at war and facing immense hardships, but open, hopeful, democratic and my own—and I could hardly bear to tear myself away from it again. On the first of those two visits—which was after our elections in January, 1949—Ben-Gurion asked me if I would join the cabinet he was forming. "I want you to serve as a minister of labor," he said. Mapai, the Labor Party, had won an overwhelming victory at the polls by receiving 35 percent of the total vote (20 percent more than Mapam, its nearest rival) in an election in which 87 percent of all the eligible voters in Israel had gone to the polls. The state's first government was formed by a coalition which included the United Religious Front, the Progressive Party (made up largely of middle-class professionals who were Mapai-oriented, though they stressed a nonpartisan point of view) and the Sephardim (a tiny party that represented the interests of the so-called Oriental Jews).

The religious bloc balked a bit at the idea of a woman minister but eventually accepted the argument that in ancient Israel Deborah had been a judge—which was at least equivalent to, if not more important than being, a cabinet minister! The religious bloc's objection to my holding office, based on my being a woman, came up again in the 1950s, when I was a candidate for the mayoralty of Tel Aviv, although on that occasion it was not overcome as it was in 1949. Anyhow, I was overjoyed by Ben-Gurion's offer. At last I would be where I wanted to be, doing what I most wanted to do and what, for a change, I felt completely qualified to do. Not that I, or anybody else in the government, knew at that point exactly what fell within the jurisdiction of a Ministry of Labor. But I couldn't imagine a more constructive and gratifying task than one which—whatever else it encompassed—would certainly have much to do with employing and housing the hundreds of thousands of immigrants who were already arriving in Israel. I said yes to Ben-Gurion at once, without a moment's hesitation, and I never regretted it. My seven years in the Ministry of Labor were, without doubt, the most satisfying and the happiest of my life.

But before I could plunge into my new job, I had to return to Moscow for another few weeks. It didn't take long for the effects of my trip home to wear off. The obvious social inequalities, the general anxiety and fear of the population, the isolation in which the diplomatic corps went through its paces—all depressed me unspeakably, and

I felt very guilty knowing that I would soon be out of it while Namir, Levavi and the rest of the staff stayed on. Sarah and Zechariah were both dying to leave, as was Lou, but they still had to serve several more months in the legation. I embarked on a round of farewell parties and said good-bye to the few Soviet officials with whom I had dealt directly—all of whom had been unfailingly courteous, though also unfailingly evasive about nine out of every ten requests or queries we had. Still, we had been treated no worse (if no better) than other legations, and like other legations, we too became accustomed to the practically total absence of affirmative replies—or of any replies at all, for that matter. Most of all, of course, I wanted to say not good-bye but *au revoir* to the Jews; but almost none of them dared come to the legation anymore, and there were no more crowds at the synagogue.

On April 20, 1949, I returned to Israel. At this point, I think it is important to describe what was happening there because in the course of 1949 and 1950 Israel underwent a process that no other country has ever undergone in quite the same way and that was to result in the doubling of our population within only two years. The War of Independence ended (to the extent that it ever ended) in the spring of 1949, and armistice agreements—though not peace treaties—had been signed with Egypt, Lebanon, Jordan and Syria, through the good offices of Dr. Ralph Bunche (who had taken Count Bernadotte's place as UN mediator). Unfortunately, however, their signatures didn't mean that the Arab states were now reconciled to our existence. On the contrary, it meant that the war which they were so anxious to wage against us and which they had lost on the battlefield would now be fought differently and in a manner less likely to result in their defeat but just as likely, they hoped, to destroy the Jewish state. Having been trounced in battle, the Arabs now switched from military weapons to economic ones. They boycotted any companies or individuals that traded with us. They closed the Suez Canal to Israeli shipping, in the face of the international convention which stipulated that the Canal must be open to all nations at all times.

But they didn't stop killing Jews altogether. For years there was a steady infiltration across our borders of armed Arab gangs that murdered and robbed Israelis, set fields and orchards on fire, stole cattle and generally made life a misery in our border settlements. Whenever we protested or tried to convince the United Nations that these constant raids were, in fact, a continuation of the war and a major violation of the armistice agreements, the Arab states, loudly proclaiming their innocence, said that there was nothing whatsoever they could do about these "incidents"—although we knew that they were providing the money, arms and backing, and what's more, we could prove our allegations. Under normal circumstances, I suppose this continuous, malicious and very dangerous harassment would have so enraged us that we would have retaliated in a way, and on a scale, appropriate to a sovereign state. But since, at that point, we were all so preoccupied with the problem of feeding, housing and employing the 684,201 Jews from seventy countries who arrived in Israel between May 14, 1948, and the end of 1951, all we did, at first, was to complain to the United Nations about the raids and hope that something would be done about them.

It may be difficult today to imagine what that flood of human beings was like. These were not immigrants of the kind that had come when Sheyna and I did—sturdy young idealists in good physical condition who couldn't wait to settle on the land and who regarded the discomforts of pioneering as part of the great Zionist experiment in which they had so eagerly involved themselves. Nor were they the professionals, tradesmen or artisans who came in the 1930s with some means of their own and whose contribution to the *yishuv*'s economy began as soon as they reached Palestine. The hundreds of thousands of Jews who streamed into Israel in those early years of statehood were utterly destitute. They had nothing at all except the will to live and the desire to get away from their past. Most of them were broken in body, if not in spirit, and many thousands were broken in both. All the Jews of Europe had suffered crippling tragedies; as for the Jews from the Arab lands of the Middle East and North Africa they had lived, for the most part, uneducated, poverty-stricken and terrorized in the ghettos and casbahs of some of the most repressive countries on earth, and they knew little or nothing about twentieth-century life. It was, in short, a flood of Jews from opposite ends of the earth who spoke different languages, came from widely contrasted backgrounds, ate different foods and were frequently quite ignorant of each other's traditions and customs. The one thing they had in common was that they were all Jews, but that was a great deal—everything, in fact.

I know that statistics make dull reading—at least they do for me, but perhaps I will be forgiven for citing a few now in order to illustrate the scope of the problems we faced—problems which, to some extent, Israel's minister of labor was called upon to solve. By 1949, 25,000 European Jews had come to Israel from the camps on Cyprus, and 75,000 from the DP camps of Germany and Austria. Of the 80,000 Jews living in Turkey at the beginning of 1948, 33,000 were in Israel by the end of 1950. Czechoslovkia was letting its surviving Jews leave at the rate of 20,000 a year, and 37,000 Bulgarian Jews plus 7,000 Yugoslav Jews—almost all who were left after the Holocaust—had made their way to Israel by the autumn of 1950. The news of the birth of the Jewish state gave rise to the immigration in less than three years of 5,000 Jews from China and of 35,000 Jews from Morocco, Tunis and Algiers. At first Poland and Rumania would not let their Jews go, but toward the end of 1949 their governments had a brief change of heart, and between December, 1949, and February, 1951, 28,000 Jews came from Poland, and in 1950 and 1951, 88,000 Rumanian Jews were gathered in. In 1950 a movement of 3,000 Jews per month began from Hungary, and emigration from Persia, once a clandestine trickle, turned into a wave carrying along with it refugees who had congregated in Persia from surrounding countries. Nineteen fifty was also the year that a law was passed in Iraq permitting Jewish emigration within a twelve-month period, and a grand total of 121,000 Iraq Jews were airlifted into Israel while there was still time!

Each of these migrations, of these mass responses to the establishment of the State of Israel, had its own special history, and each was different. But certainly the airlift of the Jews of Yemen from southwest Arabia to the Jewish state was the most remarkable migration of all. No one knows exactly when the Jews first came to Yemen. It may have been in the days of King Solomon, or perhaps there were Jews who crossed the mountains of Arabia with the Roman troops that fought there at the beginning of the Christian

*The first photograph
taken of Golda in Milwaukee.*

*Golda (center) at the age of eighteen,
as photographed for the yearbook
of the Milwaukee Normal School, 1916.*

LOUISE G. BORN

Classical Course; Girls' Club; Lincoln; Pageant.

*"Ready to make a day of night,
Goddess excellently bright!"*

Louise Born.

HARRY MARTENS

Science Course; President M. N. D.;
Football, '12, '14, '15; Senior Play;
Track, '12, '13; Basket Ball, '12, '13,
'14; Cap't. Indoor Baseball, '15.

"Has a smile for everybody."

Harry Martens

GOLDIE MABOWEHZ

Elective Course, 3 yrs.; Lincoln Society; Science Club; Pageant.

*"Those about her
From her shall read the perfect ways
of honor."*

WILLIAM L. KICKHAEFER

Science Course; Lincoln; Gridiron;
Senior Vaudeville, '15; Pageant.

*"Frequently seen in public places,
Social dances, sports and races."*

PEARL GILBERT

Commercial Course, 3½ yrs.; Palladium; Girls' Club.

*"The learning ear is always found
close to the speaking tongue."*

*Golda and Morris Myerson
were married on December 24, 1917.*

The precious photograph taken outside
Moscow's Great Synagogue in 1948.
Golda Meir is ringed.

Golda Meir with her sisters,
Sheyna (left) and Clara (center).

As foreign minister,
out for a stroll with one of her grandchildren.

Mrs. Meir, after being nominated as Israel's prime minister.

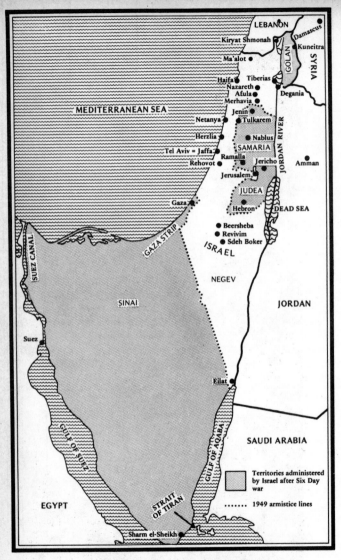

*Map showing the 1949 armistice lines
and the territories administered
by Israel after the Six-Day War.*

Era. At any rate, Jews had lived in Moslem Yemen for many centuries, cut off from the rest of the Jewish world, persecuted, deprived of political rights and impoverished, but always loyal to their faith and to the Bible, which served as their only source of knowledge and learning for hundreds of years. They survived as serfs, as the property of the ruler of Yemen, forbidden to work in trades that were open to others or even to walk on the same side of the street as Moslems. In that backward, bigoted and poverty-stricken country, the Jews were the poorest and lowest of citizens, but unlike the rest of the population, they were literate. In their synagogues and schools they taught their male children to read and write Hebrew, and I remember that one of my first impressions of the Yemenite Jews was that they were able to read upside down. Because books were so rare, the children, who sat in a circle in the mud-baked huts that served as schools in the Jewish quarters of Yemen, had to learn to read the Bible from every possible angle.

How did they keep themselves alive? They became master craftsmen, silversmiths, jewelers, weavers and carpenters. All over Israel today you can see—and buy—their delicate, exotic filigreed work. Of course, those who couldn't keep their families alive by craftsmanship became itinerant workmen and peddlers, but for all of them life was more than degrading; it was also very precarious. Out of every 1,000 Jewish children born in Yemen, nearly 800 died, and all orphaned Jewish boys were forced to convert. But somehow the Jewish community of Yemen never disappeared, and every now and then either Yemenite Jews were given permission by the imam to leave Yemen or they escaped from it across the desert into Aden, hoping from there to reach the Holy Land—although very few ever did.

Still, when I came to Palestine in 1921, there were already some Yemenite Jews there. I was fascinated by them. I knew that they were capable of great feats of strength but to me they looked like dark-skinned, fragile dolls in their colorful traditional clothing (in Yemen they were not allowed to wear the same clothes as Arabs). Most of the Yemenite women in Palestine then wore lovely hooded garments and dresses over narrow, beautifully embroidered trousers, while the men, all of whom had long earlocks, were dressed in loose striped robes. During the war years a

few thousand Yemenite Jews who received permission from
the British to leave Aden and enter Palestine, sailed up the
Red Sea and through the Suez Canal. But the majority
were still trapped. In 1947, a few days after the UN vote
on partition, there were dreadful Arab riots in Aden, and
the situation of the Jews inside Yemen itself also worsened.
In their despair and terror, thousands of Yemenite Jews—
hearing that the State of Israel was at last coming into being—finally took their lives in their own hands and fled.
They left their few possessions behind, gathered up their
families and—like the Biblical Children of Israel—began
to walk out of slavery into freedom, believing implicitly that
somehow or other they would get to the Holy land. They
had learned of the renewed settlement activity in Palestine
from Samuel Yaurich, an Eastern European Jew who had
made his way through Yemen as early as 1908, finding these
"lost remnants" of people and bringing them the message
of the return to Zion. They walked in groups of thirty or
forty, set upon by Arab brigands, eating only the pitta (flat
Arab bread), honey and dates they could carry and paying
exorbitant ransoms to the various desert sultanantes they
passed en route for each man, newborn baby and Bible.
Most of them did reach Aden and the camps organized for
them there by the Joint Distribution Committee and staffed
by Israeli doctors and social workers, where they rested,
prayed and read their Bibles. But since the Egyptians had
closed the Suez Canal to Israeli shipping, there was only one
way for them to reach Israel—and that was by air. Each
day 500 or 600 Yemenite Jews were flown to Israel, packed
into giant converted transport planes that flew them along
the Red Sea route in what soon became known as Operation
Magic Carpet. The airlift went on all through 1949, and by
the time it ended it had brought 48,000 Yemenite Jews to
Israel.

Sometimes I used to go to Lydda and watch the planes
from Aden touch down, marveling at the endurance and
faith of their exhausted passengers. "Had you ever seen a
plane before?" I asked one bearded old man.

"No," he answered.

"But weren't you very frightened of flying?" I persisted.

"No," he said again, very firmly. "It is all written in the
Bible. In Isaiah. 'They shall mount up with wings of ea-
gles.'" And standing there on the airfield, he recited the

entire passage to me, his face lit with the joy of a fulfilled prophecy—and of the journey's end. Today there are virtually no more Jews in Yemen, and the scars of their long exile have begun to fade. Ben-Gurion used to say that his happiest day would come when a Yemenite Jew would be appointed chief of staff of the Israel Defense Forces, and I myself think that day is not far off now.

Reading over what I have just written, I am still amazed by the sheer number of the immigrants we absorbed. But we weren't dealing with abstract numbers then. It wasn't the arithmetic of the Law of the Return—the bill passed by the Knesset in July, 1950, giving the right of immigration to all Jews and automatic Israeli citizenship to all Jewish immigrants—that most concerned us. What worried us was how were we ever going to feed, clothe, house, educate and generally care for those thousands of immigrants. How and with what? By the time I arrived back in Israel there were 200,000 people living (if that's the word) in tents all over the country, more often than not two families to a tent—and not necessarily families from the same country or even the same continent. Apart from the fact that none of the services we improvised in such a rush really worked well or was geared for so many thousands of people, there were also a great many sick, undernourished and handicapped people who might have managed better had they been housed differently but who just couldn't cope at all under the circumstances. The man who had lived through years of Nazi slave labor, survived the DP camps and braved the trip to Israel and who was, at best, in poor health and, at worst, badly damaged physically and entitled to the best possible conditions found himself and his family (if he still had one) living in unbearable proximity with people with whom he didn't even have a common language. Nine times out of ten, he even regarded his new neighbors as primitive because they had never seen a flush toilet. Even then, he might have pulled himself together faster if we had been able to give him a job at once or to move him into more adequate housing or somehow to give him the sense of permanence for which, like all refugees, he longed. Or consider the illiterate woman from Libya or Yemen or the caves of the Atlas Mountains who was stuck with her children in a drafty, leaky tent with Polish or Czech Jews who prepared their food differently, ate things that made

her feel sick and, by her standards, weren't even Jews at all
either because they weren't observant or else because their
prayers and rituals were totally unfamiliar to her.

In theory, none of this should have mattered. In theory,
no overcrowding, no misery, no cultural or intellectual differences should have been at all important for people who
had experienced the Holocaust or for those who had literally walked out of Yemen through the robber-infested,
scorching desert. But theory is for theoreticians. People are
people, and the tensions and discomforts of those hideous
tent cities that I saw everywhere in 1949 were really unbearable. Something had to be done at once about housing,
and jobs had to be created for those unhappy people as
soon as possible. Their health and their nutrition were
taken care of more or less adequately: The TB, trachoma,
ringworm, malaria, typhoid, dysentery, measles and pella-
gra that the immigrants brought with them were all being
coped with, although I don't know how our overworked
and exhausted doctors and nurses did it. And all the tent
cities had schools of some sort where Hebrew was being
taught intensively. But in 1949 housing seemed an insur-
mountable problem.

As for our resources, despite the magnificent response of
world Jewry, there was never enough money. Thanks to
our neighbors, our defense budget had to stay sky-high,
and anyhow, all the other essential needs of the state had to
be met somehow. We couldn't close down our schools or
our hospitals or our transportation or our industries (such
as they were) or put too tight a rein in any way on the
state's development. So everything had to be done at the
same time. But there were things that we could do without,
after all—so we did without them. We rationed almost everything—food, clothing and shoes—and got used to the
idea of an austerity that lasted for years. Recently I came
across one of my own ration books, a drab little booklet
issued by the Ministry of Commerce and Industry in 1950,
and I recalled the hours I stood in line for a few potatoes
or three eggs or the frozen fish on which we feasted so gratefully—when we got it.

Luckily, I still had clothes from my stay in Russia. But
most Israelis had a very hard time indeed. Their standard
of living dropped drastically. Whatever had been sufficient
for one family in 1948 now had to be shared with two or

three other families. Old-timers, who had just emerged from months of a terrible war, might have been forgiven for rebelling against the new demands made on them. But no one rebelled. A few people said that perhaps the immigrants should wait wherever they were until times were better here. But no one, no one at all, ever suggested that the burden was too heavy or that the infant state might collapse under it. The national belt was tightened—and tightened again—and still we all managed to breathe. And about one thing we all were in agreement: Without those Jews, Israel wasn't worth having.

But there had to be priorities, and for me, at least, housing and jobs for the immigrants headed the list. Not all my colleagues agreed with me. A barrage of experts explained to me in detail, with charts and graphs, why a housing program of the kind I envisaged was not a good idea. It would lead only to inflation, they said. It would be far wiser to put the little money at our disposal into factories or streamlined methods of agriculture. But I couldn't accept or support any recommendation that didn't deal with the absorption of immigrants, first and foremost, from the human point of view. And I certainly didn't believe that anything could ever be as "productive"—in terms of Israel's future—as decent housing. To me it seemed absolutely clear that good citizenship, a real sense of belonging, the beginning of integration—in other words, the creation of a good society—depended to an overwhelming degree on how people lived, and there was no point in our talking loftily about social responsibility, education or even public health unless we got at least some of the new immigrants out of those dreadful tents and into proper housing as soon as possible.

A few weeks after I returned from Moscow, I went to the Knesset with a plan for building an initial 30,000 housing units and got it through, despite the objections. But we couldn't make houses out of milk and honey (not that those commodities were available either), so I took myself off to the States in search of the necessary funds and once again asked the Jews of America for help—this time "not to win a war but to maintain life." I told them:

> I went to our Parliament two weeks ago last Tuesday and presented a project for thirty thousand housing units by the end of this year. Parliament approved

it, and there was great joy in the country. But actually
I did a strange thing: I presented a project for which I
didn't have the money.

What we want to do is to give each family a luxurious apartment of one room; one room which we will
build out of concrete blocks. We won't even plaster
the walls. We will make roofs, but no ceilings. What
we hope is that since these people will be learning a
trade as they build their houses, they will finish them,
and eventually, one day, add on another room. In the
meantime, we will be happy, and they will be happy,
even though it means putting a family of two, three,
four or five into one room. But this is better than putting two or three families in a single tent. . . .

It is an awful thing to do—to forge a signature to a
check—but I have done it. I have promised the people
at home and the people in the camps that the government is going to put up these thirty thousand units,
and we have already started to do so with the little
money we have. But there isn't enough for these thirty
thousand units. It is up to you either to keep these
people in camps and send them food packages or to
put them to work and restore their dignity and self-
respect.

I got the money, and we began to build those units. Of
course, at first we made all kinds of mistakes—some of
them serious—both in planning and in execution. We mis-
calculated, sited badly, fell behind the flow of immigration.
In the end we couldn't build quickly enough or well
enough, and by October, 1950, we had constructed only a
third of the units we had undertaken to build because an
unusually severe winter forced us to divert funds ear-
marked for building to the emergency purchase of thousands of metal huts, which were better than tents in the
winter but like roasting ovens all through Israel's long, hot
summer. Still, not a single family that entered Israel in
those great waves of immigration ever lacked shelter of
some kind. Somehow we found or invented accommoda-
tions for everyone. When the corrugated metal huts ran
out, we used canvas and nailed it to wooden frames and
created tens of thousands of fabric shacks; when these ran

out, we went unhappily back to tents for a while. But no one slept out of doors, and we never stopped building.

By the end of 1950, however, we knew that we couldn't go on thinking of those "temporary camps" as reception centers that could be neatly folded away within a few months. They were obviously going to have to do for several years, and that being the case, their entire character would have to change. They would have to be turned into work villages and moved to the outskirts of towns and cities, so that the new immigrants could live near places where labor was in demand. They would have to be so organized that the people in them could become more or less self-sufficient, cooking for themselves, rather than eating in public food kitchens, and participating in the upkeep of public services. We couldn't levy rates and taxes on penniless men and women, but we could prevent them from feeling that they were the objects of charity.

The new camps were called *ma'abarot,* the plural of the Hebrew word *ma'abara* (place of transit), and by November, 1951, we had set up 112 *ma'abarot,* housing a total population of 227,000 new immigrants. But if we were not to create two classes of Israelis—the relatively well-established old-timers, on the one hand, and the new immigrants in their crowded ugly *ma'abarot,* on the other—we would have to supply a lot more than just housing. We would have to see to it that the new immigrants worked and got paid for their work, and I believed that there was only one way of doing this: a public works program would have to be established.

That was not easy either. The majority of the so-called Oriental Jews (those from the Middle East and North Africa) had virtually no skills that were applicable to the circumstances in the new state. We feared that many of them would get used to doing nothing but living on a dole for years and years, while the gap between them and us widened. But social welfare, however enlightened, certainly wasn't the answer. Employment opportunities had to be created, and we would have to create them, so we set in motion a chain of special projects that offered work to people who had never used drills or held bricks in their hands or even worked in fields. The Ministry of Labor launched a massive road-building scheme throughout the country, and hundreds upon hundreds of acres of stony, stubborn land were cleared, terraced, and afforested by hand. And all the time we went on building and training the immigrants, although the tide of immigration didn't slow down until 1952.

The real problem, of course, wasn't the difficulty of creating a labor force or building houses or absorbing thousands of immigrants into our economy. Those were all urgent matters, but they were never at the core of our concern. What really preoccupied us in those days—and, what, in part, still preoccupies all thinking Israelis—was how to weld together people who on the surface had so little in common and found it so hard to understand each other. But, again because we had no alternative, we often succeeded where success seemed impossible. I remember, for instance, how pessimistic—not to say disapproving—some of my colleagues were about the road building. Not only didn't we need all those approach roads, but importing the building materials was in itself a luxury, and anyhow, the roads would be no good because we didn't have the kind of workers we needed. But I relied on three things: the dedication and ingenuity of the old-timers; the growing desire of the new immigrants to earn an honest day's wage and not to be turned into perpetual wards of the state or the Jewish Agency; and the understanding and generosity of world Jewry, which responded again and again to our endless pleas for help. Looking back, I must say that I was very rarely disappointed, although anyone watching the way in which those roads were built in 1949 and the early 1950s would have been justified in considering us all a little mad. We used to take one skilled construction worker from Jerusalem or Tel Aviv, turn him overnight into the foreman of a road-building crew somewhere in the south and leave him to cope with the problem of supervising ten men who spoke ten different languages, came from ten different countries and had been in Israel for only a few intolerably confusing months. But somehow or other, though perhaps inefficiently and too expensively, the roads (wryly nicknamed the golden roads in my honor) were built.

In 1952, when the immigration began to taper off at last—to 1,000 a day—we started to direct newcomers away from the *ma'abarot* into regular quarters in new development areas and border villages all over Israel and to stress agriculture, rather than public works. We gave each immigrant family not only a tiny house, but also a plot of land, livestock and lessons in farming. We made mistakes about that, too. We tried, probably too soon, to turn the pressure cooker into a melting pot. We created villages populated by combinations of people like the road-building crews. They had nothing much in common with each other and found it difficult (sometimes impossible) to live together in a totally isolated part of the country, and they usually had neither any experience nor any taste for farming. Many of them rebelled and drifted away to the towns, where they settled into slums. But most of them stayed and became first-rate farmers, whose children today grow the Israeli fruit, flowers and vegetables that are bought around the world.

I'm not at all sure that my constant visits to building sites, the new roads and the new settlements were always appreciated by the engineers and architects responsible for them. I couldn't walk into one of those tiny houses and not notice that the wall between what was to be the eating area and the kitchen only made the whole house smaller than necessary, or not see that the kitchen counter was so designed that no one could keep it clean, least of all women who had never cooked in an indoor kitchen before, or not observe that two steps leading to a house built on a slope weren't enough and that a third step was essential—especially for families that comprised eight or nine small children, a pregnant mother and at least one (if not two or three) grandparents. "But it will cost much more," was the inevitable response to my suggestions.

Of course, it would have been easier to accept the argument that most of the immigrants—particularly those from Yemen and North Africa—were better off even in badly designed houses than they had been before. "They don't know how to live in the kind of houses you want them to have," I was told often. "They don't know what bathrooms or flush toilets are. They'll just turn the space into storage rooms for junk." It was true. They didn't know what bathrooms were or how to use showers, but that didn't mean that they weren't entitled to them or shouldn't be taught how to use them. And the same applied to kitchens, schools and the state itself, for that matter. But it was also true that we couldn't do anything without money.

So, though I begrudged every minute that I was away

from Israel, I went on with my fund-raising speeches abroad, traveling often to Europe, the United States and South America. But fund raising, too, had to be suited to our new circumstances. The United Jewish Appeal had become a magnificent instrument for the raising of money; but it was still an appeal, and the money was still "gift" money. I had been troubled for years by the picture of a Jewish state that relied on charitable funds, which, apart from everything else, could never begin to meet our growing needs for development capital. I wasn't an economist any more than I was a construction engineer, but just as I didn't need to be able to use a slide rule in order to understand how high a kitchen sink should be, so I didn't require years of experience as a financier in order to know that a falloff in philanthropic funds was inevitable. But it wasn't only the amount of money that worried me; it was also the kind of money we were getting. It seemed to me that a continued dependence on philanthropy violated the most elementary concepts of Zionism, of self-reliance and self-labor, to say nothing of national independence, and I began to think of other possible sources of funds, sources that would make world Jewry fuller partners in the Zionist enterprise and in the "ingathering of the exiles." After my 1948 visits to the United States I had corresponded steadily on this subject in dozens of letters and cables with Henry Montor, and whenever he and I and Eliezer Kaplan (Israel's first minister of finance) met, we talked in depth about the feasibility of entering into a new economic activity that would express itself in the floating of an Israel bond issue.

The first time that the bond idea surfaced in public was September, 1950 at a special three-day conference convened in Jerusalem by Ben-Gurion and attended by the leaders of the major Jewish communities in the United States. At the beginning there was very little enthusiasm for the idea. What if the sale of bonds undermined the efforts of the UJA? And who wanted either to make money out of Israel or, as seemed more likely and worse, lose it? Philanthropic contributions were tax-deductible, but the bonds would not be. And what if the U.S. government did not look with favor on a bond issue? Underlying all these reservations and anxieties, I felt, was a general unease about an altered relationship with Israel. No one came out and bluntly said that Israel wasn't a good financial risk, but I couldn't help sensing a feeling that the whole notion of an assumption of indebtedness by us at this time was most undesirable. The bonds, however, found one very powerful champion—far more influential than Ben-Gurion, Kaplan, Montor and myself put together. Henry J. Morgenthau, the former U.S. secretary of the treasury, with whom I had traveled to so many communities in 1948 and who had served as general chairman of the UJA, understood at once and immediately approved. He did more than that. He went to see President Truman at the White House and we discovered that the president also understood and approved. So another conference was convened—this time in Washington, D.C.—and I was handed the "choice" assignment of trying to convert the nonbelievers and turn their skepticism and resistance into support and cooperation.

I didn't waste much time on preliminaries or phraseology. If Israel was to develop, to grow and to thrive, even to be able to feed itself, we needed $1.5 billion over the next three years! We ourselves—all 1,000,000 of us—would be responsible, I said, for a third of that staggering sum. But $1 billion would have to be provided by the Jews of America in various ways, including the purchase of bonds.

> Part of that money will have to be given as donations, but part of it, the major part, must be money we can invest profitably, money that will be returned, money that can bear interest. In addition to a large, strong UJA, we want investment capital; we want to sell bonds; we want you to lend us money. I don't know what security we can give you or what security you can ask for. There is only one kind of security that I think I can offer you on behalf of the government of Israel. I can offer you the gilt-edged security of the people of Israel, the hundreds of thousands of Jews who will still come to Israel and the tens of thousands of Jews in Israel who live in tents. But also I can offer you our children, the children of the old-timers and the little Yemenite children and the Iraqi children and the Rumanian children who are growing up in Israel—proud, safe, self-respecting Jews. They will pay back this debt, which they are honor-bound to pay back, with interest.

As I spoke, I saw before my eyes those children and their fathers, in the long processions that left the tents, the wooden barracks and the canvas huts early each morning to plant trees on hillsides or build roads. They were not all young men, their clothes were tattered, their bodies were frail, but only a few months ago they had walked with bent backs and downcast heads in the streets of Yemen or sat, despondent and listless, in the DP camps of Europe. Now their heads were up, and their backs were straight, and they held picks and shovels in their hands. I knew that they were a sound investment—and thank God, I was right. From the time that the first Israel bond campaign was launched in May, 1951, up to the present, close to $3 billion worth of bonds have been sold, of which $1 billion has already been repaid. Flowing into Israel's economy by way of a development budget, the bonds helped substantially and dramatically to establish the new state's economic viability.

But work was not everything for me during that period. There were also the private joys and sorrows of every life. One day in 1951, when I was away from home on one of those interminable trips to raise money, a cable arrived informing me that Morris was dead. I flew back to Israel at once to attend his funeral, my head filled with thoughts about the life we might have lived together if I had only been different. It was not a bereavement that I either could or wanted to talk about with other people, even my own family. Nor am I prepared to write about it now, except to say that although we had been apart for so long, standing at his graveside, I realized once again what a heavy price I had paid—and made Morris pay—for whatever I had experienced and achieved in the years of our separation.

There was also Sarah's pregnancy, illness and stillborn first baby and the days of unbearable worry about her recovery when Zechariah and I tried to force the doctors to tell us that everything would be all right and, instead, heard with horror that there was little hope for her life. I couldn't believe it, perhaps because I had heard those same words so many years before or perhaps because they are words one never really believes. But she pulled through this time, too, and characteristically insisted on returning to Revivim as soon as she could and starting another baby. It took me months, however, to recover from the fright I had

had, and every time I remembered how desperately ill she had been I wanted to rush down to Revivim and drag her back to Jerusalem with me so that I could take care of her myself. But I knew that my mission would fail and that I had to let her live her own life where and how she chose, regardless of how much I worried about her.

One of the greatest personal pleasures of my life during the time that I was minister of labor was the apartment in which I lived in Jerusalem. I had never been particularly interested in my immediate surroundings, as long as they were clean, neat and reasonably attractive. After all, a house is only a house, and I have lived in a number of houses since the state was born: the official residence of the foreign minister, that of the prime minister and now the small semidetached house in a garden suburb of Tel Aviv in whose other half live Menachem, Aya, their three sons and a cocker spaniel called Daisy—who is a lot fonder of me than I am of her. But none of those houses has ever meant as much to me as the lovely flat that was mine from 1949 to 1956. Its story is far more than just the tale of a piece of real estate. At the end of 1949, on Ben-Gurion's instructions, the Knesset and most of the government offices moved from Tel Aviv to Jerusalem. It was not a simple decision for Ben-Gurion to make, but it was entirely typical of him. Although the opening session of the Knesset had taken place in Jerusalem, and Dr. Weizmann had been sworn in as Israel's president there, only the Israelis themselves seemed aware of the unique place that Jerusalem has occupied throughout the ages in the hearts of Jews everywhere. The rest of the world managed to disregard the tie that has always existed between us and the City of David. Both the Peel Commission and UNSCOP had taken the position that Jerusalem must not be included either in the proposed Jewish or Arab state, and the UN General Assembly decided that Jerusalem should be internationalized, administered through a special council and its own governor and guarded by an international police force. The point of all this, ostensibly, was to protect the holy places so that "order and peace" might reign in Jerusalem forever. The Arabs, of course, rejected this plan, lock, stock and barrel, along with the entire partition proposal. But we accepted it, though very unhappily, and comforted ourselves with the UN promise that at the end of ten years there would be a referendum "leading to certain modifications." Since there were 100,000 Jews and only 65,000 Arabs in Jerusalem in 1948, it seemed not impossible that in the end Jerusalem would be ours. Not that we ever intended to expel its Arab population (as has, I think, been amply proved by the events in the city since the Six-Day War), nor that we didn't bitterly resent the implication that we were likely to disturb the "order and peace" of a city that has been scared to us for more than 2,000 years. After all, we knew by heart—even if others had forgotten it—the record of Arab disturbances and violence in Jerusalem ever since 1921, and we knew that not one incident there had ever been caused by Jews.

That special council never came into existence, but Jerusalem came—and remained for months—under Arab fire. During that siege of Jerusalem, when the city was mercilessly shelled by the Egyptians and Jordanians, all the great international concern for the holy places just vanished into thin air. Apart from a few feeble resolutions at the United Nations, no one, except the Jews, said or did anything to halt the Arab assault on the city, and no one, except the Jews, moved to rescue either its people or its ancient sites. The Arab Legion occupied the Old City, and every single Jew in it who remained alive was thrown out. In fact, we became the only people to be denied access to the holy places, but still no one, except the Jews, said a word. Nobody even asked: "How is it that the Jews can no longer go to the synagogue in the Jewish Quarter of the Old City or pray at the Western Wall?" In view of the deafening silence, we could hardly be expected ever again to rely on anyone else to protect Jerusalem or take seriously any Christian or Moslem protestations of anxiety about the holy places. Anyhow, we were perfectly capable of guarding them ourselves, along with all the other historical and religious sites in Israel. And what's more, there was no longer any reason for us to wait for a referendum about Jerusalem. We had had a war forced on us instead.

Nonetheless, it took considerable courage on Ben-Gurion's part—in the face of a UN resolution passed in December, 1949, calling for the internationalization of Jerusalem at once—to decide to move the government there before any such resolution could be implemented. Even in Israel there were voices raised against the possible perils—

both political and military—of the move; but Ben-Gurion's inner voice was stronger yet, and although most of the foreign missions (and therefore our Foreign Ministry) stayed on in Tel Aviv, my ministry and most of the others packed up and moved to Jerusalem, the capital.

This meant that I had to find somewhere to live in Jerusalem. I certainly didn't want to settle in an hotel or take a room with a strange family. So even though I knew better than most people just how scarce housing was, I implored my co-workers at the Ministry of Labor to scour the city in search of a room for me. "All that I need," I said, "is one room with a private entrance. Surely that is available."

It took some time, but finally my phone rang. "Golda, we have found a room with a private entrance, but we don't think it is at all suitable for you. Still, if you'd like to see it. . . ."

I went to look at the room immediately, of course, It was in the Talbieh section of the city, in a house called the Villa Haroun al-Raschid (of all things), which had once served as a British headquarters. The house had two floors and an enormous roof with one broken-down room on it, and it was all indescribably dirty. The engineer was right. The whole house, let alone the rooftop room, was not only unsuitable, but impossible. Nonetheless, I went up to see the roof. I spent five minutes looking around me at the spectacular view of Jerusalem and then came down with an announcement. "This is it. I'll make myself comfortable in the filthy little room while you go ahead and fix up a small flat for me on another part of the roof." There was an instant barrage of disapproval. It wasn't large enough for a minister. It was too near the border. It would take too long to build a small apartment for me, and I'd have to live in that dreadful room for months. But I just smiled and said that I would move in as soon as the room was cleaned up. It did take several months before the apartment was finished, but it was well worth waiting for. From its one big bay window I could see the whole of Jerusalem perched on the Judean Hills, and I never got tired of looking at it. It didn't matter how hard or how long the day had been, how many new settlements I had visited or how many meetings I had attended. When I closed the door of the rooftop flat, made myself a cup of tea and sat down at last, with the lights of the city spread out before me, I was as happy as I have ever been. I could, and did, sit like that for hours sometimes, with or without friends dropping in, just feasting my eyes on Jerusalem's beauty. Later Menachem and Aya were married in that apartment, and it became part of our family history.

As I write about that period in my life, I can't help reflecting on how lucky I was to have been in on the beginnings of so many things—not that I influenced the course of events, but that I was so much a part of what was happening all around me, and sometimes my ministry and I were even able to play a decisive role in the upbuilding of the state. I suppose that if I were to limit myself—as I must—to singling out the two or three developments that were the most rewarding and most meaningful for me during those seven years, I would have to start with the legislation for which the Ministry of Labor was responsible. For me, that, more than anything else, symbolized the kind of social equality and justice without which I couldn't even imagine the state functioning at all. Old age pensions, widows' and orphans' benefits, maternity leaves and grants, industrial accident insurance, disability and unemployment insurance were essentials in any self-respecting society, and whatever else we lacked or postponed, these were basic.

Even if we couldn't afford to cover all of the labor movement's achievements by law at once, we were at least dutybound, I felt, to legislate as many as possible as soon as possible, and it meant a great deal to me to be able to present Israel's first National Insurance Bill—based largely on the voluntary insurance schemes of the Histadrut—to the Knesset in January, 1952, thus paving the way for the National Insurance Act that came into effect in the spring of 1954. National insurance wasn't a magic remedy. It didn't eliminate poverty in Israel, or close the educational or cultural gap between our citizens, or solve our security problems. But it did mean, as I told the Knesset that day, "that the State of Israel will not tolerate within it poverty that shames human life, the possibility that the happiest hours of a mother's life will be marred by worry about food or the possibility that men and women who reach old age will curse the day they were born." A drain on our resources? Of course it was—which was why we had to do it in stages. But it had economic as well as social significance and the merit of accumulating capital and withdrawing money from circulation, which helped us fight inflation. Above all, it equalized the financial burden, made one age group responsible for the other and spread the risk. It also had another by-product that mattered to me: Because the percentage of babies born in hospital rose as a result of the maternity benefits (which included the cost of hospitalization), infant mortality—which was high among the new immigrants and the Arabs—dropped. I went to Nazareth myself to hand the first check to the first Arab woman who had her baby in a hospital there, and I think I was more excited than she was.

Another of the Ministry of Labor's projects with which I became very involved had to do with vocational training, both for adults and for youngsters. Again, it wasn't a question of waving a wand and turning new immigrants into craftsmen or skilled technicians overnight. It took years to qualify people for new professions or trades, and hundreds of the new immigrants never became fully employable, because they were already too old, too sick, too psychologically addicted to not working or simply unable to adjust to the demands of modern life. But thousands of other men and women attended vocational schools and courses, learned to handle machinery, raise poultry, become plumbers and electricians, and I never got tired of watching the transformation take place. Everyone pitched in to make the vocational training program a success; the Ministry of Labor joined forces with the Ministry of Social Welfare, the Ministry of Education, the army, the Histadrut and veteran voluntary organizations such as ORT (Organization for Rehabilitation through Training), Hadassah and WIZO (Women's International Zionist Organization), which were financed by Jews abroad. We pushed and pulled together until we turned out workers who made knitwear, polished industrial diamonds, became part of assembly-line teams and drove tractors. And all this was quite apart from the really titanic efforts that were required to battle plain ordinary illiteracy and teach Hebrew.

Then there were the new towns that began to mushroom in those years all over Israel. They didn't all live up to the promise of the drawing board, and some of them failed altogether; but some of them sprouted and bloomed and did great credit to both their planners and their inhabitants, and in all of them the building was carried out mostly by

the government. One of those new towns was Kiryat
Shmonah in the extreme north, the Upper Galilee,
which always held a special appeal for me, perhaps because
it was located in such breathtaking surroundings or because
I was so sure from the start that despite all the obstacles,
Kiryat Shmonah would make it. Anyhow, my connection
with it from 1949 on was never merely formal.

It began life as a transit camp, a *ma'abara* made up of
tin huts and bewildered immigrants who had been taken
there directly from the planes or ships and who didn't
really know where they were or why they were there. It
was a very far cry from the enticements of Tel Aviv. There
were no towns in the vicinity at all, just a few kibbutzim
with their fields and orchards, and the nearby swamps of
the Huleh Valley that we were just starting to reclaim. But
the government had decided to found an urban center there
that would be the dynamic core of a newly populated region, and we sat for weeks poring over maps and blueprints
and trying to anticipate the needs of the future. The *ma'a-
bara* was replaced by the rudiments of a town. Schools, a
community center, light industry, even a swimming pool
were built in Kiryat Shmonah, and everything was planned
down to the last nail—except the reaction of the new immigrants to life there. Yes, the scenery was wonderful, and,
yes, the climate was bracing, and yes, the spick-and-span
new houses were fine, they told me; but it was very lonely,
and there weren't enough jobs for everyone. The European
Jews said that we had dumped them down in the middle of
nowhere, and the "Oriental" Jews made it clear that we
were forcing new ways on them too quickly, disrupting
their mode of life and treating them like second-class citizens.

There was a constant turnover of population, and
each time I went to Kiryat Shmonah I listened to the complaints and saw the discontent and came back to Jerusalem
with a list of new suggestions, which there usually wasn't
enough money to implement. It broke my heart to see
houses that we had built with such difficulty sitting there
empty. But we increased the subsidies, and new batches of
immigrants came—and most of these stayed. They stayed
even when, after the Six-Day War, Kiryat Shmonah was
picked as a favorite target for the rockets of Arab terrorists
operating across the Lebanese border, and even much more

recently, when the terrorists entered and killed people in the town itself. Whenever I can, I go back to Kiryat Shmonah to sit in the city square with some of the old hands and exchange stories with them about the days when they and I thought that the town might never develop. Not that I don't still come back with a list of new suggestions or that even today there is enough money for everything that should be done there.

Something else may come as a surprise to certain of Israel's "constructive critics," particularly those of the so-called New Left: Along with all the rest of the building and settlement we did in those hectic seven years, we also built for the Arabs, because when *we* talked about the citizens of Israel, we meant all the citizens of Israel. Whenever I had arguments with local people in Kiryat Shmonah and similar places, there was always someone in the crowd who shouted that the Arabs were better off. It wasn't true, of course, but it is equally untrue—and far more wicked—to claim that we ignored the Arabs altogether. The truth is that we used the houses of those Arabs who ran away from the country in 1948 for new immigrant housing whenever we could, although the properties remained under the supervision of a special custodian. At the same time we allocated more than 10,000,000 pounds for new Arab housing and rehoused hundreds of Arabs who remained in Israel but were displaced as a result of the fighting. There was such an outcry about the way we used absentee property— as though there were a better way to use it—that in 1953 we passed a Land Acquisition Law under which at least two-thirds of all the Arabs who put in claims were paid compensation, given back their property or given other property in its place—and none of them was asked to take a loyalty oath before his claim was honored.

Whenever I read or hear about the Arabs whom we allegedly dealt with so brutally, my blood boils. In April, 1948, I myself stood on the beach in Haifa for hours and literally beseeched the Arabs of that city not to leave. Moreover, it was a scene that I am not likely to forget. The Haganah had just taken over Haifa, and the Arabs were starting to run away—because their leadership had so eloquently assured them that this was the wisest course for them to take and the British had so generously put dozens of trucks at their disposal. Nothing that the Haganah said or tried did any good—neither the pleas made via loud-speakers mounted on vans nor the leaflets we rained down on the Arab sections of the town ("Do not fear!" They read in Arabic and Hebrew. "By moving out, you will bring poverty and humiliation upon yourselves. Remain in the city which is both yours and ours"). They were signed by the Jewish Workers' Council of Haifa. To quote the British general, Sir Hugh Stockwell, who was in command of the troops then, "The Arab leaders left first, and no one did anything to halt what began as a rush and then became a panic." They were determined to go. Hundreds drove across the border, but some went to the seashore to wait for boats. Ben-Gurion called me in and said, "I want you to go to Haifa at once and see to it that the Arabs who remain in Haifa are treated properly. I also want you to try to persuade those Arabs on the beach to come back. You must get it into their heads that they have nothing to fear." So I went immediately. I sat there on the beach, and I begged them to return to their homes. But they had only one answer: "We know that there is nothing to fear, but we have to go. We'll be back." I was sure that they went, not because they were frightened of us, but because they were terrified of being considered traitors to the Arab "cause." At all events, I talked myself blue in the face, and it didn't help.

Why did we want them to stay? There were two very good reasons: First of all, we wanted to prove to the world that Jews and Arabs could live together—regardless of what the Arab leadership was trumpeting—and secondly, we knew perfectly well that if half a million Arabs left Palestine at that point, it would create a major economic upheaval in the country. This brings me to another issue with which I might just as well deal now. I should very much like, once and for all, to reply to the question of how many Palestinian Arbas did, in fact, leave their homes in 1947 and 1948. The answer is: at the very utmost, about 590,-000. Of these, some 30,000 left right after the November, 1947, UN partition resolution; another 200,000 left in the course of that winter and the spring of 1948 (including the vast majority of the 62,000 Arabs of Haifa); and after the establishment of the state in May, 1948, and the Arab invasion of Israel, yet another 300,000 Arabs fled. It was very tragic indeed, and it had very tragic consequences; but at least let everyone be clear about the facts as they were—and still are. The Arab assertion that there are "millions" of "Palestinian refugees" is as dishonest as the claim that we made the Arabs leave their homes. The "Palestinian refugees" were created as a *result* of the Arab desire (and attempt) to destroy Israel. They were not the *cause* of it. Of course, there were some Jews in the *yishuv* who said, even in 1948, that the Arab exodus was the best thing that could have happened to Israel, but I know of no serious Israeli who ever felt that way.

Those Arabs who stayed in Israel, however, had an easier life than those who left. There was hardly an Arab village with electricity or running water in all Palestine before 1948, and within twenty years there was hardly an Arab village in Israel that wasn't connected to the national electric grid or a home without running water. I spent a lot of time in those villages when I was minister of labor, and I felt as delighted with what we were doing for them as I was when the *ma'abarot* disappeared. Hearsay and propaganda are one thing; facts are another. It was I—and not members of the New Left—who as minister of labor opened roads and visited new housing units in Arab villages all over Israel. One of my favorite recollections of that era, by the way, is of the village in Lower Galilee that needed a road because it was on a hill, while the village well was below, and carrying water uphill was no joke. So we built the road, and when it was done, there was a celebration with refreshments, speeches and flags. Then, all of a sudden, a young woman got up to speak—which is not customary among Arabs. She looked very pretty, in a long purple dress, and made a very charming speech. "We want to thank the Ministry of Labor and the minister for easing the burden of the feet of our men," she said. "But now we would like to ask the minister if she could ease the burden also of the heads of our women." She put it poetically, but what she meant was that she wanted running water so that she needn't carry those heavy jars on her head anymore, even on the new road. So, a year later, I went to another celebration there, and this time I turned on tens of taps!

It was during that time that I almost lost my job as minister of labor. In 1955 elections were coming up. Mapai was very anxious to have a laborite mayor in Tel Aviv, and Ben-Gurion decided that I was the only candidate who had a chance. I wasn't very pleased because I didn't want to give up the ministry, but since that was the party's decision, I felt I had no choice. "You must understand, though, that it will mean leaving the cabinet," I said to Ben-Gurion.

"That is out of the question," he retorted. "We'll make you a minister without portfolio."

"No," I said. "If I am going to be mayor, then I'm going to be a full-time mayor."

He was very angry, but, fortunately for me, we didn't get a majority on the Tel Aviv Council. And since my election by the council depended on the votes of two men belonging to the religious bloc, one of whom refused to vote for a woman, I didn't become a mayor and went on with the Ministry of Labor—which, I devoutly hoped, I would be allowed to do for many years more.

Although, personally, I was very relieved, I was enraged by the fact that the religious bloc had managed—at the last minute—to exploit the fact that I was a woman, as if the women of Israel hadn't done their full share—and more—in the building of the Jewish state. There wasn't a settlement in the Negev or the Galilee that hadn't, from its first days, included women. And it wasn't as if the representatives of the religious bloc weren't at that very minute sitting together with women in the Knesset, just as they had accepted the presence of women in the Jewish Agency and the Va'ad Le'umi. To have objected to my being mayor of Tel Aviv because I was a woman was a political tactic for which I had great contempt, and I said so without mincing any words.

The religious question—by which I mean the extent to which the clerical parties had their way—flared up sporadically all through the 1950s. We were determined not to be drawn (if it could be avoided) into open conflict with the religious bloc because we had troubles enough without that particular headache. Nonetheless, every now and then there were explosions which brought cabinet crises in their wake. Suffice it to say that no easy way was ever found of getting around the place of religion in the Jewish state. It bedeviled us then, and to some degree it bedevils us now.

One of the jokes which Israelis told in those days was about the man who said with a sigh, "Two thousand years we waited for a Jewish state, and it had to happen to me!" I think that all of us probably felt that way—though very fleetingly—at one time or another during those first years of statehood. At all events, since nothing in Israel ever stays static, in 1956 Ben-Gurion had a new plan for me.

10. The Right to Exist

Before I go on to tell about that plan and what became of me, I must explain that it was while I was minister of labor that Ben-Gurion—physically and spiritually worn out—decided to resign as prime minister and minister of defense. The past twenty years had utterly exhausted him, and he asked for a two-year leave of absence. He needed a change of scene, and he was going off to a small Negev kibbutz, Sdeh Boker, not far from Beersheba. There, he told us, he would live as a pioneer again, devoting himself to reclaiming the wilderness as a member of a collective settlement. It was like a thunderclap. We begged him not to go. It was far too soon; the state was only five years old; the ingathering of the exiles was far from completed; Israel's neighbors were still at war with her. It was no time for Ben-Gurion to desert the country that had looked to him for guidance and inspiration for so many years—or us. It was inconceivable that he should leave. But he was determined to go, and nothing we said had any effect on him. Moshe Sharett, retaining the portfolio of foreign affairs, became Israel's prime minister, and in January, 1954, Ben-Gurion went off to Sdeh Boker (where he stayed until 1955, when he returned to public life first as minister of defense and then as prime minister, while Sharett went back to being a full-time foreign minister).

As prime minister Sharett was the same intelligent, cautious, man he had been before. I must admit that although the leadership of Mapai had tremendous respect and affection for him—most of us were fonder of Sharett than of Ben-Gurion—whenever there was a really difficult problem to be solved, it was to Ben-Gurion that people still turned for advice—and that included Sharett himself. There was a steady stream of visits and correspondence to Sdeh Boker—which became one of the most famous places in

Israel overnight—and although Ben-Gurion liked to think of himself as a simple philosopher-shepherd who tended the kibbutz sheep for half the day and spent the other half reading and writing, he still kept his hand very near, if not actually on, the helm of the ship of state. That, I think, was inevitable under the circumstances, but what made for trouble was that Ben-Gurion and Sharett never really got on together, despite all the years of their partnership. They were too different in their basic personalities, although they were both ardent socialists and ardent Zionists.

Ben-Gurion was an activist, a man who believed in doing rather than explaining and who was convinced that what really mattered in the end—and what would always really matter—was what the Israelis did and how they did it, not what the world outside Israel thought or said about them. The first question he asked himself—and us—about almost any issue that came up in those days was: "Is it good for the state?" And what he meant was: *"In the long run,* is it good for the state?" Ultimately, history would judge Israel on the record of its deeds, not its statements or its diplomacy and certainly not on the number of favorable editorials that appeared in the international press. Being liked or not—or even being approved of or not—was not the kind of thing that interested Ben-Gurion. He thought in terms of sovereignty, security, consolidation and real progress, and he regarded world opinion, or even public opinion, as relatively unimportant compared to these.

Sharett, on the other hand, was immensely concerned with the way in which policymakers elsewhere reacted to Israel and what was likely to make the Jewish state look "good" in the eyes of other foreign ministers or the United Nations. Israel's image and the verdict of his own contemporaries—rather than history or future historians—were the criteria he tended to use most often. And what he really wanted most for Israel, I think, was for it to be viewed as a progressive, moderate, civilized European country of whose behavior no Israeli, least of all himself, ever need be ashamed.

Luckily, for many years, until the 1950s in fact, the two worked together very well. Sharett was a born diplomat and negotiator. Ben-Gurion was a born national leader and fighter. And the Zionist movement in general, as well as the labor movement in particular, benefited tremendously from their combined talents and even, I would say, from their very different temperaments and attitudes. They weren't similar, and they weren't really friends; but they did complement each other, and of course, they did share the same fundamental aims. But after the establishment of the state their basic incompatibility grew—or maybe it simply became more obvious and more significant. At all events, when Ben-Gurion came back from Sdeh Boker in 1955 (for reasons which I shall go into a little later on), the tension and disagreements grew to such a point that they became intolerable.

One major area of conflict between them then was the question of Israeli retaliation for terrorist activities. Sharett was just as convinced as Ben-Gurion that the incessant incursions across our frontiers by gangs of Arab infiltrators had to end, but they disagreed sharply on the method that should be used. Sharett did not rule out retaliation. But he believed more strongly than most of us did that the most effective way of dealing with this very acute situation was by continuing to put maximum pressure on the powers-that-be so that they, in turn, would put maximum pressure on the Arab states to stop aiding and abetting the infiltrators. Well-worded protests to the United Nations, skillful and informed diplomatic notes and clear, repeated presentation of our case to the world would, he was sure, eventually succeed, whereas armed reprisals by Israel could only result in a storm of criticism and make our international position even less comfortable than it was. He was 100 percent right about the criticism. It was more than just a storm; it was a tornado. Whenever the Israel Defense Forces retaliated against the infiltrators—and sometimes, unavoidably, innocent Arabs were wounded or killed along with the guilty—Israel was promptly and very severely censured for "atrocities."

But Ben-Gurion still saw his primary responsibility, not to the statesmen of the West or to the world tribunal, but to the ordinary citizens who lived in the Israeli settlements that were under constant Arab attack. The duty of the government of any state, he believed, was first and foremost to defend itself and to protect its citizens—regardless of how negative the reaction abroad might be to this protection. There was also another consideration of great importance to Ben-Gurion: The citizens of Israel—that conglomeration of people, languages and cultures—had to be taught that the government, and *only* the government, was responsible for their security. It would obviously have been much simpler to have permitted the formation of a number of anti-terrorist vigilante groups, shut an official eye to private acts of retaliation and vengeance and then loudly disclaim all responsibility for the resultant "incidents." But that was not our way. The hand extended in peace to the Arabs would remain extended, but at the same time the children of Israeli farmers in border villages were entitled to sleep safely in their beds at night. And if the only way of accomplishing this were to hit back mercilessly at the camps of the Arab gangs, then that would have to be done.

By 1955 dozens of such Israeli punitive raids had been carried out, all of them in answer to our growing death toll, the mining of our roads and the ambushing of our traffic. They didn't end the terror; but they did put a very high price on the lives of our settlers, and they did teach the Israelis that they could rely on their own forces. In fact, they underlined, at least for the new half of the population, the real difference between living in a country on sufferance and living in a country that belonged to one. But unfortunately, they also served to widen the breach between Ben-Gurion and Sharett, who continued to disapprove of some of the reprisals.

After a while Ben-Gurion stopped calling Sharett by his first name and began to talk to him as though he were a stranger. Sharett was terribly hurt by Ben-Gurion's coldness. He never said anything about it in public, although he would sit at home at night and fill the pages of his diary with furious analyses of Ben-Gurion's character and maltreatment of him. In 1956 it so happened that Mapai was looking for a new secretary-general. Ben-Gurion decided that this would be an ideal job for me, and he asked me what I thought about it, suggesting that we meet with some of our colleagues at his Jerusalem home to talk about the idea. Not everybody was equally enthusiastic; but although it meant that I would have to part from the cabinet and the labor ministry, I was prepared to leave the decision up to the party, and I listened with great interest to the ensuing discussion. I certainly didn't want to turn my ministry over to anyone else, but on the other hand, I was extremely concerned about the future of Mapai (which had suffered in the July, 1955, elections). I thought that its membership should—and, what's more, could—be substantially broadened, and that the threat to Mapai—both from the extreme left and the extreme right—could be overcome provided that an intensified effort was made on the part of the Mapai leadership which tended, not unnaturally I suppose, to rely on Ben-Gurion to do much of its work for it. All of a sudden I heard Sharett say, jokingly, "Well, maybe *I* should become the secretary-general of the party." Everyone laughed—except Ben-Gurion, who jumped at Sharett's little joke. I don't think he would ever have brought himself to ask Sharett to leave the cabinet; but here the opportunity had unexpectedly presented itself, and Ben-Gurion was certainly never one to ignore opportunities.

"Marvelous," he said at once. "A wonderful idea! It will save Mapai." The rest of us were a bit taken aback and embarrassed, but on second thought, it did seem like a very good idea to the party, too. Cabinet meetings were increasingly turning into open disputes on policy between Ben-Gurion and Sharett, and although it wasn't an elegant solution, it was—or at least it looked like—a way of lessening the growing strain, on all of us, created by the perpetual wrangling between the two men. "Don't *you* think it is a good idea for Moshe to become secretary of the party?" Ben-Gurion asked me a day or two later.

"But who will be foreign minister?" I wanted to know.

"You," he said calmly.

I couldn't believe my ears. It had never occurred to me, even as the remotest possibility, and I wasn't at all sure that I could or wanted to cope with it. In fact, I was only sure of one thing: I didn't want to leave the Ministry of Labor, and I told this to Ben-Gurion. I also told him that I didn't want to step into Sharett's shoes in this manner. But Ben-Gurion wouldn't listen to my objections. "That's that," he said—and it was.

Sharett was very bitter. I think he always imagined that had I refused to take over his beloved Foreign Ministry, Ben-Gurion would have acquiesced in his staying on indefinitely. But he was wrong. The tension between Ben-Gurion and Sharett would have never merely blown over; it was far too late for that, although Sharett didn't seem to realize this for a long time. It was only when two very close friends of his, Zalman Aranne and Pinchas Sapir, told him in so many words that unless he resigned from the cabinet, Ben-Gurion might bid us all farewell once more that Sharett gave in. Levi Eshkol once said, "As prime minister Ben-Gurion is worth at least three army divisions to Israel." And in a way, it is as good a measure as any of Ben-Gurion's prestige and personal strength at that time that Sharett, too, agreed with his assessment. Of course, later on some of Ben-Gurion's opponents charged him with having rid himself of Sharett so that he could go ahead and plan the Sinai Campaign without being burdened by Sharett's lack of sympathy for it, but I myself am sure that there was no such "plot." The story of their relationship didn't end then. Sharett removed himself from public life for a while and later became the chairman of the Jewish Agency. In 1960, when the so-called Lavon Affair exploded, Sharett—already stricken by the illness that was to kill him in 1965—became one of the most outspoken critics of Ben-Gurion's refusal to let the "affair" die a natural death.

As a matter of fact, since I've raised the subject of the Lavon Affair, I might as well go into it now, although I hardly intend to write an exhaustive tract on it. The original issue dated back to a security blunder related to an espionage mission in Egypt in 1954 (disastrous in its very conception, to say nothing of its execution). That was at the time when Sharett was prime minister and foreign minister. The new minister of defense, who had been hand-picked by Ben-Gurion himself, was Pinchas Lavon, one of the most capable, if least stable, members of Mapai, a handsome, complicated intellectual who had always been a great dove, but who turned into the most ferocious sort of hawk as soon as he began to concern himself with military matters. Many of us thought that he was extremely unsuitable for that very sensitive ministry. He had neither the necessary experience nor, we thought, the necessary powers of judgment. Not only I but Zalman Aranne, Shaul Avigur and various other colleagues had tried—in vain—to argue Ben-Gurion out of his choice of successor. As usual, he wouldn't change his mind. He went off to Sdeh Boker, and Lavon took over the defense ministry. But he couldn't get along with the bright young men who had been Ben-Gurion's most devoted disciples—among them Moshe Dayan, who was Israel's chief of staff then, and Shimon

Peres, who was director general of the Defense Ministry. They neither liked nor trusted Lavon, and they made this quite clear to him, while he, for his part, made it equally clear that he was not going to live in Ben-Gurion's shadow and that he was going to make his own mark. So the seeds of trouble were already sown.

When the security blunder, which was the start of the whole affair, occurred, a committee was appointed to look into its whys and wherefores. I am not free to go into any details about the actual mishap, nor do I want to. It is enough, I think, to say that Lavon claimed to have known nothing at all about the operation and accused the head of intelligence of having planned it behind his back. The committee didn't come up with any really conclusive findings one way or the other, but it also did not fully absolve Lavon of responsibility for what had happened. At all events, the public was unaware of the entire top-secret episode, and the few people who did know about it assumed that it was now a closed chapter. Nonetheless—and regardless of who was to blame—a terrible mistake had been made. Lavon had no alternative other than to resign, and Ben-Gurion was summoned back to the Defense Ministry from Sdeh Boker.

Then, six years later, the whole thing flared up again— and this time it turned into a major political scandal with the most tragic aftereffects inside Mapai itself. It upset and confused the Israeli public for months, and it led, indirectly, to my own break with Ben-Gurion and to his second and final resignation as prime minister. In 1960 Lavon claimed that false evidence had been given at the initial inquiry and even that documents had been forged. Lavon therefore demanded that Ben-Gurion publicly clear his name. Ben-Gurion refused; he had not accused Lavon of anything, he said, and therefore he couldn't acquit him. That would have to be done by a court of law. A committee was formed at once to inquire into the conduct of the army officers whom Lavon had charged with conspiring against him. But before it could complete its work, Lavon had brought the entire matter to the attention of an important Knesset committee, and it eventually reached the press.

The rest of the Lavon–Ben-Gurion battle was fought out largely in public. Levi Eshkol, characteristically, undertook to try to calm everyone concerned, but Ben-Gurion was adamant about the need for a juridical inquiry. He was evidently quite prepared to injure his closest colleagues and the party he led in order to solve the problem in the only way he believed was right—and to prevent anyone from casting any aspersions either on the army or on the Defense Ministry. He went on demanding legal procedures, while Eshkol, Sapir and I tried to get the conflict resolved at the cabinet level—decently and discreetly. Seven ministers were appointed to a special committee of investigation, and we all were thankful that Ben-Gurion raised no objection to this. But in due course the ministerial committee, which Ben-Gurion hoped would back him in his demand for legal proceedings, announced that nothing further need be done: Lavon had not been responsible for giving the order that led to the blunder, and there was no need to go on pursuing the matter. Ben-Gurion was furious and argued that if the committee was sure that Lavon had not given the order, then the blame could only fall on the head of military intelligence. Since, however, there was no proof of this, only a judicial committee could decide who had been responsible. Furthermore, he said the ministerial committee had behaved most improperly. It had not done what it was supposed to do, it had covered up for Lavon, and generally, it was a disgrace. In January, 1961, Ben-Gurion resigned again, Levi Eshkol became prime minister at Ben-Gurion's suggestion, and Ben-Gurion started up his campaign for a judicial inquiry all over again. But Eshkol had had enough of the Lavon Affair. He rejected the idea. Ben-Gurion was like a man possessed. He had counted on Eshkol to obey him, and Eshkol had refused. So now poor Eshkol and all his supporters within the party became the prime targets of Ben-Gurion's fury.

I couldn't forgive Ben-Gurion either for the ruthless way in which he was pursing Eshkol or for the way in which he treated and spoke about the rest of us, myself included. It was as though all the years that we had worked together counted for nothing. In Ben-Gurion's eyes we had turned into personal enemies, and that was how he behaved toward us. We didn't see each other for years after that. I even thought that feeling as I did, it wouldn't be right for me to attend Ben-Gurion's eightieth birthday party in 1969 (from which Eshkol had been excluded), though

Ben-Gurion had sent a special emissary to invite me. I knew that it would hurt him very much if I refused, but I just couldn't say yes. He had injured all of us too badly, and I couldn't get over it. If we were really as stupid as he had said we were, well, when people are born stupid, not much can be done about it, and it isn't anyone's fault. But no one is born corrupt, and that is a terrible accusation! If other party leaders were willing to overlook the fact that Ben-Gurion thought, or at any rate said, that they were corrupt, well and good. Eshkol wasn't and neither was I. I couldn't pretend that it never happened. I couldn't rewrite history, and I wouldn't lie to myself. I didn't go to that birthday party.

In 1969, when I presented my first cabinet to the Knesset, Ben-Gurion—who in the meantime had broken away from Mapai to form Rafi (the Israel Workers List) together with Dayan and Peres—abstained from voting. But he did make a statement. "There is no doubt at all," he told the Knesset, "that Golda Meir is capable of being a prime minister. But it must never be forgotten that she lent her hand to something immoral." And he went on and on again about the Lavon Affair. Toward the end of his life, however, we made up. I went down to Sdeh Boker on his eighty-fifth birthday, and though we didn't have a formal reconciliation, we were friends again. He, in turn, made a point of coming to Revivim when Sarah's kibbutz gave me a seventy-fifth birthday party in 1973. Of course, by then Ben-Gurion wasn't really Ben-Gurion anymore. Still, we had at least repaired that awful and unnecessary breach—for which I have no adequate explanation to this day. That, in a very small nutshell indeed, was the Lavon Affair, the first installment of which was already behind us in 1956, when I became Israel's second foreign minister.

Although it is customary for the formal handing over of a ministry to be performed by the outgoing minister in the presence of the incoming one, Sharett took leave of his ministry differently. He went there alone, called in the heads of departments and said good-bye to them. Then he asked me to come see him, and for three days he briefed me about as thoroughly as I have ever been briefed on anything by anybody. It was typical of Sharett that he knew everything down to the last detail about the ministry, including the name, family status and personal problems of everyone who worked there. He even knew the names of all their children. But he said he was not going to accompany me to the ministry on my first day. I would have to go there alone. So one day I made my appearance at the Foreign Ministry all by myself, feeling and probably looking miserable and fully aware of the fact that I was succeeding a man who not only had founded the ministry but had headed it ever since 1948.

My first few months as foreign minister were not much happier. It wasn't only that I was a novice among experts. It was also that Sharett's style was so different from mine, and the kind of people he had chosen to work with him—though they were all remarkably competent and genuinely dedicated—were not necessarily the kind of people with whom I was accustomed to work. Many of the more senior ambassadors and officials had been educated at British universities, and their particular brand of intellectual sophistication, which Sharett admired so much, was not always my cup of tea. Nor, to be honest, could I have any illusions about the fact that some of them obviously didn't think I was the right person for the job. I was certainly not known either for my subtle phraseology or for my great concern with protocol, and seven years at the Ministry of Labor wasn't their idea of the most suitable background for a foreign minister. But after a while we all got used to each other, and I must say that on the whole we worked very well together, perhaps because there was always so much at stake.

I had entered the Foreign Ministry in the summer of 1956, when the activities of the Arab terrorists—especially of the fedayeen (the bands of armed raiders supported and trained by Egypt)—had reached an intolerable peak. The fedayeen operated mainly from the Gaza Strip; but they also had bases in Jordan, Syria and Lebanon, and Jews were being killed by them right in the center of Israel, in such places as Rehobot, Lydda, Ramle and Jaffa. The Arab states had long ago explained their position. "We are exercising a right of war," an Egyptian representative had said in 1951 in defense of Egypt's refusal to let Israeli ships go through the Suez Canal. "An armistice does not put an end to a state of war. It does not prohibit a country from exercising certain rights of war." That these "rights" were still being fully upheld in 1955 and 1956 we knew all too well.

Colonel Gamal Abdel Nasser, who had to come to power in Egypt in 1952 and was now the most powerful figure in the Arab world, openly applauded the fedayeen. "You have proven," he told them, "that you are heroes upon whom our entire country can depend. The spirit with which you enter the land of the enemy must be spread." Cairo Radio also praised the murderers endlessly in language that was crystal clear. "Weep, oh Israel," was one refrain, "the day of extermination draws near."

The United Nations did nothing effective to put a halt to the fedayeen outrages. The UN secretary-general, Dag Hammarskjöld, did succeed in arranging a cease-fire that lasted for a few days in the spring of 1956, but when the fedayeen went back to crossing the border, he let it go at that and didn't return to the Middle East. I know that today a small cult has grown up around the personality and fine perceptions of Mr. Hammarskjöld, but I am not a party to it. I used to meet with him often, after he had seen Ben-Gurion and talked to him for an hour or two about Buddhism and other philosophical topics, in which they had a common interest. Then he and I would discuss such commonplace subjects as a clause in the armistice agreement with Jordan that was being contravened or some complaint we had against the United Nations. No wonder Hammarskjöld thought that Ben-Gurion was an angel and that I was impossible to get along with. I never considered him a friend of Israel, and although I tried hard not to show it, I expect he sensed my feeling that he was less than neutral as far as the situation in the Middle East was concerned. If the Arabs said no to something—which they did all the time—Hammarskjöld never went any further. Not that U Thant (the Burmese statesman who followed him at the United Nations) was a great improvement. Despite all the years of Burmese-Israeli friendship and his own really warm personal relationship with the country and with us, the moment that U Thant became secretary-general we were in for a very hard time. He also found it absolutely impossible, apparently, to be firm either with the Russians or with the Arabs, though he had no trouble at all being exceedingly firm with Israel.

But that is all by the way. Certainly it was not the UN secretary-general who was responsible for the almost daily murder, robbery and sabotage carried out by the fedayeen.

In one of those attacks a group of archaeologists working in Ramat Rachel near Jerusalem was fired upon from the Jordanian border. Four people were killed, and many others wounded. One of the four was part of my family. He was Menachem's father-in-law, Aya's father, a distinguished and gentle scholar who had never harmed anyone in his whole life, and I remember thinking to myself bitterly that there was something crazy about a world that calmly accepted the concept of "rights of war" but was so indifferent about the "rights of peace." But the real responsibility lay—not for the last time—with the Russians.

In 1955 an agreement was concluded between Czechoslovakia (read the Soviet Union) and Egypt as a result of which Egypt was receiving an almost unending supply of arms, ranging from submarines and destroyers to tanks and troop carriers. It may well be asked how it happened that the Soviet Union suddenly decided to arm a state that was making no bones whatsoever about its intention of "reconquering Palestine," as Colonel Nasser put it. The answer is that it was not really sudden at all. In the global struggle of the 1950s, known (not very accurately as far as we were concerned) as the cold war, both the United States and the Soviet Union were busy outbidding each other for the favors of the Arab states, especially those of Egypt. The United States and Britain may have felt a little uneasy about their courtship of Nasser's Egypt, but the Soviet Union had no qualms at all. The fact that the USSR was making possible the fulfillment of the Egyptian dream of a second round of war against Israel was justified—to the extent that the Russians ever feel that they have to justify themselves—on the grounds that Zionism, which was such an evil thing, had to be suppressed everywhere. And to prove how evil it was, the so-called Doctors' Plot was invented in Moscow in 1953. The Russian people were informed that nine doctors (no less than six of whom were Jewish) had tried to murder Stalin, as well as a number of other Soviet leaders, and an infamous trial was staged as part of an anti-Jewish campaign set in motion throughout the Soviet Union.

Then, one night, a small bomb exploded in the garden of the Soviet legation in Tel Aviv. The Russians at once accused the government of Israel of having engineered the incident and broke off diplomatic relations. But even when diplomatic relations were renewed a few months later, the anti-Semitic propaganda campaign in the USSR, with its constant references to Zionism, went on, and the chant about the "Zionist stooges of imperialist warmongers" was taken up in Czechoslovakia, which mounted its own despicable campaign against the Jews.

Despite all this—and the unconcealed Soviet-Arab preparations for another war—the United States and Britain refused to sell us arms. It didn't matter how often or how loudly we knocked on their doors. The answer was always negative, although at the very beginning of 1956 the United States—still refusing to sell us arms—indicated to France and Canada that it didn't mind if *they* did so. But France hadn't waited for U.S. permission. For its own reasons, it had decided to come to Israel's aid, and while there was no possibility of matching the boundless Soviet "generosity" to Egypt, we were now at least no longer totally defenseless nor alone.

In the summer of 1956, just as I was settling into my new office and getting used, among other things, to being called Mrs. Meir—the closest I could get to a Hebrew version of Meyerson and still obey Ben-Gurion's order that I take a Hebrew name (Meir means illuminate in Hebrew)—the noose tightened a bit more around our necks. Nasser made his most dramatic gesture. In July he nationalized the Suez Canal! No Arab leader had ever done anything so spectacular before, and the Arab world was profoundly impressed. There was, indeed, only one more thing that Nasser needed to do in order for the Egypt he ruled to be acclaimed as the supreme Moslem power, and that was to annihilate us. Elsewhere in the world, the nationalization of the Canal was anxiously discussed in terms of big-power politics, but we in Israel were more worried about the increase in the military strength of Egypt and Syria, which had signed a pact to unite their high commands. There was no longer any doubt that war was inevitable and that the Egyptians had once again fallen prey to a fantasy of victory over Israel—a self-glorifying fantasy, incidentally, which Nasser himself had developed in his *Philosophy of a Revolution*.

There is already so much literature (some of it fact and some of it fiction) about the Sinai Campaign that I think my own contribution can be quite modest. But I must stress one fact: Regardless of the abortive French and British attempt to seize the Suez Canal, Israel's own strike against the Egyptians in 1956 had one goal and one goal only—to prevent the destruction of the Jewish state. The threat was unmistakable. As I later said at the UN General Assembly, "Even if no one else chose to do so, *we* recognized the symptoms." We knew that dictatorships—including those given disarmingly to informing the world of their plans—usually keep their promises, and no one in Israel had forgotten the lesson of the crematoria or what total extermination really meant. Unless we were prepared to be killed off, either piecemeal or in one sudden attack, we had to take the initiative, although God knows, it was not an easy decision to make. Nonetheless, it was made. We began secretly to plan the Sinai Campaign (known in Israel as Operation Kadesh).

The French offered us arms and began making their own secret plans for the joint Anglo-French assault on the Suez Canal. In September they invited Ben-Gurion to send a delegation to France for talks with Guy Mollet (who headed the French socialist government), Christian Pineau, (the French foreign minister) and Maurice Bourges-Manoury (the French minister of defense), and he asked me, as Israel's foreign minister, to join the group. It included Moshe Dayan, Shimon Peres and Moshe Carmel (our minister of transport, who had served with great distinction as a brigadier general during the War of Independence). Needless to say, I couldn't even hint to Sarah that I was going abroad. As a matter of fact, you could count on the fingers of one hand the number of people, other than those who were actually traveling, who knew anything about the whole idea at that stage. It was a truly watertight secret. Even the cabinet was told about the interaction with th French and British and decided on the details of the campaign only a few days before it started, on Monday, October 29, and the opposition leaders were informed by Ben-Gurion even later than the new cabinet. Everybody, in short, was taken by surprise—not only Nasser!

We flew to France from a secret airfield in a rickety old French army plane that was very badly lit. We were all very silent and, of course, tense. And no one's frame of mind was helped much when Moshe Carmel, while walking through the plane, almost fell out of the bomb bay, which was not properly closed. Fortunately, he managed to pull himself back into the plane, breaking three ribs in the process!

Our first stop was in North Africa, where we were put up at a very pleasant French guesthouse and given a marvelous meal. Our hosts had no idea of our identity, and I remember how astonished they were when they discovered that the mysterious mission included a woman. Anyhow, we flew on from there to a military airfield outside Paris and to our meetings with the French. I didn't even venture into Paris, and I remember being furious with Dayan, who did—although luckily, no one recognized him. The main point of those talks was to work out various details of the military aid the French had promised us, especially the essential French undertaking to protect our skies, should we request it. But this was only the first of a series of such conferences, one of which was attended by Ben-Gurion himself.

On October 24, in total secrecy, we began to mobilize our reserves. The public—and, by the same token, I suppose, Egyptian intelligence—was given the impression that because Iraqi troops had ominously moved into Jordan (which had recently joined the United Egyptian-Syrian command), we were preparing for an assault against that country, and our troops massing on the Jordanian border helped lend authenticity to the rumor. A week before the Sinai Campaign was to start, a conference of Israeli ambassadors took place at the Foreign Ministry, partly so that I could meet with some of our more important representatives abroad before the UN General Assembly convened. They went back to their respective posts four days before the war broke out not knowing anything about it. Sharett, who had gone to India as soon as I took over at the ministry, was actually talking to Nehru when they got word that the Sinai Campaign had begun, and Nehru couldn't believe that his guest knew nothing about it. But total secrecy was vital.

Every now and then during the last week or two before the campaign began, working at the Foreign Ministry or trying to get organized in the foreign minister's residence (to which I had moved in the summer), I found myself longing to talk to someone about what I knew was going to happen on October 29. There is nothing lonelier or less natural for a human being than to have to keep a secret that affects the lives of everyone around her, and one can only do it, I think, by an enormous, almost superhuman effort. Wherever I went and whatever I did, I was never, for one instant, unaware of the fact that within a few days we would be at war. I had no doubt that we would be victorious, but however great our victory might be, there would still be great suffering and danger I used to look at the young men in the Foreign Ministry or at the boy who delivered my newspapers or at the builders working across the street from my home and wonder what would happen to them when the war started. It was not at all a good feeling, but there was no other way for us to get rid of the fedayeen or force the Egyptians to understand that Israel was not expendable. I spent the last weekend during that long, hot October with Sarah, Zechariah and the children at Revivim. Shaul was six months old then, a beautiful baby whom I had hardly seen since he was born. I tried not to think about the war on my way to the kibbutz, but it was impossible. If something went wrong, it was through the Negev and through Revivim itself that the Egyptian army would smash its way into Israel, bent on destruction. I played with the children, sat with Sarah and Zechariah in the shade of the young trees of which Revivim was so proud, spent an evening with friends of theirs (and mine), talking, as Israelis always do, about the "situation"—which means, whatever the year, the current danger to Israel's survival. And all the time I thought to myself: "Must we really go on like this forever, worrying about children and grandchildren and fighting, killing and being killed?" But I couldn't even warn them of what was ahead.

Just before I left Revivim to return to Jerusalem, a young man came up to me. I knew his face (he was one of the old-timers in the kibbutz), but I couldn't recall his name. He introduced himself to me, explained that he was in charge of security at Revivim and said that he already knew that something was about to happen. He didn't use the word "mobilization," but we understood each other perfectly. "I know that you can't tell me anything," he said very apologetically, "and that I ought not even ask you this. But should we start to dig trenches?"

I looked around at the little kibbutz, so exposed and vulnerable in the middle of the Negev, and into the grave eyes of the young man. "I think perhaps I would if I were you," I replied, and got into my car. All the way back to Jerusalem I saw signs of the call up that was already under way by word of mouth, telegram and telephone; at almost every bus stop men in civilian clothes were lining up for buses to take them to their units.

The Sinai Campaign began as scheduled after sunset on October 29 and ended as scheduled on November 5. It took the Israel Defense Forces, made up mainly of reservists traveling in a crazy assortment of military and civilian vehicles, less than 100 hours to cross and capture from the Egyptians the whole of the Gaza Strip and the Sinai Peninsula—an area two and a half times larger than Israel itself. We had counted on surprise, speed, and utterly confusing the Egyptian army, but it was only when I myself flew to visit Sharm el-Sheikh at the southernmost tip of the Sinai and toured the Gaza Strip by car afterward that I really understood the extent of our victory—the sheer size and desolation of the territory through which those tanks, half-tracks, ice-cream trucks, private cars and taxis had raced in under seven days. The Egyptian defeat was absolute. The nests of the fedayeen were cleaned out. The elaborate Egyptian system to defend the Sinai—the fortresses and the battalions concealed in the desert—was put totally out of commission. The hundreds of thousands of weapons and the millions upon millions of rounds of ammunition—mostly Russian—stockpiled for use against us were worthless now. A third of the Egyptian army was broken. Of the 3,000 Egyptian soldiers whom we found pathetically wandering in the sand, 5,000 were taken as prisoners to save them from dying of thirst (and eventually exchanged for the one Israeli the Egyptians had managed to capture).

But we hadn't fought the Sinai Campaign for territory, booty or prisoners, and as far as we were concerned, we had won the only thing we wanted: peace, or at least the promise of peace for a few years, perhaps even for longer. Although our casualties were "light," we desperately hoped that the 172 Israelis who were killed (some 800 were wounded) would be the last battle casualties we would ever have to mourn. This time we would insist that our neighbors come to terms with us—and with our existence.

Of course things didn't turn out that way. Although we had won our war against Egypt, the French and the British had lost theirs—to some extent owing to their ineptness, but mostly to the overwhelmingly negative public reaction in France and Great Britain to what was viewed as an imperialist assault on an innocent third party. I have always thought that had the Anglo-French attack on Suez been more swift and efficient, the storm of protest in those countries would have died down in the face of a *fait accompli*. But as it was, the combined assault failed, and the French and British backed down as soon as the United Nations, under intense U.S. and Soviet pressure, demanded that they withdraw their troops from the Suez Canal zone. It also demanded Israel's withdrawal from the Sinai Peninsula and the Gaza Strip.

That was the beginning of the four and a half heartbreaking months of diplomatic battle that we waged—and lost—at the UN in our attempt to persuade the nations of the world that if we retreated to the armistice lines of 1949, war would again break out in the Middle East one day. Those people, those millions of people who even today have still not quite grasped the realities of Israel's struggle to stay alive and who are so quick to condemn us for not being "more flexible" and for not retreating pleasantly to our former borders each time we are forced to go to war might do well to ponder the course of events following 1956 and ask themselves what was gained by the fact that we did reluctantly withdraw then from the Sinai and the Gaza Strip. The answer is: nothing, only more wars, each one bloodier and far more costly than the Sinai Campaign had been. Had we been allowed to stay where we were until the Egyptians agreed to negotiate with us, the recent history of the Middle East would certainly have been very different. But the pressure was intense, and in the end we gave in. President Eisenhower, who had been kept totally in the dark by his European allies, was furious and said that unless Israel withdrew at once, the United States would support sanctions against it at the United Nations.

The source of the greatest pressure, however, was the Soviet Union, which not only had witnessed a complete Egyptian defeat—all the Soviet support notwithstanding—but was also now able to becloud the issue of the recent Soviet invasion of Hungary by screaming to high heaven about the terrible colonialist conspiracy against Egypt and, most of all, about Israel's "unrestrained aggression." In retrospect, it is unlikely that Soviet Prime Minister Nikolai Bulganin's threats of direct Soviet intervention in the Middle East would have resulted in a third world war, but at the time that was what was being read into his grim warnings. It looked as though virtually the whole world was against us, but I didn't believe that we should give in without a fight.

In December, 1956, I left for the United Nations, filled with forebodings. But before I went, I wanted to see the Sinai and the Gaza Strip for myself, and I am glad that I did, because otherwise I would never have really comprehended the full gravity of the situation we had been in prior to the Sinai Campaign. I shall never forget my first sight of the elaborate Egyptian military installations—built in defiance of the United Nations itself—at Sharm el-Sheikh for the sole purpose of maintaining an illegal blockade against our shipping. The area of Sharm el-Sheikh is incredibly lovely; the waters of the Red Sea must be the bluest and the clearest in the world, and they are framed by mountains that range in color from deep red to violet and purple. There, in that beautiful tranquil setting, on an empty shore, stood the grotesque battery of huge naval guns that had paralyzed Eilat for so long. For me, it was a picture that symbolized everything. Then I toured the Gaza Strip, from which the fedayeen had gone out on their murderous assignments for so many months and in which the Egyptians had kept a quarter of a million men, women and children (of whom nearly 60 percent were Arab refugees) in the most shameful poverty and destitution. I was appalled by what I saw there and by the fact that those miserable people had been maintained in such a degrading condition for more than five years only so that the Arab leaders could show the refugee camps to visitors and make political capital out of them. Those refugees could, and should, have been resettled at once in any of the Arab countries of the Middle East—countries, incidentally, whose language, traditions and religion they share. The Arabs would still have been able to continue their quarrel with us, but at least the refugees would not have been kept in a state of semistarvation or lived in such abject terror of their Egyptian masters.

I couldn't help comparing what I saw in the Gaza Strip to what we had done—even with all the mistakes we had made—for the Jews who had come to Israel in those same eight years, and I suppose that is why I began my statement to the UN General Assembly on December 5, 1956, by talking not about the war we had won, but about the Jewish refugees we had settled:

> Israel's people went into the desert or struck roots in stony hillsides to establish new villages, to build roads, houses, schools and hospitals, while Arab terrorists, entering from Egypt and Jordan, were sent in to kill and destroy. Israel dug wells, brought water in pipes from great distances; Egypt sent in fedayeen to blow up the wells and the pipes. Jews from Yemen brought in sick, under-nourished children believing that two out of every five would die; we cut that number down to one out of twenty-five. While we fed those babies and cured their diseases, the fedayeen were sent in to throw bombs at children in synagogues and grenades into baby homes.

Then I went on to those celebrated "rights of war," to that discredited excuse of a "belligerent status" against Israel, the screen behind which Colonel Nasser had trained and unleashed the fedayeen.

> A comfortable division has been made. The Arab states unilaterally enjoy the "rights of war"; Israel has the unilateral responsibility of keeping the peace. But belligerency is not a one-way street. Is it then surprising if a people laboring under this monstrous distinction should finally become restive and at last seek a way of rescuing its life from the perils of the regulated war that is conducted against it from all sides?

The real point of that address, however, was not to make the familiar accusations—however justified they were—or even to try to bring home again to the so-called family of nations the immediate background to the Sinai Campaign. It was not even to put on the record what we knew to have been the very well-laid Egyptian plans for the annihilation of Israel. It was something else, something far more important: to try once again, and in public, to explore the source of the hatred the Arab leaders bore toward Israel and to

make some concrete proposals for a possible peace. I want
to emphasize the fact that I made this speech at the end of
1956, twenty years ago. If it is in any way familiar, that is
only because we have gone on saying the same thing ever
since, with about as much success as we had in 1956!

The fundamental problem in the whole situation is
the systematically organized Arab hostility against Israel. This Arab enmity is not a natural phenomenon.
It is artificially fostered and nurtured. It is not, as has
been alleged here, Israel which is an instrument of co-
lonialism. It is the Israel-Arab conflict which keeps the
area at the mercy of dangerously contending outside
forces. Only by the liquidation of that conflict will the
people of the region be able to work out their own
destinies in independence and hope. Only in that prospect lies hope for a brighter future of equality and
progress for all the peoples concerned. If hatred is
abandoned as a principle of Arab policies, everything
becomes possible.

Over and over again the Israeli government has
held out its hand in peace to its neighbors. But to no
avail. At the ninth session of the General Assembly,
the Israeli representative suggested that if the Arab
countries were not yet ready for peace, it would be
useful, as a preliminary or transitory stage, to conclude agreements committing the parties to policies of
nonaggression and pacific settlement. The reply was
outright rejection. Our offer to meet the representatives of all or any of the Arab countries still stands.
Never have we heard an echo from across our borders
to our call for peace.

The concept of annihilating Israel is a legacy of Hitler's war against the Jewish people, and it is no coincidence that Nasser's soldiers had an Arabic translation
of *Mein Kampf* in their knapsacks. Those concerned
sincerely with peace and freedom in the world would,
I think, have been happier had some more ennobling
literature been offered these men as a guide. Still, we
are convinced that these dangerous seeds have not yet
succeeded in corrupting the Arab peoples. This fatal
game is one which the Arab political leaders should

halt in the interests of the Arab peoples themselves. . . .

What ought to be done now? Are we to go back to an armistice regime which has brought anything but peace and which Egypt has derisively flouted? Shall the Sinai Desert again breed nests of fedayeen and be the staging ground of aggressive armies posed for the assault? Must the tragedy again be reenacted in the tinderbox of the Middle East? The peace of our region and perhaps of more than our region hangs on the answers which will be given to these questions.

Or, I asked, would the General Assembly now apply itself to thinking of the future "with the same vigor and insistence" with which it was calling upon us to withdraw our troops from across a boundary that could not continue to be "open to the fedayeen but closed to Israeli soldiers"? Surely, peace was not only necessary, but also possible. Only a few days before my speech, I had heard the representative of Egypt, speaking from the same rostrum, make a speech which—though it was perhaps not very original—at least sounded a note that, for a change, was not warlike. Listening to him, I had for a minute seen a picture of the Middle East as it might be if the barriers (they had actually become barricades) between the Arabs and ourselves ever fell. When the time came for me to speak, I thought I could do a lot worse than to repeat his words:

> With the great majority of the peoples of the world, Egypt has been saying, and will continue to say, that all nations can and should, for their own good, moral as well as material, live together in equality, freedom and fraternity, and with modern science and its vast potentialities at the service of man, enabling him, carried by the momentum of liberty and faith, to live an infinitely more productive and honorable life.

I had asked for a transcript of that speech, and now I read those lines out loud to the General Assembly and continued:

> With that statement we wholeheartedly concur. We are ready to make it a practical reality. . . . The

countries of the Middle East are rightly listed in the category of the "underdeveloped": The standard of living, disease, the illiteracy of the masses of people, the underdeveloped lands, desert and swamp—all these cry out desperately for minds, hands, financial means and technical ability. Can we envisage what a state of peace between Israel and its neighbors during the past eight years would have meant for all of us? Can we try to translate fighter planes into irrigation pipes and tractors for the people in these lands? Can we, in our imagination, replace gun emplacements by schools and hospitals? The many hundreds of millions of dollars spent on armaments could surely have been put to a more constructive purpose.

Substitute cooperation between Israel and its neighbors for sterile hatred and ardor for destruction, and you will give life and hope and happiness to all its people.

But walking back to my seat, I could see that no one else in that vast hall had shared the brief vision of the future with me, and I remember how surprised I was when a delegate sitting somewhere behind me applauded me as I sat down. The seating at the United Nations is always alphabetical; lots are drawn at the first meeting of each session as to which country should be seated first, and all the others are then seated in alphabetical order. At that session Holland happened to be behind us. I nodded my head very gratefully to the Dutch delegate—one of the few not to vote against us—but I still took my place with a sense of great emptiness and utter disbelief. I had spoken to the United Nations, and one would have thought from the expression on the faces of most of the delegates that I had asked for the moon, when in fact all I had done—all that Israel has ever done at the United Nations—was to suggest that the Arabs, fellow members of that organization, recognize our existence and work together with us toward peace. That no one had jumped up to seize the opportunity, to say, "All right, let's talk. Let's argue it all out. Let's make an effort to find a solution," was like a physical blow to me—not that I had many illusions left about the kind of family that family of nations was. Anyhow, I promised myself then that before the session was over, whatever else happened, I would try once again to reach the Arabs, to make a person-to-person appeal to them because unless something was done soon, the future, as I saw it, looked pretty grim.

Those were terrible months. Our phased-out withdrawal from the Gaza Strip and Sinai was going on all the time, but nothing was being said or done to force the Egyptians to agree to enter into negotiations with us, to guarantee the lifting of the blockade of the Strait of Tiran or to solve the problem of the Gaza Strip. The four questions we had asked in November, 1956, were still unanswered in February, 1957. And I still couldn't get through to the Americans—least of all to the U.S. secretary of state, that cold, gray man John Foster Dulles—that our very life depended on adequate guarantees, real guarantees with teeth in them, and that we couldn't return to the situation which had existed before the Sinai Campaign. But nothing helped. None of the arguments, none of the appeals, none of the logic, not even the eloquence of Abba Eban, our ambassador to Washington. We just didn't talk the same language, and we didn't have the same priorities. Dulles was obsessed by his own "brinkmanship," by his fear of a looming world war, and he told me in so many words, and more than once, that Israel would be responsible for that war, if it broke out, because we were so "unreasonable."

There were many days during that period when I wanted to run away, to run back to Israel and let someone else go on hammering away at Dulles and Henry Cabot Lodge, the head of the U.S. delegation at the United Nations. I would have done anything just not to have to face another exhausting round of talks that always seemed to end in recriminations. But I stayed where I was, and tried to swallow my bitterness and sense of betrayal, and at the end of February we arrived at a compromise of sorts. The last of our troops would leave the Gaza Strip and Sharm el-Sheikh in return for the "assumption" that the United Nations would guarantee the right of free passage for Israeli shipping through the Strait of Tiran and that Egyptian soldiers would not be allowed back in the Gaza Strip. It wasn't much, and it certainly wasn't what we had been fighting for; but it was the best we could get—and it was better than nothing.

On March 3, 1957, having first had each last comma of

it checked and cleared by Mr. Dulles in Washington, I made our final statement:

> The government of Israel is now in a position to announce its plans for full and prompt withdrawal from the Sharm el-Sheikh area and the Gaza Strip. In compliance with Resolution 1 of February 2, 1957, our sole purpose has been to ensure that on the withdrawal of Israeli forces, continued freedom of navigation will exist for Israel and international shipping in the Gulf of Aqaba and the Strait of Tiran.

And then, as I had promised myself I would do, I said:

> Now may I add these few words to the states in the Middle East area and, more specifically, to the neighbors of Israel? Can we from now on, all of us, turn a new leaf, and instead of fighting among each other can we all, united, fight poverty, disease, illiteracy? Can we, is it possible for us to put all our efforts, all our energy, for one single purpose—the betterment and progress and development of all our lands and all our peoples?

But no sooner had I taken my seat than Henry Cabot Lodge got up. To my astonishment, I heard him reassure the United Nations that while the rights of free passage for all nations through the Strait of Tiran would indeed be safeguarded, the future of the Gaza Strip would have to be worked out within the context of the armistice agreements. Perhaps not everyone at the United Nations that day understood what Cabot Lodge was saying, but *we* understood all too well. The U.S. State Department had won its battle against us, and the Egyptian military government, with its garrison, was going to return to Gaza. There was nothing I could do or say. I just sat there, biting my lip, not even able to look at the handsome Mr. Cabot Lodge while he pacified all those who had been so worried lest we refuse to withdraw unconditionally. It was not one of the finest moments of my life.

But reality had to be faced, and we had not lost everything. For the time being, the fedayeen terror was over; the principle of freedom of navigation through the Strait of

Tiran had been upheld; the UN Emergency Force moved into Gaza and the Sharm el-Sheikh area; and we had won a victory that had made military history, proving again our ability—if need be—to take up arms in our own defense.

I went back to the United Nations later that year, in October, and once again tried to break the ten-year-old deadlock between the Arab states and ourselves. I spoke to them out of the very depths of my conviction that the time had come for us to deal directly with each other, and I spoke on the spur of the moment, without any preparation and without a text.

Israel is approaching her tenth anniversary. You did not want it to be born. You fought against the decision in the United Nations. You then attacked us by military force. We have all been witnesses to sorrow, destruction and the spilling of blood and tears. Yet Israel is here, growing, developing, progressing. . . . We are an old tenacious people and, as our history has proved, not easily destroyed. Like you, the Arab countries, we have regained our national independence, and as with you, so with us, nothing will cause us to give it up. We are here to stay. History has decreed that the Middle East consists of an independent Israel and independent Arab states. This verdict will never be reversed.

In the light of these facts, what is the use or realism or justice of policies and attitudes based on the fiction that Israel is not here or will somehow disappear? Would it not be better for all to build a future for the Middle East based on cooperation? Israel will exist and progress even without peace, but surely a future of peace would be better both for Israel and for her neighbors. The Arab world with its ten sovereignties and 3,000,000 square miles can well afford to accommodate itself to peaceful cooperation with Israel. Does hate for Israel and the aspiration for its destruction make one child in your country happier? Does it convert one hovel into a house? Does culture thrive on the soil of hatred? We have not the slightest doubt that eventually there will be peace and cooperation between us. This is a historic necessity for both peoples.

We are prepared; we are anxious to bring it about now. . . .

I could have saved my breath. Our few friends in the General Assembly clapped their hands politely, maybe even enthusiastically, but the Arabs didn't as much as look up.

During my term of office as foreign minister, I visited the United Nations often. I was there at least once a year as head of Israel's delegation to the General Assembly, and there wasn't a single time that I didn't make an attempt to contact the Arabs somehow—or, to my sorrow, a single time that I succeeded. I remember once, in 1957, seeing Nasser there from a distance and wondering what would happen if I just went over to him and began to chat. But he was surrounded by his bodyguards, and I had my bodyguards, and it obviously wouldn't work. But Tito was at that same session, and I thought perhaps I could talk to him and he would arrange something. So I asked someone in our delegation to talk to a member of the Yugoslav delegation and try to set up a meeting between Tito and me. I waited and waited and waited. I even postponed my return to Israel, but there was no reply. Then, the day after I had left New York, we got an answer: Tito would meet me in New York. But I was already back home. We tried again. There was silence again.

There wasn't one possible intermediary whom I didn't approach during that period. At one Assembly session, I became quite friendly with the wife of the acting head of the Pakistani delegation, that country's ambassador to London. One day she approached me, of her own accord, and said, "Mrs. Meir, if we women are in politics, *we* ought to try and make peace." Well, that was just what I had been waiting for.

I said to her, "Let me tell you something. Never mind about peace. Invite a few of the Arab delegates to your home and invite me. I promise you, on my word of honor, that as long as the Arabs don't want anyone to know about our meeting, no one will know. And I don't want to meet them for peace negotiations. Just to talk. Just to sit in one room together."

She said, "That's wonderful. I'll do it. I'll start to organize it at once."

So I waited and waited, but nothing happened. One day

I asked her to have a cup of coffee with me in the delegates' lounge, and we were sitting there when the foreign minister of Iraq came in. (He was the gentleman who had once pointed at me from the General Assembly rostrum and said, "Mrs. Meir, go back to Milwaukee—that's where you belong.") She turned white. "My God," she said, "he'll see me talking to you," and she got up in a panic and left. That was the end of that.

And so it went, even down to the casual meetings we might have had at diplomatic luncheons. Every head of a UN delegation learned very quickly that if he wanted the Arabs to come, then he mustn't invite us. There was one foreign minister who was new to the game and who did invite both the Arabs and the Israelis. He not only invited us, but even seated an Iraqi delegate across the table from me. Well, the Arab sat down, started to eat his smoked salmon, raised his eyes, saw me, stood up and left. Of course, at the large receptions or the cocktail parties for hundreds of people, it was possible for a host to invite Arabs and Israelis, but for a dinner or a luncheon—never! As soon as an Arab delegate caught sight of one of the Israelis, he would walk out of the room, and there was nothing we could do about it.

But there were brighter moments during those years, and some very memorable meetings. The most interesting and most memorable, perhaps, were those with John F. Kennedy, Lyndon Johnson and Charles de Gaulle. I met Kennedy twice. The first time was right after the Sinai Campaign, when he was a senator from Massachusetts. The Zionists of Boston had organized a tremendous demonstration and a gala dinner in support of Israel, which was attended by the entire consular corps, the state's two senators—and the Israeli foreign minister. I was seated next to Kennedy, who was one of the speakers, and I remember being tremendously impressed by him, by how young he was and how well he spoke, although he was not really easy to talk to. I had a feeling that he was very shy, and we exchanged only a few words. The next time I met him was shortly before he was assassinated. I went down to Florida, where he was vacationing, and we talked for a very long time—and very informally. We sat on the porch of the big house in which he was staying, and I can still see him, in his rocking chair, without a tie, with his sleeves rolled up,

listening very attentively as I tried to explain to him why
we so desperately needed arms from the United States. He
looked so handsome and still so boyish that it was hard for
me to remember that I was talking to the president of the
United States—although I suppose he didn't think I looked
much like a foreign minister either! Anyhow, it was a
strange setting for such an important talk. There were two
or three other people with us, including Mike Feldman,
one of Kennedy's right-hand men, but they didn't participate in the conversation.

At first, I went into the current situation in the Middle
East. Then, suddenly, it occurred to me that this bright
young man might not understand very much about the
Jews and what Israel actually meant to them, and I decided
that I ought to explain that to him before I went on talking
about why we had to have arms. So I said, "Mr. President,
let me tell you in what way Israel is different from other
countries." To do so, I had to go back a long way because
the Jews are such an ancient people. I said: "The Jews
came into being more than three thousand years ago and
lived alongside nations that have long since disappeared—
the Ammonites, the Moabites, the Assyrians, the Babyloni-
ans and others. In ancient times, they were all subject to
oppression from foreign powers at one time or another, and
in the end they all accepted their fate and became part of
whatever the dominant culture was. All of them, that is,
except the Jews. Like these other peoples," I said, "the Jews
had their land occupied by foreign powers. But the fate of
the Jews was very different, because, of all these nations,
only the people of Israel were determined to remain what
they were. The people of other nations stayed in their lands
but abandoned their identity, while the Jews, who were dispersed among the nations of the world and lost their land,
never let go of their determination to remain Jewish—or of
their hope of returning to Zion. Well, now we are back
there, and that places a very special burden on the leadership of Israel. In many ways, the government of Israel is no
different from any other decent government. It cares for the
welfare of the people, for the development of the state and
so on. But, in addition, there is one other great responsibility, and that is for the future. If we should lose our sovereignty again, those of us who would remain alive—and
there wouldn't be very many—would be dispersed once

more. But we no longer have the great reservoir we once had of our religion, our culture and our faith. We lost much of that when six million Jews perished in the Holocaust."

Kennedy didn't take his eyes off me, and I went on: "There are five and a half or six million Jews in the United States. They are wonderful, generous, good Jews, but I think that they themselves would be the first to agree with me if I say that I doubt very much whether they would have the tenacity which those lost six million had. And if I am right, then what is written on the wall for us is: 'Beware of losing your sovereignty again, for this time you may lose forever.' If *that* should happen, then my generation would go down in history as the generation that made Israel sovereign again, but didn't know how to hold onto that independence."

When I finished, Kennedy leaned over to me. He took my hand, looked into my eyes and said very solemnly, "I understand, Mrs. Meir. Don't worry. *Nothing* will happen to Israel." And I think that he did truly understand.

I met Kennedy again at a formal UN reception where he was greeting the heads of delegations; but we only said hello to each other then, and I never saw him again. But I did go to his funeral, and afterward—with all the other heads of delegations—I went to shake Mrs. Kennedy's hand. I never saw her again either, but I can't forget how she stood there, pale and with tears in her eyes, but still finding something special to say to each one of us. It was also at Kennedy's funeral—or, more accurately, at the state dinner given that evening by the new president—that I met Lyndon B. Johnson. I had met him before, during the General Assembly of 1956–57, when he was the Democratic majority leader of the Senate and came out, strongly and publicly, against President Eisenhower's threat of sanctions against us, so I already knew how he felt about Israel. But when I came up to him that night in the receiving line, he put his arm around me, held it there for a minute and said, "I know that you have lost a friend, but I hope you understand that I, too, am a friend"—which he certainly proved himself to be.

Often, throughout the period of the Six-Day War, when President Johnson backed our refusal to return to the pre-1967 lines unless we could do so within the framework of a peace settlement—and helped us achieve the military and economic means to maintain that position—I used to think back to the night of Kennedy's funeral and to the words that he said to me then, when he had so much else to think and worry about. I never saw him again either, although I wasn't at all surprised that he got along so well with Levi Eshkol when he was prime minister. They were very similar in many ways—open, warm and easy to establish contact with. I know how unpopular Johnson eventually became in the United States; but he was a very staunch friend indeed, and Israel owes a lot to him. I think he was one of the very few leaders abroad who understood what a mistake had been made by the Eisenhower administration after the Sinai Campaign, when we were forced to retreat before any negotiations with the Arabs got under way.

When Johnson died in 1973, I was prime minister, and of course, I wrote a letter of condolence to Mrs. Johnson. I have her reply before me now. It, too, moved me greatly, particularly since I knew how sincere it was.

"Dear Mrs. Meir," she wrote. "You must know how much my husband looked forward to your forthcoming visit here. Often he talked of visiting Israel someday. His concern for your country was real and deep and his respect for your people came from the depths of his heart. . . ."

Another of the personalities who were to have such a decisive effect on Israel's future and whom I met at President Kennedy's funeral was General de Gaulle. I had seen him for the first time in 1958, when the French ambassador to Israel, Pierre Gilbert (who is a whole story unto himself), made up his mind that I must visit the general. Gilbert was as ardent a Gaullist as he was a Zionist, and there was no talking him out of this plan, although I must say that I was very nervous about meeting De Gaulle. Everything I had heard about him—including the fact that he expected everyone to know French perfectly, while I didn't know it at all—scared me. But once Gilbert had set my visit in motion, there was no pulling back, and I went to Paris for a few days. First, I met with the then French foreign minister, Maurice Couve de Murville, the most British Frenchman I ever encountered. He had served in various Arab countries. He was very correct, very cold and, on the whole, unfriendly—none of which helped me look forward to meeting De Gaulle the next day. I was received at the Elysée palace with all the standard pomp and circumstance. Walking up the steps, I felt as though I were reviewing the entire French army, and I wondered what those splendid French guards in their red cloaks thought of me as I trudged up to the general's office, feeling very ill at ease. And there he was, in all his height and glory, the legendary Charles de Gaulle. Walter Eytan, who was the director general of our Foreign Ministry then and who afterward served as our ambassador to France, had come with me, and between De Gaulle's interpreter and Eytan, the general and I managed to converse. He was remarkably cordial and very kind. It only took a few minutes for me to feel quite relaxed, and we had a most satisfactory talk about the problems of the Middle East, with his assuring me of his undying friendship for Israel.

Then at Kennedy's funeral I saw him again, first at the cathedral (the only people who were not kneeling, I believe, were De Gaulle, Zalman Shazar—who was president of Israel—and myself) and later at the dinner which I've already mentioned. Before we went into dinner, I spotted De Gaulle (not a great feat, considering how he towered over everyone) at the other end of the room. I was just considering whether I ought to go over to him or not when he moved in my direction. There was a great flurry all around. *Who* was De Gaulle going to? "He never goes over to anyone himself; people are always summoned to him," someone standing next to me explained. "He must be going to talk to a very important person." It was like the Red Sea parting so that the Children of Israel could get through; De Gaulle walked straight ahead, and everyone scuttled out of his way. I almost fell over when he stopped in front of me and did something that was really unprecedented for him: He spoke to me in English. "I am enchanted to see you again, even on this so tragic occasion," he said, and bowed. It made an enormous impression on everyone, but most of all on me. In the course of time, I even became very good friends with Couve de Murville, who used to tell me that De Gaulle had a soft spot in his heart for me. I only wish it had stayed that way, but we didn't do what he told us to do (which was to do nothing) in 1967, and he never forgave us for that disobedience. In those dreadful days before the Six-Day War he told Abba Eban that there were two things Israel should know: "If you are in real danger, you can depend upon me; but if you move first, you will be destroyed, and you will bring a catastrophe on the entire world." Well, De Gaulle was wrong. We weren't destroyed, and there wasn't a world war; but our relationship with him—and with the French government—was not the same from that day on. The same De Gaulle who, in 1961, toasted "Irsael, our friend and ally" summed up his attitude toward the Jews after the Six-Day War by describing us as "an elitist, self-confident and domineering people."

The most exciting and, I think, the most important contribution I made as foreign minister, however, was in a totally different sphere. It had to do with Israel's new role in the developing countries of Latin America, Asia, and in particular, perhaps Africa, and it opened up an entirely new chapter in my own life, too.

11. African and Other Friendships

I suppose that as far as my personal feelings were concerned, at least some of the impetus for my initial involvement with Africa and with the Africans in the late 1950s came as an emotional response to the situation in which we found ourselves after the Sinai Campaign—in many respects entirely alone, less than popular and certainly misunderstood. France was an ally and a good friend, and one or two other European countries were sympathetic to us; but our relationship with the United States was strained, with the Soviet block it was worse than strained, and in Asia—despite all our efforts to secure real acceptance—we had for the most part, come up against a stone wall. True, we had established missions in Burma, Japan and Ceylon and consular offices in the Philippines, Thailand and India; but although we were among the first nations to recognize the People's Republic of China, the Chinese were not at all interested in having an Israeli embassy in Peking, and Indonesia and Pakistan, as Moslem states, were openly hostile to us. The Third World, in which Nehru, on the one hand, and Tito, on the other, played such a decisive role, looked toward Nasser and the Arabs—and away from us. And when in the spring of 1955 a conference of Asian and African nations took place at Bandung, although we had greatly hoped to be invited, the Arab states threatened to boycott it if Israel participated, and we were excluded from that "club" as well. I used to look around me at the United Nations in 1957 and 1958 and think to myself: "We have no family here. No one who shares our religion, our language or our past. The rest of the world seems to be grouped into blocs that have sprung up because geography and history have combined to give common interests to their peoples. But our neighbors—and natural allies—don't want to have anything to do with us, and we really belong nowhere and to no one, except to ourselves." We were the firstborn of the United Nations; but we were being treated like unwanted stepchildren, and I must admit that it hurt.

Still, the world was not made up exclusively of Europeans and Asians. There were also the emerging nations of Africa, then on the verge of achieving independence, and to the black states in the making there was a great deal that Israel could and wanted to give. Like them, we had shaken off foreign rule; like them, we had had to learn for ourselves how to reclaim the land, how to increase the yields of our crops, how to irrigate, how to raise poultry, how to live together and how to defend ourselves. Independence had come to us, as it was coming to Africa, not served up on a silver platter, but after years of struggle, and we had had to learn—partly through our own mistakes—the high cost of self-determination. In a world neatly divided between the haves and the have-nots, Israel's experience was beginning to look unique because we had been forced to find solutions to the kinds of problems that large, wealthy, powerful states had never encountered. We couldn't offer Africa money or arms, but on the other hand, we were free of the taint of the colonial exploiters because all that we wanted from Africa was friendship. Let me at once anticipate the cynics. Did we go into Africa because we wanted votes at the United Nations? Yes, of course, that was one of our motives—and a perfectly honorable one—which I never, at any time, concealed either from myself or from the Africans. But it was far from being the most important motive, although it certainly wasn't trivial. The main reason for our African "adventure" was that we had something we wanted to pass on to nations that were even younger and less experienced than ourselves.

Today, in the wake of the post-Yom Kippur War rupture of diplomatic relations between most of the African states and Israel, the chorus of cynics also includes disillusioned Israelis. "It was all a waste of money, time and effort," they say, "a misplaced, pointless, messianic movement that was taken far too seriously in Israel and that was bound to fall apart the moment that the Arabs put any real pressure on the Africans." But of course, nothing is cheaper, easier or more destructive than that sort of after-the-fact criticism, and I must say that in this context I don't think it has the slightest validity. Things happen to countries as they do to people. No one is perfect, and there are setbacks, some more damaging and painful than others; but not every project can be expected to succeed fully or quickly. Moreover, disappointments are not failures, and I have very little sympathy indeed for that brand of political expediency that demands immediate returns. The truth is that we did what we did in Africa not because it was just a policy of enlightened self-interest—a matter of *quid pro quo*—but because it was a continuation of our own most valued traditions and an expression of our own deepest historic instincts.

We went into Africa to teach, and what we taught was learned. No one regrets more bitterly than I that, for the time being, the African nations—or many of them—have chosen to turn their backs on us. But what really matters is what we—and they—accomplished together, what the thousands of Israeli experts in agriculture, hydrology, regional planning, public health, engineering, community services, medicine and scores of other fields actually did throughout Africa between 1958 and 1973, and what the thousands of Africans who trained in Israel during those years took home with them. Those benefits can never be lost, and those achievements should never be minimized. They are of enduring worth, and nothing can erase them, not even the current loss to Israel of whatever political or other benefits we derived from our ties with the governments of the African states. Ungrateful those governments most certainly have been, and it will take a great deal of effort on their part to remove the bad taste left by their desertion of us in a time of crisis. But that is no excuse for disowning, or belittling, what I honestly believed to have been a profoundly significant, not to say unprecedented, attempt on the part of one country to better human life in other countries, and I am prouder of Israel's International Cooperation Program and of the technical aid we gave to the people of Africa than I am of any other single project we have ever undertaken.

For me, more than anything else, that program typifies the drive toward social justice, reconstruction and rehabilitation that is at the very heart of Labor Zionism—and Judaism. The philosophy of life that impelled the men and women of Merhavia in the 1920s to dedicate themselves to pioneering within a cooperative framework, that led my daughter and her comrades to continue in that same demanding pattern in the Revivim of the 1940s and that is responsible today for each new kibbutz established in Israel is identical, I believe, with the vision that took Israelis into African countries for years to share with the Africans the practical and theoretical knowledge that alone could answer Africa's needs in a changing world in which it was, at last, responsible for its own destiny. Not that all those who took part in the sharing of our national experience with the Africans were socialists. Far from it. But for me, at least, the program was a logical extension of principles in which I had always believed, the principles, in fact, which gave a real purpose to my life. So, of course, I can never regard any facet of that program as having been "in vain," and equally I cannot believe that any of the Africans who were involved in it, or reaped its fruits, will ever regard it in that light either.

One other thing: We shared with the Africans not only the challenge posed by the need for rapid development, but also the memory of centuries of suffering. Oppression, discrimination, slavery—these are not just catchwords for Jews or for Africans. They refer not to experiences undergone hundreds of years ago by half-forgotten ancestors, but to torment and degradation experienced only yesterday. In 1902 Theodor Herzl wrote a novel in which he described the Jewish state of the future as he imagined it might be. The novel was called *Altneuland* ("Old-New Land"), and on its title page were written the words: "If you will it, it is no dream"—words that became the motto and inspiration of the Zionist movement. In *Altneuland* there is a passage about Africa which I used to quote sometimes to African friends and which I should like to quote now:

> . . . There is still one other question arising out of the disaster of the nations which remains unsolved to this day, and whose profound tragedy only a Jew can comprehend. This is the African question. Just call to mind all those terrible episodes of the slave trade, of human beings who, merely because they were black, were stolen like cattle, taken prisoner, captured and sold. Their children grew up in strange lands, the objects of contempt and hostility because their complexions were different. I am not ashamed to say, though I

may expose myself to ridicule in saying so, that once I have witnessed the redemption of the Jews, my people, I wish also to assist in the redemption of the Africans.

I think that passage speaks for itself!

Also, although I think, and hope, that I was responsible for much of the initial scope and intensity of the nearly 200 development programs that Israel has carried out to date with more than eighty countries of Africa, Asia, Latin America and, more recently, the Mediterranean basin, drawing upon the sheer enthusiasm, perseverance and talent of some 5,000 Israeli advisers, I cannot claim to have invented the idea. The first Israeli to have explored the possibility of this form of international cooperation was my good friend Reuven Barkatt, who, as head of the Histadrut's Political Department, brought several Africans and Asians to Israel to see for themselves how we had gone about solving various problems. And by the time I became foreign minister in 1956—on the eve of the independence of Ghana—a young Israeli diplomat appointed by Sharett, Chanan Yavor, was already packing his bags and getting ready to represent Israel there. When Ghana became independent in 1957, Ehud Avriel was appointed Israel's ambassador to that state and to Liberia, and he suggested that I attend the first anniversary of Ghana's independence in 1958 and that I also visit Liberia, Senegal, the Ivory Coast and Nigeria. So I started to plan the journey, on which, we decided, Ehud and our then ambassador to France, Jacob Tzur, would accompany me.

I had met Africans before, of course, chiefly at various international socialist meetings; but I had never been to Africa, and I couldn't really imagine it at all. I remember packing for the trip (one of my great drawbacks as a traveler, incidentally, is that I unfailingly take much more than I ever need) and losing myself in a daydream for hours about Africa and the role that we might be able to play in the waking of that great continent. I didn't have any illusions whatsoever about the fact that this role would inevitably be small, but I was fired by the prospect of going to a part of the world to which we were so new and which was so new to us. I was as excited as a child about what lay ahead.

My first stop was Monrovia, the capital of Liberia,

where I was the guest of President William Tubman. Liberia's social and economic elite lived in incredibly luxurious conditions—bordering very often on the fantastic—while the rest of the population was destitute. But I hadn't come to Africa to preach, to interfere or to convert. I had come to meet the Africans, and I was well aware of the fact that President Tubman was a devoted friend of the Jews, chiefly, as I recall, because in the long history of his complicated relationship with the United States he had been befriended by a Jewish congressman, that wonderful man Emanuel Celler, who—alone of all of Tubman's contacts in Washington—had understood the loneliness of a black leader at a time when it was neither fashionable nor necessary to consider the feelings of any black. Liberia was the world's first black state, born of an impulse not entirely dissimilar to the Zionist impulse, and I couldn't help responding both to Tubman's evident affection for Israel and to his strong feeling that we had much in common. But what most charmed and interested me was not the Liberia of Monrovia, but the Africa I saw in the interior of the country.

We traveled for miles in Liberia. I talked to hundreds of people and answered thousands of questions about Israel, many of them about Israel as the land of the Bible. A very nice young woman from the Liberian Foreign Office accompanied me, and I remember that on the last day of my visit she said very bashfully to me, "I have an old mother to whom I explained that I would be busy all week with a visitor from Jerusalem. My mother just stared at me. 'Don't you know,' she said, 'that there is no such place as Jerusalem? Jerusalem is in heaven.' Do you think, Mrs. Meir, that you could possibly see her for a minute and tell her about Jerusalem?"

Of course, I went to meet her mother that day and took with me a little bottle of water from the Jordan River. The old woman just walked around and around me, though she never actually touched me. "You come from Jerusalem," she kept on saying. "You mean, there's a *real* city, with streets and houses where *real* people live?"

"Yes, I live there," I answered, but I don't think she believed me for a moment. It was a question that I was asked all over Africa, and I used to tell the Africans that the only thing that was heavenly about Jerusalem was that it still existed!

The highlight of that visit to Liberia, for me, was the ceremony in which I was made a paramount chief—an honor rarely bestowed on women—of the tribe of Gola (when I told the story later, it was regarded as a remarkable coincidence in Israel that the Hebrew word for the Diaspora is also *Gola*) in northern Liberia. It was certainly one of the most extraordinary things that ever happened to me, and I confess that as I stood there in the blazing sun, with the tribesmen singing and dancing all around me, I could hardly believe that it was I, Golda Meir, from Pinsk, Milwaukee and Tel Aviv, to whom this great tribute was being paid. Two thoughts were uppermost in my mind: "I must behave as though an initiation ceremony in the middle of Africa is something to which I have been accustomed all my life" and "I wish that the grandchildren could see me now." When the dancing was finished, I was led by about 200 women of the tribe into a tiny, airless, straw hut, where I was dressed in the bright robes of a paramount chief and underwent a secret initiation—the details of which I have no intention of disclosing. But I shall never forget the looks in the eyes of my Israeli escorts (including Ehud and my security officers) when I vanished to the sound of African drums and the chant of the women into the darkness of that hut—or the relief on their faces when I walked out of it intact and very pleased with myself. What I can say about that ceremony is that I was immensely impressed and delighted by the colorfulness, the naturalness and the wholeheartedness of the proceedings. They had the kind of warmth and joy about them that made me feel immediately at home wherever I went in Africa and that I never found to quite the same degree anywhere else, certainly not in Asia.

From Liberia, we moved on to Ghana, Africa's first decolonized independent state, where I met with Dr. Kwame Nkrumah, the charming demigod of African nationalism in those days. It was impossible not to like or admire Nkrumah, but the long talk I had with him as soon as I arrived in Accra nonetheless left me with reservations about his reliability and candor. There was something very unrealistic and even unattractive about his rhetoric and his evident eagerness to remain *the* symbol of African liberation. He talked about the problems of Africa as though all that mattered were formal independence, and he seemed far less interested in discussing the development of Africa's resources or even how he could raise the standard of life for his people. He talked on one level, and I talked on another. He talked about the glories of freedom, and I talked about education, public health and the need for Africa to produce its own teachers, technicians and doctors. We spoke for hours, but I think that neither of us convinced the other.

I couldn't help being pragmatic and trying to stress technique and know-how, while Nkrumah, I imagine, couldn't help his rather high-flown oratory. At one point, for instance, he explained to me why he had had an enormous statue of himself put up in front of the parliament building in Accra and why the new coins in Ghana were decorated with a bust of himself: "Independence doesn't signify anything to the people in the bush. They don't understand what the word means. But when they pick up a coin and see Nkrumah's portrait on it instead of that of the queen of England *then* they will know the meaning of independence." It was a fundamental difference of approach, but it didn't get in the way of the eventual establishment of a very close relationship indeed between Ghana and Israel, which was to express itself in the dozens of training programs we launched both in Israel and in Ghana and construction work and engineering services that were carried out by Israeli personnel there. We also helped create and run Ghana's Black Star shipping line. In fact, today there are hundreds of Israelis for whom Ghana was a second home and to whom Ghana's future mattered almost as much as Israel's.

Later, I met other African leaders, for example, President Houphouët-Boigny, of the Ivory Coast, whose personal order of priorities was much closer to mine. Houphouët-Boigny (who, by the way, belonged to the same tribe as Nkrumah and could converse with him only in their tribal language because Nkrumah knew no French while Houphouët-Boigny knew no English) was convinced, in 1958, that development is as important as independence. He saw much more clearly than Nkrumah ever did the dangers that would certainly face the Africans if they continued to press for independence without adequate preparation: Moslem extremism; the even more lethal combination of communism—Russian or Chinese—with Islam; the return—in a slightly altered guise—of the former masters of Africa; and the weakening of moderate progressive elements throughout the continent. And he was able to resist Nasser's blandishments and threats for many years. In November, 1973, however, even Houphouët-Boigny gave in and broke relations with us, explaining sadly that he had to choose "between his Arab 'brothers' and his Israeli 'friends.' " But of course, in 1958, all that lay in the future, and it was just as well that it did.

Although I was rather dejected about my first meeting with Nkrumah, my visit to Ghana turned out to be not only fascinating but also crucial to our entire African enterprise. As part of the anniversary celebrations, Ghana was playing host to the First All-African Peoples' Conference, a gathering of the representatives of all of the African liberation movements, including the Algerian FLN. I had already met Dr. George Padmore, a brilliant West Indian ex-communist, then the most important ideologist of the forces of "progressive" pan-Africanism who had fathered a concept of African development that rested, among other things, on massive financial support from the U.S. black community—along the lines, as he put it, of the United Jewish Appeal. He was extremely interested in Israel and insisted that I meet with the other African leaders who were assembled in Accra. It was a God-sent opportunity, he said, for me and for them. The conference was due to start at 4 P.M. at the Ambassador Hotel, Ghana's one brand-new modern hotel, but a special meeting was called for three o'clock, and when I entered the conference room with Padmore, some sixty men were already sitting around an enormous table, waiting for me.

It was a curious and dramatic confrontation. Here we were in the first African country to achieve independence (excluding, of course, Liberia and Ethiopia): I, the foreign minister of a Jewish state that was all of ten years old, and sixty men whose countries would achieve their freedom within only two or three years. We all had lived through so much, all struggled so hard for our liberty—they, representing still uncounted millions upon millions of people spread over the vastness of Africa, and we, in our one tiny country that had been battered and besieged for so long. It seemed to me that afternoon that this was a truly historic meeting of the kind that perhaps Herzl himself had envisaged. I couldn't identify most of the Africans by name, but Padmore told me who they were: the leaders of fighting Algeria, of all the other French colonies, of Tanganyika, of Northern and Southern Rhodesia. The atmosphere in the room was very charged. I could feel the tension and the suspicion, neither of which was much allayed by Padmore's opening words. "I have called this meeting," he said, "so that you can meet the foreign minister of a young country that has just achieved its independence and that has taken remarkable strides forward in every field of human endeavor."

For a few seconds there was an uncomfortable silence; then the representative of Algeria rose. In an ice-cold voice, he asked the most provocative—and relevant—of all possible questions. "Mrs. Meir," he said, "your country is being armed by France, the arch-enemy of all those who sit around this table, a government that is fighting a ruthless and brutal war against my people and that uses terror against my black brethren. How do you justify your intimacy with a power that is the primary foe of the self-determination of the African people?" And he sat down. I was not at all surprised by the question, only by the fact that it opened the meeting. Somehow I had expected more phraseology and more time. But I was glad that we were not going to indulge in any amenities or shadowboxing, and I didn't need time for preparation.

I lit a cigarette and looked around the table again. Then I answered the question. "Our neighbors," I said to the sixty African leaders staring at me with such coldness and hostility, "are out to destroy us with arms that they receive free of charge from the Soviet Union and for very little money from other sources. The one and only country in the world that is ready—for hard currency, and a lot of it—to sell us some of the arms we need in order to protect ourselves is France. I do not share your hatred for De Gaulle, but let me tell you the truth—whether or not you like it: If De Gaulle were the devil himself, I would regard it as the duty of my government to buy arms from the only source available to us. And now let me ask you a question. If you were in that position, what would you do?"

I could almost hear the sigh of relief that swept the room. The tension was over. The Africans knew that I had told them the truth and that I was not trying to put anything over on them, and they relaxed at once. Now there was no stopping the barrage of their questions about Israel. They were hungry for information—about the kibbutzim, the Histadrut, the army—and they bombarded me with queries. They were also quite frank in return. One young man from Northern Nigeria (which is almost entirely Moslem) even stood up and said, "We have no Jews in Northern Nigeria, but we know that we are supposed to hate them!"

That dialogue with the African revolutionaries went on for the duration of my stay in Ghana, and it laid the foundation for our International Cooperation Program. I won the respect and the friendship of the African leaders, and they were anxious to meet and work with other Israelis. They were not used to white men who labored with their own hands or to foreign experts who were willing to leave their offices and work at the site of a project, and the fact that we were what they termed color-blind was tremendously important. Things that came quite naturally to me filled the Africans with amazement—whether it was my not very graceful but very sincere attempts to learn African dances or my enthusiasm for teaching the stiff young officials of Ghana's Foreign Office how to dance Israel's hora. Most of all, they couldn't help feeling how much I liked them. I remember sitting under an enormous mango tree in Ghana and combing my hair one morning when, as if from nowhere, ten or eleven little girls appeared who had apparently never seen long hair before. One little girl, braver than the rest, came up to me. I could see that she wanted to touch my hair, so for the next half hour I let them take turns combing it and didn't even notice the crowd of awe-struck Africans who had gathered behind me.

By not behaving as they had learned to expect foreigners to behave, I think we helped build much more than farms, industrial plants, hotels, police forces or youth centers for so many of the African countries; we helped build the self-confidence of the Africans. We proved to them, by working with them, that they could become surgeons, pilots, citrus growers, community workers and foresters and that technical ability was not—as they had been made to believe for so many decades—the permanent prerogative of the white race.

Of course, the Arabs did their best, even then, to convince the Africans that we were fundamentally no different
from other "colonialists," but the Africans, for the most
part, knew better. They knew that when Israeli poultry experts were engaged by Zambia, it didn't turn Zambian
chickens into "colonialist" chickens and that the fish-
processing program that Israelis developed in Mali didn't
result in "imperialist" fish. They also knew that the
hundreds of African trainees who studied agriculture in Israel were not being trained in exploitation. In fact, we set
up three basic criteria for our program, and I think that it
is not immodest to claim that even these criteria were a
new departure. We asked ourselves, and the Africans, three
questions about each proposed project: Is it desired, is it
really needed, and is Israel in a position to help in this
particular sphere? And we only initiated projects when the
answer to all three questions was yes, so the Africans knew
that we didn't regard ourselves as being able, automatically, to solve all their problems.

I returned to Africa over and over again and got used to
being told before each trip that it was "too much" for me. I
learned to accustom myself to the heat, to the frequent lack
of cleanliness, to washing my teeth with boiled water (and,
when I couldn't get that, with coffee) and to spending
hours doing things that I had never in my wildest dreams
expected to do, such as presiding over the election of a
beauty queen during the Independence Day festivities of
Cameroun, or going out to dinner in Abidjan, on the Ivory
Coast, with a group of African leaders and hearing an African band strike up a stirring rendition of "Die Yiddishe
Mama" as soon as I walked in. The more I traveled in
Africa, the more I liked it and fortunately the more the
Africans liked me. To this day, I correspond with some of
the many African parents who named a daughter after me.
Recently I received a letter from a man in Rivers State,
Nigeria. "I acknowledge with grateful thanks," he wrote,
"the receipt of your kind letter in which you enclosed a
necklace for little Golda. Please find enclosed here little
Golda's picture given you as a token of our appreciation for
your good work in helping mankind." And I was deeply
flattered by the many other ways in which the Africans
showered me with affection.

In December, 1959, I visited Cameroun, returned to

Ghana, went for the first time to Togo (where, apart from other projects, we helped set up a national youth movement and organize a cooperative village), visited President Tubman in Monrovia again and toured Sierre Leone and Gambia. I also traveled to Guinea and had my first encounter with Sekou Touré. It was not, however, an unqualified success. He was one of the few African leaders with whom I didn't manage to develop a personal relationship, although I was greatly impressed by his intellectual abilities. Like Nkrumah and, to a lesser extent, Tanzania's Nyerere, Sekou Touré was more concerned with his country's international standing than with its well-being. Although he was a radical left-winger, he seemed to have no real social concepts, and there was very little, therefore, that we could offer him—although we did extend aid to Guinea, and there is a beautiful vocational high school in Conakry which we helped to bring into existence. But Guinea was never really friendly to Israel, and when, after the Six-Day War, it broke relations with us—the only African state to do so then—I wasn't particularly surprised. Not that I think the attitude of a given state toward Israel is inevitably a conclusive test of the caliber of that state's leadership, but it was certainly a fact that the more an African leader concerned himself with his nation's progress, rather than with playing games with one power bloc or another, the more that state wanted our assistance and the better we got along together.

I put some of my feelings about this—and about other aspects of my African experiences—into a speech that I made before the General Assembly toward the end of 1960, by which time sixteen independent African states were already represented there. As I spoke, I saw before me the men, women and children I had met all over Africa, with many of whom I couldn't even speak without an interpreter, but with all of whom I had always felt a genuine bond, the bond of real brotherhood and of shared aspirations, and I also saw in my mind's eye the deprived, underprivileged, ill-educated masses of Jews that had come to Israel—in the hundreds of thousands—expecting a paradise on earth. What I was really talking about was the pitfall of unrealistic expectations and of political fantasies either about the past or about the future—things to which we ourselves were not immune, so it was natural for me to talk in terms of "us" and not "them":

> There are two dangers that face those of us who have emerged as newly independent states: first, lingering in the past and, secondly, the illusion that political independence will provide instant solutions for all our problems.
>
> What do I mean by lingering in the past? It is natural that many new peoples should have unhappy and, in some cases, bitter memories. It is understandable that many of them should feel a sense of grievance against their former rulers and should view their present plight as the legacy of the past. It is to them a painful paradox that while some countries have problems of surpluses and overproduction, they should have been left behind in poverty. As they look about them at their lands, rich with minerals and vegetation—gold and diamonds, bauxite, iron and copper, cocoa and cotton, sugar and rubber—they must come to the conclusion that it was not God's will that they should be hungry.
>
> How can we expect Africans to be impressed by the feats of the space age, when so many of their own people still are illiterate? You cannot expect a mother in an African village to be elated over the advance of medicine in the world when she sees her children suffering from trachoma, tuberculosis and malaria. All this must be understood. It is natural that their former suffering and degradation should be remembered by these new free peoples. No people can build its future if it does not remember its past. But a people cannot live only by brooding over the past; it must invest all its energy and ability in the future.

And then I spoke about the challenge of the future:

> We, the new countries, have gained our independence in an era of man's greatest achievements. In some parts of the world, the standard of living and development has reached fantastic heights. We should not be told to go slow in our development; we should not be told that the advances of the developed coun-

tries have taken generations and centuries to attain. We cannot wait. We must develop quickly. As a friend from Kenya who visited Israel said: "Must I walk in an age of jet planes just because those that now have jets were walking generations ago?"

This challenge is one not only for the new nations, but for the entire world. Much has been said and done about what I would call "first aid": the sharing of food; the transfer of surplus to the hungry. But I wish to say that we will never be really free as long as our children need to be fed by others. Our freedom will be complete only when we have learned to bring forth the food that we need from our own soil. The cry that goes out from the African and Asian continents today is: Share with us not only food, but also your knowledge of how to produce it. The most frightening inequality in the world today lies in the gap between those that literally reach for the moon and those who do not know how to reach efficiently into their own soil to produce their daily necessities.

In addition to Israel's International Cooperation Program and the Histradrut-established (with the aid of the AFL) Afro-Asian Institute, we have participated in the various specialized UN agencies that concern themselves with the developing countries. There were—and still are—two Israeli activities that hold a particular appeal for me and that—to some extent, at least—answered the question I had asked at the United Nations. In the summer of 1960, under the guidance of Abba Eban—who had just returned from his spectacularly successful years of service as Israel's ambassador to Washington and representative to the United Nations (and who, in 1966, became my successor as Israel's foreign minister)—the first International Conference on Science in the Advancement of New States was held in Rehovot on the beautiful campus of the Weizmann Institute of Science. Its purpose was to try to build a real bridge between the developed and the developing nations of the world by exploring the way in which science and technology could most effectively be harnessed on behalf of states that had just achieved independence. Half the participants were Africans and Asians, the other half were leading European and U.S. scientists. For almost all of the participants, as well as for me, it was an intensely moving and extremely stimulating gathering, the first of its kind to take place anywhere.

Some of the speeches were too long, some of the scientific papers were too abstruse, some of the questions, and answers, were out of place; but it was a giant step in the direction of true international cooperation, the kind of step that meant more in a way even than the formal equality bestowed by membership in the United Nations. In Rehovot representatives of two cultures met to chart together the specific pathways by which one part of mankind could most usefully assist the other, and I never tired of watching African statesmen (many of them in their native robes) whom I had last met in Africa—new ministers of education, of health and of technology—deep in conversation with Nobel Prize winners and other world-famous members of the international scientific community, with whom they were slowly developing a common language. That first Rehovot Conference was to turn into a tradition. Every two years since 1960 a similar meeting has taken place on the campus of the Weizmann Institute, dealing, in turn, with topics such as public health, economics, education and agriculture, and each one of those conferences has given to its participants something that money alone can certainly never buy: the feeling that, when all is said and done, this is indeed one world.

The other project that remains as exciting and as interesting to me as it was when we began it in 1960 is the Mount Carmel Center (known more formally, as the International Training Center for Community Services), which concentrates on training women from the developing countries of Asia, Africa and Latin America in social services. Over the past fifteen years, I have seen the center make it possible for hundreds of women—whether a kindergarten teacher from Nepal, a nutritionist from Lesotho, a social welfare worker from Kenya or a teacher of reading from Malawi—to play a vital role in the development of their own countries. For all these women, Israel itself served as a living laboratory because, as a student from Kenya once said to me, "If I had gone to study in the United States, I might have learned the history of development, but here in Israel I have seen development as it takes place."

The center has always held a very special place in my

heart, not only because I helped found it, together with Sweden's Inga Thorsson and Israel's Mina Ben-Zvi, but also because I so greatly admire these women from developing countries who leave their towns and villages and their families and travel so far to a strange country in order to learn the skills that will eventually make the life of their people easier and richer. There is something heroic, I think—and this is not a word I use easily or often—in the effort made by such women to ensure a better and fuller existence for themselves, for their children and for their children's children through the long difficult process of self-education. Among the women I met at the center, I remember most clearly a striking woman judge from Ghana, a shy young midwife fom Swaziland, an impressive elderly woman doctor who had led the family-planning activities of Nigeria and an articulate committed Ethiopian dietitian. All of them were wives and mothers who had become pioneers in their respective fields and whose greatest hope was that the women of Africa would one day take their rightful place in African society as full contributors to Africa's future, much as they had seen the women of Israel do in the Jewish state. I don't think I have ever encountered a more hardworking, enthusiastic or attractive group of women than those I used to talk to for hours in Haifa. On the surface, our life experiences had been entirely different, but in reality we were struggling for much the same things.

Our involvement in the training of Africans was not restricted to activities held in Israel, though, and my visit to the training school for social workers that was established with the support and help of the Mount Carmel Center— originally as a joint Kenya-Israel enterprise—at Machakos, Kenya, was one of the highlights of my first tour of East Africa in 1963, when I flew thousands of miles, mostly in very small planes, across Kenya, Tanganyika, Uganda and Madagascar. Every now and then we would touch down at some tiny village where an Israeli adviser was hard at work, and I would spend an hour or two with him and his family and see for myself the trust and fondness with which they were treated by the Africans, marveling at the determination and personal involvement that kept those young Israelis, living under such unfamiliar and primitive conditions, at their self-imposed jobs.

Not that there weren't Israelis who failed or that every-

thing was always sweetness and light. It often took an Israeli family months to adjust to the climate, to the food, to
the slower, traditional African way of doing things, to understand what underlay African sensitivity and superstition
and to curb the sort of impatience and even arrogance that
might have undone all the good work. There were quarrels,
projects that came unstuck and hurt feelings on both sides.
But for the most part, because both the Africans and Israelis so deeply understood the value of what they were
trying to do, the cooperation worked. And nothing delighted me more than meeting Africans who had trained in
Israel and who showed me around their African clinics,
farms or schools, cheerfully explaining everything to me in
fluent Hebrew—to say nothing of the African sabras I met
everywhere, the black children who had been born in Israel
and whose first language had been Hebrew. African children—however "radicalized" they may become—will
never, I know, think of the friends they made in Beersheba,
Haifa or Jerusalem or, for that matter, of me as their "enemy," regardless of what they may say in public.

One of the most instructive though not most important
things I learned on that grand tour of East Africa was that
we ourselves had to alter the way in which we entertained
official guests to Israel. Like the Israelis, the Africans insisted on sightseeing that often lasted for twelve hours or
more a day and that was mercilessly followed by a full-
scale banquet, complete with speeches in which every one
endlessly congratulated everyone else. I used to sit through
those banquets in a state of total exhaustion, knowing that
in a few hours we would be off on another sun-scorched
tour that was doomed to end with another banquet and
more speeches. So I took an oath that when I got back to
Israel, I would see to it that we cut down on our own
overly zealous hospitality, although I can't honestly say
that my efforts in this direction were very successful.

At all events, in the end I fell ill and had to cut short
that particular trip although it meant canceling a reception
for me given by Milton Obote, the levelheaded intelligent
president of Uganda who was later so ruthlessly removed
by Idi Amin. In a certain sense, it occurs to me now, Obote
and Idi Amin perhaps represent the two extremes of the
current African dilemma. Obote was everything that Amin
is not—rational, serious, hardworking and effective—and I

am afraid that Uganda's progress has been set back many years by the rise to power of someone like Idi Amin, who has been so hopelessly injured by having been placed in a position of virtually unlimited control over a country that is still so new to independence. I hadn't known Idi Amin when he was training as a paratrooper in Israel (Israeli "wings" are still worn proudly not only by him, but by a number of other African leaders, including Zaire's President Mobutu), but I had heard even then, when he thought that the sun rose and set on Israel, that he was very eccentric—to put it politely. And my last meeting with him, in Jerusalem when I was prime minister, convinced me that he was really quite mad. In fact, our discussion might have been staged by Charlie Chaplin.

"I have come to see you," he said to me very seriously, "because I want a few Phantoms from you."

"Phantoms! We don't manufacture Phantoms," I answered. "We buy them from the United States, when we can—which is not always or often enough. They aren't things that you buy and sell. Anyhow, why do you need Phantoms?"

"Oh," he said blandly, "to use against Tanzania."

Then he sent me a message: "I need ten million pounds sterling at once." I couldn't give him that either, so he left Israel in a tremendous huff, went off to Colonel Qaddafi of Libya—and Uganda broke diplomatic relations with us in 1972, a year and a half before the Yom Kippur War. But Idi Amin is not Uganda, and even he can't remain a dictator forever, which is some consolation.

Thinking back on the African leaders I met—Kenya's splendid old man Jomo Kenyatta, and the late Tom Mboya, Zambia's Kenneth Kaunda, Senegal's poet-president Senghor, and General Mobutu Sese Seko of Zaire, to name just a few—I must say that, the tragedy of their break with us apart, they were and are a credit to their peoples and to the African liberation movement. One of the reasons, I think, that I got along so well with them—even though we did not always see eye to eye on everything—was that I practiced what I preached, and they saw me do it. In 1964, for instance, I attended the Independence Day ceremonies of Zambia (formerly Northern Rhodesia), including a visit for all the guest VIPs to the Victoria Falls, which are partly in Zambia and partly on the territory of what was then still called Southern Rhodesia. We were taken to the falls in buses, and when we reached the border between the two countries, the police of Southern Rhodesia had the effrontery to refuse to let the blacks on my bus get out, although they were all African dignitaries and President Kaunda's personal guests. I couldn't believe my ears when I heard a police officer say, "Whites only." "In that case," I said, "I'm sorry, but I won't be able to enter Southern Rhodesia either." There was great consternation, and the Rhodesians tried very hard to get me to leave the bus, but I wouldn't hear of it. "I have no intention of being separated from my friends," I repeated. The whole busload of us then happily traveled back to Lusaka, where Kaunda received me as though I were Joan of Arc rather than just a woman who couldn't and wouldn't tolerate racial discrimination in any form.

On that trip I was also involved in another incident that helped clarify further to the Africans that we really meant what we said—a characteristic which they had previously had little reason to attribute to Europeans. I was scheduled to visit Nigeria on my way home from Zambia. En route, I stopped over in Nairobi, where a special plane had been rented to fly me to Lagos, since there was no other way I could get there from East Africa unless I overflew or touched down in an Arab state. In Nairobi, our ambassador to Nigeria awaited me, looking very troubled. He told me that I would be greeted by anti-Israel demonstrations in Lagos. The wives of all the ambassadors of Arab countries had got together to organize protests against my visit. It might be wise if I canceled my trip. Nigeria was on the eve of elections, and many of the ministers were away from Lagos in any case; it was not the best time to go. What if something happened to me? I was very tired at that point and didn't at all relish being the object of violence on the streets of a major African city. On the other hand, I was certainly not going to be bullied, I answered, by Arab ambassadors hiding behind their wives' skirts. "I won't impose myself on the Nigerian government," I said, "but if the government doesn't recall its invitation to me, I intend to go."

As we reached the airport at Lagos, I saw masses of people waiting on the ground, hundreds and hundreds of Africans. "This is it," I thought, "and it's going to be very unpleasant." But instead of hysterical demonstrators, I was being met by a huge crowd of men and women who either had trained in Israel or had been trained by Israelis in Nigeria. All of them were singing "Hevenu Shalom Aleichem" (We Bring Peace Unto You, the "theme song" of Israel's International Cooperation Program), which I have heard literally thousands of times but have never been as touched by as I was on that night. The next morning I was received by President Azikiwe. "We respect and greet you as an ambassador of true goodwill," he said, and that trip to Nigeria turned out to be a great success after all.

I spent less time in Asia, although there, too, I always felt welcome. Still, I missed the vividness and the drama that I associate with Africa. Maybe it was because I never quite understood the elaborate codes of behavior in the Far East, or maybe it was because Jews, the Jewish heritage and the Jewish ethic are all less known in Asia than they are in Africa, where Christianity brought with it a real familiarity with the Bible. Even the place-names of Israel—Galilee, Nazareth, Bethlehem—have meaning for educated Africans, and I met almost as many Moseses, Samuels and Sauls in Africa as I do at home. But Asia was something else. It lay outside the traditions of the Old Testament, and there was more need to explain and interpret who we were and where we came from. Even a man as cultured as the former Burmese Prime Minister U Nu once told our ambassador to Rangoon, David Hacohen, that he had known nothing at all about us until one day "by accident, I came across a book," and it was only then, when he read the Bible as an adult, that he discovered the existence of the Jews. As a matter of fact, what may well have made U Nu's relationship with Ben-Gurion so warm was that Ben-Gurion had also learned about Buddhism only relatively late in life.

But before I write anything about my own travels in the Far East, I want to say again that the one Asian nation with which we have, alas, made no headway whatsoever is China, a fact to which I referred briefly before. There are Israelis, David Hacohen among them, who believe that we simply didn't try hard enough to make friends with the Chinese, but I am not at all sure that we could have done more than we did. In 1955, we sent a trade mission, headed by Hacohen, to China, and of course we invited the

Chinese to send a mission to us. They never as much as answered the invitation, and at the Bandung Conference later that year the Chinese-Egyptian rapprochement began. It resulted in a violent Chinese response to the Sinai Campaign and eventually in open Chinese identification with Arab anti-Israel terror. The Chinese government, in fact, is totally committed to the Arab war against Israel, and Mr. Arafat and his comrades are constantly given arms, money and moral support by Peking, though I, for one, have never really understood why and for years lived under the illusion that if we could only talk to the Chinese, we might get through to them.

Two pictures come to my mind when I mention China: The first is the horror with which I once picked up a mine manufactured in China—so far away and remote from us—which had put an end to the life of a six-year-old girl in a border settlement in Israel. I stood there near that small coffin, surrounded by weeping, enraged relatives. "What on earth can the Chinese have against us?" I kept thinking. "They don't even know us." Then I remember, at the celebration of Kenya's independence, sitting with Ehud Avriel at a table near that of the Chinese delegation. It was a very relaxed, festive occasion, and I thought to myself, "Perhaps if I go over and sit down with them, we can talk a bit." So I asked Ehud to introduce himself to the Chinese. He walked over, held out his hand to the head of the delegation and said, "My foreign minister is here and would like to meet you." The Chinese just averted their gaze. They didn't even bother to say, "No, thank you, we don't want to meet her."

But Israelis don't easily take no for an answer, least of all I. Not long ago my dear friend and fellow socialist the Italian statesman Pietro Nenni was invited to China. Before he went, he visited me in Jerusalem. We sat on the porch of my house there, drank coffee and talked, as old socialists always do, about the future. Inevitably, in this connection, we also talked about China. "Look," I said to him, "the Chinese will listen to you. Please try to discuss Israel with them." So he did. He tried to explain to various important Chinese statesmen what sort of country Israel is, how it is run, what it stands for—but they weren't interested. They didn't tell Nenni, as they usually do, that Israel is only "a puppet of the United States"; someone just said that if every group of 3,000,000 people tried to set up their own state, what would the world come to?

I tried several times to persuade each of my children to accompany me on my travels, but Sarah wouldn't be dislodged from Revivim and Menachem was just as reluctant to be parted from Aya and the boys (they had three sons, Amnon, Daniel, and Gideon by then) or from his cello. Each time I went to Africa, I came back with basketfuls of masks, carvings, handwoven cloth and more anecdotes about what I had seen, but of course, it wasn't the same as actually sharing these experiences with them. I longed for the children to take at least one trip with me—not because they hadn't traveled enough (we had all done more than our share of that), but because I wanted them to see some of the things that I was seeing and meet some of the people whom I was meeting. I often wondered in those years, and even more later on when I was prime minister, how they felt—or how my grandchildren really felt—about the way I lived. It wasn't something we ever talked about much, but I don't think that any of them especially enjoyed being "related to Golda Meir." We always talked a great deal together, and very freely, about politics, both domestic and international, and my grandchildren were never excluded from these conversations, even when they were very small. But other than the fact that I was a potential source of valuable autographs for classmates or that they grew up knowing that what they heard around my table was not to be repeated, I don't think they were in any way different from other children. They certainly treated me like a very ordinary grandmother. Visitors were always amazed that Menachem's boys ran in and out of my house with such freedom and amused by the fact that they were clearly so much more interested in the contents of my refrigerator than in the world-famous guests I entertained so often. As for me, like all grandmothers, I fussed over them more than was necessary, and I still do. But then my five grandchildren are my greatest joy in life, and nothing is too good for them, as far as I am concerned. I only wish that I could be sure they will not have to go through any more wars but of course, that is the one thing that I cannot promise them.

At any rate, it was a great deprivation for me to be away from all of them so frequently, and I kept on at Menachem and Sarah until each of them, in turn, agreed to make one

journey with me. In 1962 Sarah traveled with me to Kenya
and to Ethiopia, where I introduced her to Haile Selassie
and we visited the large community of Israelis working in
that country in agriculture, fishing, transportation, helping
train the police and the army and teaching at the University of Addis Ababa. Even Ethiopia, with which we had
had such a very special relationship for so many years,
broke with us in 1973, but at the time of which I write the
ties were still very strong—although never publicized by
the Ethiopians and therefore also not by us. For me, Haile
Selassie was almost a storybook character, a man from a
far-off, exotic land who dared stand up in 1936 and call the
attention of an indifferent world to the Italian invasion of
Ethiopia. He and his family had spent a year in Jerusalem
as refugees during the Italian occupation, and I used to see
him sometimes—a dark, bearded little man with huge, sad
eyes—walking with his empress in the street, while his
adored little dogs ran after them. He was not just another
refugee from fascism; he is descended from that line of
Ethiopian kings who claim that their ancestor was the son
born to King Solomon and the Queen of Sheba and that
they are therefore our distant kin. The Lion of Judah has
always been the symbol of the Ethiopian monarchy, and
the links between the Jews and Ethiopia have always been
unique.

But although Ethiopia is a Christian country, it is part of
Africa and, as such, was subjected for years to strong anti-
Israeli pressure by the Arabs. For a long time, however,
Haile Selassie warily trod a tightrope; many of his dealings
with Israel were kept secret, and we only sent an ambassador in 1961. The Sinai Campaign—because it opened up
the Strait of Tiran—became the start of an even closer relationship, and Israeli ships and planes helped develop a
steady flow of trade between the Ethiopians and ourselves.
At the same time we did a great deal to develop the educational facilities of Ethiopia, and several Israeli professors
settled in Addis Ababa for a few years. Sarah was too
young, I expect, to feel about Haile Selassie as I did. For
her he was only the ruler of a fascinating country, for me
he was always much more. I can't say that we became
fast friends, but when I saw him in his own place and remembered the lonely exiled figure I used to see in Jerusalem in
the 1930s, I felt that justice had—for a change—been

done, and I was immensely disappointed when even Haile Selassie—for all his own experience with appeasement—did not stand by us. It proved to me once again—although I didn't need very much more proof by then—that one can count on no one but oneself.

Anyhow, that same year, to my delight, Menachem also agreed to make a journey with me, and we went to the Far East together. It was really very noble both of Aya and of him because Gidi had just been born. We spent more than a week in Japan, where I was received by the emperor, the prime minister and the foreign minister. I don't know what I expected Hirohito to be like, but I was certainly not prepared for the modest, very pleasant gentleman with whom I exchanged courtesies—never quite sure, I suspect, that we were getting through to each other. I found the Japanese very courteous but very noncommittal. I knew that they were extremely cautious about their relationship with us and handled it as though the Middle East were a flower arrangement in which all the elements had to be balanced just so.

One rather funny thing that happened in connection with my Japanese trip was the excessive worry of the Japanese officials regarding my visiting a geisha house. On the plane going to Japan, Ya'akov Shimoni (then the head of our Far Eastern desk), who accompanied us, told Menachem that "since Golda is both a woman and a foreign minister, the Japanese have not suggested giving her the traditional geisha party, which they usually throw for foreign distinguished guests. They don't think it would be proper in her case." When we got to Tokyo, I told Menachem to make it clear to the Japanese that I certainly did want to go to a geisha party and that I had nothing at all against geishas. In the end a lovely geisha party was laid on for me in Kyoto by the governor and his wife, and everyone was satisfied, though I think Shimoni never got over the sight of me sitting on cushions while the geishas fluttered around me like butterflies.

Like most people, I was tremendously impressed by the beauty of Japan and even more by the ability of the Japanese to create beauty in their everyday surroundings. And of course, we met Jews there, too, in particular some of the many Japanese who have become converts to Judaism, including—to my astonishment—a member of the imperial family who chatted away with me in Hebrew. In recent years, by the way, there have been regular visits to Israel of large ardently pro-Israel groups from Japan, and I am no longer so taken aback as I used to be by the sight and sound of dozens of Japanese singing "Jerusalem the Golden," in perfect Hebrew, near the Western Wall.

From Japan we flew to the Philippines, where I received an honorary degree from the Catholic University of Manila and found myself marching in solemn procession down a hall filled with lavishly robed church notables, with priests holding crosses on either side of me. I knew that it was a very great honor that this Catholic institution was bestowing on a Jewish woman, from a Jewish state, and as I walked I thought to myself that Jews were not always welcome in all universities and that there were still institutions of higher learning, even in the free world, that could only tolerate a small number of us in their midst. As I spoke, I recalled—not for the first time—the letter that Sheyna, who always worried lest my head be turned, had once written to me: "Never forget who you are," she had warned me. But she needn't have worried. I have never forgotten that I came from a poor family or ever fooled myself into thinking that I was honored anywhere—Manila included—for my beauty, wisdom or erudition.

Manila, Hong Kong, Thailand, Cambodia—I could write pages about my impressions of the people we met and the sights we saw in those countries, but the heart of that trip to the Far East was our visit to Burma, a country with which we had had close ties ever since 1952, when a delegation of Burmese socialists had first visited Israel. Sharett had gone to Rangoon a year later to attend the first Asian Socialist Congress, and by 1955 there were full diplomatic relations between Burma and Israel. David Hacohen opened the Israeli embassy in Rangoon, and Burma's prime minister, U Nu, came to Israel as Ben-Gurion's guest.

I think there was no developing country in the world— not even Ghana or Kenya—with which we conducted such an ardent love affair. For years there seemed to be nothing about Israel that the Burmese did not admire or want to emulate, and as Asia's only socialist state, it was natural for them to be profoundly interested in our special brand of socialism, the Histadrut, the kibbutz movement and the way in which we had created a citizen army and turned it into one of our most effective educational institutions, with an education corps that was teaching thousands of culturally deprived children from immigrant families (and in many cases their mothers, too) to read and write. The Burmese were also fascinated by the methods we had used to combine military service with pioneering on the land, and they took over from us, almost intact, the idea that people could work as farmers and at the same time be trained in self-defense. For the Burmese, whose border with China was a constant source of harassment and who couldn't maintain a large standing army, Israel's Nahal (the initials of the Hebrew words for Fighting Pioneer Youth) was the perfect answer. It gave idealistic young people the opportunity to get simultaneous agricultural and military training within the framework of existing kibbutzim so that they could go on to establish their own collective settlements. I had suggested to the Burmese that they create border settlements of their own in this way, and I invited them to send a large group of demobilized Burmese soldiers with their families to Israel for a year or so to work on our kibbutzim and mainly *moshavim* (cooperative villages) and accustom themselves to the communal or cooperative way of life, while we would send Israelis to Burma to help plan Burmese-style *moshavim* there. And that was just what happened. The *moshav* seemed to suit the Burmese temperament more.

There were many other joint Burmese-Israeli enterprises, including the establishment of a major pharmaceutical industry in Burma, the training of dozens of Burmese doctors and nurses and the creation of vast irrigation schemes, but for me personally, the *moshavim* of the Namsang region in the north of Burma were more exciting than anything else. I had, of course, followed their progress with enormous interest, but I still could hardly believe that I was not dreaming when we landed at a northern airport and all the Burmese wives and children who had once been in Israel greeted me with Hebrew songs and Israeli flags. I don't think I will ever forget walking up to one of the little houses in Namsang and saying in Hebrew to a young Burmese who stood in the doorway, *"Shalom, ma nish'mah?"* (Shalom, how are things?) and hearing him answer, like a real Israeli, *"Beseder, aval ein maspeek mayim."* (Fine, but there isn't enough water.) I might have been in Revivim.

I traveled all over Burma with Ne Win, then Burma's chief of staff. Within a few weeks he had taken over in Burma with a new policy that was pro-Russian, anti-American and emphasized noninvolvement with any non-Burmese interests. It didn't end trade relations between Burma and Israel, but it did end the love affair.

I was very much taken by the Burmese, and I felt comfortable with them, although I can't say that Burmese delicacies are *my* idea of good food. There was very little I wouldn't have done in 1963 for Burma, but I just couldn't eat the fish paste on which the Burmese live or even taste the roasted leopard offered to me in Namsang, let alone drink soup made of birds' nests that we served at the dinner I gave in Rangoon in honor of U Nu. Menachem explained all about the subtlety of Oriental food to me, but I didn't think it would seriously impair Israel's relationship with Burma if I left a thousand-year-old egg—which it would have killed me to swallow—untouched on my plate. Of course, there were also things about us that it took the Burmese a long time to understand. I remember, on U Nu's first visit to Israel, when Ben-Gurion was driving with him through the young forests that line part of the road from Tel Aviv to Jerusalem—of which we are so proud because such a tremendous effort went into afforesting the rocky land there—U Nu looked very worried indeed. "You must be extremely careful," he said to Ben-Gurion. "Take it from me that those trees will *grow*." His problem, of course, was keeping jungles at bay, and he couldn't imagine that for us each tree was a gem to be treasured!

By the time we returned to Israel I had seen enough rice paddies and rickshas to last me for several years—if not for a lifetime—and I wanted and badly needed a rest; but in 1964, 1965 and 1966 I was in orbit again. I traveled back to Europe, Africa and to Latin America, and I was frequently ill. I had begun to feel the strain of perpetual travel; I seemed always to be either en route to somewhere or from somewhere or sick. Besides, I was no longer as young as I had been. In 1963 I had celebrated my sixty-fifth birthday. I didn't feel at all old or depleted of energy, but I was beginning to think how nice it would be to have a day to myself or to visit old friends again without having a bodyguard follow me around, and the children and my doctor kept telling me that the time had come for me to

take it easy. I tried, but I never succeeded in learning how
to do so. There was always a pressing commitment—either
abroad or in Israel—and however early I began my
workday, it never ended until the early hours of the next
morning. Sometimes I did treat myself to doing what I
wanted to do, but very rarely.

One such occasion was the party I gave in July, 1961, to
the friends with whom I had come to Palestine aboard the
Pocahontas forty years earlier. I can't remember now how
or when I got the idea of an anniversary celebration, but I
was very curious to meet the group again, to find out who
had settled in Israel and who had gone back to the States,
and I wanted to see their children. One of the topics of
conversation and debate between myself and my colleagues
in Mapai in those days was why there was such a relatively
small emigration of Jews from the West. "They have it too
good," was one explanation. "They will come to us only
when they face real anti-Semitism elsewhere." But I felt
this to be a very unjust oversimplification, and I used to
have long arguments with Ben-Gurion about the unimpressive rate of emigration from such countries as the United
States, Canada and Britain. "They will come, one day, if
we are patient," I used to tell him. "It is not as simple to
transplant oneself and one's family as it used to be. Also
people are not as idealistic, as romantic or as dedicated
anymore. It takes a tremendous amount of determination
and guts for a Zionist from Pittsburgh, Toronto or Leeds to
decide one day to settle permanently in Israel. It means
much more than merely moving to another country. It involves learning a new language, accepting a different standard and way of life, and getting used to the sort of tensions
and insecurities that we take for granted." I was no less
anxious than Ben-Gurion for Western Jews to join us in
their hundreds of thousands, millions even; but I was not as
intolerant of their hesitation, and I was certainly not prepared—at this point in Israel's history—to demand of Jews
who supported the State of Israel without actually living
there that they should no longer consider themselves Zionists but rather "friends of Zion," a very diluted formula
angrily suggested by Ben-Gurion.

But the nineteen men and women who had taken that
trip on the *Pocahontas* with Morris and me in 1921 had
made that great decision, and I had a sudden urge to see

them again. I didn't have their addresses, so I put an advertisement in the paper: "The foreign minister invites all the members of the *Pocahontas* contingent to an evening at her home; not only the original group but husbands, wives, children and grandchildren."

Most of the people who had made that dreadful journey with me in 1921 did not come. They were either dead or too infirm, and one had gone back to the United States for good. But seven or eight of the original group loyally turned up and, what's more, brought their children and grandchildren with them. We had a wonderful party, reminiscing, singing and eating cake and fruit in my garden. There weren't any formal speeches, and I refused to let the press attend—although the journalists implored me to let them come "only for a few minutes." But it was a personal marking of a very personal anniversary, and I wanted it to be a private gathering.

I suppose that some of the songs we sang (which were the same songs with which we had tried to boost our morale on that miserable ship) must have sounded very sentimental and naïve, maybe even banal to our children. They were all about building the land and pioneering. Nonetheless, they reminded us of the days when we believed we could do anything and everything, and we sang for hours. Afterward, when the party was over and all the guests had gone home, I sat on for a while in the dark garden, thinking about those forty years and wishing that Morris could have been with us. Of one thing I was quite sure that night: None of us had ever regretted, for one moment, having remained on the *Pocahontas* until she finally sailed from Boston, taking us most of the way to Palestine.

By the end of 1965 even I began to realize that I needed a change. The election campaign in the summer of that year had exhausted me. I have never felt really well in the heat, and now the migraine headaches from which I had suffered off and on for years were getting worse. I couldn't avoid coming to the conclusion that the responsibilities I had shouldered for more than thirty years were starting to weigh on me too heavily. I didn't want to live forever, but also I didn't want to turn into a semi-invalid. However, it wasn't only my health that bothered me; it was also the need to recharge my emotional batteries, which seemed to be running down slightly because I was tired. And the internal situation in Israel was not good. There was a severe economic depression, emigration—which we call *yerida* (descent) as opposed to the "ascent" of immigration—and the aftermath of the Lavon Affair, which was demoralizing the public and wreaking havoc in the ranks of the labor movement. My own battles with Ben-Gurion were, of course, not the least of my headaches. Nothing catastrophic would happen if I left public life: The party would heal its own wounds, and I couldn't do much to solve Israel's economic plight, which was largely caused by the fact that German reparations were coming to an end while neither our defense budget nor the Arab boycott was reduced at all.

To add to my dispiritedness, Sheyna was not at all well. She, too, was growing old and, like our mother before her, was aging in both body and mind. Eshkol, who became prime minister in 1963, and Pinchas Sapir, who was minister of finance, tried valiantly to keep me from resigning; but I knew that Abba Eban was waiting in the wings to become foreign minister, and I could see no reason, under the circumstances, for my clinging to the ministry. Eshkol offered me the deputy prime ministership, but it held no appeal for me at all. Better, I thought, to be a full-time grandmother than a part-time minister, and I told Eshkol that I really wanted to retire. "I won't go into a political nunnery," I assured him, "but I do want to be able to read a book without feeling guilty or go to a concert on the spur of the moment, and I don't want to see another airport for several years."

12. We Are Alone

It took me some time, several months in fact, to "organize" my retirement. To begin with, there was the move from Jerusalem to the small, semidetached house on a quiet, treelined street of a Tel Aviv suburb, right next door to Menachem and Aya. It wasn't just a matter of moving from one city to another; it involved hours and hours of sorting things out, deciding what was mine and what belonged to the government, what I wanted to take with me and what I was going to give away. I had traveled so extensively for the past twenty-five years and accumulated so many mementos of my trips that going through them was almost a full-time job—and not one that I particularly relished. But Clara came from the States to visit me, and she, Lou and I finally disposed of everything. Luckily, by nature I am not a collector, and living in a private museum is certainly not my idea of comfort, so it wasn't difficult for me to shed most of the possessions and presents and keep only those books, paintings, scrolls and keys to cities that had some special meaning for me. Of course, I was quite sure at that point that I would never have to go through the ordeal of selecting, packing and unpacking again—and the feeling of blessed finality also helped.

My new home—which is where I still live—was probably a quarter of the size of the foreign minister's residence that I had occupied for nine years; but it was exactly what I wanted and needed, and I felt comfortable in it from the very first day. I had planned it to suit my own requirements—a combined living room-dining room lined with bookshelves that opens onto the garden I share with Menachem's family, a kitchen that is big enough for me to work in efficiently, and an upstairs with one bedroom and a study that serves also as a guest room. This year I hope, at last, to add one more room to the house, but even without that extra room it has always been big enough for me, and it was wonderful in 1965 to feel that I was settling in somewhere for good.

Even my immediate family, I suspect, didn't really believe that I would enjoy the transition to life as an ordinary citizen, but I was as happy as I had known I would be. For the first time in years I was free—to do my own shopping, to use public transportation instead of being driven everywhere and being concerned about the fact that a driver was forever waiting for me outside and, most of all, to call my time my own. I really felt like a prisoner released from jail. I made long lists of the books I wanted to read, called up old friends whom I hadn't seen for years and planned a series of visits to Revivim. What's more, I cooked, ironed and cleaned house with enormous pleasure. I had stepped out of office at exactly the right time, of my own accord and before anyone could say "For God's sake, when is that old woman going to realize that it's time for her to quit?" and I felt as though I had taken on a new lease on life.

The public got used to my new role almost as quickly as I did, although every now and then, I must confess, I was accorded special treatment. Shopkeepers in the neighborhood often volunteered to deliver my orders to the house because they didn't think it was right for the former foreign minister to be carrying bags of groceries, and bus drivers were equally kind about making unscheduled stops so I could get off nearer home sometimes—and once or twice I was even driven in state right up to my door. But I didn't care at all what I carried or how far I had to walk; my liberation from obligatory appointments and official receptions was like a daily miracle. Nor did I for a moment feel isolated or out of touch with what was happening in the country. I had remained a member of the Knesset and of the Mapai executive and in both places did as much work as I felt like doing—but no more than that. All in all, I was very satisfied with my lot.

I should have guessed, I suppose, that this newfound tranquillity with which I was so pleased wouldn't last long. There was a succession of interruptions, of which by far the most pressing was the appeal made by my colleagues in the party that I return on a full-time basis—at least for a while—to help bring about the unification of all or most of the various sectors of the labor movement, which had recently been so seriously shaken by the Lavon Affair. If ever there was a time for unification, this was certainly it. The economic situation in Israel, and the national mood, were such that for the first time it was possible to imagine an end to the labor leadership of the country unless a united labor front could be brought into effective existence very soon. Mapai itself had been critically weakened by the secession of Rafi (the splinter party headed by Ben-Gurion and Dayan) and, to tell the truth, had never quite recovered from the much earlier split (in 1944) of Achdut Ha Avodah or from the formation, four years later, of the anti-Western, Marxist Mapam, whose chief support lay in the membership of the more radical kibbutzim and a number of young intellectuals who still cherished the idea that an Israel-Soviet rapprochement was possible and could be achieved simply by wanting it enough!

The ideological differences between Mapai, Rafi and Achdut Ha Avodah were not, however, so great that a united labor party was out of the question. But someone would have to undertake the actual job of bridge building, of reconciling the various points of view and personalities, of healing old wounds without making fresh ones and of creating a new and viable structure. Whoever that person was, it would have to be someone utterly committed to the vision of a single labor party able to contain within itself political factions that had been at odds with each other for years and believing implicitly in the urgent need for a labor coalition. There was, said my colleagues (who took to coming to talk to me in relays), only one person who had all the necessary qualifications—and time. If I were unwilling to take the job, for purely selfish reasons, it would never be done. All that they were asking of me was that I become secretary-general of Mapai until the unification was achieved—and assured. Then I could go back into my retirement.

It was the one appeal that I couldn't turn down. Not because I was so sure that I would succeed or because I so yearned to be in the middle of a crucial struggle all over again—and not because I was bored, as many people probably thought—but for a much simpler and much more important reason: I truly believed that the future of the labor movement was at stake. And although I could hardly bear the idea of giving up the peace and quiet I had finally attained—even if for only a few months—I couldn't turn my back at this stage of my life either on my principles or on my colleagues. So I said yes and went back to work, to traveling, to incessant meetings and to the bondage of an appointment book, but I promised myself—and my children—that this was the last job I would ever do.

In the meantime, a number of events had occurred in the Middle East which were to place Israel's future in far greater jeopardy than labor disunity at home could ever have done. In 1966 preparations were already being made by the Arabs for another round of war. The symptoms were all familiar. As a matter of fact, in a way the prelude to the Six-Day War of 1967 was identical to the prelude to the Sinai Campaign: Terrorist gangs—as actively encouraged and supported by President Nasser as the fedayeen had been in the fifties—were operating against Israel from both the Gaza Strip and Jordan. They included a new organizaion, founded in 1965, known as the El Fatah, which, under Yasir Arafat's leadership, subsequently became the most powerful and well-publicized element in the Palestine Liberation Organization. Also, a united Egyptian-Syrian high command had been established, and vast sums of money were allocated at an Arab summit conference for the express purpose of stockpiling weapons to be used against Israel—and, of course, the Soviet Union was still pumping both arms and money into the Arab states. The Syrians seemed bent on an escalation of the conflict; they kept up an endless bombardment of the Israeli settlements below the Golan Heights, and Israeli fishermen and farmers faced what was sometimes virtually daily attack by snipers. I used to visit those settlemets occasionally and watch the settlers go about their work as though there were nothing at all unusual in plowing with a military escort or putting children to sleep—every single night—in underground air-raid shelters. But I never believed them when they said that they had got quite used to living under perpetual fire. I don't think parents ever get "used" to the idea that their children's lives are in danger.

Then, in the autumn of 1966, the Soviet Union suddenly began to accuse Israel of readying its forces for a full-scale attack against Syria. It was an absurd charge, but it was duly investigated by the United Nations and, naturally, found to be without any basis. The Russians, however, kept on making the same accusations and talking about the Israeli "aggression" that was bound to cause a third round of the Arab-Israeli war, while the Syrians, receiving arms and financial aid from the Soviet Union, kept up their raids on our border settlements. Whenever the Syrian terror reached an intolerable point, Israel's air force would go into action against the terrorists, and for a few weeks the border settlements could relax. But by the early spring of 1967 these periods of relative relaxation were becoming fewer and shorter. In April, 1967, the air force was sent up in an action that turned into an air battle and resulted in the downing by Israeli plans of six Syrian MIGs. When this happened, the Syrians, egged on as always by the Soviet Union, once again screamed that Israel was making preparations for a major offensive against Syria, and an official complaint to this effect was even made on Syria's behalf to Prime Minister Eshkol by the Soviet ambassador to Israel, Mr. Chuvakhin. Not only was this one of the most grotesque incidents of the period, but it actually helped trigger the war that broke out in June.

"We understand," Chuvakhin said very unpleasantly to Eshkol, "that in spite of all your official statements, there are, in fact, extremely heavy concentrations of Israeli troops all along the Syrian border." This time Eshkol did more than merely deny the allegation. He asked Chuvakhin to go up north and look at the situation along the border for himself, and he even offered to accompany the ambassador on the trip. But Chuvakhin promptly said he had other things to do and refused the invitation, although all that was involved was only a few hours' drive. Of course, had he gone, he would have been forced to report to the Kremlin—and to the Syrians—that no Israeli soldiers were massed on the border and that the supposed Syrian alarm was absolutely unjustified. But this was exactly what he didn't want to do. By refusing to take that trip, he successfully breathed new life into the lie that helped set in motion Nasser's entry into the picture and therefore the Six-Day War.

At the beginning of May, responding to what he termed the "desperate plight" of the Syrians, Nasser ordered Egyptian troops and armour to mass in the Sinai, and just in case anyone misunderstood his intentions, Cairo Radio shrilly announced that "Egypt, with all its resources . . . is ready to plunge into a total war that will be the end of Israel."

On May 16 Nasser moved again—only now he gave orders not to his own army but to the United Nations. He demanded that the UN Emergency Force that had been stationed both at Sharm el-Sheikh and in the Gaza Strip since 1956, get out at once. Legally, he had a right to evict the UNEF because it was only with Egypt's consent that the international police force had been stationed on Egyptian soil, but I don't for a minute believe that Nasser actually expected the United Nations to do his bidding meekly. It was against all rhyme or reason for a force that had come into existence for the sole purpose of supervising the cease-fire between Egypt and Israel to be removed at the request of one of the combatants the very moment that the cease-fire was seriously threatened, and I am sure that Nasser anticipated a long round of discussions, arguments and haggling. If nothing else, he almost certainly reckoned that the United Nations would insist on some kind of phasing-out operation. However, for reasons which have never been understood by anyone—least of all by me—the UN secretary-general, U Thant, gave in to Nasser at once. He didn't refer the matter to anyone else. He didn't ask the Security Council for an opinion. He didn't even suggest a delay of a few days. Entirely of his own accord, U Thant instantly agreed to the immediate withdrawal of the UNEF. It started to move out of Sharm el-Sheikh and the Gaza Strip the very next day, and by May 19, to the tune of wild Egyptian applause, the last unit of the UNEF had pulled out, leaving the Egyptians in full control of their border with Israel.

I don't think that anyone could have felt more bitter than I did about U Thant's ludicrous surrender to Nasser. Not, God forbid, because I was the only person to understand what was happening. Far from it. But because it brought back to me, in an almost intolerable rush of pain and anxiety, the memory of those frightful months in New York after the Sinai Campaign, when the entire world seemed bent on forcing us to withdraw our troops from the Sinai and the Gaza Strip, regardless of what we knew, and said, would inevitably happen as a result. I went over and over those months in my mind: the hours of difficult fruit-

less conversation with Mr. Dulles, the equally difficult and
fruitless behind-the-scenes negotiations we had held with
the delegates of other powerful states, the incessant efforts
we had made—without the slightest success—to explain
that there was only one way to ensure peace in the Middle
East, not by continuing to appease the Arabs at our expense, but by insisting on a nonaggression pact between the
Arab states and Israel, on regional disarmament and on
direct negotiations. Why had it seemed so simple and so
obvious to us but so impossible of attainment to everyone
else? Hadn't we explained the realities of life in our part of
the world properly? Had I made some dreadful mistake or
left something crucial unsaid? The more I thought about
those months in 1956 and 1957, the more apparent it became to me now that nothing at all had changed since then
and that the Arabs were once again being permitted to de-
lude themselves that they could wipe us off the face of the
earth.

That delusion was further strengthened on May 22,
when Nasser, intoxicated by the success of his dismissal of
the UNEF, made another test of the world's reaction to his
stated intention of entering an all-out war with Israel. He
announced that Egypt was reimposing its blockade of the
Strait of Tiran, despite the fact that a score of nations (including the United States, Britain, Canada and France) had
guaranteed Israel's right of navigation through the Gulf of
Aqaba. It was without any question another deliberate
challenge, and Nasser waited to see how it would be met.
He didn't have to wait very long. No one was going to do
much about that either. Of course, there were protests and
angry reactions. President Johnson described the blockade
as "illegal" and "potentially disastrous to the cause of
peace" and suggested that an international convoy, including an Israeli vessel, sail through the strait to call Nasser's
bluff. But even he couldn't persuade the French or British
to join him. The Security Council met in an emergency
session, but the Russians saw to it that no conclusions were
reached. The British prime minister, my good friend Harold Wilson, flew to the States and to Canada to suggest that
an international naval task force be organized to police the
Strait of Tiran, but he also got nowhere with his suggestion.
Even U Thant—realizing at last what a terrible mistake he

had made—finally bestirred himself sufficiently to go to Cairo and try to reason with Nasser, but it was too late.

Nasser had drawn his own conclusions: If the so-called guarantees that had been given to Israel after the Sinai Campaign by the maritime powers were as worthless as they now appeared to be, then what and who were to stop the Egyptians from winning that final, glorious and total victory over the Jewish state that would make Nasser the supreme figure of the Arab world? To the extent that he had any remaining doubts regarding the adventure into which he was about to plunge himself and his nation, they were swept away by the Russians. The Soviet minister of defense brought Nasser a last-minute message of encouragement from Kosygin: The Soviet Union would stand by Egypt in the battle that lay ahead. So the stage was set. As for war aims, to the extent that Nasser felt obliged to explain anything to the Egyptian people—who were already in the first throes of war hysteria—it was enough to go on repeating the clause "We aim at the destruction of the State of Israel" and to tell the Egyptian National Assembly, as he did in the last week of May, "The issue is *not* the question of Aqaba, the Strait of Tiran or the UNEF. . . . The issue is the aggression against Palestine that took place in 1948." In other words, the war that was now in the making was to be the *ultimate* Arab war against us, and on the face of it, Nasser had every reason for thinking that he would win it.

By June 1 there were 100,000 Egyptian soldiers and more than 900 Egyptian tanks in the Sinai, plus six Syrian brigades and nearly 300 Syrian tanks straining at the leash in the north. Also—after having hesitated for a few weeks—Jordan's King Hussein had finally decided to take the risk of joining Nasser in the great exploit. Although we had sent him constant messages promising that if he kept out of the war nothing would happen to him (the last of these messages was sent to Hussein by Eshkol through the good offices of the UN Truce Supervision Organization on the very morning that the war broke out), the temptation of participating in the victory—as well as his fear of defying Nasser—finally got the better of Hussein, and he, too, threw his lot in with the Egyptians—which provided the Arab war effort with seven more brigades, about 270 more tanks and a small but competent air force. The last to join in the coalition against Israel was Iraq, which signed a mu-

tual defense pact with Egypt a day before the war began.
It was certainly a most formidable array of military
might, and since the West seemed to be either paralyzed or
totally indifferent, while the Russians were backing the
Arabs to the hilt, one can't really blame Nasser very much
for having assumed that at last he was in a position to deal a
deathblow to Israel.

Well, so much for the Arab mood and the Arab dream.
What was happening to us? I neither want nor do I think it
is necessary to retell in detail the story of the Six-Day War,
about which so much has already been written. But no one
who lived in Israel during the weeks that preceded it will
ever, I believe, forget the way in which we faced the terrible danger that confronted us. And no one can possibly
understand Israel's reaction to its current situation without
first understanding what we learned about ourselves, about
the Arab states and about the rest of the world in the
course of those three weeks in the spring of 1967 that came
to be known in Hebrew as the period of *konnenut* (preparedness). Of course, I was not a member of the cabinet any
longer, but it was only natural that in the developing crisis
I should be called on to help arrive at some of the life–
or–death decisions that faced the cabinet, and it was taken
for granted, I think, by everyone that I had to make myself
available.

From the beginning there was no question in anyone's
mind that war had to be averted—at almost any cost.
There was no question that if we had to fight, we would do
so—and win—but first, every possible avenue had to be
explored. Eshkol, his face gray with weariness and tension,
set in motion a search for some kind of diplomatic intervention. That was the sum total of his requests; needless to
say, we never asked for military personnel. Eban was sent
on a round of missions to Paris, London, and Washington,
and at the same time Eshkol quietly gave the signal for the
nation to ready itself for the third time in nineteen years to
defend its right to exist. Eban came back with nothing except the worst possible news. Our gravest fears had been
confirmed. London and Washington were sympathetic and
worried, but still not prepared to take any action. It was
too bad, but maybe the Arab frenzy would wear itself out.
At all events, they recommended patience and self-control.
There was no alternative other than for Israel to wait and

see. De Gaulle had been more direct: Whatever happened he told Eban, Israel must not make the first move until and unless the Arab attack actually began. When that happened, France would step in to save the situation. To Eban's question "But what if we are no longer there to be saved?" De Gaulle chose not to reply, but he made clear to Eban that France's continued friendship with us depended entirely on whether or not we obeyed him.

Within a matter of a few days our survival was suddenly at stake. In the most literal sense of these dreadful words, we were alone. The Western world, of which we had always considered ourselves to be a part, had heard what we had to say, had listened to our assessment of the extreme danger confronting us, though in the streets and assembly halls everywhere, the people were with us. So we began to get ready for the inevitable war. The army turned to its contingency plans. Eshkol ordered a general mobilization. The overage men and the women and children of Israel buckled down to clean out basements and cellars for use as makeshift air-raid shelters, to fill thousands of sandbags with which to line the pathetic homemade trenches that fathers and grandfathers dug in every garden and schoolyard throughout the country and to take over the essential chores of civilian life, while the troops waited, under camouflage nets in the sands of the Negev—waited, trained and went on waiting. It was as though some gigantic clock were ticking away for all of us, although no one except Nasser knew when the zero hour would be.

By the end of May ordinary life—as we had known it in the previous months—came to an end. Each day seemed to contain double the normal number of hours, and each hour seemed endless. In the heat of the early summer I did what everyone else was doing: I packed a little overnight bag with a few essential belongings that might be needed in the shelter and put it where it could most easily be grabbed as soon as the sirens started to wail. I helped Aya make identification disks out of oilcloth for the children to wear and blacked out one room in each house so that we could put on the light somewhere in the evenings. I went to Revivim one day to see Sarah and the children. I watched the kibbutz that I had known from its first day calmly prepare itself for the Arab onslaught that might turn it into rubble, and I met with some of Sarah's friends—at their request—

to talk about what might happen. But what they really wanted to know was when the waiting would end, and that was a question I couldn't answer. So the clock ticked on, and we waited and waited.

There were also the grim preparations that had to be kept secret: the parks in each city that had been consecrated for possible use as mass cemeteries; the hotels cleared of guests so that they could be turned into huge emergency first-aid stations; the iron rations stockpiled against the time when the population might have to be fed from some central source, the bandages, drugs and stretchers that were obtained and distributed. And of course, above all, there were the military preparations, because even though we had by now absorbed the fact that we were entirely on our own, there wasn't a single person in Israel, as far as I know, who had any illusions about the fact that there was no alternative whatsoever to winning the war that was being thrust on us. When I think back on those days, what stands out in my mind is the miraculous sense of unity and purpose that transformed us within only a week or two from a small, rather claustrophobic community, coping—and not always well—with all sorts of economic, political and social discontents into 2,500,000 Jews, each and every one of whom felt personally responsible for the survival of the State of Israel and each and every one of whom knew that the enemy we faced was committed to our annihilation.

So the issue was not, as it is perhaps for other countries, how best to remain intact and least damaged by an inevitable war, but rather how to survive as a people. The answer to that question was never in doubt. We could survive only by being victorious, and everything else—all the complaints, pettinesses and dissensions—fell away from us; we became, to put it very simply, one family, determined not to budge. Not one Jew left Israel during those awful weeks of waiting. Not one of the mothers in the settlements below the Golan Heights or in the Negev took her children and ran. Not one survivor of the Nazi death camps, many of whom had lost their children in the gas chambers, said, "I cannot bear to suffer again." And hundreds upon hundreds of Israelis who had gone abroad returned, although no one had called them back. They returned because they just could not stay away.

More than that, world Jewry looked on, saw our extreme peril and our isolation and asked itself, for the first time I think: What if the State of Israel ceases to exist? To this question there was also only one possible and short answer: No Jew anywhere in the world would ever feel free again if the Jewish state were to be eradicated. After the war—on its last days, to be accurate—I flew to the United States for a few days, and I spoke at a huge rally that was organized at Madison Square Garden by the United Jewish Appeal. My schedule was very crowded, and I was in a great hurry to get home again; but I very much wanted to meet some of the thousands of young American Jews who had besieged Israeli consulates throughout the United States in their clamor to be with us in the war. I wanted to know what had impelled them—and others, like the young British Jews who rioted at London Airport because El Al (the only airline flying to Israel during the war) couldn't possibly take all the volunteers who wanted to come—to put their heads in the noose that was already being so tightly bound around our throats. After all, it wasn't a romantic border skirmish that awaited them in Israel. A tremendous apparatus for killing, mutilating and destroying us had been assembled on our frontiers, and every day that apparatus was moving in, closer and closer. Like us, they had been treated to the revolting nightly spectacle of televised mobs throughout the Arab world clamoring hysterically for the bloodbath that was to spell the end of Irael. So they had certainly known the score. In the end most of them had not managed to come to Israel. The State Department had stopped them, and anyhow the fighting was over in six days; but I felt an overwhelming need to ascertain for myself what Israel really meant to them, and I asked my friends in New York to arrange a meeting for me with at least some of the 2,500 young Jews from that city who had volunteered to go to Israel during the war.

It wasn't easy to arrange the meeting within twenty-four hours, but it was done, and more than 1,000 of those youngsters came to talk to me. "Tell me," I asked them, "why did you want to come? Was it because of the way you were brought up? Or because you thought it would be exciting? Or because you are Zionists? What did you think about when you stood in line last month and asked to be allowed to go to Israel?"

There wasn't a uniform answer, of course, to my question, but it seemed to me that one young man spoke for all of them when he got up and said, "I don't know how to explain it to you, Mrs. Meir, but I do know one thing. My life will never be the same again. The Six-Day War—and the fact that Israel came so close to being destroyed—has changed everything for me: my feelings about myself, my family, even my neighbors. Nothing will ever be quite the same for me as it was before."

It wasn't a very coherent reply; but it came from his heart, and I knew what he was talking about. It was about his identity as a Jew and about the larger family to which he suddenly knew he belonged, for all of the differences between us. The threat we were experiencing, to be very blunt, was the threat of extinction, and to that Jews respond in the same way, whether they go to the synagogue or not, whether they live in New York, Buenos Aires, Paris, Moscow or Petach Tikva. It is a deeply familiar threat, and when Nasser and his associates made it, they doomed their war to failure because we had decided—all of us—that there was to be no repetition of Hitler's "Final Solution" and no second Holocaust.

In a certain respect, that great coming together of a nation to meet a collective threat was responsible also for the demand that arose in Israel for a "wall-to-wall" coalition of all our political parties (except the communists), and for the assumption of the defense portfolio by someone with more practical military experience than Levi Eshkol. I must say that I was not in favor of either development. National coalitions—with which I was subsequently to have some experience myself—may be all very well under normal circumstances, when there is time for lengthy discussions that represent contrasting points of view; but they are positively counterproductive, in my opinion, at moments when truly fateful decisions must be taken and when only shared ideologies, attitudes and backgrounds make it possible for a cabinet to do its job in the most efficient and harmonious way. If it were necessary, in those last few days before the war to strengthen Eshkol's government—which I doubted—I thought that this could and should be done without making major alterations and without major changes of personnel. I knew—although many people in Israel did not know this then—that Eshkol in his dual role as prime minister and minister of defense had seen to it, without fanfare or drawing attention to himself in any way, that the Israel Defense Forces were ready for the task that lay ahead of them. His relationship with the army, his understanding of its needs and his ability to secure for it what it needed were never in doubt.

I was no blinder than anyone else to Eshkol's somewhat tentative manner. He addressed the nation once or twice during the worst days of the *konnenut*, and he said all that anyone else could or should have said; but he said it hesitantly and without any flair, when what the country wanted was more dynamic leadership. Personally, I didn't think—and don't think even in retrospect—that any of this mattered. He was a very wise and dedicated man who found himself shouldering about as staggering a responsibility as any statesman has ever shouldered and who felt weighed down by it. Only a fool would have felt differently, and if he stuttered a little when he spoke about sending his people to war, it was only to his eternal credit.

I myself have learned since then how it feels, and I thought about Eshkol more than once during the Yom Kippur War, when I had to appear on television and did so feeling and looking as grim as death because what I had to say—and what no one else could say for me—was so serious that I couldn't worry much about my choice of words or how I delivered my speech. But like other things, if you have never been there yourself, it is hard to imagine, and many Israelis—their nerves stretched close to the breaking point—felt let down by Eshkol's broadcast and by his continued desperate attempts to find some way other than war that would break the impasse. What was the point of sending Eban to knock on yet another door? How much longer could the uncertainty last? Were we going to remain like this forever—mobilized and waiting? Eshkol seemed too uncertain, too reluctant to take action. These were heroic times, but where was the hero?

In all this storm of criticism there was no real demand that Eshkol resign; there was only a growing, though unreasonable, dissatisfaction with him, which turned into growing pressure for the appointment of a new minister of defense, someone bolder and much more charismatic. By the end of May it was clear that thousands of Israelis were looking to Moshe Dayan to express the national determination to endure and to prevail. It was as though the Israelis (not all of them, but a great many) were counting on Dayan to provide something which Eshkol couldn't offer. Even now, I can't define exactly what it was they sought. Maybe it was the assurance of being led, in a time of such stress, by a fighter, or maybe it had to do with that quality of fearlessness that is so strong a part of Dayan's personality. Whatever it was, there was no withstanding the pressure. In the end Eshkol, hurt to the core, but realizing that it was essential to maintain maximum unity, gave in, and I stopped asking myself how come, if Dayan was such an obvious candidate to head the Ministry of Defense, even Ben-Gurion had never given him the portfolio.

Dayan remained Israel's minister of defense until 1974; he was the only minister of defense to serve in my cabinet, and we worked together extremely well. Nevertheless, I hope he will forgive me for saying that I still don't believe that his appointment in 1967 changed the course of the Six-Day War in any basic way, or that he was the main architect of our victory. The Israel Defense Forces had not waited until June 1 either to plan their strategy or to train for it, and the real heroes of that victory were, of course, the people of Israel. It is hard for me to imagine that the war would have ended differently had Dayan not entered the government. Having said this, I must in all fairness admit, however, that although I felt that a great injustice was being done to Eshkol, the Israeli public had at last acquired the dynamic and dramatic military leadership it so badly wanted, and perhaps even needed, and I was grateful that the issue was settled.

There are two other general comments I must make about the Six-Day War. The first should go without saying; but I have learned not to take anything for granted, and there may still be people who do not understand that we fought that war so successfully not only because we were made to fight it, but also because we most profoundly hoped that we would achieve a victory so complete that we would never have to fight again. If the defeat of the Arab armies massed against us could be made total, then perhaps our neighbors would finally give up their "holy war" against us and realize that peace was as necessary for them as for us and that the lives of their sons were as precious as the lives of our sons. We were wrong about that. The defeat *was* total, and the Arab losses *were* devastating; but the Arabs still couldn't, and didn't, come to grips with the fact that Israel was not going to accommodate them by disappearing from the map. The second point of which I would like to remind my readers is that in June, 1967, the Sinai, the Gaza Strip, the West Bank, the Golan Heights and East Jerusalem all were in Arab possession, so that it is ludicrous to argue today that Israel's presence in those territories *since* 1967 is the cause of tension in the Middle East or was the cause of the Yom Kippur War. When Arab statesmen insist that Israel withdraw to the pre-June, 1967, lines, one can only ask: If those lines are so sacred to the Arabs, why was the Six-Day War launched to destroy them?

The war began early in the morning of Monday, June 5. As soon as we heard the whine of the air-raid sirens, we knew that the waiting was over, although it was not until very late that night that the dimensions of Israel's strike were revealed to the nation. All day, while wave after wave of our planes flew over the Mediterranean to blast the Egyptian airfields and demolish the aircraft poised to attack us, we waited for news, ears glued to the transistor radios that we all carried around with us but on which there was nothing to hear except music, Hebrew songs and the passwords that were used to call up reservists who had still not been mobilized. It was only after midnight that the official and almost incredible story of the first of those six days was unfolded to the civilian population by the chief of the air force and that, sitting in their blacked-out rooms, the people of Israel learned that they had been delivered from destruction within the six hours that it had taken the air force to put out of action more than 400 enemy planes, including those parked on Syrian and Jordanian airfields, and to gain full command of the air from Sinai to the Syrian border. I had been kept informed all day of the general situation, but even I had not quite grasped the implications of what had happened until after the broadcast. I stood alone for a few minutes at the door of my house, looked up at the cloudless and undisturbed sky and realized that we had been rescued from the terrible fear of air raids that had haunted us all for so many days. True, the war had only started; there would still be death and mourning and misery. But the planes that had been readied to bomb us were all mortally crippled, and the airfields from which they had

been about to take off were now in ruins. I stood there and
breathed in the night air as though I had not drawn a
really deep breath for weeks.

It was not only in the air that we had won a conclusive
victory, however. That same day, racing along the three
routes they had taken in 1956, our ground forces, backed
by the air force, had pushed their way deep into the Sinai,
were already gaining the upperhand in tank battles that involved even more armor than had clashed in the Western
Desert in World War II, and were already well on their
way to the Suez Canal. Israel's hand, held out in peace for
so long, turned into a fist, and there was no stopping the
forward advance of the Israeli Defense Forces. But Nasser
was not the only Arab ruler whose plans were shattered on
June 5.

There was also Hussein, who had measured Eshkol's
promise that nothing would happen to Jordan if he kept
out of the war against the message he had received from
Nasser that very morning informing him that Tel Aviv was
being bombed by the Egyptians—never mind that Nasser
didn't have a single bomber to his name by then. Like his
grandfather before him, Hussein had carefully weighed the
odds and made a mistake. On June 5 he ordered his troops
to start shelling Jerusalem and the Jewish settlements on
the Jordan-Israeli border. His army was to serve as the
eastern arm of the pincer movement that was to do us in,
but failed in its mission. As soon as the Jordanian shelling
began, the Israeli Defense Forces struck at Hussein also, and
although the fighting on the Jerusalem front cost the lives
of very many young Israelis—who fought hand to hand
and street by narrow street, rather than resort to the mortars
and tanks that might have damaged the city and the Christian and Moslem holy places—it was already clear that night
that Hussein's greed was going to lose him his hold on eastern Jerusalem, at the very least. At the risk of repeating myself, I must emphasize, at this point, that just as in 1948 the
Arabs had hammered at Jerusalem without the slightest regard for the safety of its churches and holy places, so in
1967 Jordanian troops didn't hesitate to use churches and
even the minarets of their own mosques for emplacements.
This may explain why we resent the fears that are sometimes expressed for the sanctity of Jerusalem under Israeli
administration, to say nothing of what we discovered when

we finally entered East Jerusalem: Jewish cemeteries had been desecrated, the ancient synagogues of the Jewish Quarter of the Old City had been razed to the ground, and Jewish tombstones from the Mount of Olives had been used to pave Jordanian roads and Jordanian army latrines. So let no one ever try to convince me that Jerusalem is better off in Arab hands or that we cannot be trusted to take care of it.

It took all of three days for the Egyptians to be beaten and two days for Hussein to pay for his error of judgment. By Thursday, June 8, the governor of the Gaza Strip had surrendered, Israeli forces were settled in on the east bank of the Suez Canal, the Strait of Tiran was back under Israel's control and 80 percent, if not more, of Egypt's military equipment had been destroyed. Even Nasser, not the most accurate of men, admitted that 10,000 Egyptian soldiers and 1,500 Egyptian officers had been lost, and we had nearly 6,000 Egyptian prisoners. The whole of the Sinai and the Gaza Strip had fallen to Israel again. So had East Jerusalem, the Old City and virtually half of the kingdom of Jordan. But we had still not learned how many of our boys had died in the fighting, and there was still one more aggressor to deal with. On Friday, June 9, the Israel Defense Force turned their attention to Syria and to rectifying the Syrian mistake in believing that the guns on top of the Golan Heights that had been pounding away relentlessly at the Jewish villages in the valley below were really invincible. I must confess that there was some justification for the Syrian self-confidence. After the war, when I visited the Golan Heights and saw for myself the miles upon miles of reinforced concrete bunkers bristling with barbed wire and filled with antitank guns and artillery, I understood why the Syrians had been so sure of themselves and why it took two bloody days and one terrible night for the Israel Defense Force to scale the Golan Heights, inch by inch, and then force their way into those bunkers. But it was done— by the army, the air force, the paratroopers and brave engineers in bulldozers—and by June 10 the Syrians were begging the United Nations to arrange a cease-fire. General David Elazar (our chief of staff during the Yom Kippur War) was then the commander of the northern front. When the fighting was over, he sent a message to those Israeli settlements in the valley: "Only from these heights can I see how really great you are."

It was all over. The Arab states and their Soviet patrons had lost their war. But this time, the price for our withdrawal was going to be very high, higher than it had been in 1956. This time the price would be peace, permanent peace, peace by treaty based on agreed and secure borders. It had been a lightning war, but it had also been a cruel one. All over Israel there were military funerals again, many of them the funerals of boys whose fathers or older brothers had fallen in the War of Independence or the fighting that had plagued us ever since. We were not going to go through that anguish again if we could possibly help it. We were not going to be told what a wonderful people the Israelis are. They win wars every ten years, and they have done it again. Fantastic! Now that they have won this round, they can go back where they came from, so that Syrian gunners on the Golan Heights can again shoot into the kibbutzim, so that Jordanian legionnaires on the towers of the Old City can again shell at will, so that the Gaza Strip can again be a nest for terrorists and the Sinai Desert can again become the staging ground for Nasser's divisions.

"Is there anybody," I asked at that rally in New York, "who is bold enough to say to us: 'Go home! Start preparing your nine-and ten-year-olds for the next war.' I am sure that every decent person in the world will say no, and—forgive me for being so blunt—most important of all, we ourselves say no."

We had fought alone for our existence and our security and paid for them, and it seemed to most of us that a new day was really about to dawn, that the Arabs—trounced on the battlefield—might agree at last to sit down and thrash out the differences between us, none of which ever was, or is, insoluble.

There was no sense of triumph, only an enormous surge of hopefulness. And in the sheer relief of the victory, in the delight of finding ourselves alive and relatively unscathed and dazed momentarily by the prospect of peace, the whole of Israel went on a sort of holiday that lasted most of the summer. I don't think that there was a single family, including my own, that didn't take off a few days right after the Six-Day War to indulge in what looked to strangers like mass sightseeing, but was really a kind of pilgrimage to those parts of the Holy Land from which we had been excluded for nearly twenty years. In the first place, of course, the Jews streamed to Jerusalem; thousands and thousands of people daily crowded the Old City, praying in front of the Western Wall and picking their way through the ruins of what had been the Jewish Quarter. But we also went to Bethlehem, Jericho, Hebron and Gaza and Sharm el-Sheikh. Offices, factories, kibbutzim and schools—all participated in the endless excursions, and hundreds of cars, buses, trucks and even taxis, packed to the brim, crisscrossed the country for months en route to Mount Hermon in the north or Mount Sinai in the south. Everywhere we went during that elated, almost carefree summer, we met the Arabs of the territories that we now administered, smiled at them, bought their produce and talked to them, sharing with them—even if not always in words—the vision of peace that suddenly seemed about to become a reality and trying to convey to them our joy that now we would all be able to live together normally.

Everyone was on wheels in those days because the Arabs in the administered territories were traveling around almost as much as we were. They flocked to Tel Aviv, to the seashore and to the zoo, stared at the shopwindows in West Jerusalem and sat in the cafés of all the main streets. Most of them were as excited and as curious as we were and, like us, were absorbed in looking at landscapes which the adults had forgotten and the children had never seen. All this may sound too good to be true, and I certainly don't want to convey the impression that the Arabs turned to Mecca five times a day to thank Allah for their good fortune in having been defeated or that there were not Jews who preferred to stay home rather than participate in what they felt to be an indecent celebration of peace before the scars of war had had time to heal. But anyone who visited Israel in the summer of 1967 will testify to the extraordinary euphoria that gripped the Jews and appeared also to affect the Arabs. It was, in short, as though a death sentence had been lifted—which was, after all, literally true.

If I have to choose one particular aspect of that immediate post war period as an illustration of the general atmosphere, I would certainly point to the tearing down of the concrete barricade and barbed-wire fences that had separated the two halves of the city of Jerusalem ever since

1948. More than anything else, those hideous barricades had signified the abnormality of our life, and when they were bulldozed away and Jerusalem overnight became one city, it was like a sign and symbol of a new era. As someone who came to Jerusalem then for the very first time said to me, "There is light from within the city," and I understood exactly what he meant. "Very soon," I told my grandchildren, "the soldiers will come home; there will be peace; we will be able to travel to Jordan and to Egypt; and all will be well." I honestly believed it, but it wasn't to be.

In August, 1967, at a summit conference in Khartoum, the Arab leaders reviewed the situation and came to an altogether different conclusion. They issued their notorious three noes: There would be no peace with Israel, no recognition of the Jewish state and no negotiations. No, no, no! Israel must withdraw, totally and unconditionally, from the territories taken in the Six-Day War, and the Arab terrorists who were invited to the conference added a fourth helpful statement of their own: Israel must be destroyed, even within the pre-1967 boundaries. This was their answer to the Israeli government's appeal: "Let us meet not as conqueror and conquered, but as equals to negotiate peace—with no preconditions." Never mind who started the war, and never mind who won it. As far as the Arabs were concerned, nothing had changed. So the so-called fruits of the victory turned into ashes before they could ripen, and the lovely dream of immediate peace faded away. But if the Arabs had learned nothing, we had learned something. We were not prepared to repeat the exercise of 1956. Discuss, negotiate, compromise, concede— all these, yes! But not go back to where we had been on June 4, 1967. That accommodating we couldn't afford to be, even to save Nasser's face or to make the Syrians feel better about not having destroyed us! It was a great pity that the Arab states felt so humiliated by losing the war which they had started that they just couldn't bring themselves to talk to us, but on the other hand, we couldn't be expected to reward them for having tried to throw us into the sea. We were bitterly disappointed, but there was only one possible reply: Israel would not withdraw from any of the territories until the Arab states once and for all put an end to the conflict. We decided—and, believe me, it was not a painless decision, that whatever it cost us in terms of public opinion, money or energy, and regardless of the pressures that might be brought to bear on us, we would stand fast on the cease-fire lines. We waited for the Arabs to accept the fact that the only alternative to war was peace and that the only road to peace was negotiation.

In the meantime, the close to 1,000,000 Arabs living in the territories on our side of the cease-fire lines—about 600,000 on the West Bank of the Jordan and some 365,000 in the Gaza Strip and the Sinai, plus the Druze villagers who had opted to stay on the Golan Heights after the Syrian army had gone—would live pretty much as they had lived before the Six-Day War. It is never a great pleasure to be accountable to a military government, and none of the Arabs in the territories enjoyed having Israeli patrols move around in their midst. But the army kept a very low profile indeed, and the military government —thanks largely to Dayan's concept of its role—interfered with daily life as little as possible. Local laws were retained, and so were local leaders. The bridges over the Jordan were open, and the Arabs on the West Bank went on trading with the Arab states, studying in the Arab states and visiting their relatives there, while their relatives were free to visit them—which they did by the thousands. It was only going to be an interim arrangement anyhow; no sane Israeli ever assumed that all the territories were going to remain under Israeli rule. Jerusalem, of course, would stay united, but an arrangement could be made regarding Moslem control over the Moslem holy places. New borders would have to be drawn up between Jordan and Israel; it was unlikely that the Golan Heights would be handed back, lock, stock and barrel, to the Syrians or that all of Sinai would be returned at once to the Egyptians, and the Gaza Strip was certainly a problem. But there was no point whatsoever in drawing maps of what the Middle East would look like or even to arguing among ourselves what territory would be returned to whom until these matters could be taken up with the only other people to whom they were of real concern—our neighbors. After all, you can't return territory by parcel post. So, we went on waiting for a response to our repeated call for talks.

In the meantime, the Security Council passed a resolution—the celebrated Resolution 242, sponsored by the British—which outlined a framework for the peaceful settlement of "the Arab-Israel dispute" and appointed a special representative, Dr. Gunnar V. Jarring, who was charged with supervising a "peaceful and accepted settlement." So much has been written and said about Resolution 242, and it has been so thoroughly distorted by the Arabs and the Russians, that I think it might be useful for me to quote it, particularly since it isn't very long:

The Security Council,

Expressing its continuing concern with the grave situation in the Middle East.

Emphasizing the inadmissibility of the acquisition of territory by war and the need to work for a just and lasting peace in which every State in the area can live in security.

Emphasizing further that all Member States in their acceptance of the Charter of the United Nations have undertaken a commitment to act in accordance with Article 2 of the Charter.

1. Affirms that the fulfillment of Charter principles requires the establishment of a just and lasting peace in the Middle East, which should include the application of both the following principles:

    (i) Withdrawal of Israeli armed forces from territories occupied in the recent conflict;

    (ii) Termination of all claims or states of belligerency and respect for and acknowledgement of the sovereignty, territorial integrity and political independence of every State in the area and their right to live in peace within secure and recognized boundaries free from threats or acts of force; and

2. Affirms further the necessity

    (i) For guaranteeing freedom of navigation through international waterways in the area;

    (ii) For achieving a just settlement of the refugee problem;

    (iii) For guaranteeing the territorial inviolability and political independence of every State in the area, through measures including the establishment of demilitarized zones.

It will be noted that it does *not* say that Israel must withdraw from all territories, nor does it say that Israel must withdraw from *the* territories; but it *does* say that every state in the area has a right to live in peace within "secure and recognized boundaries" and it *does* specify the termination of belligerency. Furthermore, it does *not* speak of a Palestinian state, while it *does* speak of a refugee problem. But it wasn't only Resolution 242 that was misinterpreted, but also our attitude that was being misinterpreted. After the Six-Day War, Israel's leading satirical writer, Ephraim Kishon, together with the Israeli cartoonist Dosh, published a book called *So Sorry We Won.* It was a bitter title, but not in the least ambiguous to its Israeli readers. In fact, it summed up rather succinctly the way we were beginning to feel, by 1968, which was that the only receipe for improving Israel's rapidly deteriorating image was to forget all about peace. Our crime appeared to be that we kept saying to the Arabs, "Let's negotiate." Not, as we were entitled to do, "This is the new map; sign on the dotted line," but "Let's negotiate."

In some mysterious way, this made us the villians. I couldn't for the life of me ever grasp, for instance, why Willy Brandt when he recognized the Oder-Neisse border because the time had come to put right the wrong that Germany had done to Poland in World War II, got (and richly deserved) the Nobel Prize for it and was hailed as a great statesman and a man of peace, while Eshkol and later I were branded as expansionists for wanting exactly the same kind of border adjustments between Israel and its neighbors. And not only were we called expansionists by our critics, but we were constantly being asked by our friends whether we weren't worried about Israel's turning into a militaristic nation (" a little Sparta" was the phrase most often used) that had to rely on its "brutal" occupation forces to preserve law and order in the administered territories. And, of course, "intransigent" was to become my middle name. But neither Eshkol nor I nor the overwhelming majority of other Israelis could make a secret of the fact that we weren't at all interested in a fine, liberal, antimilitaristic, *dead* Jewish state or in a "settlement" that would win us compliments about being reasonable and intelligent but that would endanger our lives. Dr. Weizmann used to say that he had become the president of a country where everybody is a president; Israeli democracy is so lively that there were, and are, also as many doves as hawks, but I have yet to come across any Israeli who thinks that we should turn ourselves, permanently, into clay pigeons—not even for the sake of a better image.

At all events, I still had an assignment to complete: the unification of the labor movement, which kept me busy through the winter of 1967 and the beginning of 1968. I was also, of course, at Eshkol's disposal whenever a new crisis broke out, either in connection with the stepped-up activities in the administered territories of El Fatah and the other smaller Arab terrorist groups that now declared themselves the only true representatives of the Arab people, or in connection with the incessant attempts that were being made to use Resolution 242 as a device for forcing on Israel withdrawal from all the territories in a way and at a time that was not acceptable to us. In January, 1968, the Israel Labor Party was formed—a union of Mapai, Achdut Ha Avodah and Rafi—and in February I was elected its secretary-general. It was really only a partial unification at this stage, a federation of three parties, and it wasn't until the next year that the larger alignment—Ma'arach, as it is called in Hebrew—which also involved an alliance with Mapam, was created. But despite the looseness of the ties that bound the three parties, at least they were now under one political roof, which was what I had undertaken to accomplish. So I thought that I could allow myself at last to go back into retirement, and in July I did so.

Now I was seventy. It is not a sin to be seventy but it is also no joke. I had been ill again in 1967, and neither the Six-Day War nor the creation of the Ma'arach was exactly what the doctor had ordered. I felt that I owed myself some peace and quiet, and this time nothing and no one would change my mind. I went to the States for an Israel bond drive and visited Menachem, Aya and the children in Connecticut, where Aya was working on a university research grant and Menachem was teaching cello. I even spent a few weeks in Switzerland on what I think, was the first complete holiday I had ever taken, and I came back home feeling as fit as a fiddle.

The situation at home, however, hadn't progressed much. Despite the cease-fire, there was still a war of sorts going on at the Suez Canal. The Egyptians, secure in the knowl-

edge that the Russians had already replaced all the guns,
tanks and planes that they had lost in the Six-Day War, were
keeping up a constant barrage of bombardments again just
as soon as they dared. "When the time comes, we will
strike," Nasser roared, and he repeated what he called "the
principles of Egyptian policy": no negotiations with Israel,
no peace with Israel, no recognition of Israel. And in the
spring of 1969 he launched what was to become known
as his war of attrition.

I suppose that from a distance, that continuous shelling
of the Israel Defense Forces positions on the Canal might
have seemed merely like another one of the protracted "incidents" that had been going on in the Middle East since
anyone could remember, another demonstration of the supposed inability of Jews and Arabs to get along together, and
I imagine that at first no one abroad took the reports about
the endless Egyptian violations of the cease-fire very seriously. But we did, because we knew what those violations
foretold, and we began to build a fortified defense line—the
Bar-Lev line—to protect our troops on the banks of the
Canal.

At the same time, when the Arab terrorist organizations
found they were unable to persuade or provoke the population of the administered territories into taking any major action against the Israelis—other than an occasional, though
certainly deeply felt, protest march in Hebron or strike in
Jenin—they decided to go in for terrorism thousands of
miles away from Israel. It was obviously much safer for
them and a great deal more effective, and there was a wide
choice of potential targets, including civilian aircraft and
innocent passengers in foreign air terminals. Besides, the
terrorists would then not have to restrict their terror to Jews.
The Saudi Arabians saw to it that El Fatah didn't lack
money; Nasser again bestowed his official blessings on them
("El Fatah," he proclaimed, "fulfills a vital task in drawing
the enemy's blood"); and King Hussein took another stroll
on his tightrope. Although the terrorists were soon to fight
him, tooth and nail, for control of Jordan and to endanger
him more than they had ever endangered us, Hussein—
with the same lack of foresight that he had shown in the
Six-Day War, gave them his enthusiastic support. In 1970,
when he found himself in such trouble with the so-called
Palestinian terrorist organizations and began looking around

everywhere for aid, I couldn't help thinking that he was like a man who murders his mother and father and then begs for mercy on the grounds that he·is an orphan!

In the north there was also no peace. Southern Lebanon was gradually being turned into a playground for the terrorists; Israeli towns, villages and farms—even school buses filled with children—were regularly being shelled and fired upon from what was now nicknamed Fatahland, while the Lebanese government wept crocodile tears and said it could do "nothing" about the activity of the terrorists or even the fact that they were trained and operating from Lebanese territory.

But we had decided that we were going to defend the cease-fire lines regardless of Nasser or El Fatah and, what's more, press on with our search for peace, however disheartening that search had become. Somehow we managed to cope with everything, without losing hope, mostly because our young men, for the sake of Israel's future, were willing to sit for weeks on Mount Hermon, or in Sinai, or in the Jordan Valley, holding those cease-fire lines, which was a very small joy. Let there be no misunderstanding of the extent of the sacrifice involved. This was an army made up of the reserves—farmers, waiters, students, owners of dry-cleaning establishments, doctors, truck drivers and so forth—none of whom was a professional soldier drawing decent pay for his military service. They were men who had answered the call to arms, done their duty magnificently and badly wanted to go home. They had other things to do and other obligations, and I don't think that there was ever a sadder victorious army in history because the war it had fought never came to a real end. The reservists went home for a few weeks or months, and then were called up again. They grumbled and muttered, but no one questioned the need to stay on those lines until a permanent peace was attained.

Then, on February 26, 1969, my dear friend Levi Eshkol, with whom I had worked for so many years and whom I had loved and admired so much, had a heart attack and died. I was at home alone when the news reached me, and I was stunned. I sat by the phone for several minutes in a state of shock, unable to pull myself together enough to find someone to drive me to Jerusalem. It seemed impossible that Eshkol was gone. I had talked to him only the night before, and we were to meet the next day. I couldn't imagine what would happen now or who would take his place as prime minister. In Jerusalem I immediately went to Eshkol's home. While the cabinet met in an emergency session, I sat in someone's office and waited for it to end so that I would know what had been decided about the funeral arrangements. As I sat there, an Israeli newspaperman came in.

"I know how you must feel," he said to me. "But I have just come from the Knesset. Everyone says there is only one solution. Golda must come back."

"I don't know what you are talking about," I answered furiously. "Please don't bother me now. This is no time to talk politics. Please, please, go away."

"Well," he said, "my editor wants to know where you'll be tonight. *He* wants to talk to you."

"Look," I said, "I don't want to see anyone now. I don't know anything, and I don't want to know anything. I just want you to leave me alone."

The cabinet meeting ended. Yigal Allon, who was deputy prime minister, took over as acting prime minister. I went with a group of cabinet ministers to see Miriam Eshkol again. Then, toward evening, I returned to Tel Aviv. At about 10 P.M. the editor rang my doorbell. "I come to tell you," he said, "that everybody has decided that you must take Eshkol's place. You are the only person with enough authority, experience and credit within the party to be acceptable to almost everyone."

If I had been in a different mood, I might have reminded him then and there that in a recent poll, when the public was asked about its choice of the next prime minister, I had won exactly 3 percent of the votes, which was all right by me, but not what one would call a landslide. The greatest number of votes had been received by Moshe Dayan, and Yigal Allon had not done so badly either. But I was in no frame of mind to discuss the matter. "Eshkol isn't even buried yet," I said to the editor. "How can you talk to me about these things?" and I sent him away.

But within a few days the party began to press me. "National elections are scheduled to take place in October; an interim prime minister will have to be appointed; it is only a question of a few months! And there is no one else." Even Allon himself beseeched me, for the sake of the party, so recently unified, and for the sake of the country, which was still in such peril, to perfom this last service. Not that the entire Labor Party was so keen on me. The ex-Rafi faction, headed by Dayan and Peres, was less than anxious to have me as prime minister, and I could certainly understand the reservations of those other people in the country who thought that a seventy-year-old grandmother was hardly the perfect candidate to head a twenty-year-old state.

As for me, I couldn't make up my mind. On the one hand, I realized that unless I agreed, there would inevitably be a tremendous tug-of-war between Dayan and Allon, which was one thing that Israel didn't need then. It was enough that we had a war with the Arabs on our hands; we could wait for that to end before we embarked on a war of the Jews. On the other hand, I honestly didn't want the responsibility, the awful stress and strain of being prime minister. I wanted to talk to the family, so I telephoned Menachem and Aya in Connecticut; and then I called up Sarah and Zechariah in Revivim and told them that I had to see them but was much too tired to go the Negev. Could they possibly come to me? They managed to get in by truck at midnight, and we sat up all through the night, talking, smoking and drinking coffee. In the morning, Sarah told me that Zechariah and she had made up their minds. They agreed with Menachem and Aya; I had no choice. "Ima, we know it will be terribly hard for you, harder than anyone will ever guess. But there is simply no way out—you must say yes. So I did. On March 7 the Central Committee of the Labor Party voted to nominate me as prime minister; there were seventy votes in favor, none against, and the Rafi faction abstained. I have often been asked how I felt at that moment, and I wish that I had a poetic answer to the question. I know that tears rolled down my cheeks and that I held my head in my hands when the voting was over, but all that I recall about my feelings is that I was dazed. I had never planned to be prime minister; I had never planned any position, in fact. I had planned to come to Palestine, to go to Merhavia, to be active in the labor movement. But the position I would occupy? That never. I only knew that now I would have to make decisions every day that would affect the lives of millions of people, and I think perhaps that is why I cried. But there wasn't much time for reflection, and any thoughts I had about the path that had begun in Kiev and led me to the prime minister's office in Jerusalem had to wait. Today, when I can take time for those reflections, I find I have no appetite for them. I became prime minister because that was how it was, in the same way that my milkman became an officer in command of an outpost on Mount Hermon. Neither of us had any particular relish for the job, but we both did it as well as we could.

13. The Prime Minister

So I moved again, this time to the large, not especially attractive prime minister's residence in Jerusalem—in
which Ben-Gurion, Sharett and Eshkol had lived before
me—and began to accustom myself to the permanent presence of police and bodyguards, to a workday of at least
sixteen hours and to the minimum of privacy. Obviously
some days were easier, shorter and less tense than others, and
I have no intention of pretending that I spent the five years
that I was prime minister of Israel in a state of martyrdom
or that I never enjoyed myself at all. But my term of office
began with one war and ended with another, and I can't
help thinking how symbolic it was that the very first in-
struction I gave to anyone in my capacity as prime minister
was to tell my military secretary Yisrael Lior, that I
was to be informed as soon as the reports from any military
action came in—even if it was in the middle of the night.

"I want to know the moment that the boys get back," I
told him, "and I want to know how they are." I didn't use
the word "casualties" but Lior understood and was horrified by the request.

"You don't really want me to phone you at three A.M.?"
he said. "After all, there is nothing you can do about it if
there are any casualties. I promise to call you first thing in
the morning."

But I knew that I wouldn't be able to bear the idea of
sleeping soundly through the night not even knowing if soldiers had been killed or wounded, and I forced poor Lior
to obey me. When the news was bad, of course, I couldn't
fall asleep again, and I spent more nights than I
care to remember padding around that big, empty house,
waiting for morning and for more detailed information.
Sometimes the bodyguards outside the house would see
that the kitchen light was on at 4 A.M., and one of them

would look in to make sure that I was all right. I'd make us both a cup of tea, and we'd talk about what was happening at the Canal or in the north until I felt that I could go back to bed again.

The Egyptian War of Attrition had started at the beginning of March, 1968, and went on, with increasing ferocity, till the summer of 1970. Not only did the Soviet Union refrain from pressuring Nasser to end the violence and the killing, but it rushed to Egypt thousands of Soviet instructors, to help retrain the battered Egyptian army and lend it a helping hand in combat against us and a flood of military equipment, conservatively valued at some $3.5 billion. Egypt was not the sole beneficiary of this Soviet largess; it went to Syria and Iraq also. But Nasser was certainly the main beneficiary. Two-thirds of all the hundreds of tanks and fighter aircraft that Russia poured into the area immediately following the Six-Day War were earmarked for Egyptian use in the hope that in the face of the incessant fire and our own mounting losses, we would be unable to maintain our position along the Canal and that broken in spirit as well as in body, we would finally agree to withdraw from the Canal zone without achieving peace or any kind of end to the conflict.

In theory, I suppose it looked simple to Nasser and to the Russians. If they could keep up their hammering of our fortifications on the Canal—making life a hell on earth for Israeli troops there—then, sooner or later (but probably sooner), we would have to cry uncle. After all, it was no secret either to the Egyptians or to the Soviet Union that each Israeli casualty, each of the many Israeli military funerals that went on all through that period, each bereaved Israeli family were like knives being turned in the heart of the entire nation, and I can understand all too well why Nasser and his patrons were sure that we would eventually give up. But we didn't—because we couldn't afford to. We weren't very eager to go on fighting anyone—not the Egyptians and even less the Russians—but we had absolutely no alternative. The only way we could possibly prevent that total war which Nasser himself proclaimed day and night to be the ultimate goal of his War of Attrition was by striking back, and striking hard, at the Egyptian military installations, by bombing Egyptian military targets, not only at the ceasefire line but inside Egypt itself, and, if and when necessary, even by bringing our message to the very doorstep of the Egyptians by raiding deep into Egyptian territory. It wasn't an easy decision to make, particularly since we knew that the Soviets might extend their involvement in Egyvt even further. (Incidently, this was the first actual Soviet intervention anywhere outside the accepted Soviet sphere of influence since World War II.) So we reluctantly began our strategic "in-depth" retaliatory bombardments, using our planes as flying artillery and trusting that the Egyptian people, hearing those planes over the military airfield near Cairo, would understand that they couldn't have it both ways: war for us and peace for themselves.

So much has happened since then that reading about the War of Attrition today may not be very vivid for most people. Even the terrible story of the Soviet ships that sailed secretly to Egypt laden with the SA-3 ground-to-air missiles that were to be installed, manned and operated by Soviet specialists throughout the Canal zone is probably not of any great interest now, though, we all know how those missiles were used against Israel in the autumn of 1973. But for us the War of Attrition was a real war, and it took all the determination, courage, strength and skill of our soldiers and pilots to hold the cease-fire lines and to try, regardless of the cost, to stop the forward movement of the missile pads that the Egyptians and their Russians were so busy setting up adjacent to the cease-fire lines. Still, there was a limit to our ability to go it alone. We had to have support and help, aircraft and arms, and we had to have them soon.

There was only one world power to whom we could turn: the United States, our traditional and great friend, which was selling us planes but did not, at that point, seem fully to understand our situation and might, we feared, cut that aid at any moment. President Nixon was more than just friendly. But neither he nor his secretary of state, William Rogers, was sympathetic to our refusal to accept any solution for the Middle East that would be imposed upon us by others nor to my strong opposition to Mr. Rogers' idea that the Russians, the Americans, the French and the British should sit down comfortably somewhere to work out a "feasible" compromise for the Arabs and for us. Such a compromise, I had repeatedly explained to Mr. Rogers, might satisfy the demands of the U.S.-Soviet détente, but it would almost certainly not result in any binding guarantees for Israel's safety. How could it? The Russians were feeding and manipulating the entire Egyptian war effort; the French were almost as pro-Arab as the Russians; the British were not far behind the French; only the Americans were at all concerned with Israel's survival. At best, it would be three against one, and I couldn't envisage a workable solution ever being achieved under such conditions. On the other hand, if we went on incurring both President Nixon and Mr. Rogers' displeasure, we might get no arms at all. Something had to be done at once to break the impasse.

Let me say at the outset that personally I always liked William Rogers. He is a very nice, very courteous and extremely patient man, and in the end it was he who proposed and brought about the cease-fire in August, 1970. But (and I hope he will forgive me for writing this) I suspect that he never really understood the background to the Arab wars against Israel or ever realized that the verbal reliability of the Arab leaders was not, in any way, similar to his own. I remember how enthusiastically he told me about his first visits to the Arab states and how immensely impressed he was by Feisal's "thirst for peace." As is true of many other gentlemen I have known, Rogers assumed— wrongly, unfortunately—that the whole world was made up solely of other gentlemen.

All my attempts to establish direct contact with the Arab leaders had failed miserably—including the appeal I made on the first day I assumed office, when I had declared that "we are prepared to discuss peace with our neighbors, any day and on all matters," only to read, within seventy-two hours, Nasser's reply that "there is no voice transcending the sounds of war . . . and no call holier than the call to war." Nor were the responses from Damascus, Amman or Beirut any more encouraging. To quote just one example of the reaction of the Arab world to my plea that we enter into negotiations at once, here is an excerpt from an article published in a leading Jordanian newspaper in June, 1969:

> . . . Mrs. Meir is prepared to go to Cairo to hold discussions with President Nasser but, to her sorrow, has not been invited. She believes that one fine day a world without guns will emerge in the Middle East.

Golda Meir is behaving like a grandmother telling bedtime stories to her grandchildren. . . .

I felt as if we were caught in a vise. All the time the war was going on, people abroad were asking whether our real intention was not to bring Nasser down—as though we had set him up and were now preoccupied with plans to replace him. What enraged me, though, was that we were also being questioned whether our bombing in depth was "really" necessary and a matter of self-defense, as though one must wait till a murderer actually reaches one's home before it is morally permissible to stop him from trying to kill one, particularly when—as in Nasser's case—we were being left in no doubt whatsoever as to his intentions.

It was, in short, a difficult period, and one not made any easier for me by having inherited from Eshkol the National Unity Government which included the antisocialist bloc known as Gahal (made up of the extreme right-wing Herut Party and the far more moderate but smaller Liberal Party) and led by Menachem Begin. Quite apart from the deep-seated and very basic differences in ideology that had obviously always existed between the left and the right wings of Israel's political spectrum, there was a serious immediate difference in our approaches to the situation in which Israel now found itself. In June, Secretary of State Rogers proposed that Israel hold discussions with Egypt and Jordan, under the auspices of Dr. Jarring, with the aim of arriving at a just and lasting peace. These discussions were to be based upon "mutual acknowledgment of each other's sovereignty, territorial integrity and political independence" and on "Israeli withdrawal from territories occupied in the 1967 conflict," in accordance with Resolution 242. He also proposed that the cease-fire with Egypt, which had been shattered by the War of Attrition, be renewed for at least ninety days. Gahal, however, stood firm on the fact that the policy of the government of Israel since 1967 had been—and still was, as far as Gahal was concerned—that the Israel Defense Forces would remain on the cease-fire lines until peace was attained. Formally, of course, Gahal had a point. I knew that I would have to go to the Knesset to get its consent for this change in policy. But it didn't matter how hard I argued that the situation had changed. Though it accepted the cease-fire proposal, Gahal refused to agree to any negotiations on the subject of withdrawal from the territories until there was peace.

"But we won't have any cease-fire unless we also accept some of the less favorable conditions," I tried to explain repeatedly to Mr. Begin. "And what's more, we won't get any arms from America." "What do you mean, we won't get arms?" he used to say. "We'll *demand* them from the Americans." I couldn't get it through to him that although the American commitment to Israel's survival was certainly great, we needed Mr. Nixon and Mr. Rogers much more than they needed us, and Israel's policies couldn't be based entirely on the assumption that American Jewry either would or could force Mr. Nixon to adopt a position against his will or better judgment. But Gahal, intoxicated by its own rhetoric, had convinced itself that all we had to do was to go on telling the United States that we wouldn't give in to any pressure whatsoever, and if we did this long enough and loud enough, one day that pressure would just vanish. I can only describe this belief as mystical because it certainly wasn't based on reality as I knew it, and today I shudder to think what would have happened in October, 1973, if we had behaved in 1969 and 1970 as defiantly and self-destructively as Gahal wanted us to. There might well have been no U.S. military aid at all from 1970 on, and the Yom Kippur War would have ended very differently.

And in August, 1970, when the four Gahal ministers resigned from the cabinet on the absurd grounds that the Israeli government's acceptance of the cease-fire was the beginning of a major unconditional retreat from the cease-fire lines, I wasn't particularly taken aback. For the sake of avoiding additional problems, we asked them to stay. But they were adamant and left.

The other (though minor) bane of my life during all the time that I was prime minister—and one that it took me months to accustom myself to, even partially—was the freedom with which various ministers confided in the press, to put it very politely. The constant leaks from cabinet meetings infuriated me, and although I had my own suspicions all along as to the source of the sensational revelations by so-called diplomatic correspondents which greeted me so often in the morning papers, I could never prove them—which meant that I couldn't do much about them. But my staff very quickly got used to seeing me turn up at the office on the day after a cabinet meeting looking as black as thunder because over breakfast I had read something garbled in the paper that shouldn't have been there at all, garbled or otherwise. But these, need I say, were not my major anxieties. The real problems, as they had been for so long, were survival and peace, in that order.

Then, a number of months after I had taken office, I made a decision. I would go to Washington myself—if it could be arranged—to speak with President Nixon, to talk to congressmen and senators and to find out just what the American people thought and felt about us and what they were willing to do to help us. It wasn't that I deluded myself for a moment that I had any magical powers of persuasion. After all, I hadn't succeeded in changing Mr. Rogers' mind about the need for the Russians to participate in the Middle Eastern settlement—though I had certainly tried my best to do so. Nor did I expect to accomplish more than gifted men like our foreign minister, Abba Eban, or our new ambassador to Washington, General Yitzhak Rabin, had been able to accomplish. But I felt a deep need to establish, for and by myself, just where we stood as far as our relationship with the United States was concerned, and the cabinet thought it was a very good idea for me to go. As soon as the official invitation arrived from the White House, I began to prepare for the trip.

I certainly had doubts about its prospects for success. I had never met Richard Nixon, and I didn't even know most of the men around him. I had no idea what the president was being told about me; for all I knew, he might regard me (understandably enough) as a stopgap premier who didn't carry much weight in her own country and would probably not be reelected. But I was sure of one thing: Whatever impression I might make on him, I had to lay before the President all our problems and difficulties, quite candidly, and try to convince him, beyond a shadow of doubt, that there was a great deal that could be asked of us by way of compromise and concessions, but that we could not be expected to give up our dream of peace or to withdraw a single soldier from one inch of land until an agreement could be reached between the Arabs and ourselves. And that was not all. We desperately needed arms, and I felt that I should ask him for them myself. On the face of it, they weren't very complicated messages, but I think that I would have been less than human and a fool if I hadn't been extremely nervous about delivering them.

My personal preparations were very simple. I bought two evening dresses (including the beige lace and velvet one that I wore to the White House dinner), a knitted suit, a couple of hats (that I never wore at all) and some gloves (to hold in my hand). With the consideration that was to typify his entire relationship with me, President Nixon saw to it that Clara and Menachem and his family were also invited to the White House dinner that was to be held on my first evening in Washington, and we arranged to meet on September 24 in Philadelphia (which, for some reason—perhaps of its historic importance—is a customary first stop for presidential guests from abroad). From Philadelphia we were flown by helicopter to the lawn of the White House. With all the arrangements made, I was free to spend the weeks before my departure working overtime with my advisers, in particular with Dayan and the chief of staff, Chaim Bar-Lev, on the "shopping list" that I was going to take to Washington with me. In addition to a specific request for twenty-five Phantoms and eighty Skyhawk jets, I planned to ask the president for low-interest loans of $200,000,000 a year for five years to help us pay for the planes we hoped to be able to buy. I must explain here that the first U.S. president to authorize the sale of Phantoms and Skyhawks to Israel was President Johnson, whom Eshkol had visited in Texas and who had promised to give "sympathetic consideration" to the request. But it had taken some time before those first Skyhawks had actually been delivered to us, and I was sure that even if President Nixon agreed to sell us Phantoms, we would not be able to get them quickly unless I was able to convey to him the urgency of our situation and of the imbalance in the flow of arms to the Middle East. As for the money, I thought we would probably get that (though money is also something one can never be sure about) if for no other reason than that our credit was excellent. As a matter of fact, Israel has never fallen down on a single payment due anyone. I even cheered myself up on this score by remembering how in 1956–57, after the Sinai Campaign, when we were paying off a big loan we had received from the U.S. Import-Export Bank (and this at a time when the official U.S. attitude toward Israel was very cool indeed), we had been greatly tempted to ask for a postponement of the large repayment that had become due. A recession was going on in Israel then, and it was really very hard for us to scrape up the money we owed. But we weighed the pros and cons and finally decided that no matter how difficult it was, we were not going to be in default, even by a day. And I shall never forget Eban's description of the surprise on the usually guarded faces of the people at the Import-Export Bank in Washington when he walked in—at exactly the specified time and date—and presented our check.

Anyhow, on the plane going to the States, I was immersed in my thoughts, trying to guess what my visit to Nixon would be like and whether we would get along together. I wasn't even sure any more of the reception I would get in the United States as a whole. After the Six-Day War, I had been greeted with warmth, love and pride by American Jewry; but more than two years had passed since then, and it seemed possible that the enthusiasm for Israel's cause might have waned somewhat. But I needn't have worried so much, on either score.

At the Philadelphia airport a crowd of thousands were waiting for me; hundreds and hundreds of schoolchildren, singing "Henvenu Shalom Aleichem" were waving and carrying banners. I remember one of these banners read WE DIG YOU, GOLDA, and I thought it was the most charming expression of support for Israel—and perhaps for me— that I had ever seen. But I had no idea, other than smiling and waving at them, how to make clear to those youngsters that I certainly "dug" them, too. So I just smiled and waved and was delighted when I spotted my own family. At Independence Square an even larger crowd greeted me—30,000 American Jews, many of whom had been standing there for several hours to see me. I couldn't get over the sight of all those people pressing against the police barricades and applauding. I spoke to them only very briefly, but as someone said to me, "You could have read a page from the telephone book, and that crowd would still have cheered."

We stayed overnight in Philadelphia and then flew on to Washington in the morning. It had rained all night, and the sky was still cloudy and gray, as if it were going to go on raining. But (as though that, too, had been arranged by the White House) the sun came out just after my two-minute ride in a limousine from the helicopter to the bright-green White House lawn. President Nixon put me at ease at once. He helped me out of the car, and Mrs. Nixon handed me a huge bunch of red roses. There was something about the way the Nixons received me that made me feel at home with them from the start, and I was very grateful to both of them.

The formal ceremony was very formal indeed, full of spit and polish. The president and I stood on a raised platform covered by a red carpet, while a marine band played the two national anthems. I listened to "Hatikvah," and although I made an effort to look perfectly calm, my eyes filled with tears. There I was, the prime minister of the Jewish state, which had come into existence and survived against such odds, standing to attention with the president of the United States while my country was accorded full military honors. I remember thinking, "If only the boys at the Canal could see this," but I knew, at least, that in Israel thousands of people would be watching the ceremony on television that evening and be as profoundly moved and heartened by it as I was. Perhaps other nations take these ceremonies for granted, but we don't yet. In fact, it was all a little like a dream I used to dream with my friends years ago when we sometimes talked about what it would be like when we actually had not only a state of our own, but also the trappings of statehood.

Mr. Nixon's speech was short and to the point. He talked about the U.S. stake in peace in the Middle East and paid me some nice compliments. Nothing, he said, could be solved in one meeting or even in several, but the struggle to attain peace was of the highest priority. I spoke very briefly too. I had written down a few words—also about peace and friendship—and I read them out. But I hadn't come to the White House either to hear or to make little speeches, or even to inspect troops—though I think I did it fairly well, all things considered.

My meetings with the president were as warm as his initial welcome. We were together for a couple of hours, and we talked about everything as bluntly and frankly as I had hoped we would. We were in complete agreement that Israel should stay put until some kind of acceptable agreement with the Arabs was reached and that a big power which promises assistance to a small country when it is in trouble must keep its word. We also talked about the Palestinians and I spoke my mind as openly on that topic as I did on others. "Between the Mediterranean and the borders of Iraq," I said, "in what was once Palestine, there are now two countries, one Jewish and one Arab, and there is no room for a third. The Palestinians must find the solution to their problem together with that Arab country, Jordan, because a "Palestinian state" between us and Jordan can only become a base from which it will be even more convenient to attack and destroy Israel." Mr. Nixon listened very closely to everything I had to say about the Middle East, as though he had nothing to do except to sit and talk with Golda Meir about Israel's problems, but he was still very anxious for the Big Two and the Big Four talks to go on, despite the fact that he seemed to accept my argument that Russia was most unlikely to agree to anything to which its Arab clients objected. I must say that I took some pleasure in the knowledge that at the same time as President Nixon and I were talking together, the Soviet foreign minister, Andrei Gromyko, and Mr. Rogers were meeting in New York, and I couldn't help thinking how annoyed Mr. Gromyko must have been by the timing of his sessions with the U.S. secretary of state.

As to the more substantive matters that I discussed with Mr. Nixon, I can only say that I would not quote him at the time, and I will not quote him now. The press badgered me almost to death, but all that I would say was that my impression, my own personal assessment, of the result of our talks was "that the American administration intends to continue its policy of maintaining the balance of military power in the region." Because no official communiqué was issued after my conversations with the president, some journalists assumed that I had come away with empty hands. But the truth was that I couldn't see any point to communiqués (which very rarely communicate anything), and President Nixon felt much the same way, so we decided together that no formal statement would be released. As for my shopping list, well, it eventually changed hands, as it was meant to.

That night President and Mrs. Nixon gave a state dinner in my honor. People in Washington later said that it was one of the finest White House parties of the Nixon administration—though no one could explain just what made it such a success. For me it was, from start to finish, one of the most wonderful evenings of my life, partly, I expect, because I had met with such understanding from President Nixon, and partly because I now felt sure that the United States would stand by us and I really relaxed for the first time in months. Also, everything had been superbly planned to give me pleasure—from the presence of my family to the "Charlotte Revivim" dessert that so tactfully indicated that Sarah and Zechariah were also included in the celebration. Of the 120 guests, many old friends of mine from both political parties, among them the former U.S. ambassador to the United Nations Arthur Goldberg and Senator Jacob Javits. And of course, Mr. Rogers, Dr. Kissinger, Eban and Rabin, as well as various high-ranking members of the administration were there. Throughout the dinner Israeli music was played, and then—as a special treat—Leonard Bernstein and Isaac Stern performed, giving us one encore after another. I could see and hear how tremendously moved they both were, and I was so enraptured by their music and their presence that when they stopped playing, I forgot where I was and I jumped up to hug them both.

Before the dinner the Nixons and I had exchanged gifts. They gave me a covered Grecian urn, reproduced in gold and beautifully inscribed, and a lovely floral centerpiece made of blue and gold ovaline, while I had brought them Israeli antiques: a necklace of carnelian beads shaped like lotuses and dating back to the eleventh century B.C. for Mrs. Nixon, an ancient Jewish oil lamp for the president, silver candlesticks for Julie and David Eisenhower and a silver Yemenite necklace and earrings for Tricia Nixon. After the dinner there were toasts. Again, the president was very kind to Israel, and to me.

"The people of Israel," he said, "have earned peace, not the fragile peace that comes with the kind of document that neither party has an interest in keeping, but the kind of peace that will last. We hope that as a result of our meeting we will have taken a significant step forward toward that peace which can mean so much to the people of Israel, to the people of the Middle East and also to the people of the world."

I felt that he spoke from his heart, and I know that I did when I replied: "Mr. President, thank you, not only for your hospitality, not only for this great day and for every moment that I had this day, but thank you most of all for enabling me to go home and tell my people that we have a friend, a great friend in the White House. It will help. It will help us overcome many difficulties."

At about 11 P.M., the president, Mrs. Nixon and I left the party, and at my car Mrs. Nixon and I kissed each other good-night, as though we had been friends for years. The rest of the guests went on dancing until long after midnight.

In all, I spent four days in Washington. Walking in step with the bemedaled adjutant general of the United States army (not the easiest thing I have ever done), I placed a wreath of blue and white flowers on the Tomb of the Unknown Soldier at Arlington National Cemetery, preceded by a nineteen-gun salute and color-bearers carrying Israeli flags. I visited Mr. Rogers at the State Department and was entertained to lunch by him, saw Mr. Melvin Laird at the Department of Defense, met with members of the House Foreign Affairs Committee and "appeared" at the National Press Club, where I met the toughest and most experienced journalists in the United States and felt at first as if I were in a boxing ring with them. But they were very nice to me, too, and seemed to like the fact that I answered their questions as briefly and as simply as I could—though I can't say that they asked me anything that I hadn't been asked a dozen times before.

There were only two queries that were at all new. One newspaperman asked: "Would Israel employ nuclear weapons if her survival were in jeopardy?" to which I could only reply, truthfully, that I thought we hadn't done so badly with conventional weapons—an answer that was greeted by laughter and applause. The second was a request from the president of the Press Club that made me laugh. "Your grandson Gideon says that you make the best gefilte fish (stuffed fish) in Israel," he said. "Would you reveal your recipe to us?"

"I'll do better than that," I answered. "When I come here again, I promise to arrive three days in advance and make gefilte fish for lunch for all of you." Months later, incidentally, I was once interviewed in Los Angeles and asked if I made good chicken soup. "Of course, I do," I replied. Would I send the recipe? "Gladly," I said, never imagining that within a week the interviewer would get 40,000 requests for it. I only hope it resulted in 40,000 pots of good Jewish soup. Anyhow, it wasn't my skill as a cook that mattered in Washington; it was the bond of friendship between the United States and Israel and the U.S. attitude toward our counterattrition policy. Before I left, Mr. Nixon made a statement on his behalf and mine to the press which I thought summed up the results of my visit, even though it lacked any details.

"I think," he said, "that we have a very good understanding of the positions we both take, and that from this meeting there could come some progress, some solution of the terribly difficult problems confronting us in the Middle East. We do not expect them to be susceptible to instant diplomacy. On the other hand, we must try, and I was glad to find a willingness on the part of the prime minister and her colleagues to try and find a way to peace. We have no new initatives to announce, but we do think that we have a better understanding of how we should move from here on out."

From Washington I went to New York, where one function followed another so rapidly that I didn't even have time to feel tired. I got a marvelous welcome at City Hall, lunched with U Thant, held a series of meetings at my suite in the Waldorf-Astoria, attended a reception for diplomats hosted by Eban and went to a huge banquet sponsored by the United Jewish Appeal, Israel Bonds and fifty other Jewish organizations—all on the first day I was there. Then on to Los Angeles, Milwaukee and finally back to the East Coast. I had intended to return home by October 5, but there was one invitation I couldn't refuse, and I stayed on an extra day to address the AFL-CIO biennial convention in Atlantic City, New Jersey. For many years, the AFL-CIO had been very close to Israel, particularly to the Histadrut, and its president, George Meany, a dear old friend of mine, was the honorary chairman of the American Trade Union Council for the Histadrut. Talking to that immense audience of trade unionists, I felt, for the first time since I had left Israel, that I was really on home territory. I talked about exactly the same things that I had talked about in Philadelphia, Washington, Milwaukee, Los Angeles and New York, the things that I still talk about—peace between us and the Arabs. "It will be a great day," I told my friends, the workers and the trade union leaders of America, "when Arab farmers will cross the Jordan not with planes or tanks, but with tractors and with their hands outstretched in friendship, as between farmer and farmer, as between human beings. A dream it may be, but I am sure that one day it will come true."

When I got back to Israel, although I could not yet make any announcement about the Phantoms, I knew we were going to get them, and my heart was much lighter than it had been when I took off. But the War of Attrition was still being waged; the terrorists were still active; the number of Soviet military personnel in Egypt was increasing by leaps and bounds, including combat pilots and the crews of the ground-to-air missiles. In a word, peace was as remote as ever. In fact, nothing at all had changed substantially since I had assumed office. Whatever reasons existed then for my becoming prime minister were, unfortunately, still valid on the eve of our national elections—the seventh since the state was established. In the months that had passed, however, my so-called rating had improved, and although I wasn't out to win any popularity contests, it certainly feels a lot better to have a rating of seventy-five or eighty than of three! At all events, the election results weren't exactly unpredictable. The Ma'arach won 56 of the 120 Knesset seats, and I presented the Knesset with that "wall-to-wall" cabinet from which Gahal was to walk out in the summer.

Now that I was prime minister in my own right, so to speak, I very much hoped that I would be able to do something to help solve those of Israel's growing social and economic problems that were beginning to cause a real rift between various sections of the population. For years, both in the Histadrut and in the party, I had pleaded that since we unfortunately couldn't do anything about having to maintain our enormous defense budget, we should at least pull together and try to do away with the widening gap between the people who had everything they needed—if not everything they wanted—and those tens of thousands who were still ill housed, ill clothed, undereducated and sometimes even ill fed. For the most part this segment of our population belonged to what was bitterly called "the second Israel," Jews who had come to us in 1948, 1950 and 1951 from Yemen, the Middle East and North Africa and whose standard of living in the late 1960s and early

1970s still left a great deal to be desired. Of course, we could go on congratulating ourselves on the fact that between 1949 and 1970 we had built more than 400,000 units of public housing and that there wasn't a single place in the country—however isolated—that didn't have a school, a kindergarten and, in most cases, also a nursery school. But no amount of justified pride in what we had managed to achieve could possibly eliminate the other less pleasant facts. There was poverty in Israel, and there was also wealth. Neither the poverty nor the wealth was great, but they both existed.

There were, and still are, Israelis who live ten to a two-room house, whose children are dropouts (even though they would probably be totally exempt from paying secondary-school fees) and delinquents (largely because of their disadvantaged background) and who, because they believe that they are in danger of turning into permenently underprivileged second-class citizens, regard all other newer immigrants as inevitably making their own situation worse. There are also Israelis, though not many, who live in relative luxury, who drive large cars, entertain lavishly, dress in the height of fashion ane have adopted a life-style that is imported from abroad and has nothing whatsoever to do either with our real national economic capacity or with the real circumstances of our national life. In between these two groups are the masses of skilled laborers and white-collar workers who have a hard time making ends meet, who can't maintain their standard of living (which is in no way immodest) on one salary, who for decades have proved themselves capable of the most remarkable self-discipline, patriotism and sacrifice, but who were nonetheless responsible, I believe, for the strikes that plagued us and guilty of insisting that each time the low-wage earners got an increase, everyone—right up the ladder—also had to get a pay raise.

It was with this strata that I tried, though not very successfully, to reason. Something was happening to the rank and file of the Histadrut, to the good sense of the Israeli worker, that frightened me, and I couldn't and didn't keep quiet about it. No one believed more strongly than I that a trade union was not only entitled but obliged to safeguard the rights of workers and to call for strikes when negotiations dragged on for too long or when agreements weren't being met. But agreements that were signed had to be honored without new claims being submitted at once, and those who were not at the bottom of the nation's economic scale have to understand and accept the fact that whatever increases could be given had to be given to those whose need was greatest. There is nothing sacred about the principle of differentials. I had fought it in the Histadrut years ago, and I was prepared to fight it again. The line had to be held somewhere. God knows that Israel's doctors, nurses and teachers didn't have an easy time economically, but they could keep going while other lower-paid groups who were becoming submerged in the rising inflation and high cost of living had to be given salary increases or they couldn't have survived. It was just that simple.

I was also extremely unsympathetic to the idea of strikes in essential services, especially in a country in a state of war. I don't think that I need to explain to anyone what it meant to me personally to have to decide on issuing restraining orders when the staffs of hospitals went on strike. But there was no other way to ensure that there wouldn't be a resultant loss of life, so I grit my teeth and did it.

"The government," I told the nation repeatedly, "cannot do everything all at once. It can't wave a magic wand and meet everyone's demands simultaneously: eradicate poverty without imposing taxes, win wars, go on absorbing immigration, develop the economy and still give everyone his due. No government can do all this at one and the same time." But it wasn't only a question of money. Social equality isn't attained merely with material resources. To wipe out poverty and its aftermath, you need two partners who are equally willing to make an effort, and I didn't mince any words about this either.

"In the first place," I said, "those among us who are poor mustn't permit themselves to be turned into the passive objects of other people's concern. They must be active on their own behalf. And the more settled more affluent sections of the population will have to join in a great volunteer movement aimed at achieving social integration. The gap between those who have education and training and those who don't is at least as great and as tragic as the gap between those who can cope economically and those who can't."

Some progress was made, but nowhere near enough. I

formed a prime minister's committee for tackling the problems of underprivileged youngsters. It included distinguished educators, psychologists, doctors, probation officers and so forth, all of whom worked voluntarily. Although it took two years, instead of what I hoped would be just a few months, for it to come up with recommendations, we implemented many of its recommendations even before they were published. When we had to raise the price of staple foods, we gave tax benefits to lower-income groups, and we went on building as much low-income housing as we possibly could, while I waged a ceaseless war of my own for the building of rental housing that would be subsidized, if necessary. And of course, whatever we tried to do had to be done either in the midst of actual warfare or during periods of terrorism, and there was never enough time or money to concentrate even on our most urgent domestic problems—for which, apart from everything else, I found it impossible to forgive our neighbors. Given peace, I knew that although we might never be able to build an ideal society, we could certainly build a much better one. But where was that peace?

Then in August, 1970, Mr. Rogers' cease-fire materialized. Nasser said that as far as he was concerned, it would only last for three months, but—as though the timing were symbolic—he died in September, and Anwar el-Sadat became the president of Egypt. Not only did Sadat seem, at first glance, to be a more reasonable man who might soberly consider the benefits of an end to the war to his own people but there were also indications that he wasn't getting along too well with the Russians. And in Jordan, King Hussein, having happily sheltered the Palestinian terrorists for months, suddenly found himself so threatened by them that in September he turned on them and crushed them. So though it may have been a Black September for El Fatah, to me it looked, at long last, as if the U.S. peace initiative and Dr. Jarring might have some slim chance of success. The Arab leaders didn't modify their statements about Israel in any way or alter their demands for a total withdrawal of our troops, but there was talk about reopening the Suez Canal and rebuilding the ruined Egyptian towns along its banks, so that normal life could be restored in them—all of which gave rise to some optimism in Israel. Well, the cease-fire held, we stayed where we were, the Arabs continued to refuse to meet us or deal with us in any way, and the optimism in Israel slowly died down—but it didn't vanish altogether, and war didn't break out in 1971 or 1972! But neither did peace, and Arab terrorism mounted both in is ferocity and its inhumanity.

Certainly no one in the civilized world approved of the gunning down, at Lydda Airport, of Catholic pilgrims from Puerto Rico and one of Israel's most distinguished scientists, of the horrifying public kidnapping and murder of Israeli athletes at the Munich Olympic Games or of the slaughter of Israeli children trapped in the school building in the development town of Ma'alot. No one approved, and each outrage brought me its flood of official condolences and expressions of shock and sympathy. Nonetheless, we were expected (and still are expected by many) to come to terms with the murderers in the way that other governments had, as if these suicidal fanatics should have been allowed to blackmail us and bring us to our knees. It has certainly been proved time and again that giving in to terror only leads to more terror. No one will ever know, however, what it cost the government of Israel to say no to the demands of the terrorists or what it was like to feel that no Israeli official working abroad was entirely safe from death by letter bomb, to say nothing of the fact that any quiet border town in Israel could be turned (as several were) into the scene of massacres caused by a few demented men who had been reared on hatred and the belief that they could drain Israel of its ability to stand firm in the face of grief and pain.

But we learned to hold out against the terror, to protect our aircraft and passengers, to turn our embassies into small fortresses and to patrol our schoolyards and city streets. I walked behind the coffins and visited the bereaved families of the victims of Arab terrorism, and I was filled with pride that I belonged to a nation that was able to take these blows—these cowardly and evil blows—without saying, "Enough. We have had enough. Give the terrorists whatever they want because we have taken all that we can take." Other governments surrendered to the demands of the terrorists, put planes at their disposal and released them from jail, while the foreign press and the New Left called them "guerrillas" and "freedom fighters." For us, however, they remained criminals, not heroes, and though each funeral was a torment for me, I remained unimpressed by the "glory" of hiding mines in supermarkets and buses or the "glamor" of a holy war that required killing seven old Jews in a home for the aged in Munich. And I was literally physically sickened when the Arabs who had murdered the eleven Israeli athletes at the Olympic Games in 1972 were set free in a blaze of publicity and flown to Libya only six weeks later. The Arab states went on giving the terrorists money, arms and backing and then screaming to high heaven whenever we made clear, by raiding the terrorist bases in Syria and Lebanon, that we held the governments of those states responsible for what was happening.

The only solution, the only possible solution, was peace—not only peace with honor, but a lasting peace. And the only way of achieving it was to go on trying to convince our friends that our stand was right—since our enemies wouldn't talk to us—and to examine every single possibility that might lead to negotiations.

Many of the trips I took and talks I held must remain secret, but I think that today I can write about one of them. At the beginning of 1972 the deputy foreign minister of Rumania came to Israel on a visit, ostensibly just to meet with people in our Foreign Office. But he made one special request: He asked to see me, and he stressed that he wanted to see me alone; no one else should be present at our conversation. We had very good relations with Rumania. It was the only East European country that hadn't severed diplomatic relations with us after the Six-Day War and that consistently refused to take part in the Soviet Union's vicious anti-Israel propaganda campaign or join in the Soviet bloc's denunciations of our "aggression." We had entered into mutually profitable trade agreements with the Rumanians, exchanged art exhibitions, musicians, choirs and theatrical groups, and there was some immigration from Rumania. I had met (and liked) the attractive and energetic president of Rumania, Nicolae Ceausescu, in 1970 and I admired him for not giving way to Arab pressure and for managing to retain diplomatic links with us as well as with the Arab states. I knew that Ceausescu was anxious to promote a Middle Eastern peace settlement, and I wasn't really surprised when his deputy foreign minister announced to me as soon as we were alone that actually he had come to Israel only in order to tell me the following:

"I have been sent by my president," he said, "to inform you that when he visited Egypt recently, he saw President Sadat and that, as a result of their meeting, my president has a most important message for you. He would like to bring it to you himself, but since he can't [he was going to China], he suggests that you come to Bucharest. You can come either incognito or, if you prefer, we will gladly issue you a formal invitation." I didn't accept that going to China automatically ruled out a visit to Israel, but I said that of course, I would come to Bucharest as soon as possible. Not incognito—that didn't appeal to me as a way for the prime minister of Israel to travel (unless it was absolutely essential)—but just as soon as I got an official invitation. Ceausescu's invitation arrived shortly afterwards, and I flew to Rumania.

I spent fourteen hours (in two long sessions) with Ceausescu, who told me that he understood from Sadat himself that the Egyptian leader was ready to meet with an Israeli, maybe with me, maybe not; maybe the meeting would be on a slightly lower level than the heads of state. But a meeting of some sort could take place. I said, "Mr. President, this is the best news I have heard for many years"— as indeed it was. We talked for hours about it, and Ceausescu was almost as excited as I was. There was no question in his mind that he was delivering a historic and absolutely genuine message. He even talked to me about details. "We won't work through ambassadors or foreign officers," he said, "not mine and not yours." He suggested that his deputy foreign minister maintain personal contact with me through Simcha Dinitz, then my political secretary, who had come with me to Bucharest.

After so many years it really looked as though the ice were about to break. But it didn't. When I came back to Israel, we waited and waited—in vain. There was no follow-up at all. Whatever Sadat had told Ceausescu—and he had certainly told him something—was totally meaningless, and I suspect that the reason I never heard anything more from Ceausescu about the meeting with Sadat was that he couldn't bring himself to confess, even to me, that Sadat had fooled him.

As far as the public and press—both in Israel and Rumania—were concerned, this had just been a standard visit; Ceausescu gave me a luncheon, the prime minister gave me a dinner, and I gave him a dinner. But the only meaningful result of my visit to Bucharest—on which I had pinned such high hopes—was that I was able to attend the Friday night services at the Chorale Synagogue in Bucharest and meet many hundreds of Rumanian Jews—infinitely freer than the Jews of Moscow had been, or are, but almost as overwhelmed by my presence among them. They greeted me with such a torrent of love for Israel that I felt bodily buffeted by it, and I don't think I have ever heard Hebrew songs sung more beautifully or with greater tenderness than on that Friday night. As I walked to my car, I saw a vast crowd waiting for me in complete silence; ten thousand Jews had come from all over Rumania to see me. I turned, crossed over to them and said, *"Shabbat shalom,"* and I heard 10,000 voices call back, *"Shabbat shalom."* That encounter in itself was more than worth the trip for me. And the only tangible thing I brought back with me (though I didn't know it then) was the huge black bearskin given me by the prime minister of Rumania (a celebrated huntsman) which I later "lent" to the children of Revivim. They adored it, and for them it did not hold the bitter memories that it did for me.

There were also other journeys to other places and once even an adventure abroad that taught me that nothing I did was ever going to go unnoticed again. In the spring of 1971 I made a ten-day trip to Denmark, Finland, Sweden and Norway. Between my visit to Helsinki and to Stockholm there was a weekend and a rare chance, if I planned it properly, to be out of reach of the telephone, the telex, cables and reporters. But it isn't so simple to find a secluded place for a rest and still conform to the security regulations that increasingly governed where and how I traveled. My office in Jerusalem asked the Israeli ambassador in Stockholm to look around for some suitable spot not too far from the Swedish capital and to let us know in good time. Just before I left Israel, there was a phone call; one of the ministers wanted to say how sorry he was that he wouldn't be able to see me off, but there *was* something interesting he wanted to tell me. We chatted for a couple of minutes, and then I left for the airport.

In Helsinki I got word from our embassy in Stockholm that nothing had been found and that the best thing for me to do with those two free days was to go to Stockholm and take it easy in my hotel there until my official visit began. All of a sudden I remembered that last-minute phone call I had received just before my departure, and I asked Lou Kaddar—to her amazement—whether she fancied a weekend in Lapland. "Lapland?" She couldn't believe that I was serious.

"Well," I explained, "I forgot all about it till just now, but we have been invited to stay at a marvelous lodge in the wilds of Finnish Lapland that belongs to a devoted friend of Israel. He has promised to give us a very good time there, and I, for one, would like to go."

There were all kinds of objections: My bodyguards said it was much too isolated and much too far away; Lou said that we didn't have the right clothes and that we'd freeze to death; the Finnish and Swedish security people were appalled at the idea of my taking off for a place that was only about 100 miles from the Soviet border; and everyone decided that it was mad to travel a total of 1,200 miles for a two-day vacation. But I wanted to go—and go we did.

Our trip was veiled in the utmost secrecy, of course. We went to Stockholm and flew on to Lapland in a small plane, arriving at Rovaniemi, the capital of Finnish Lapland, in the brilliant sunshine of the early afternoon. At the airport, which was the size of a small tennis court, there were some taxis waiting for us, and the mayor of Rovaniemi with his wife. He had only been told that some important guests were coming, but he hadn't even been told who they were. There was also, it turned out, one newspaperman who just happened to be there and just happened to notice that the mayor's wife was holding a rose. Who sees roses in Lapland? He took another look at the people who were getting off the plane, stared at the short woman in a heavy coat who was obviously the VIP traveler for whom that precious rose was intended, told himself it was impossible and then, when we were already on our way through the snow to the lodge, suddenly realized that it was really me and immediately sent a cable off to his editor.

I had a wonderful time in Rovaniemi, rested and came back to Stockholm in great shape only to discover that the whole world wanted to know about my clandestine meeting with the Russians. Why else would Golda Meir have gone to Finnish Lapland? What had we talked about? With whom had I met? No one in Scandinavia or anywhere else, for that matter, believed the truth until Mr. Tsarapkin, the Soviet deputy foreign minister, arrived in Oslo the day before I left it—without seeing me. The press then finally resigned itself to the undramatic fact that all I had done in Lapland for forty-eight hours was eat, sleep, buy souvenirs made of reindeer fur for my grandchildren and drive around the lovely, silent, frozen lakes.

There were times during those five years when I would have gladly run away from it all if I had felt free to do so, not because my strength was giving out or because the pace was too much for me, but primarily because I was so tired of repeating myself so often, saying the same things over and over again and getting nowhere. I was also tired of hearing about my supposed complexes from people who thought we should act in a way that would result in handing Israel over either to President Sadat or, better yet, to Mr. Arafat. This meant, I gathered, that I should stop remembering the lessons of the past and try to persuade the population of Israel that because our national home had been broken into once, twice, three times, we should now move out and go elsewhere, instead of putting up iron bars on the windows and extra strong locks on the doors. Yes, I had complexes. They had started, if not in Kiev, then at the Evian Conference, in 1938, and nothing that had happened to us since was conducive to lessening them. Even in Israel itself, there were people who thought—and said loudly—that the government wasn't doing "enough" to find common ground with the Arabs, though they never managed to suggest anything that we hadn't tried ourselves.

There was also a constant uproar from a numerically small but exceedingly vocal segment of the population about such things as the government's decision, after the Six-Day War, to allow a number of Jews to settle in Hebron, a town on the West Bank of the Jordan River (some thirty-five kilometers south of Jerusalem) in which, according to Jewish tradition, the Biblical Patriarchs are buried and which was King David's capital before he moved it to Jerusalem. The Crusaders had expelled the Jews from Hebron, but during Ottoman rule in Palestine some Jews had returned there, and the town had had a Jewish community right up to the time when a terrible Arab massacre finally drove the surviving Jews out of the town in 1929. After 1948 the Jordanians wouldn't even let the Jews visit the holy Cave of Machpelah to pray at the Tomb of the Patriarchs. But Hebron remained holy to the Jews, and on Passover eve, 1968, after it had come under Israeli administration, a group of young and militant Orthodox Jews, defying the military ban on settlement in the West Bank, moved into the Hebron police compound and remained there without permission. There was no question but that they were behaving most improperly and in a manner that was very damaging to Israel's "image." The Arabs at once set up a great hue and cry about the "Jewish annexation" of Hebron, and Israeli public opinion was very divided on the subject. On the one hand, the would-be settlers were obviously trying to create a *fait accompli* and force the Israeli government to make up its mind prematurely about the future of the West Bank and Jewish settlement there. On the other hand, although I deplored the way in which they had taken the law into their own hands, as though they were in the Wild West, I thought that the real issue was not really what they had done or even how they had done it, but something far more serious.

Was it logical, I asked myself and my colleagues, for the world (including our own superpious doves) to demand of a Jewish government that it pass legislation expressly forbidding Jews to settle anywhere on earth?

I didn't know any more than anyone else did exactly what would happen to Hebron eventually. But let's suppose, I said, that one day, please God, we will sign a peace treaty with Jordan and "return" Hebron. Would that mean that we would agree that no Jews would ever be allowed to live there again? Obviously, no Israeli government could ever obligate itself to a permanent banning of Jews from any part of the Holy Land. And Hebron was not an ordinary market town; it meant a lot to believing Jews.

We debated and argued and examined the pros and cons for months, and then, in 1970, we permitted the building of a limited number of housing units for Jews in an area on the outskirts of Hebron that the settlers named Kiryat Arba (The Town of the Four, Hebron's other Hebrew name)— and that particular storm died down. But other subsequent attempts at illegal settlements were more firmly dealt with—however painful it was for the government to have to order Israeli soldiers to drag Jews away from places in the West Bank in which they wanted to settle. We did allow Jews to settle in certain spots in the administered territories, but only when such settlement was fully in accordance with our political and military interests.

Another constant focus of international attention was the Christian holy places both in the West Bank and in Jerusalem. So, needless to say, I was very glad to be able to go to the Vatican in January, 1973, when I was received by Pope Paul VI in an eighty-minute audience. It was the first time that a prime minister of Israel had been given an audience by the pope, though, on his one-day visit to Israel in 1964, when he came to the Holy Land as a pilgrim, the pontiff had met President Shazar, Eshkol and virtually the entire Israeli cabinet. It had not been the happiest of meetings. The pope had made it clear that his visit in no way constituted full recognition by the Vatican of the State of Israel; he had made Jordan, rather than Israel, his headquarters for three days, and the parting message he had sent us from his plane was carefully addressed to Tel Aviv, not Jerusalem.

The relations between the Vatican and the Zionist movement had always been delicate, ever since Theodor Herzl, who had been granted an audience by Pius X in 1904, had been told by the pope, "We cannot prevent Jews from going to Jerusalem, but we could never sanction it . . . the Jews have not recognized our Lord; we cannot recognize the Jews." Other popes had been friendlier. Sharett was received twice (once as Israel's foreign minister) by Pius XII. Pope John XXIII had been sympathetic and even warm to Israel, and we were invited to send a representative both to his funeral and to Paul VI's coronation. In 1969 Paul had received Abba Eban in an official audience, and our ambassadors to Rome always had good and fairly close contacts with various high-ranking Vatican personalities. Although the Vatican has recognized all the Arab states, recognition is still withheld from Israel, and the exact stand of the Vatican on the question of Jerusalem has still to be clarified. But it seems to me that the Vatican has indeed reconciled itself after all, to the reality of the Jewish state.

The story of my audience with the pope began, not in Rome, but in Paris. For years I have attended the annual

meetings of the Socialist International (of which I am a
vice-president) wherever they are held. In 1973 a socialist
leadership meeting was to take place in Paris—about a
month and a half before the French national elections—
and, of course, I planned to go, as did the socialist heads of
other governments, including Austria, Denmark, Finland
and Sweden, as well as heads of parties that were in opposition. To everybody's amazement, Georges Pompidou
promptly charged me with coming to Paris chiefly in order
to sway the "Jewish vote" (which is nonexistent in France)
in favor of the socialists. As a result of the subsequent uproar in France, the Socialist International—to which no
one unfortunately pays much attention as a rule—got an
enormous amount of publicity, and so did the French government's apparently uncontrollable hostility toward Israel.
In any case, since I was going to France, our ambassador
to Rome, Amiel Najjar, suggested that perhaps it would be
a good time to take up the recommendation, made to him
on several occasions by friends of his at the Vatican, that I
meet with the pope. I said that I would be delighted to do
so, and after a while we were told to request an audience
for me. Within a few days a letter addressed to me arrived
at the embassy in Rome. It was from the prefettura of the
Vatican, and it read: "Your Excellency. I have the honor
of informing you that the Holy Father will receive you in
audience on Monday, January 16, 1973."

I was immensely impressed—it is impossible not to be—
not only (or even mostly) by the Vatican, but by the pope
himself, by the simplicity and graciousness of his manner
and the penetrating gaze of his deepset dark eyes. I think I
would have been much more nervous about our talk if he
hadn't started it by telling me that he found it hard to accept
the fact that the Jews—who, of all people, should have been
capable of mercy toward others because they had suffered
so terribly themselves—had behaved so harshly in their
own country. Well, that is the kind of talk that I can't bear
and particularly since it is simply not true that we have
mistreated the Arabs in the territories. There is still no
death penalty in Israel, and the most we have ever done is
to jail terrorists, blow up the houses of Arabs who have
gone on sheltering terrorists, despite repeated warnings,
and sometimes, when we have had no alternative, even expelled Arabs who have openly incited and encouraged the

terrorists. But I challenge anyone to cite chapter and verse about brutality or repression. I was very tempted to ask the pope what his sources of information were since they were obviously so different from mine, but I didn't. Instead, I said, and I could hear my own voice trembling a little with anger: "Your Holiness, do you know what my own very earliest memory is? It is waiting for a pogrom in Kiev. Let me assure you that my people know all about real 'harshness' and also that we learned all about real mercy when we were being led to the gas chambers of the Nazis."

It may not have been a conventional way of talking to the pope, but I felt that I was speaking for all Jews everywhere, for those who were alive and for those who had perished while the Vatican maintained its neutrality in World War II. I had a sense of participating in a truly historic confrontation, and the pope and I stared at each other for a second. I think he was quite surprised by my words, but he didn't say anything. He just looked at me, right into my eyes, and I looked back at him in the same way. Then I went on to tell him, very respectfully, but very firmly and at some length, that now that we had a state of our own, we were through forever with being "at the mercy" of others. "This is truly a historic moment," he said, as though he had read my mind.

Then we went on to talk about other matters, the status of Jerusalem and the Middle East in general. There would have to be special provisions for the holy places, and that, I gathered, could be taken up in the "continuing dialogue" between the church and ourselves, to which he enthusiastically referred. He also went out of his way to express his deep appreciation for the care that Israel had taken of the Christian holy places. For my part, I assured the pope that we would make whatever arrangements would be required of us for the administration not only of the Christain but also of the Moslem holy places in Israel, but that Jerusalem itself would remain the capital of Israel. I also asked the pope to use his influence to try to bring about a settlement in the Middle East and to do whatever he could to secure the return to Israel of the Israeli prisoners who had been in Egyptian and Syrian jails ever since the War of Attrition and whom the Arab states had refused to release.

After the first difficult minute or two the atmosphere was very relaxed and cordial. We sat in the pope's private

library on the second floor of the Apostolic Palace and
conversed without any strain—all of which made the unpleasant episode that immediately followed my visit very
hard to understand. Along with the customary statement
that had been initially agreed upon, the pope's spokesman,
Professor Alessandrini, issued an unsual "verbal note" to
the press. It was an obvious attempt to appease the Arab
states about the implications of my meeting with the pope.
Announcing that "it was not a gesture of preference or exclusive treatment," Professor Alessandrini went on to say,
"The pope accepted the request of Mrs. Meir because he
considers it his duty not to let slip any opportunity to act in
favor of peace, in defense of all religious interests, particularly of the weakest and most defenseless, and most of all
the Palestinian refugees."

Najjar telephoned to the Vatican at once and protested
most strongly about the utterly misleading statement. And I
didn't mince words either. I hadn't broken into the Vatican, and I told that to the journalists at the press conference I held that afternoon at the Israeli embassy in Rome.
Regardless of whether or not the Vatican tried to play
down the importance of my audience with Paul VI, "it was
greatly appreciated," I said, "by me and by my people. . . .
In the quest for peace and goodwill all over the world,
there is a complete identity of views between the pope and
the Jews."

The next day I got lovely gifts from the Vatican: a magnificent silver dove of peace with an inscription to the
prime minister of Israel from the pope, a beautiful Bible
and—as a gesture, I suspect, to make up for Professor
Alessandrini's inaccurate "note"—a catalogue of all the
Hebrew publications in the Vatican Library, as well as a
medallion each for Lou and Simcha. All in all, it was an
intensely interesting and intensely meaningful experience
for me, and I hope that, in a small way, it brought the
Vatican closer to understanding Israel, Zionism and the
feeling of Jews like me about themselves.

When I think back on the spring and summer of 1973, I
must say that I do so with very little pleasure. There were
days when I fell into bed at two in the morning and lay
there, telling myself that I was crazy. At seventy-five I was
working longer hours than I had ever worked before and
traveling more, both inside Israel and abroad, than was

good for anyone. Although I really did my best to cut down on appointments and delegate more work, it was much too late for me to turn myself into another person. Regardless of all the good advice I was given by the people closest to me—the children, Clara (who was now coming fairly regularly from Bridgeport to stay with me for a few weeks at a time), Galili, Simcha and Lou—there was only one way I could be prime minister, if that was what I had to be, and that was by talking to the people who wanted to talk to me and listening to the people who had something to tell me.

I couldn't just go to the opening of a symposium being held by the teachers' union, for instance, without preparing myself for it ahead of time, and reading memos wasn't my idea of doing my homework properly. Memos always left unanswered questions in my mind that often turned out to be the most crucial questions. I was very worried about the rate of dropouts from schools in the development towns and thought that might be a topic for the speech that the teachers had asked me to give. But I couldn't get the *exact* number of dropouts from anyone—not from the chairman of the teachers' union, not from the Ministry of Education—and that bothered me. How come no one knew exactly how many children had dropped out of school in each town? If teachers reported nonattendance to principals and principals reported to the Ministry of Education, then why were the specific figures unavailable? The more questions I asked, the more I understood about the dropout situation, about the way that schools and the ministry operated, and, most of all, about life in the new towns and the standards of teaching in them. And when I went to that symposium, I had something to say, more questions to ask and a chance of getting more answers that would eventually help me to suggest ways of doing something about a problem that vitally concerned Israel's future.

I also wasn't about to make myself unavailable to anyone. When I invited Jews who had just immigrated from the Soviet Union after months, often years, of persecution and suffering and who wanted and deserved to talk to the prime minister, I tried to spend as much time as possible with them. And when party leaders came to talk to me in the evening about urgent local political matters, I also didn't want to cut these sessions short. Either I was the head of the Labor Party or I was not, but if I was, then I wasn't going to be a figurehead. Nor was I going to limit the amount of time I spent with delegations of "Oriental" Jews or students or landlords or anyone else who wanted to tell me how badly (or sometimes even how well) I was conducting the affairs of the nation. There were also the constant visitors from abroad who felt themselves entitled—and rightly so—to spend half an hour with me. Some were American Jews who had given Israel the staunchest moral and financial support for years; some were European would-be investors whom we needed like lifeblood; others were people sent to me by other people whom I had met and who had helped us in the States, or in Africa, or in Latin America.

I liked seeing people, and I felt that it was my duty to do so, but the more people I saw in my office or at home, the more papers and mail I had to plow through at night. I tried to get home for lunch whenever I could; sometimes there were official lunches, but sometimes I would just drive back home with Lou around two o'clock, eat quickly and be back at the office by three for another round of meetings and phone calls. If I was lucky, and no evening functions were planned, I would leave the office by seven or eight, go home, shower, change and have some supper. I had a maid, of course. She left as soon as she had done the lunch dishes (unless there was an official luncheon, in which case we got outside help), but she usually left something in the refrigerator for my evening meal. Occasionally I could stay home in the evenings and someone from the office would come over with piles of correspondence that had to be attended to. And sometimes, but very rarely indeed, I could just sit in an armchair and look at an old movie on television or fiddle around with little things, like tidying up my shelves, which always relaxed me.

Now and then different members of the cabinet dropped in so that we could talk about specific problems in a relaxed and informal way. These were not official meetings, and no decisions were ever taken at them, of course. But I am convinced that they helped make the process of government more efficient just because we could talk things out over a cup of coffee or a bit to eat around my kitchen table. Every two or three weeks Pinchas Sapir, my minister of finance (and now chairman of the Jewish Agency), came over so that we could discuss in depth suggestions that he wanted to bring before the cabinet. Sapir is a man with an immense capacity for work, and he is also Israel's most successful fund raiser. When Sapir meets a Jew abroad, he says, "How much money have you got?" And the funny thing is the man tells him! One of his great preoccupations is the bettering of life—and in particular of education—in the development towns, for which he has done a great deal more than most people know. We always worked very well together, despite the fact that we were poles apart on a number of policy questions, and I personally couldn't have imagined heading a cabinet without him.

Another indispensable member of my cabinet was Yisrael Galili, a minister without portfolio, upon whom I relied very heavily for advice. Galili is not only a wise and unusually modest man, but also someone with a unique talent for getting to the heart of complicated issues and formulating things in the most lucid way possible. I suspect I shall go on asking Galili for his opinions on important matters for a long time.

Generally speaking, I was very fortunate in having good people around me: The director general of my ministry, the late Ya'akov Herzog, was among the most intellectually sophisticated men I have met. And no one could have asked for more devoted aides than Mordechai Gazit (who took over after Herzog's untimely death); Yisrael Lior, Eli Mizrachi and, of course, Simcha Dinitz and Lou.

One nice thing that happened in 1973 was that Sarah decided to take a year's leave of absence from the kibbutz and study English literature at the Hebrew University, which meant that I wasn't alone at night anymore. But the penalty for that was that she and I would sit up until all hours talking, mostly about whether I should head the party list again and run for office (to the extent that one can "run" for anything at seventy-five!) in the elections that were scheduled to take place that autumn. I thought a great deal about retiring, but wherever I turned, I heard the same arguments that I had heard in 1969: The problem of my so-called succession was no less acute than the problem of Eshkol's succession had been; the three elements that made up the Labor Party were still very uneasy partners; the military situation—though it was fairly quiescent since the War of Attrition—was certainly liable to worsen at any time; my relationship with President Nixon was one of great rapport and not likely to be established quickly by anyone else; and so on and so forth. I loathed being the subject of endless speculation—will she or won't she?—but I couldn't honestly counter any of those arguments with effective arguments of my own, other than the fact that I felt I owed it to myself to retire. All through the spring the conversations went on with my colleagues in the party, followed avidly by the press, as though Israel had no other worries. In the end, I said, "All right. There is no point to dragging the decision out any longer, and there are other things to think about." Later I often thought to myself bitterly that even if I had then refused to head the party list again, I would still have been prime minister in October, 1973, because the elections were due to take place only in November.

In March I visited Washington again. There had just been a most unfortunate incident that might have cast something of a cloud over my visit: The Israeli air force had shot down a Libyan Boeing 727 that had strayed over the Sinai Peninsula, and the lives of 106 people had been lost. It was one of those tragedies that can't be avoided when a nation has to stay on the alert, night and day, against terrorism. We had been warned that a possible suicide attack was being readied against us somewhere in Israel by terrorists who would try to land a plane loaded with explosives, and we were in no mood to take chances—though we would have done so if we had had even the slightest inkling that there were any passengers aboard that plane. But the pilot had ignored all our attempts to identify him, as was proved later when the "black box" was found. Both President Nixon and the House Foreign Affairs Committee listened sympathetically to my explanation of what had happened and why, and in the ninety minutes that I spent with the president, he again assured me warmly that U.S. aid to Israel would continue and that we would go on getting U.S. backing for our demand for negotiations with our neighbors. But I was no less eager to explain our position to the nations of Europe, and when the president of the Council of Europe invited me to attend the meeting of the council's Consultative Assembly in Strasbourg, I said I would be glad to come. This time, however, I would not go to Paris. I asked our ambassador only to notify the French

Foreign Office that I would be visiting France and not in any way, directly or indirectly, to give the French the impression that I wanted to be invited to Paris. So I went directly to Strasbourg.

But just before I left Israel, I got some devastating news. Arab terrorists had succeeded in "convincing" the Austrian government to shut down the Jewish Agency transit camp at Schonau Castle, near Vienna, which had served for a number of years as the indispensable halfway station for Jews leaving the Soviet Union en route to Israel. Before I got into the story of this surrender to blackmail and what I tried to do about it, let me say something about the function of Schonau. As most people probably know by now, those courageous Soviet Jews who have dared to apply for an exit permit in order to emigrate to Israel are usually forced to wait for it for years. And when it is granted, there is no prior notice whatsoever—only the curt stipulation that its recipient must leave the USSR within a week or, at most, ten days. There have been exceptions, of course, some Jews have even been told that if they want to go, they must clear out within a matter of hours. But most of the time prospective emigrants are given a few days to put all their personal affairs in order: arrange for those possessions that they are allowed to send to Israel to be packed, cleared by customs and dispatched; organize their own passage; give up their Soviet citizenship; and go through a whole host of other formalities, while finding time to say their good-byes to people whom they will probably never see again as long as they live. It is not the way that most emigrants leave their countries; it is neither human nor decent, but it is the only way that Jews can leave the Soviet Union, as though they are criminals who are being deported.

The first stop for the trains that bring them into freedom, generally via Prague, is a little railway crossing on the Cechoslovak-Austrian frontier, where the Austrian authorities issue on the spot the vital transit visas that make it possible for the emigrants to enter the free world and for the Jewish Agency officials in Austria, who welcome them into it, to learn the number and names of the Jews aboard a particular train. From the frontier, the trains—with their special compartment for the Jewish immigrants—continue on to Vienna, where buses stand ready to take the emigrants to the transit camp. Schonau, a large white stucco *Schloss* rented to the Jewish Agency by an Austrian countess, was much more, however, than just a place for the immigrants to rest and realize that they were at last on their way to the Jewish state. It was a place where the immigrants—confused and exhausted—could be given information about Israel, be classified according to their professions and prepared, if only very minimally, for the new life they were going to lead in a new land.

No one stayed long in Schonau. The average emigrant family spent only two or three days there before being bused to the airport and to the El Al planes that brought them, still weary but ecstatic, to us. I had visited Schonau the year before and seen for myself the state of mind and body in which those people had come from the Soviet Union, and I knew the importance of that gateway to freedom. I also knew that there was virtually no other way for the Jews to leave the Soviet Union except through Austria, and I knew that for millions of Russian Jews who were still there, Schonau was a symbol of liberty and hope.

But the Arab terrorists knew all this, too, and at the end of September, 1973, two gunmen broke into one of those trains just as it crossed into Austria, kidnapped seven Russian Jews (including a seventy-one-year-old man, an ailing woman and a three-year-old child) and brazenly informed the Austrian government that unless it instantly put an end to the assistance it had given the Soviet Jewish immigrants and closed down Schonau, not only would the hostages be killed, but there would be violent retaliation against Austria. To our astonishment and horror, the Austrian cabinet, led by Chancellor Bruno Kreisky, gave in at once, to the tunes of loud rejoicing both from the gunmen (who were immediately whisked away to Libya) and from the entire Arab press, which could hardly contain its glee at what it called "the successful commando blow to the movement of Russian Jews emigrating to Israel."

I had known Kreisky for quite a long time and fairly well. He served for several years as the foreign minister of Austria, and we used to meet at the United Nations. He was also a socialist, and I had, in fact, seen him last at the Socialist International that had taken place in Vienna two years before. I remember that once I invited him to come to Israel and he began to hem and haw and generally look rather unhappy. "I know exactly what you want to say," I told him. "You want to say that if you come to Israel, you'll have to go to Egypt and to the other Arab countries first. So go ahead. We don't mind in the least who goes where first, but do come and visit us." I could see that he was very relieved that I had said it for him.

"Yes, I will come," he said, and he did. As a Jew Mr. Kriesky had not displayed any interest in Israel, although in 1974 he was to visit us as the head of a delegation of European socialist leaders.

There were many socialists in Austria, some Jews, some not, with whom we had a much closer relationship. But I wanted to talk to Kreisky himself and explain to him the full implications of closing Schonau and what it would do not only to Austria, but to the Jews of Russia. I told our ambassador in Vienna to ask Kreisky whether he would see me on my way to Strasbourg.

To be quite fair, I must note that although I don't believe there is ever a good enough excuse for knuckling under to terrorism, the Austrian decision was not altogether unreasonable. To begin with, Schonau had become far too well known, although we had all tried very hard to discourage visitors from going there and the press from writing about it too often, and there were rumors all the time that the terrorists would attack it. The Austrian security was very good indeed; the trains were met; the emigrants were escorted to Schonau; the castle itself was well guarded. The Austrians were extremely helpful in this regard and very efficient. But if Schonau were closed, then whatever other place was made available would also be held to ransom. I felt that if I could discuss it all with Kreisky, I might get him to change his mind. I waited very tensely for a reply; when it came, I learned that Kreisky couldn't see me on my way to Strasbourg but would see me on my way back.

I had prepared an address for presentation at the Council of Europe meeting, in which I thanked the council and individual European parliaments and political parties for having raised their voices in the demand that Soviet Jewry be permitted to emigrate and touched upon a variety of other subjects, including the refusal of the Arab states to deal with us and the prospects, as we saw them, of Arab-Jewish coexistence. I had ended that address by appealing to the council to help enable the Middle East to "emulate the model that the council itself has established," and my last words were to be a quotation from that great European statesman Jean Monnet, who once said, "Peace depends not only on treaties and promises. It depends essentially on the creation of conditions which, if they do not change the nature of men, at least guide their behavior toward each other in a peaceful direction." I thought those words summed up better than any words of mine could have what it was that the State of Israel wanted from the Arabs—and from the rest of the world.

But by the time I arrived in Strasbourg it seemed idiotic to read that speech. There were other more urgent things I had to say to the council now.

"I have written a speech," I said. "I think you have it before you. But I have decided, at the last minute, not to place between you and me the paper on which my speech is written, especially in the context of what has happened in the course of the past two or three days." And I went on to talk about the Austrian decision:

Having failed in Israel itself the Arab organizations, aided by Arab governments, have taken their terror into Europe. . . . I fully understand the feelings of a prime minister and other members of the government of a country who say, "We have nothing to do with this conflict. Why has our territory been chosen for these activities?" I also understand that such a government may reach the conclusion that the only way to free itself from this headache is to make its country out of bounds, either for the Jews (and then certainly for Israelis) or for the terrorists. It is a choice that every government must make these days. . . . *But there can be no deals with terrorism.* What has happened in Vienna is that, for the first time, a government has come to an understanding, an agreement, with the terrorists. A basic principle of the freedom of movement of peoples has been put under question, at any rate for Jews, and this in itself is a great victory for terrorism and for terrorists. Believe me, we are most grateful to the Austrian government for all that it has done for the tens of thousands of Jews who have gone through Austria from Poland, Rumania and the Soviet Union. But if it has decided that rather than do away with terrorism, it will set terrorists free and give them whatever they ask for, then it will have raised the question of whether any country can permit itself to be involved in allowing Jews to use its soil for transit. . . .

I stayed in Strasbourg for two days and attended the necessary luncheons and dinners; but my mind was fixed on Schonau all the time, and when I got to Vienna, I went straight to Kreisky's office. The prime minister listed for me all the reasons for his government's capitulation to the Arabs and asked why Austria should be the only country to have the problem of the Russian Jews. Why not the Dutch? They could let emigrants through also. I told him that I thought the Dutch were surely prepared to share this burden with him. But it didn't depend on them; it depended on the Russians. And the Russians had agreed to let the Jews out via Austria. Then Kreisky said something I really couldn't accept. "We belong to two different worlds," he told me. Under normal circumstances, there wouldn't have been more for me to say; but I wasn't there for my own sake, and I had to continue the conversation.

Kreisky was adamant about closing Schonau. "I will never be responsible for any bloodshed on the soil of Austria," he repeated. "Other arrangements must be made."

"But if you close Schonau," I pleaded, "you will be handling the Russians the perfect excuse for not letting the Jews go, because they will certainly say that if there is no possibility of transit, then they won't allow any emigrants to leave Russia."

"Well," Kreisky said, "There isn't anything I can do about that. Let the Jews be picked up by your people just as soon as the trains arrive."

"That is impossible," I said, "since we never know how many Jews are on each train. Anyhow, I don't think it is safer to have dozens of people waiting at the airport for an El Al plane to collect them." But I could see that it was no use. Nothing I said would make any difference. Above all, Kreisky wanted to avoid more trouble with the Arabs. I thanked him for having received me, and I left.

A press conference had been called so that both Kreisky and I could answer questions, but when we passed the room in which the press was waiting for us and Kreisky held the door open for me, I shook my head. "No," I said. "I have nothing to say to the press. I don't want to come in." I don't know to this day whether he spoke to the press alone or canceled the conference; I only know that I felt as though my mouth were filled with ashes. *We* belonged to different worlds! The things that Kreisky had said to me just went around and around in my head. Of course, I had no idea what awaited me in Israel.

14. The Yom Kippur War

Of all the events upon which I have touched in this book, none is so hard for me to write about as the war of October, 1973, the Yom Kippur War. But it happened, and so it belongs here—not as a military account, because that I leave to others, but as a near disaster, a nightmare that I myself experienced and which will always be with me.

Even as a personal story, there is still a great deal that cannot be told, and what I write is far from being definitive. But it is the truth as I felt and knew it in the course of that war, which was the fifth to be forced on Israel in the twenty-seven years that have passed since the state was founded.

There are two points I should like to make at once. The first is that we won the Yom Kippur War, and I am convinced that in their heart of hearts the political and military leaders of both Syria and Egypt know that they were defeated again, despite their initial gains. The other is that the world in general and Israel's enemies in particular should know that the circumstances which took the lives of the more than 2,500 Israelis who were killed in the Yom Kippur War will never ever recur.

The war began on October 6, but when I think about it now, my mind goes back to May, when we received information about the reinforcement of Syrian and Egyptian troops on the borders. Our intelligence people thought that it was most unlikely that war would break out; nonetheless, we decided to treat the matter seriously. At that time I went to general headquarters myself. Both the minister of defense and the chief of staff, David Elazar (who is known throughout the country by his nickname, Dado) briefed me thoroughly on the armed forces' state of preparedness, and I was convinced that the army was ready for

any contingency—even for full-scale war. Also, my mind
was put at rest about the question of a sufficiently early
warning. Then, for whatever reason, the tension relaxed.

In September we started to receive information about a
buildup of Syrian troops on the Golan Heights, and on the
thirteenth of that month an air battle took place with the
Syrians, which ended in the downing of thirteen Syrian
MIGs. Despite this, our intelligence people were very reassuring: It was most unlikely they said, that there would be
any major Syrian reaction. But this time, the tension remained, and what's more, it had spread to the Egyptians.
Still our intelligence assessment remained the same. The continued Syrian reinforcement of troops was, they explained,
caused by the Syrians' fear that *we* would attack, and
throughout the month, including on the eve of my departure
to Europe, this explanation for the Syrian move was repeated
again and again.

On Monday, October 1, Yisrael Galili called me in
Strasbourg. Among other things, he told me that he had
talked to Dayan and that they both felt that as soon as I
got back, we should have a serious discussion about the
situation in the Golan Heights. I told him that I would
definitely return the next day and that we should meet the
day after.

Late on Wednesday morning I met with Dayan, Allon,
Galili, the commander of the air force, the chief of staff
and, because the head of intelligence was sick that day, the
head of military intelligence research. Dayan opened the
meeting, and the chief of staff and the head of intelligence
research described the situation on both fronts in great detail. There were things that disturbed them, but the military
evaluation was still that we were in no danger of facing a
joint Syrian-Egyptian attack and, what's more, that it was
very unlikely that Syria would attack us alone. The buildup
and movement of Egyptian forces in the south was probably due to the maneuvers that were always held around this
time of year, and in the north the bolstering and new de-
ployment of forces were still explained as they had been
before. The fact that several Syrian army units had been
transferred only a week before from the Syrian-Jordanian
border was interpreted as part of a recent détente between
the two countries and as a Syrian gesture of goodwill toward Jordan. Nobody at the meeting thought that it was

necessary to call up the reserves, and nobody thought that war was imminent. But it was decided to put a further discussion of the situation on the agenda for Sunday's cabinet meeting.

On Thursday, as usual, I went to Tel Aviv. For years I had been spending Thursdays and Fridays in my Tel Aviv office, Saturdays at my house in Ramat Aviv and returning to Jerusalem either late Saturday evening or early Sunday morning, and there seemed to be no reason for changing the pattern that week. In fact, it was a short week in any case, because Yom Kippur (the Day of Atonement) was to begin on Friday evening, and most people in Israel were taking a long weekend.

I suppose that by now, thanks in part to the war, even non-Jews who had never heard of Yom Kippur before know that this is the most solemn and the most sacred of all the days in the Jewish calendar. It is the one day in the year that Jews throughout the world—even if they are not very pious—unite in some sort of observance. Believing Jews, totally abstaining from food, drink and work, spend Yom Kippur (which, like all Jewish holidays and the Sabbath itself, begins in the evening of one day and ends in the evening of the next) in the synagogue, praying and atoning for sins that they may have committed in the course of the past year. Other Jews, including those who do not actually fast, usually find their own individual way of marking Yom Kippur, by not going to work, by not eating in public and by going to the synagogue, even if for only an hour or two, to hear the great opening prayer, Kol Nidrei, on the eve of Yom Kippur or to listen to the ritual blowing of the shofar, the ram's horn, that closes the fast. But for most Jews everywhere, regardless of how they observe it, Yom Kippur is a day unlike any other.

In Israel it is a day on which the country comes to a virtual standstill. For Jews, there are no newspapers, no television or radio broadcasts, no public transportation, and all schools, shops, restaurants, cafés and offices are closed for twenty-four hours. Since nothing, however, not even Yom Kippur, is as important to Jews as life itself, danger to life overrides everything, and all essential public services function, though many make do for those twenty-four hours with skeleton staffs. The most essential public service for all in Israel, unfortunately, is the army, but as many soldiers as possible are always given leave so that they can be at home with their families on this day.

On Friday, October 5, we received a report that worried me. The families of the Russian advisers in Syria were packing up and leaving in a hurry. It reminded me of what had happened prior to the Six-Day War, and I didn't like it at all. Why the haste? What did those Russian families know that we didn't know? Was it possible that they were being evacuated? In all the welter of information pouring into my office that one little detail had taken root in my mind, and I couldn't shake myself free of it. But since no one around me seemed very perturbed about it, I tried not to become obsessive. Besides, intuition is a very tricky thing; sometimes it must be acted upon at once, but sometimes it is merely a symptom of anxiety and then it can be very misleading indeed.

I asked the minister of defense, the chief of staff and the head of intelligence whether they thought this piece of information was very important. No, it hadn't in any way changed their assessment of the situation. I was assured that we would get adequate warning of any real trouble, and anyway, sufficient reinforcements were being sent to the fronts to carry out any holding operation that might be required. Everything that was necessary had been done, and the army was placed on high alert, particularly the air force and the armored corps. When he left me, the head of intelligence met Lou Kaddar in the corridor. Later she told me that he had patted her shoulder, smiled and said, "Don't worry. There won't be a war." But I was worried; furthermore, I couldn't understand his certainty that all was well. What if he were wrong? If there was even the slightest chance of war, we should at least call up the reserves. At any rate, I wanted a meeting at least of those cabinet ministers who would be spending the Yom Kippur weekend in Tel Aviv. It turned out that very few of them were around. I was reluctant to ask the two National Religious Party ministers who lived in Jerusalem to come to a meeting in Tel Aviv on the eve of Yom Kippur, and several other ministers had already left for their kibbutzim, which were all fairly far away. Still, nine ministers were in town, and I told my military secretary to schedule an emergency meeting for Friday noon.

We gathered in my Tel Aviv office. In addition to the cabinet members, the meeting was attended by the chief of staff and the head of intelligence. We heard all the reports again, including the one that concerned the rushed—and to me still inexplicable—departure of the Russian families from Syria, but again, no one seemed very alarmed. Nevertheless, I decided to speak my mind. "Look," I said, "I have a terrible feeling that this has all happened before. It reminds me of 1967, when we were accused of massing troops against Syria, which is exactly what the Arab press is saying now. And I think that it all means something." As a result, although as a rule a cabinet decision is required for a full-scale callup, that Friday we passed a resolution, suggested by Galili, that if necessary, the minister of defense and I could do so by ourselves. I also said that we should get in touch with the Americans so that they could get in touch with the Russians and tell them in no uncertain terms that the United States was not in the mood for trouble. The meeting broke up, but I stayed on at the office for a while, thinking.

How could it be that I was still so terrified of war breaking out when the present chief of staff, two former chiefs of staff (Dayan and Chaim Bar-Lev, who was my minister of commerce and industry) and the head of intelligence were far from sure that it would? After all, they weren't just ordinary soldiers. They were all highly experienced generals, men who had fought and led other men in spectacularly victorious battles. Each one of them had an outstanding military record, and as for our intelligence services, they were known to be among the best in the world. Not only that, but foreign sources with whom we were in constant touch agreed absolutely with the assessment of our experts. So why was it that I was still so ill at ease? Was I perhaps talking myself into something? I couldn't answer my own questions.

Today I know what I should have done. I should have overcome my hesitations. I knew as well as anyone else what full-scale mobilization meant and how much money it would cost, and I also knew that only a few months before, in May, we had had an alert and the reserves had been called up; but nothing had happened. But I also understood that perhaps there had been no war in May exactly because the reserves had been called up. That Friday morning I should have listened to the warnings of my own heart and ordered a callup. For me, that fact cannot and never will be erased, and there can be no consolation in anything that anyone else has to say or in all of the commonsense rationalizations with which my colleagues have tried to comfort me.

It doesn't matter what logic dictated. It matters only that I, who was so accustomed to making decisions—and who did make them throughout the war—failed to make that one decision. It isn't a question of feeling guilty. I, too, can rationalize and tell myself that in the face of such total certainty on the part of our military intelligence—and the almost equally total acceptance of its evaluations on the part of our foremost military men—it would have been unreasonable of me to have insisted on a callup. But I know that I should have done so, and I shall live with that terrible knowledge for the rest of my life. I will never again be the person I was before the Yom Kippur War.

Then, however, I sat in the office, thinking and agonizing until I just couldn't sit there anymore and I went home. Menachem and Aya had invited a few friends to drop in after dinner. Jews eat dinner early on the eve of Yom Kippur because traditionally it is their last meal for twenty-four hours, and by the time the stars are out the fast has begun. We sat down to eat; but I was very restless and had no appetite at all, and although they wanted me to stay on with their friends, I excused myself and went to bed. But I couldn't sleep.

It was a still, hot night, and through the open window I could hear the voices of Menachem and Aya's friends talking quietly in the garden below. Once or twice the children's dog barked, but otherwise it was a typically silent Yom Kippur night. I lay awake for hours, unable to sleep. Eventually I must have dozed off. Then, at about 4 A.M., the phone next to my bed rang. It was my military secretary. Information had been received that the Egyptians and the Syrians would launch a joint attack on Israel "late in the afternoon." There was no doubt anymore. The intelligence source was authoritative. I told Lior to ask Dayan, Dado, Allon and Galili to be in my office before 7 A.M. On the way there, I caught sight of an old man going to synagogue, his prayer shawl over his shoulders holding the hand of a small child. They looked like symbols of Judaism itself, and I remember thinking sorrowfully that all over Israel, young men were fasting in synagogues today and that it was from their prayers that they would soon be called to arms.

By eight o'clock the meeting had begun. Dayan and Dado differed as to the scale of the callup. The chief of staff recommended the mobilization of the entire air force and four divisions and said that if they were called up at once, they could go into action the next day—that is, Sunday. Dayan, on the other hand, was in favor of calling up the air force and only two divisions (one for the north and one for the south), and he argued that if we had a full mobilization before a single shot was fired, the world would have an excuse for calling us the "aggressors." Besides, he thought that the air force plus two divisions could handle the situation, and if toward evening the situation worsened, we could always call up more within a few hours. "That's my suggestion," he said, "but I won't resign if you decide against me." "My God," I thought, "*I* have to decide which of them is right?" But what I said was that I had only one criterion: If there really was a war, then we had to be in the best position possible. "The callup should be as Dado suggested." But, of course, it was the one day of the year that even our legendary ability to mobilize rapidly partly failed us.

Dado was in favor of a preemptive strike since it was clear that war was inevitable in any case. "I want you to know," he said, "that our air force can be ready to strike at noon, but you must give me the green light now. If we can make that first strike, it will be greatly to our advantage." But I had already made up my mind. "Dado," I said, "I know all the arguments in favor of a preemptive strike, but I am against it. We don't know now, any of us, what the future will hold, but there is always the possibility that we will need help, and if we strike first, we will get nothing from anyone. I would like to say yes because I know what it would mean, but with a heavy heart I am going to say no." Then Dayan and Dado went to their offices and I told Simcha Dinitz (now our ambassador to Washington, who happened to be in Israel that week) to fly back to the States immediately and I called in Menachem Begin to tell him what was happening. I also asked for a cabinet meeting for noon and called the then U.S. ambassador, Kenneth

Keating, and asked him to come and see me. I told him two things: that according to our intelligence, the attacks would start late in the afternoon and that we would not strike first. Maybe something could still be done to avert the war by U.S. intervention with the Russians or maybe even directly with the Syrians and the Egyptians. At all events, we would not make a preemptive strike. I wanted him to know that and to relay that information as soon as possible to Washington. Ambassador Keating had been a very good friend to Israel for many years, both in the U.S. Senate and in Israel itself. He was a man I liked and trusted and on that dreadful morning I was grateful to him for his assistance and understanding.

When the cabinet met at noon, it heard a full description of the situation, including the decision to mobilize the reserves and also my decision regarding a preemptive strike. Nobody raised any objections whatsoever. Then, while we were meeting, my military secretary burst into the room with the news that the shooting had started, and almost at once we heard the wailing of the first air-raid sirens in Tel Aviv. The war had begun.

Not only had we not been warned in time, but we were fighting on two fronts simultaneously and fighting enemies who had been preparing themselves for years to attack us. We were overwhelmingly outnumbered—in guns, tanks, planes and men—and were at a severe psychological disadvantage. The shock wasn't only over the way in which the war started, but also the fact that a number of our basic assumptions were proved wrong: the low probability of an attack in October, the certainty that we would get sufficient warning before any attack took place and the belief that we would be able to prevent the Egyptians from crossing the Suez Canal. The circumstances could not possibly have been worse. In the first two or three days of the war, only a thin line of brave young men stood between us and disaster. And no words of mine can ever express the indebtedness of the people of Israel to those boys on the Canal and on the Golan Heights. They fought, and fell, like lions, but at the start they had no chance.

What those days were like for me I shall not even try to describe. It is enough, I think, to say that I couldn't even cry when I was alone. But I was very rarely alone. I stayed in the office most of the time, although now and then I went to the war room and sometimes Lou made me go home and lie down until the phone summoned me back. There were meetings all through the day and all through the night, incessantly interrupted by phone calls from Washington and bad news from the front. Plans were presented, analyzed and debated. I couldn't bear to be away from the office for more than an hour at a time because Dayan, Dado, Foreign Office people and various ministers were constantly coming in either to report to me on the most recent developments or to ask my advice on various matters.

But even on the worst of those early days, when we already knew what losses we were sustaining, I had complete faith in our soldiers and officers, in the spirit of the Israel Defense Forces and their ability to face any challenge, and I never lost faith in our ultimate victory. I knew we would win sooner or later; but each report of the price we were paying in human lives was like a knife being turned in my heart, and I shall never forget the day when I listened to the most pessimistic prediction I had yet heard.

On the afternoon of October 7 Dayan returned from one of his tours at the front and asked to see me at once. He told me that in his opinion the situation in the south was so bad that we should pull back substantially and establish a new defensive line. I listened to him in horror. Allon, Galili and my military secretary were in the room. Then I asked Dado to come in too. He had another suggestion—that we should go on with the offensive in the south. He asked if he could go to the southern front to supervise things himself and for permission to make whatever decisions might have to be made on the spot. Dayan agreed and Dado left. That night I called a cabinet meeting and got the ministers' approval for us to launch a counterattack against the Egyptians on October 8. When I was alone in the room, I closed my eyes and sat perfectly still for a minute. I think that if I hadn't learned, during all those years, how to be strong, I would have gone to pieces then. But I didn't.

The Canal had been crossed by the Egyptians, and our forces in the Sinai had been battered. The Syrians had penetrated in depth on the Golan Heights. On both fronts the casualties were already very high. One burning question was whether at this point we should tell the nation how bad the situation really was, and I felt very strongly that we should wait for a while. The very least we could do for our soldiers, and for their families, was to keep the truth to ourselves for a few more days. Nonetheless, some kind of statement had to be made at once, so on that first day of the war I addressed the citizens of Israel. It was one of the most difficult assignments of my life because I knew that, for everyone's sake, I could not tell all the facts.

Talking to a nation that had no idea yet of the terrible toll being taken in the north and in the south or of the peril that Israel faced until the reserves were fully mobilized and in action, I said, "We are in no doubt that we shall prevail. But we are also convinced that this renewal of Egyptian and Syrian aggression is an act of madness. We did our best to prevent the outbreak. We appealed to quarters with political influence to use it in order to frustrate this infamous move of the Egyptian and Syrian leaders. While there was still time, we informed friendly countries of the confirmed information that we had of the plans for an offensive against Israel. We called on them to do their utmost to prevent war, but the Egyptian and Syrian attack had started."

On Sunday Dayan came in to my office. He closed the door and stood in front of me. "Do you want me to resign?" he asked. "I am prepared to do so if you think I should. Unless I have your confidence, I can't go on." I told him—and I have never regretted this—that he had to stay on as minister of defense. We decided to send Bar-Lev to the north for a personal assessment of the situation. Then we began our negotiations to get military aid from the United States. Decisions had to be taken very quickly—and they had to be the right ones. There was no time nor any margin for mistakes.

By Wednesday, the fifth day of the war, we had pushed the Syrians back across the 1967 cease-fire line and begun our attack into Syria, while in Sinai the situation was sufficiently static for the cabinet to consider our crossing of the Canal. But what if our troops crossed and then were trapped? I also had to consider the possibility that the war would not be a short one and that we might find ourselves without the planes, tanks and ammunition we needed. We needed arms desperately, and, in the beginning they were slow in coming.

I talked to Dinitz in Washington at all hours of the day

and the night. Where was the airlift? Why wasn't it under way yet? I remember calling him once at 3 A.M., Washington time, and he said, "I can't speak to anyone now, Golda. It is much too early." But I couldn't listen to reason. I knew that President Nixon had promised to help us, and I knew from my past experience with him that he would not let us down. Let me, at this point, repeat something that I have said often before (usually to the extreme annoyance of many of my American friends). However history judges Richard Nixon—and it is probable that the verdict will be very harsh—it must also be put on the record forever that he did not break a single one of the promises he made to us. So why was there a delay? "I don't care what time it is," I raged at Dinitz. "Call Kissinger now. In the middle of the night. We need the help today because tomorrow it may be too late."

The story has already been published of that delay, of the U.S. Defense Department's initial reluctance to send military supplies to us in U.S. planes and of the problems that arose when we feverishly shopped around for other planes—when all the time huge transports of Soviet aid were being brought by sea and air to Egypt and Syria and we were losing aircraft at a disturbing rate (not in air battles but to the Soviet missiles on both fronts). Each hour of waiting that passed was like a century for me, but there was no alternative other than to hold on tight and hope that the next hour would bring better news. I phoned Dinitz and told him that I was ready to fly to Washington incognito to meet with Nixon if he thought it could be arranged. "Find out immediately," I said. "I want to go as soon as possible." But it wasn't necessary. At last Nixon himself ordered the giant C-5 Galaxies to be sent, and the first flight arrived on the ninth day of the war. On October 14 the airlift was invaluable. It not only lifted our spirits, but also served to make the American position clear to the Soviet Union, and it undoubtedly served to make our victory possible. When I heard that the planes had touched down in Lydda, I cried for the first time since the war had begun, though not for the last. That was also the day on which we published the first casualty list—656 Israelis had already died in battle.

But even the Galaxies that brought us tanks, ammunition, clothing, medical supplies and air-to-air rockets couldn't bring all that was required. What about the planes? The Phantoms and Skyhawks had to be refueled en route, so they were refueled in the air. But they came—and so did the Galaxies that landed in Lydda, sometimes at the rate of one every fifteen minutes.

When it was all over, in the spring, the U.S. colonel who had been in charge of the airlift came back to visit Israel with his wife, and they came to see me. They were lovely young people, filled with enthusiasm for the country and with admiration for our ground crews, who had learned, almost overnight, to use the special equipment for unloading those giants. I remember going out to Lydda once to watch the Galaxies come in. They looked like some kind of immense prehistoric flying monsters, and I thought to myself: "Thank God I was right to reject the idea of a preemptive strike! It might have saved lives in the beginning, but I am sure that we would not have had that airlift, which is now saving so many lives."

In the meantime, Dado shuttled from one front to the other. Bar-Lev returned from the north, and we sent him to the south to straighten out the confusion that had arisen there because the generals on the spot had such critical differences of opinion about the tactics to be employed. He was asked to stay there as long as necessary. On Wednesday he phoned me from the Sinai. It was right after a collossal tank battle in which our forces had smashed the Egyptian armored advance. Dado has a slow, very deliberate way of speaking, and when I heard him say, "G-o-l-d-a, it will be all right. We are back to being ourselves and they are back to being themselves," I knew that the tide had turned, although there were still bloody battles ahead in which hundreds of young men, and older ones too, lost their lives. It was not for nothing that people bitterly suggested later that this war should be known, not as the Yom Kippur War, but as the War of the Fathers and Sons, for all too often they fought side by side on both fronts.

For days I was tormented by the fear that a third front would be opened and that Jordan would join in the attack on us. But apparently King Hussein had learned his lesson in the Six-Day War, and luckily his contribution to the Yom Kippur War was only one Jordanian armored brigade sent to help the Syrians. But by then we were already attacking strategic targets inside Syria, and our artillery had come well within range of the suburbs of Damascus, so Hussein's tanks were not much use after all.

On October 15, the tenth day of the war, the Israel Defense Forces began their crossing of the Canal in order to establish a bridgehead on the other side. I spent that night in my office and thought that it would never end. The time for the actual crossing had been set, originally, for 7 P.M., and I decided to call a meeting of the cabinet an hour earlier so that I could inform the ministers of what was happening. Then I was told that the crossing had been delayed until 9 o'clock, and we rescheduled the cabinet meeting for 8 P.M. But the crossing was postponed again, this time till 10 P.M. and then delayed once more because there was trouble with the bridge. In the meantime, however, the ministers had already come to my office, and they stayed there with me all that night, waiting for news about the operation. Every ten or fifteen minutes someone would come in and say, "It will be very soon now. Only another quarter of an hour." That was how the night passed, in an agony of suspense. The paratroops had crossed on time, but the crossing by the infantry, artillery and tanks was held up by fierce fighting. But I couldn't go home until I knew that the crossing had taken place.

The next day I addressed the Knesset. I was very tired, but I spoke for forty minutes because I had a lot to say, although most of it didn't make pleasant hearing. But at least I could tell the Knesset that, as I was speaking, a task force was already operating on the west bank of the Canal. I wanted also to make public our gratitude to the president and the people of America, and, equally clear, our rage at those governments, notably the French and British, that had chosen to impose an embargo on the shipments of arms to us when we were fighting for our very lives. And most of all, I wanted the world to know what would have happened to us had we withdrawn before the war to pre-Six-Day War lines of 1967—the very same lines, incidentally, that had not prevented the Six-Day War itself from breaking out, although no one seems to remember that.

I have never doubted for an instant, that the true aim of the Arab states has always been, and still is, the total destruction of the State of Israel or that even if we had gone back far beyond the 1967 lines to some miniature enclave, they would not still have tried to eradicate it and us. Nor am I so naïve as to believe that speeches inevitably persuade everyone of everything. But on October 16, 1973, when Israel was still in such peril, I felt that it was my duty to remind the member states of the United Nations and the Arabs just why it was that we had held on, so stubbornly— pending peace talks—to the terrorists we took in 1967. As I said to the Knesset that day:

> One needn't have a fertile imagination to realize what the situation of the State of Israel would have been if we had been on the June 4, 1967 lines. Anyone who finds it difficult to visualize this nightmarish picture, should direct his mind and attention to what happened on the northern front—on the Golan Heights—during the first days of the war. Syria's aspirations are not limited to a piece of land but to deploying their artillery batteries once again on the Golan Heights against the Galilee settlements, to setting up missile batteries against our aircraft, so as to provide cover for the breakthrough of their armies into the heart of Israel.
>
> Nor is a fertile imagination required to imagine the fate of the State of Israel had the Egyptian armies managed to overcome the Israel Defense Forces in the expanses of Sinai and to move in full force toward Israel's borders. . . . War has been launched once more against our very existence as a state and a nation. The Arab rulers pretend that their objective is limited to reaching the lines of June 4, 1967, but we know their objective: the total subjugation of the State of Israel. It is our duty to realize the truth; it is our duty to make it clear to all men of goodwill who tend to ignore it. We need to realize this truth in all its gravity, so that we may continue to mobilize from among ourselves and from the Jewish people all the resources necessary to overcome our enemies, to fight back until we have defeated our attackers.

Also, I wanted to put on record the culpability of the Soviet Union and to stress the evil role Russia was once again playing in the Middle East:

The hand of the Soviet Union is obvious in the equipment, the tactics and the military doctrines that the Arab armies are trying to imitate and adopt. Above everything else, the Soviet Union's all-out support for Israel's enemies in the course of the war has been manifested in the airlift reaching our enemies' airfields and the ships calling at their ports. The Soviet planes and ships carry military equipment, including missiles of various types, and it may be assumed that the planes are also bringing in advisers and experts on operational matters, as well as on equipment and armament.

The Soviet airlift up to October 15 included: to Syria, a hundred twenty-five Antonov-12 planes; to Egypt, forty-two Antonov-12 planes and sixteen Antonov-22 planes; to Iraq, seventeen Antonov-12 planes.

Intelligence reports indicate that the Soviet Union has succeeded in involving other countries of the Soviet bloc in the supply of aid to Egypt and Syria. Such conduct on the part of the USSR goes beyond the limits of unfriendly policy. It is a policy of irresponsibility not only toward Israel, but toward the Middle East and toward the world.

Then I returned to my office for what was perhaps my grimmest duty, another of the many meetings I held with the distraught parents of boys who were missing in battle. One of the most terrible aspects of the Yom Kippur War was that for days we could not determine the fate of soldiers who had failed to communicate in any way with their families since the attacks began. Israel is a very small country, and its army, as everyone knows, is a citizens' army, made up of a limited standing force and of reserves. We have never fought far from our own borders, and contact between our soldiers and their homes is always closely maintained. But this war was already lasting longer than any other war we had ever had to fight—with the exception of the War of Independence—and we had been taken by surprise.

Reservists throughout the country had been called away from the synagogue and their homes. In the rush, some had not even taken time to look for dog tags or been able to find their units. Reservists in the armored corps had joined improvised tank crews, jumped from one burning tank to another and then from that, when it exploded, into a third. And, of course, the war against us had been waged with terrifying weapons, the antitank missiles supplied to the Egyptians and Syrians by the Russians which left tanks in flames and their crews so badly burned that often identification was almost impossible. One of the proudest traditions of the Israel Defense Forces is that our dead and wounded are never left to the enemy; but in the first days of the Yom Kippur War, there was often no alternative, and hundreds of parents were now beside themselves with worry. "Is he dead? If so, where is his body? Is he a prisoner of war? If so, why doesn't anyone know?"

I had been through this torment with the parents of boys taken prisoner in the War of Attrition, and there were days in the winter of 1973 when I could hardly bring myself to face yet another group of parents, knowing that I had nothing to tell them and that the Egyptians and Syrians had not only refused to give the Red Cross lists of captured Israelis months after the cease-fire, but even to let our army chaplains search the battlefields for our dead.

But how could I say no to parents and wives who thought that if they reached me, I would, magically, have some sort of answer for them, although I knew that in their hearts some of them blamed me for the war and for our lack of preparedness. So I saw them all and for the most part they were very brave indeed. All they wanted from me was some scrap of information, a fact or two, however bitter, that they could cling to, something concrete to ease their pain. But for weeks there was nothing I could say. After one such meeting with the parents, I thought of *their* parents in 1948, when 6,000 had fallen—1 percent of the entire *yishuv* killed in the course of eighteen months.

I spent dozens of hours with those poor parents, although all that I could tell them in the beginning was that we were doing whatever we could to find their boys and that we would not agree to any arrangement that did not include the return of prisoners. But how many prisoners were there? I don't think I ever wanted anything as desperately as I wanted those POW lists that were dangled in front of us so long and so cruelly. There is much for which I personally shall never forgive the Egyptians or the Syrians, but above all, I shall never forgive them for withholding that information for so many days, out of sheer malice, and for trying to use the anguish of Israeli parents as a political trump card against us.

After the cease-fire and after the months of negotiations that led at last to the disengagement of troops on both fronts, when our prisoners finally returned from Syria and Egypt, the world at last learned for itself what we had already known for years: that amenities such as the Geneva Convention go by the board when Jews fall into the hands of Arabs—particularly into the hands of the Syrians—and perhaps our anxiety about our POWs was better understood. Often when I sat with those frantic parents, wives and sisters, listening to their plans for yet another petition or demonstration, and when all that I could tell them for weeks on end was that we were doing everything possible to get the lists, I thought to myself that torture by our enemies is worse than death.

By October 19, the thirteenth day of the war, although the fighting had certainly not ended, Mr. Kosygin had already made a rushed visit to Cairo. His "clients" were obviously losing the war they had begun with his assistance, and it was, therefore, not only Egyptian "face" that needed saving, but also that of the Soviet Union itself. It was bad enough that the Egyptians hadn't managed to destroy the Israeli bridgehead on the west bank of the Canal, but worse than that they now had to admit to their patron that the Israel Defense Forces were entrenched west of the Canal, some 60 miles away from Cairo, in an area that soon became known in Israel as Africa. As for the situation of the Soviet Union's other protégé, Syria, it was even graver. That being the case, the Russians did what they have always done: They began a full-scale campaign for a quick cease-fire. Never mind who started the war, and never mind who lost it. The important thing was to get the Arabs out of the mess they had got themselves into and to rescue the Egyptian and Syrian forces from total defeat.

But although we had neither wanted nor started the Yom Kippur War, we had fought and won it, and we had a war aim of our own—peace. For once, we were not going to bury our dead quietly, looking on, while the Arabs and their supporters were solacing themselves at the United Nations for their humiliation. This time the Arabs were going to have to meet us, not only on battlefields but at the negotiating table, and together with us find a solution to a problem that had taken thousands of young lives—theirs and ours—over the past three decades. For years we had been shouting "peace" and hearing the echo "war" come back from the other side. For years we not only had seen our sons killed but had tolerated a situation so grotesque that it is almost unbelievable: The only time that Arab states were prepared to recognize the existence of the State of Israel was when they attacked it in order to wipe it out.

I remember driving back from the office through Tel Aviv's blacked-out streets on one of those nights when the Brezhnev-Kissinger talks about a cease-fire were going on in Moscow and taking a silent oath that, to the extent that it depended in any way at all on me, this war would end in a peace treaty obliterating, for all time, the famous three "noes" of the Arabs declared in Khartoum after the Six-Day War, when their response to our plea that we sit down with them and negotiate was no recognition, no negotiation, no peace! I looked at the dark windows of the houses I passed and wondered behind which of them families were sitting *shiva* (the traditional first week of mourning) and behind which other families were trying to carry on as usual, although there was still no answer to the question Where is he? Dead somewhere in the Sinai, dead on the Golan Heights or a prisoner of war? That night I swore that I would do whatever lay in my power to bring about the peace which the Arab people needed no less than we did and which could be secured only in one way—by negotiation.

I had held a press conference a few days before, on October 13, and a journalist had asked me then if Israel would agree to a cease-fire on the basis of the lines that had existed on October 5, one day before the Arab attack.

"There is no sense whatsoever," I had answered, "in speculating on what Israel will or will not agree to as long as our neighbors to the south and our neighbors to the north have still not indicated any desire to stop the fighting. When we come to a proposition for a cease-fire, we will consider it very seriously and decide because we wish to end this war as quickly as possible.

"But," I had added, "although we are a very small people and there is no comparison between the numbers in our army and those in any of the countries fighting us, and although we do not have the wealth of arms and ammunition they have, we do have two things that give us an advantage over them—our hatred for war and for death."

Now that we were about to be placed under extreme pressure regarding a cease-fire, I felt more strongly than ever that we must make no substantive concession of any sort that did not include direct negotiations—at any time or in any place that the Arabs chose. Not that I made light of the oil embargo with which Saudi Arabia, Libya, Kuwait and other enlightened Arab states were holding the West, including the United States, to ransom, but a limit had to be set as to how accommodating we were going to be.

In the final analysis, to put it bluntly, the fate of small countries always rests with the superpowers, and they always have their own interests to guard. We would have liked the call for a cease-fire to have been postponed for a few more days so that the defeat of the Egyptian and Syrian armies would be even more conclusive than it was, and on October 21 there was every reason to believe that, given just a little more time, this would have happened. North of Ismailia we were pressing hard on the Egyptian Second Army. South of Suez we were completing the encirclement of the Egyptian Third Army. On the Golan Heights the Syrian positions on Mount Hermon had fallen to our forces. We had complete air supremacy on both fronts and thousands of prisoners. But Sadat, of course, was in a far stronger position than we were diplomatically, and the bait he held out to the United States was very tempting: its reentry into the Middle East, plus the removal of the oil embargo. Nor was the Soviet Union without its own means of persuasion. The stakes in Moscow were very high indeed. So I was not at all surprised when, early on the morning of October 22, the Security Council, meeting in an emergency session, predictably enough passed a resolution calling for a cease-fire to go into effect within twelve hours.

There was no question but that Resolution 338, passed with such indecent speed, was intended to avert the total destruction of the Egyptian and Syrian forces by us, though the pill was sugar-coated, to some extent. The resolution for "negotiations to start between the parties concerned under appropriate auspices aimed at establishing a just and durable peace in the Middle East," but it did not spell out how this would be done. The U.S. secretary of state flew from Moscow to Jerusalem to convince me that we ought to accept the cease-fire, and we announced that we would do so. But the Syrians did not accept it at all, and although the Egyptians declared their acceptance, they did not stop shooting on October 22. The fighting went on, and we completed the encirclement of the Third Army and gained control of parts of the city of Suez.

On October 23 I made a statement in the Knesset about the cease-fire. I wanted the people of Israel to know that we had not accepted it out of military weakness, nor had we asked for it. If the Egyptians did not conform to it, I said, we would certainly not remain silent. Our position on both fronts was better than it had been when the war broke out. True, Egypt held a narrow strip on the east bank of the Suez Canal, but the Israel Defense Forces sat firmly on a large section of the Canal's west bank, and in the north, on the Golan Heights, we had occupied all the territory that had been under our control before the war and moved into a salient in Syria. Nonetheless, I said, and I meant everyword with all my heart, "Israel wants peace negotiations to start immediately and concurrently with the cease-fire. It can display the inner strength necessary to bring about an honorable peace within secure borders." But unless and until the Egyptians and Syrians felt the same way and acted accordingly, these would, of course, remain just words.

The war entered its nineteenth day with a new crisis. Knowing that the request had no chance of being accepted by us, Sadat asked that a Soviet-U.S. force be entrusted with supervising the cease-fire, and the Russians themselves made active preparations to step in to that area. The story of the subsequent U.S. alert is not for me to tell. There is only one thing that I wish to say about it. I know that in the United States at that time many people assumed that the alert was "invented" by President Nixon in order to divert attention from the Watergate problem, but I didn't believe that then, and I do not believe it now. I have never claimed to be unusually perceptive about people, but I think that at this stage of my life I can probably tell when someone speaks with true conviction.

One of my most vivid recollections of President Nixon is a conversation we had in Washington at the time that two

U.S. diplomats were murdered by terrorists in Khartoum. The evening before they were killed, I was dining at the White House. Before we went into dinner, President Nixon, Mrs. Nixon, Yitzhak Rabin (then our ambassador to the United States) and I stood talking about what was happening in Khartoum, and President Nixon said to me very quietly, "You must know, Mrs. Meir, that I will never give in to blackmail. Never. If I compromise with the terrorists now, I shall be risking the lives of many more men in the future." He was as good as his word. Then, on his visit to Israel in 1974—when we ourselves had just been through the unspeakable outrage of the slaughter of children by terrorists at Ma'alot—Nixon returned to the subject. "I was brought up," he told me when he visited me at my home in Jerusalem, "to abhor capital punishment. I come from a Quaker background. But terrorists cannot be dealt with in any other way. You must never give in to blackmail."

I was absolutely sure, on both occasions, that the man speaking to me—without the benefit of press or TV cameras—spoke with complete sincerity, and I am still sure that President Nixon ordered the U.S. alert on October 24, 1973, because, détente or no détente, he was not about to give in to Soviet blackmail. It was, I think, a dangerous decision, a courageous decision and a correct decision.

But it brought about an escalation of the crisis, and someone had to pay to bring about a relaxation of tension. The price demanded, needless to say from Israel, included our agreeing to permit supplies to reach the encircled Egyptian Third Army and to accept a second cease-fire that was to go into effect under the supervision of a UN force. The demand that we feed the Third Army, give it water and generally help its 20,000 soldiers recover from their defeat was not, in any way, a matter of humanitarianism. We would gladly have given them all this had the Egyptians been willing to lay down their arms and go home. But this was exactly what President Sadat wanted to avoid. He was desperately anxious not to make public within Egypt the fact that Israel had prevailed in yet another attack upon it—the more so since for a few days in October the Egyptians were intoxicated by their apparent victory over us. So once again there was the standard concern for those tender feelings of the Arab aggressor, rather than for those of the victims of Arab aggression, and we were urged to compromise in the name of "world peace."

"At least," I told the cabinet that week, "let's call things by their right name. Black is black and white is white. There is only one country to which we can turn and sometimes we have to give in to it—even when we know we shouldn't. But it is the only real friend we have, and a very powerful one. We don't have to say yes to everything, but let's call things by their proper name. There is nothing to be ashamed of when a small country like Israel, in this situation, has to give in sometimes to the United States. And when we do say yes, let's for God's sake, not pretend that it is otherwise and that black is white."

But we didn't agree to everything. We had minimum demands of our own, which I had listed in the Knesset on October 23 as follows:

> It is our intention to clarify and ensure, *inter alia,* that the ceasefire shall be binding upon all the regular forces stationed in the territory of a state accepting the cease-fire, including the forces of foreign states, such as the armies of Iraq and Jordan in Syria and also forces sent by other Arab states which took part in the hostilities.
>
> The cease-fire shall also be binding upon irregular forces acting against Israel from the area of the states accepting the cease-fire.
>
> The cease-fire shall assure the prevention of a blockade or interference with free navigation, including oil tankers in the Bab el Mandeb Strait on their way to Eilat.
>
> It shall ensure that the interpretation of the term referring to "negotiations between the parties" is direct negotiations and, naturally, it must be assured that the procedures, the drawing up of maps and the subject of cease-fire supervision shall be determined by agreement.
>
> A subject of great importance . . . is the release of prisoners. The government of Israel has decided to demand an immediate exchange of prisoners. We have discussed this with the government of the United States, which was one of the initiators of the cease-fire.

There was nothing new in the list, nothing untoward and nothing that was not—by any criteria—our due.

At this point the outstanding personality in the Middle East became not President Sadat, or President Assad, or King Feisal or even Mrs. Meir. It was the U.S. secretary of state, Dr. Henry Kissinger, whose efforts on behalf of peace in the area can only be termed superhuman. My own relationship with Henry Kissinger had its ups and downs. At times it became very complicated, and at times I know I annoyed and perhaps even angered him—and vice versa. But I admired his intellectual gifts, his patience and his perseverance were always limitless, and in the end we became good friends. I met and spent time in Israel with his wife, too, and liked and admired her immensely. I think that possibly one of the most impressive of Kissinger's many impressive qualities is his fantastic capacity for dealing with the minutest details of whatever problems he undertakes to solve. He told me once that two years ago he had never heard of a place called Kuneitra. But when he became involved in negotiating the disengagement of the Syrian and Israeli forces on the Golan Heights, there wasn't a road, a house or even a tree there about which he didn't know everything there was to know. As I said to him then, "With the exception of the former generals who are now members of the Israeli cabinet, I don't think we have a single minister who knows as much about Kuneitra as you do."

When he first started on the long and rocky road that was to lead to the disengagement of forces on the Golan Heights, and we said that we could not give up certain positions on the hills near Kuneitra because to do so would mean endangering the Israeli settlements below, he was very skeptical. "You talk about those hills as though they were the Alps or the Himalayas," he said to me. "I've been to the Golan Heights and I couldn't see any Alps there." But, as he always did, he listened very attentively, learned every detail of the topography for himself, and when he was quite satisfied that we were making sense, he was prepared to spend days upon days persuading Assad that on such and such a point the Syrians must give way. And in the end they did. But all the time Kissinger went back and forth as though he had never heard of the word "fatigue."

Several times the negotiations with the Syrians were almost broken off, and Kissinger was already writing out drafts of statements for them and for us so that at least it could be said that the negotiations would only be postponed, not terminated altogether. Then, on the last day, he came to us with yet another new demand from Assad, and we said, "No. Not this. *This* is unacceptable." So Kissinger said, "All right. Then this is the end. Sisco will go to Damascus today with instructions to say that there will be 'no more negotiations' and that we suggest a joint communiqué be issued." That afternoon Kissinger came in to see me—he was supposed to leave at night—and said again, "Well, this is the end." Then he looked at me and said, "Do you think perhaps I should go to Damascus instead of Sisco?" "I didn't dare ask it of you," I said. "You told me that you would never meet with Gromyko in Damascus, and this is exactly where Gromyko is right now." Kissinger thought for a minute and then said, "Yes, I must see him, even if it's just a brief courtesy call. What do you think? I'll do what you suggest." So I said, "Look, I know one thing. If you yourself go, there is some chance that you will make it this time. Otherwise, there is no chance at all." Joseph Sisco, who was in the room with us, nodded his head and said, "I agree absolutely." "OK," said Kissinger, "I'll go. Maybe I can do something after all." And he went at once.

He came back to Israel at about 1:30 A.M. and sent a message from his plane to say that he wanted us to meet that night, at 2:30 in the morning. He turned up, as fresh as though he had spent the past month in a summer resort, although everyone else around him was wilting. He bounced in and said, "It's all right. That's it. We've done it." Of course, even with that really brilliant mind and with that astounding capacity for hard work, if Kissinger had been the foreign minister of Gabon, he wouldn't have got far with the Syrians, but he had everything: intelligence, diligence, stamina *and* the fact that he represented the greatest power in the world, which made for a very effective combination indeed.

As for his being Jewish, I don't think it either aided or hindered him in all those months of negotiation. But if he was emotionally involved with us, such an involvement never reflected itself, for one moment, in anything he said to us or did on our behalf. The first time he went to Saudi Arabia, he was treated to a long lecture by Feisal on

"Communists, Israelis and Jews." Feisal's theory—which he didn't hesitate to explain in detail to Kissinger—was that the Jews had created the communist movement in order to conquer the world. Part of the world was already theirs, but in that part which the Jews couldn't conquer, they placed Jews in important governmental positions. Then he continued, "Did you know that Golda Meir was born in Kiev?"

"Yes," Kissinger replied.

"Doesn't that mean anything to you?"

"No," said Kissinger, "not necessarily."

"Kiev, Russia, communism, that's the formula," declared Feisal.

Afterward Feisal had tried to give Kissinger the *Protocols of the Elders of Zion,* that notorious czarist Russian forgery, as a present, but of course, he didn't accept it.

I had one or two very difficult conversations with Kissinger regarding the Soviet and Egyptian allegations that we had violated the cease-fire. Kissinger apparently was inclined to believe this, and at one point Dinitz called from Washington to implore me to give Kissinger my personal assurance that we had done no such thing. All that week there had been an exchange of messages between us in which President Nixon and Kissinger had asked us to yield—first on one thing, then another, then on a third— and while I understood the U.S. position in regard to the Soviet Union only too well, I found this stream of requests very disturbing. I wrote a letter to Kissinger asking him to tell us everything he wanted all at once, so that we could meet and make some decisions ourselves, rather than get a new request every few hours. So when Dinitz called in such a state, I decided to pick up the phone and talk to Kissinger, rather than send yet another letter. I said, "You can say anything you want about us and do anything you want, but we are *not* liars. The allegations are *not* true."

On October 31 I flew to Washington to try to straighten out the rather strained relationship that had come into being with Washington and to explain, in person, exactly why some of the demands being made of us were not only unfair, but unacceptable. The day before, I had gone to "Africa" myself with Dayan and Dado to visit the commanders there, get their explanations about the terrain and spend some time with the troops. We made three stops at the front, and I must say that the soldiers were all rather surprised to see me in the middle of the desert, and I myself had certainly never expected to be answering questions showered at me by Israeli boys on Egyptian territory. I spoke to large gatherings of soldiers once deep underground, once in the sand outside a tent and once in a battered Egyptian customshouse at Suez. Most of the boys' questions had to do, naturally, with the cease-fire. Why had we allowed supplies to be brought to the Third Army? Why had we agreed to a premature cease-fire? Where were our prisoners of war? I did my best to explain the facts of political life to them, and later I flew to the Golan Heights, and had the same conversation there.

I also had questions that weren't answered to my satisfaction. I was still enraged over the refusal of my socialist comrades in Europe to let the Phantoms and Skyhawks land for refueling as part of the airlift operation. One day, weeks after the war, I phoned Willy Brandt, who is much respected in the Socialist International, and said, "I have no demands to make of anyone, but I want to talk to my friends. For my own good, I need to know what possible meaning socialism can have when not a single socialist country in all of Europe was prepared to come to the aid of the only democratic nation in the Middle East. Is it possible that democracy and fraternity do not apply in our case? Anyhow, I want to hear for myself, with my own ears, what it was that kept the heads of these socialist governments from helping us."

The leadership meeting of the Socialist International was called in London, and everyone came. Such meetings consist of the heads of socialist parties, those in government and those that are in parliamentary oppositions. On that occasion, since I had asked that the meeting be called, I opened it. I told my fellow socialists exactly what the situation had been, how we were taken by surprise, fooled by our own wishful thinking into believing the interpretation we were given of our intelligence reports, and how we had won the war. But it had been touch and go for days. Then I said, "I just want to understand, in the light of this, what socialism is really about today. Here you are, all of you. Not one inch of your territory was put at our disposal for refueling the planes that saved us from destruction. Now, suppose Richard Nixon had said, 'I am sorry, but since we have nowhere to refuel in Europe, we just can't do anything for you, after all.' What would all of you have done then? You know us and who we are. We are all old comrades, long-standing friends. What did you think? On what grounds did you make your decisions not to let those planes refuel? Believe me, I am the last person to belittle the fact that we are only one tiny Jewish state and that there are over twenty Arab states with vast territories, endless oil and billions of dollars. But what I want to know from you today is whether these things are decisive factors in socialist thinking too?"

When I got through, the chairman asked if anybody wanted to speak. But nobody did. Then someone behind me—I didn't want to turn my head and look at him because I didn't want to embarrass him—said, very clearly, "Of course, they can't talk. Their throats are choked with oil." And although there was a discussion, there wasn't really any more to say. It had all been said by that man whose face I never saw.

In Washington, I spent an hour and a half with President Nixon. Afterward the press wanted to know whether Israel was being pressured to make further concessions to the Arabs. I assured them that there had been no pressure. "If so, Madam Prime Minister," said one of the reporters, "then why did you come to Washington?"

"Just to find out that there is no pressure," I said. "That in itself was worthwhile!"

The focal point of my talks with Kissinger had to do with the cease-fire lines in the south, and they were not easy or pleasant talks; but then we were not discussing easy matters. I had brought a six-point proposal, and I remember that Kissinger and I sat up practically all of one night at Blair House, where I was staying. At one stage I said to him, "You know, all we have, really, is our spirit. What you are asking me to do is to go home and help destroy that spirit, and then no aid will be necessary at all."

The text of the agreement between Israel and Egypt was signed on November 11, 1973, at Kilometer 101 of the Cairo-Suez road by Israel's General Aharon Yariv and Egypt's General Abdel Gamasy. It read:

1. Egypt and Israel agree to observe scrupulously the cease-fire called for by the UN Security Council.

My Life

2. Both sides agree that discussions between them will begin immediately to settle the question of the return to the October 22 positions in the framework of agreement on the disengagement and separation of forces under the auspices of the United Nations.

3. The town of Suez will receive daily supplies of food, water and medicine. All wounded civilians in the town of Suez will be evacuated.

4. There shall be no impediment to the movemnt of nonmilitary supplies to the east bank.

5. The Israeli checkpoints on the Cairo-Suez road will be replaced by UN checkpoints. At the Suez end of the road, Israeli officers can participate with the UN to supervise the nonmilitary nature of the cargo at the bank of the Canal.

6. As soon as the UN checkpoints are established on the Cairo-Suez road, there will be an exchange of all POWs, including wounded.

For the first time in a quarter of a century there was direct, simple, personal contact between Israelis and Egyptians. They sat in tents together, hammered out details of the disengagement and shook hands. And our prisoners of war came back from Egypt, those who had been captured in the War of Attrition and those taken in the Yom Kippur War. Miraculously, they returned without a scratch on their spirits, despite everything they had gone through, although some of them wept like babies when we met. They even brought presents with them, things they made in jail, including a blue-and-white Star of David which they had knitted themselves and which had served as their flag during the long imprisonment. "Now that our 'unit' has been disbanded," a group of young officers told me, "we would like you to have it." So I framed it, and it now hangs on my living-room wall.

But we still knew nothing about our POWs in Syria, and almost every day there were military funerals for boys killed in the Sinai whose charred bodies had only now been found in the sand, identified and brought to burial. Worst of all, despite the growing feeling that perhaps this time the disengagement would grow into a real peace, the general mood in Israel was very black. From all sections of the population there came demands that the government resign, accusations that the army's poor state of preparedness was the result of faulty leadership, of complacency and of a total lack of communication between the government and the people.

A number of protest movements arose. They were different in emphasis, and they had different programs; but they shared a demand for change. And they included reservists who often expressed themselves hastily and sometimes even in a way that was painful for me. I disagreed with much of what they had to say about the past, but some of their criticism was justified. At all events, I had to hear what they had to say, and I met with many of the young people from these movements. I tried to make it easy for them to talk to me, and I came away with the feeling that they were often surprised by the difference between the woman who listened to them so attentively and the image they had of me. In that atmosphere charged by suspicion and accusation, I think they were often equally surprised by what I had to say to them.

Much of the outcry was genuine. Most of it, in fact, was a natural expression of outrage over the fatal series of mishaps that had taken place. It was not just my resignation or Dayan's that was being called for in that storm of protest; it was a call to eliminate from the scene everyone who could possibly be held responsible for what had happened and to start all over again with new people, younger people, people who were not tainted by the charge of having led the nation astray. It was an extreme reaction to the extreme situation we were in, and therefore, though it was very painful, it was understandable. But part of the outburst was vicious, and some of it was demagoguery, pure and simple, and the making of political capital by the opposition over a national tragedy.

At the first political debate in the Knesset after the war, I listened to speeches by the opposition, including Menachem Begin and Shmuel Tamir, which tore me apart. They were so full of rhetoric and theatricality that I couldn't stand it, and when I got up to close the debate, I told them that the nature of their addresses was such that I was not going to reply. "I just want to say one thing," I said. "I want to quote a very dear friend of mine, an American Labor Zionist, who once attended a debate on some very serious matter—though it wasn't nearly as serious as what we are talking about here and now—and a man got up to speak. He spoke so effortlessly and so easily that all that my friend could say was: 'If only he had stammered or hesitated occasionally.' " That is exactly how I felt about the flowing rhetoric in the Knesset. Begin and Tamir were talking about a near catastrophe, about men who had been killed or crippled, about terrible things; but they spoke smoothly, without as much as a pause, and I was disgusted.

The center of the storm was Moshe Dayan. The first open request for his resignation, as far as I can remember, was made by another minister in my cabinet, Ya'akov Shimshon Shapiro, the minister of justice. I shall never get over my anger with him for having chosen to make this demand at the height of the crisis that preceded the second cease-fire and for having made it at a meeting, where he knew it would be picked up by the press. As if that weren't enough, I was told that he had walked around the Knesset restaurant, going from one group to another to report on what he had done. So I asked him to come and see me. He came to my office and said, "Since I knew you will not ask Dayan to go, I have come to offer my resignation." I said that I had only two questions. I wouldn't ask him to stay, because I thought that he had made it impossible for me to do so. But I wanted to know, first of all, why he had picked that particular day, and he replied, "Well, because today is the day of the cease-fire." "Is that so?" I said, "I have news for you. There is still fighting going on today. Some of our men have been killed; others have been wounded. It is no day at all, in fact, for you to have made this kind of demand of another minister. And, secondly, why don't you ask me to resign? I am prime minister."

To this, Shapiro only said, "You are not responsible. You are not the minister of defense."

Afterward Dayan came to my office and once again asked, "Do you want me to resign? I am prepared to do so." Once again I said no. I knew that an official commission of inquiry would have to be formed soon—as it was under the chairmanship of Supreme Court President Shimon Agranat on November 18—and certainly until it completed its work and submitted its findings, the principle of collective cabinet responsibility still held and was at least as important as that of ministerial responsibility. The one thing that Israel did not need at that point was a cabinet crisis. Anyhow, we had rescheduled the elections from their original October 31 date to December 31, and the nation would be able to give adequate and effective vent to its feelings then. So although I myself was tremendously tempted to resign, I thought I ought to hold on for a little longer—and so should Dayan.

Of all the members of the cabinet, Dayan was, of course, the most controversial and probably the most complicated. He is, and always has been, a man who elicits very strong responses from the public. Naturally, he has his faults, and like his virtues, they are not small ones. One of the things of which I am most proud, to be quite frank, is that for more than five years I kept together a cabinet that included not only Dayan, but also a number of men who greatly disliked and resented him. But from the start I had a good idea of the problems I was likely to face in this respect. I had known Dayan for years, and I knew that he had opposed my becoming prime minister when Eshkol died. The only way in which I could operate, therefore, was to take whatever stands I would have to take on the essence of each and every issue and to prove to the cabinet—and to Dayan himself—that I was not in the habit of evaluating propositions according to who fathered them.

To his credit, I must say that when I did not support Dayan in something, he always took it very well, although he doesn't work easily with people and is used to getting his own way. In the end we became good friends, and there was not a single occasion when I could complain of any disloyalty on his part. Not once. Even on military matters, he would always come—with the chief of staff—to talk to me first. Sometimes I said to him, "I won't vote in favor of this, but you are free to take your proposal to the cabinet." But if I didn't go along with one of his ideas, he never took it any further. Considering Dayan's reputation for not being able to function as part of a team—and mine for not being able to compromise easily—I think that on the whole we did very well.

It is also not true that he is a hard man. I saw him come back shattered from those agonizing funerals following the war, when children were pushed at him by mothers who shrieked, "You killed their father," and mourners shook their fists at him and called him a murderer. I know how I felt—and I know how Dayan felt. In the first days of the

Yom Kippur War, he was very pessimistic and wanted to prepare the nation for the worst. He called a meeting of newspaper editors to describe to them the situation as he saw it—which was certainly not easy for him.

I kept him from resigning during the war, but I think perhaps he should have done so immediately after the Agranat Commission of Inquiry published its first preliminary report on April 2, 1974. That report cleared Dayan (and myself) of any "direct responsibility" for Israel's unpreparedness on Yom Kippur, but it dealt so harshly with the chief of staff and the head of military intelligence that Dado resigned at once. I have always suspected that Dayan might have retained his "charismatic" image—or at least some of it—had he then, publicly, stuck by his comrades-in-arms. He read that preliminary (and only partial) report in my office and, for the third time, asked me whether he should resign. "This time," I said, "it must be the decision of the party." But he was following a logic of his own, and I didn't feel that on such a weighty matter I should give him advice. Now I am sorry that I didn't, though he may not have taken it in any case.

As for me, the commission said that on Yom Kippur morning "she decided wisely, with common sense and speedily, in favor of the full mobilization of the reserves, as recommended by the chief of staff despite weighty political considerations, thereby performing a most important service for the defense of the state."

To many outsiders the situation in Israel appeared brighter in the winter of 1973–74 than it did to the Israelis themselves. One of my visitors around that time was the late Richard Crossman, who had been so involved in the birth of the state and couldn't understand the current gloom and despondency. "You people have gone crazy," he said to me. "What's happening to all of you?"

"Tell me," I asked him, "what would have been the reaction in England if something similar had happened to the British?" He was so astonished at my question that he almost dropped his coffee cup.

"Do you think things like that haven't happened to us?" he said. "That Churchill never made a mistake during the war? That we had no Dunkirk and a great many other setbacks as well? We just didn't take things in such an intense way."

But we are different, I suppose, and the word "trauma" that was on everyone's lips all that winter most accurately describes the national sense of loss and injury that Crossman thought was so excessive.

15.   The End of the Road

The weeks passed. The reserves were still mobilized in the south and in the now-icy north. Even the shooting hadn't come to an end, and the mood in Israel remained black, restive and very anxious. Kissinger
continued his efforts to secure a separation of forces between Syria and Israel, to produce a list of the Israeli prisoners of war in Syria and to bring about the Geneva talks
between the Egyptians, the Jordanians and ourselves—the
Syrians having announced in December that they would
not participate. Although, on the surface, we seemed to be
closer to peace than we had ever been before, the truth is
that neither I nor most other Israelis believed, in our heart
of hearts, that we would leave Geneva with peace treaties
in our hands, and we didn't go there with many illusions or
in a state of euphoria. Still, the Egyptians and Jordanians
had agreed to sit in the same room with us, and that, in
itself, was something that they had never consented to do
before.

The Geneva talks opened on December 21 and, as I had
feared, led almost nowhere. There was no real dialogue between the Egyptians and us. On the contrary, from the very
first moment it was all too clear that nothing much had
changed. The Egyptian delegation literally refused to permit
its table to be placed next to ours, and the atmosphere was
far from friendly. A military agreement was obviously a
necessity for the Egyptians, but peace, we realized once
again, was not what they were driving at. Still, even though
no political solution came of that meeting, within a few
days, at Kilometer 101, the disengagement treaty was
signed, and we went on hoping that somehow or other a
political solution could be found. Surely the Messiah had
not come all the way to Kilometer 101 and then been too
lazy to go on.

On December 31 we held our elections. The ballots showed that the country was not keen on changing horses in midstream, and although we lost some votes—as did the National Religious Party—the Ma'arach still came out as the leading bloc. But the opposition to the Ma'arach had become more forceful because the entire right wing had now combined into a bloc of its own. A coalition would have to be formed again, and it would clearly be a back-breaking job to form it, since the religious bloc, which was a traditional coalition partner of ours, was itself deeply divided on the question of who should lead it and what its policy should be at this tremendously difficult time.

I was beginning to feel the physical and psychological effects of the draining past few months. I was dead tired and not at all sure that, in this kind of situation, I could ever succeed in forming a government—or even whether I should go on trying to do so. Not only were there problems from without, but there were also difficultes within the party. At the beginning of March I felt I couldn't go on, and I told the party that I had had enough. But I was bombarded by delegations imploring me to change my mind. It was still quite likely that war would break out again since there was still no disengagement of forces with Syria and the Syrians were continually violating the cease-fire. And again I was told that the Ma'arach would disintegrate unless I stayed on.

Sometimes it seemed to me that everything that had happened since the afternoon of October 6 had happened on one endless day—and I wanted that day to end. I was deeply distressed by the breaking down of solidarity within the inner circle of the party. People who had been ministers in my government, colleagues with whom I had worked closely throughout my years in office and who had been full partners in the formation of government policy now appeared unwilling to stand up to the barrage of unjust criticism, even slander, that was being hurled against Dayan, Galili and myself on the grounds that the three of us—without consulting others—had presumed to make crucial decisions that had allegedly led to the war. I also resented the irresponsible talk of my so-called kitchen cabinet that had supposedly replaced the government to some extent by acting as a decision-making body. This accusation was utterly without foundation. It was only natural on my part to seek the advice of people whose judgment I valued. At no time and in no way, however, did these informal consulations ever take the place of government decisions.

Nonetheless, throughout March I went on with the struggle to form a government, though, increasingly, it began to look like an impossible task, particularly in the face of growing demands for a "wall-to-wall" coalition, something to which both I and most of the party were more opposed than ever. This was certainly not the time for political experimentation, and I had no more faith than I ever had in the ability of the opposition to apply good judgment, common sense or flexibility to Israel's attempts to arrive, at last, at some sort of understanding with our neighbors. I didn't want the cabinet to be burdened by an element that would refuse to negotiate—if and when the time came— because of its totally negative attitude toward any territorial compromise, especially as far as the West Bank was concerned. I knew that—for historical reasons—there was a difference in the attitude of the population regarding territorial compromise on the Sinai, for instance, and on the West Bank—though I myself felt that most Israelis would be prepared for a reasonable compromise on the West Bank, too. However, I also thought it necessary to include in the government's policy statement a clause to the effect that although the cabinet was authorized to negotiate and decide on territorial compromise with Jordan, before any actual treaty was signed, the issue would be taken to the people in the form of new elections.

Then two things happened: First, Dayan resigned, and although I persuaded him to return to the cabinet, the continuing uproar about him within the party brought the danger of a split in its ranks perilously near. There seemed to be no way of finding a formula that would satisfy the growing insistence inside the party that Dayan relinquish the Ministry of Defense and at the same time keep the Rafi faction he headed from walking out of the Ma'arach. There were also other problems: The religious bloc, which had been pressuring us for weeks and weeks to form a National Unity Government, suddenly decided, as the result of international difficulties of its own, that it was not going to become a partner in a narrower coalition and that it would not join any cabinet. This meant forming a minority government, but I didn't think that would be too serious a problem because we would have the support of various small parties in the Knesset. The really crucial issue, as I saw it, remained the possible disintegration of the Ma'arach. I managed to form a cabinet with Dayan as minister of defense, but the storm about him raged on and on. It now focused on the Interim Agranat Report, which, as I said earlier, had exonerated him from any direct responsibility for the errors of judgment that had been made by the military authorities on the eve of the Yom Kippur War.

The report, however, had not gone into the question of parliamentary or ministerial responsibility, and it was precisely over *that* issue that public opinion—within the party and outside it—now expressed itself most vehemently. Many people in the country felt that the chief of staff had been dealt with unfairly and that Dayan as minister of defense was at least as much to blame for what had happened as Dado. (Without commenting in any way on the Agranat Report, I do want, however, to say in this connection that Dado's conduct of the war itself was brilliant and beyond reproach.) There was tremendous discontent with the report's treatment of Dayan, and feelings were running very high indeed.

The more I talked with my colleagues about the ongoing conflict in the party and the more I analyzed it for myself, the more I began to feel that I couldn't go on any longer. I had reached a point where I felt that without the support of the entire party (the majority was with me all the time) I couldn't function as its head anymore. And the moment came when I said to myself, "This is it. I am going to resign, and other people will have to see what they can do about forming a coalition. There is a limit to what I can take, and I have now reached that limit."

During all those weeks of interminable talk, argument and bitterness, I had been getting the most moving letters of encouragement and support from people all over Israel whom I had never met but who seemed to understand what I was going through. Some of these were wounded soldiers, still in the hospital; others were parents of boys who had fallen. "Be well. Be strong. Everything will be all right," they wrote to me. I truly didn't want to fail them, but on April 10 I told the party leadership that I had had enough.

"Five years are sufficient," I said. "It is beyond my

strength to continue carrying this burden. I don't belong to any circle or faction within the party. I have only a circle of one to consult—myself. And this time my decision is final, irrevocable. I beg of you not to try to persuade me to change my mind for any reason at all. It will not help." Of course, attempts were made all the same to talk me out of my decision, but they were to no avail. I was about to conclude fifty years of public service, and I knew with absolute certainty that I was doing the right thing. I had wanted to do it much earlier, but now *nothing* was going to stop me, and nothing did. My political career was over.

Still, I had to stay on as head of a caretaker government until a new cabinet could be formed. Before I left office on June 4, I was able, thank God, to tell the Knesset that a disengagement agreement with Syria had been concluded through the good offices of Dr. Kissinger. On June 5 that agreement was signed in Geneva, and our POWs returned. It meant more to me than I can ever say to have been able to welcome them back—though fewer returned from their imprisonment than we had hoped.

And then I myself went home, this time for good. The new prime minister of Israel is a sabra—Yitzhak Rabin—born in Jerusalem the year that Morris and I had come to Merhavia. There are many differences between his generation and mine—differences of style, of approach and of experience. And that is how it should be, because Israel is a country of growth in which everything moves forward. But these differences are not as significant as the similarities.

Like my generation, this generation of sabras will strive, struggle, make mistakes and achieve. Like us, they are totally committed to the development and security of the State of Israel and to the dream of a just society here. Like us, they know that for the Jewish people to remain a people, it is essential that there be a Jewish state where Jews can live as Jews, not on sufferance and not as a minority. I am certain that they will bring at least as much credit to the Jewish people everywhere as we tried to bring. And at this point I would like to add something about being Jewish. It is not only a matter, I believe, of religious observance and practice. To me, being Jewish means and has always meant being proud to be part of a people that has maintained its distinct identity for more than 2,000 years, with all the pain and torment that have been inflicted upon it. Those who have been unable to endure and who have tried to opt out of their Jewishness have done so, I believe, at the expense of their own basic identity. They have pitifully impoverished themselves.

I don't know what forms the practice of Judaism will assume in the future or how Jews, in Israel and elsewhere, will express their Jewishness 1,000 years hence. But I do know that Israel is not just some small beleaguered country in which 3,000,000 people are trying hard to survive; Israel is a Jewish state that has come into existence as the result of the longing, the faith and the determination of an ancient people. We in Israel are only one part of the Jewish nation, and not even its largest part; but because Israel exists Jewish history has been changed forever, and it is my deepest conviction that there are few Israelis today who do not understand and fully accept the responsibility that history has placed on their shoulders as Jews.

As for me, my life has been greatly blessed. Not only have I lived to see the State of Israel born, but I have also seen it take in and successfully absorb masses of Jews from all parts of the world. When I came to this country in 1921, its Jewish population amounted to 80,000, and the entry of each Jew depended on permission granted by the mandatory government. We are now a population of over 3,000,000 of whom more than 1,000,000 are Jews who have arrived since the establishment of the state under Israel's Law of Return, a law that guarantees the right of every Jew to settle here. I am also grateful that I live in a country whose people have learned how to go on living in a sea of hatred without hating those who want to destroy them and without abandoning their own vision of peace. To have learned this is a great art, the prescription for which is not written down anywhere. It is part of our way of life in Israel.

Finally, I wish to say that from the time I came to Palestine as a young woman, we have been forced to choose between what is more dangerous and what is less dangerous for us. At times we have all been tempted to give in to various pressures and to accept proposals that might guarantee us a little quiet for a few months, or maybe even for a few years, but that could only lead us eventually into even greater peril. We have always been faced by the question "Which is the greater danger?" And we are still in that situation or perhaps in an even greater one. The world is harsh, selfish and materialistic. It is insensitive to the sufferings of small nations. Even the most enlightened of governments, democracies that are led by decent leaders who represent fine, decent people, are not much inclined today to concern themselves with problems of justice in international relations. At a time when great nations are capable of knuckling under to blackmail and decisions are being made on the basis of big-power politics, we cannot always be expected to take their advice, and therefore, we must have the capacity and the courage to go on seeing things as they really are and to act on our own most fundamental instincts for self-preservation. So to those who ask, "What of the future?" I still have only one answer: I believe that we will have peace with our neighbors, but I am sure that no one will make peace with a weak Israel. If Israel is not strong, there will be no peace.

My vision of our future? A Jewish state in which masses of Jews from all over the world will continue to settle and to build; an Israel bound in a collaborative effort with its neighbors on behalf of all the people of this region; an Israel that remains a flourishing democracy and a society resting firmly on social justice and equality.

And now I have only one desire left: never to lose the feeling that it is I who am indebted for what has been given to me from the time that I first learned about Zionism in a small room in czarist Russia all the way through to my half century here, where I have seen my five grandchildren grow up as free Jews in a country that is their own. Let no one anywhere have any doubts about this: Our children and our children's children will never settle for anything less.

Index

Abdullah, King, 206–13, 222, 228

Absorption, Ministry of, 76

Accra, Ghana, 311–13

Achdut Ha Avodah, 125, 338, 360

Addis Ababa, University of, 328

Aden, 249–50

Africa, 305–25

Afro-Asian Institute, 319

Agranat, Shimon, 434

Agranat Commission of Inquiry, 436, 441

Aleichem, Sholom, 43

Algeria, 314; FLN, 313

Algerian Jews, 248

Allenby, Viscount, 60

Allon, Yigal, 363–64, 406, 408, 410, 413

Altneuland (Old-New Land) (Herzl), 308

American Federation of Labor and Congress of Industrial Organizations (AFL-CIO), 379

American Jewish Congress, 56; first convention, 63

American Jews, 203–6, 226, 253–54, 259, 300–1, 347, 371, 374, 396

American Labor Zionist movement, 124

American Poalei Zion (Labor Zionists), 51

American Trade Union Council, 379

American Young Sisters Society, 35

Amin, Idi, 322–23

Am Oved publishing house, 119

Anglo-American Committee of Inquiry, 183–84, 186

Aqaba, Gulf of, 296, 342

Arab Higher Committee, 143

Arab League, 207–8

Arab Legion, 208, 228; occupation of Old City of Jerusalem, 262

Arab(s), 128–29, 142–43, 198, 200, 355 ff.; absentee property issue, 267; administration of, in Israeli-occupied territories, 357; fedayeen, 282–83, 287, 288, 290, 291, 293, 296, 339; Jerusalem, control of Old City, 99; Jerusalem, sieges of, 201, 261–62; laborers, 101; refugees, 268–69, 290; riots (1921), 65, 71; riots (1929), 127–28, 142; riots (1936), 138, 141–42, 168; terrorism, 140, 141, 166–67, 246–47, 274–75, 281–83, 339, 360, 361–62, 380, 384–85, 399, 400, 401, 402–3; and War of Attrition, 369 ff.

Arab states, 222–24, 305, 316; armistice (1949), 246; blockade of Israel, 246; oil embargo, 423; and People's Republic of China, 325–27; and United Nations, 296–99; UNSCOP partition plan vote, 201–2; and War of Independence, 222–23, 228

Arafat, Yasir, 166, 326, 339, 389

Aranne, Zalman, 276–77

Arlosoroff, Chaim, 138–39, 162

Asia, 309, 325 ff.

Asian Socialist Congress, 330

Assad, Hafez, 427, 428

Attlee, Clement, 182, 183

Austria, displaced persons camps in, 248

Austrian Jews, 152

Avigur, Shaul, 163–64, 277

Avriel, Ehud, 230, 232, 309, 311, 326

Azikiwe, Benjamin, 325

Balfour, Lord Arthur James, 60

Balfour Declaration, 60, 78, 128, 129, 188

Bandung Conference of Asian and African nations, 305, 326

Barash, Mr. and Mrs., 73, 74

Barkatt, Reuven, 170, 309

Bar-Lev, Chaim, 373, 409, 416

Bar-Lev line, 361

Baxter, Major, 176–81

Begin, Menachem, 370, 371, 411, 433–34

Ben-Gurion, David, 52, 53–54, 90, 108, 112, 113, 115, 116, 117, 118, 119, 121–23, 134–35, 138, 139, 144–48, 150, 162, 164, 165, 186, 187, 190–91, 203–4, 206–7, 213, 224, 225, 227, 228, 245, 251, 261, 268, 270, 271, 282, 284, 325, 332, 333, 335, 350, 366; declaration of independence, 217–19; first retirement, 272–73; government move to Jerusalem, 261, 262–63; and Israel bond issue, 258–59; Lavon Affair, 277–80; Peel partition proposal, 150; and Rafi, 280, 338; second retirement, 278, 279; and Sharett, relationship with, 273–77; and Sinai Campaign, 277, 285 ff.; and Weizmann, relationship with, 189; on White Paper, 154

Ben-Gurion, Paula, 145, 187

Ben-Gurion, Renana, 145

Ben Shemen, 177

Ben-Zvi, Mina, 321

Ben-Zvi, Yitzhak, 52, 53, 68, 90, 112, 115, 118, 190

Berger, Victor, 32

Bernadotte, Count Folke, 234, 246

Bernstein, Leonard, 377

Beth Israel Hospital (N.Y.), 130

Bevin, Ernest, 152, 182, 183, 186, 193, 194, 198; cantonization proposal, 191

Bialik, Chaim Nachman, 72, 171, 183

Birobidzhan, USSR, 237

"Black Saturday," 187 ff.

Black Star Shipping Line, 312

Bluwstein, Rachel, 44

B'nai B'rith, 50

Bond issue, Israel, 258–60, 360

Boston Zionists, 299

Bourges-Manoury, Maurice, 285

Boyar, Lou, 226

Brand, Samuel, 220

Brandt, Willy, 147–48, 359, 430

Brezhnev, Leonid, 422

British Army, Palestinian Jews in, 158, 160, 161–63

British Colonial Office, 116, 150

British government. *See* Great Britain

British Jews, 347

British Labour Party, 90, 128, 163, 181

Bucharest, Rumania, 386–87

Bulganin, Nikolai, 290

Bulgarian Jews, 248

Bunche, Ralph, 246

Bund (Union), 22, 56

Burma, 305, 330–32

Cario Radio, 282, 340–41

Cambodia, 330

Cameroun, 316

Camp Mafraq, 211

Canada, 342; Jewish emigration from, 333

Carmel, Moshe, 285–86

Ceausescu, Nicolae, 385–86

Celler, Emanuel, 310

Ceylon, 305

Chagall, Marc, 145

Chamberlain, Neville, 152

Chicago West Side Club, 132

China. *See* People's Republic of China

Chinese Jews, 248

Chorale Synagogue (Bucharest), 387

Christian holy places, 391, 393

Chuvakhin, Dmitri, 340

Cold war, 283

Conakry, Guinea, 317

Cossacks, 18, 20, 24

Council of Europe meeting, 401–2

Council of Jewish Federations and Welfare Funds, 204

Couve de Murville, Maurice, 302, 303

Crossman, Richard, 184, 436–37

Crum, Bartley, 184

Cunningham, Sir Alan, 196

Cyprus, displaced persons camps on, 191, 193–96, 197, 225, 248

Czechoslovakia, 152, 222; anti-Semitism campaign, 284; arms supply to Egypt, 283

Czechoslovakian Jews, 248

Daniel Sieff Research Institute, 190

Danin, Ezra, 207, 208–12

Davar (labor movement newspaper), 114, 119

David, King, 389

Dayan, Moshe, 277–78, 280, 285, 286, 357, 363, 364, 373, 435, 439; offer of resignation, 414; resignation, 440; and Six-Day War, 349–50; and Yom Kippur War, 406, 408, 410, 411, 413, 429, 433, 434–36

Dead Sea Works, 101

Declaration of Independence, 118; proclamation ceremony, 214–19

Degania kibbutz, 43, 53, 89–90, 93, 115

De Gaulle, Charles, 190, 299, 302–4, 314, 345

Denmark, 387

Denver, Colorado, 41 ff.

Development and training programs, 309, 312, 315–17, 319–22

Dinitz, Simcha, 386, 394, 395, 411, 414–15, 429

Displaced persons camps, 183, 193–96, 197, 225, 248

Dizengoff, Meier, 72

Doctors' Plot, 283

Dosh (cartoonist), 359

Dov Hos (ship), 185, 186

Dreyfus, Alfred, 21

Druze villagers, 357

Dulles, John Foster, 295–96, 342

East Africa, 321–23

Eastern European Jews, 21, 22

East Jerusalem, 351, 353

Eban, Abba, 170, 295, 303, 319, 335, 344–45, 349, 372, 374, 377, 379, 391

Education, Ministry of, 265

Education Act, 115

Egypt, 210, 277, 284; armistice (1949), 246; cease-fire (1970), 383; China rapprochement, 326; and fedayeen, 281–82; Geneva talks, 438; Israeli POW's, 393; Jerusalem, shelling of, 262; and Sinai Campaign, 286 ff.; in Six-Day War, 340–44, 351 ff., 357, 361, 362; Soviet Union, relationship with, 283, 367–68, 380; and War of Attrition, 367 ff., 380; and War of Independence, 220, 222–23, 224, 228; and Yom Kippur War, 405 ff.

Egyptian National Assembly, 343

Egyptian Second Army, 432

Egyptian-Syrian High Command, 339

Egyptian Third Army encirclement of, 423, 425, 430

Ehrenburg, Ilya, 239, 240, 242

Eichmann, Adolf, trial of, 171–74

Eisenhower, David, 377

Eisenhower, Dwight D., 289, 301, 302

Eisenhower, Julie, 377

El Al airlines, 347

Elazar, David "Dado," 353–54, 405, 410–11, 413, 416, 429, 436, 441

El Fatah, 339, 360, 361, 362, 383

Eliahu Golomb (ship), 185, 186

Emek, the, 78–80; reclamation of, 79–80

Emes publishing house, 244

Employment, 137–38, 253, 255

Enigkeit (newspaper), 244

Enzo Sereni (ship), 167

Eshkol, Levi, 90, 113, 115–18, 145, 147, 190, 277, 279–80, 302, 335, 340, 343, 344, 345, 352, 359, 360, 366, 370, 373, 397, 435; death, 362–63; and Six-Day War, 348–50

Eshkol, Miriam, 363

Ethiopia, 313, 328

Euporean Jews, 172–73, 226, 266; in displaced persons camps, 193–97; refugees, 151–53, 156–59, 164, 174, 181–86. *See also* Immigrants

Évian Conference. *See* International Conference on Refugees

Exodus 1947 (ship), 199–200

Eytan, Walter, 303

Fedayeen, 282–83, 287, 288, 290, 291, 293, 296, 339

Fede (ship), 185

Feder, Sarah, 30, 37, 40

Feisal, King, 369, 427, 428–29

Feldman, Mike, 300

Finland, 387

First All-American Peoples' Conference, 313–15

Fishman-Maimon, Rabbi, 215, 218, 239

Fourth Street School (Milwaukee), 31

France, 305, 342, 369; arms sale to Israel, 284, 314; attempt to seize Suez Canal, 285–86, 288–89

Freedom of Jerusalem Award, 99

Gahal, 370–71, 380

Galili, Yisrael, 213, 395, 397, 406, 408, 409, 410, 413, 439

Gamasy, Abdel, 431

Gambia, 317

Gaza Strip, 339, 357; capture of, in Sinai Campaign, 288 ff.; eviction of UNEF, by Nasser, 341; and Six-Day War, 351, 353

Gazit, Mordechai, 397

General Cooperative Association of Jewish Labor in Palestine. *See* Hevrat Ha-Ocdim

General Federation of Jewish Labor. *See* Histadrut

Geneva Convention, 421

Geneva talks, 438

German Jews, 152

Germany: displaced persons camps in, 248; postwar, 169–71. *See also* Hitler; Holocaust; Nazis

Ghana, 309, 311–15, 330

Gilbert, Pierre, 302

Givat Brenner, 168

Golan Heights; and Six-Day War, 339, 346, 351, 353, 354, 357; and Yom Kippur War, 406, 412, 413, 418, 423, 424, 427, 430

Gola tribe, 311

Goldberg, Arthur, 377

Goldenberg, Harold, 226

Goldman, Emma, 42

Golomb, Ada, 164, 219

Golomb, Eliahu, 162, 164–67, 175, 219

Goodman, Fanny, 130, 228

Goodman, Jacob, 130, 228

Gordon, Aaron David, 43–44, 53, 89, 125

Granados, Jorge García, 222

Great Britain, 128–29, 181–82, 342, 368, 369; Army, Palestinian Jews in, 158–59, 160, 161; Balfour Declaration, 60; "Black Saturday" occupation of Palestine, 187 ff.; blockade of immigrant ships, 174; civil administration of Palestine, 65; displaced persons camps, 193–97; Jewish emigration from, 333; Jewish immigration to Palestine, limitation of, 101, 116, 128, 140, 142, 150, 151, 155 ff., 164, 174, 181 ff., 193 ff., 198–99; mandatory government in Palestine, 78, 98, 101, 129, 140, 153, 161, 443; and Nasser, 283; resolution 242, 357–58; Suez Canal, attempt to sieze, 285, 288–89; White Paper, 153–54, 155 ff., 181–82

Great Synagogue (Moscow), 238

Gromyko, Andrei, 376, 428

Gruenbaum, Yitzhak, 214

Guatemala, recognition of Israel, 222

Guinea, 317

Ha–Am, Ahad, 72

Hacohen, David, 325, 330

Hadassah, 135, 265

Hadassah Hospital (Tel Aviv), 81

Hadera, 125

Haganah, 142, 146, 165–67, 174, 184–85, 187, 190, 197, 200–1, 203, 212, 213, 224; arms purchase, secret, 206, 222, 230; arms trial, 176–81; "illegal" immigration, 175, 184, 187; intelligence service, 164

Haifa, 267–68

Halutz (Pioneering) movement, 135

Hamburger Medzini, Regina, 30, 35, 36, 37, 40, 41–42, 47, 48, 60, 64, 73, 75, 81, 98

Hammarskjöld, Dag, 282

Hapoel Hatzair (the Young Worker), 125

Hartzfeld, Avraham, 90

Hashomer, 53

Hashomer Hatzair (the Young Guard), 125

Havlagah, 142, 143, 166

Hebron, Jewish settlement in, 389–90

Henderson, Arthur, 112

Herut Party, 370

Herzl, Theodor, 21–22, 72, 216, 217–18, 308, 314, 391

Herzlia, 102–3

Herzlia High School (Tel Aviv), 72, 114, 165

Herzog, Rabbi, 186

Herzog, Ya'akov, 397

Hevrat Ha–Ovdim (General Cooperative Association of Jewish Labor in Palestine), 105

Himmler, Heinrich, 172

Hirohito, Emperor of Japan, 329

Histadrut (General Federation of Jewish Labor), 72, 103–6, 113–14, 115, 118, 120, 134, 136–38, 141, 148–49, 159, 160, 161, 163, 178, 183, 226, 264, 309, 330, 379, 380, 382. *See also* Solel Boneh, Va'ad Ha-poel, Women's Labor Council

Hitler, Adolf, 138, 139–40, 154, 156, 158, 163, 172, 180, 292, 348

Holland, 294

Holocaust, 13, 169 ff., 174, 217, 248, 252, 301, 348

Hong Kong, 330

Hos, Dov, 163, 164, 219

Hos, Rivkah, 163

Houphoüet–Boigny, Félix, 170, 312

Housing program, in Israel, 252 ff.

Hovevei Zion (Lovers of Zion), 21

Hungarian Jews, 248

Hungary, Soviet invasion of, 289

Hussein, King, 206, 361–62, 383, 416–17; and Six-Day War, 343, 352–53

Husseini, Haj Amin el-, 101, 128, 207

Idelson, Beba, 108

Immigrants: immigration, 100–1, 104, 121, 151, 247–49, 380–81; British limitation of, 101, 116, 128, 140, 142, 150, 151, 155 ff., 164, 174, 181 ff., 193 ff., 198; employment problems of, 253, 255–56; "illegal," 121, 147, 156, 164, 184–85, 187, 191, 192; housing problems, 252–55; post-Independence, 247–53; settlement difficulties, 256–57

Imperial Labour Conference, 128–29

India, 201, 305

Indonesia, 305

International Conference on Refugees (Évian Conference), 151–52, 154, 389

International Conference on Science in the Advancement of New States, 319–20

International Cooperation Program, 307–8, 315, 319, 325

International Training Center for Community Services, 320–21

Iran, 201

Iraq, 210, 299, 426; army, 208, 211, 286; and Six-Day War, 343–44; Soviet arms aid to, 367; and War of Independence, 222–23, 228

Iraqi Jews, 168, 248

Irgun Zvai Le'umi, 166, 188, 190, 196–97

Israel, 146, 155, 227; and African nations, 306 ff.; bond issues, 258–60, 360, 379; Burma, relationship with, 330–32; China, relationship with, 325–27; development programs, 309, 312, 315–17, 319–21; elections, first, 245; emigration from, 335; immigrants, 247–57; POW's, 393, 420–21, 432, 438, 442; proclamation of, 213–19; retaliatory raids against Arab terrorists, 274–75, 368, 392–93; Rumania, relationship with, 385–87; and Sinai Campaign, 284–97, 305; Six-Day War, 345–55; Soviet Union recognition of, 221–22; United Nations, relationship with, 305–6; United States recognition of, 189, 221; Vatican, relationship with, 391; War of Attrition, 367 ff.; Yom Kippur War, unpreparedness for, 405–14

Israel Bond Organization, 226. *See also* bond issue *under* Israel

Israel Defense Forces, 370; retaliatory raids against Arab terrorists, 274; and Sinai Campaign, 288; in Six-Day War, 349, 350, 352, 353, 361; in Yom Kippur War, 413, 417, 420, 421, 424

Israel Labor Party, 360, 364, 396, 397

Israel National Opera, 233

Ivory Coast, 309, 312

Jaffa, 71

Japan, 305, 329–30

Jarring, Gunnar V., 358, 370, 383

Javits, Jacob, 377

Jerusalem, 93, 94, 95, 98, 101, 352–53, 357; Arab sieges, 200–1, 261–62; Christian holy places, 391; establishment of government offices in, 261, 262–63; liberation of, in Six-Day War, 100; Old City, 99–100; and War of Independence, 228; Western Wall, 99, 100

Jerusalem Post, 177

Jewish Agency, 76, 146, 175, 177, 180, 187, 188, 190, 201, 202, 213, 218, 256, 270, 277, 396; land settlement department, 116; political department, 162, 188, 197; Schonau transit camp, 399–400

Jewish Brigade, 162–63, 189

Jewish Center of Milwaukee, 57

Jewish Hospital for Consumptives (Denver), 34, 42

Jewish labor movement. *See* Histadrut

Jewish Legion, 50, 52–53, 78, 80, 89, 115, 165

Jewish National Fund, 135; purchase of land in Palestine, 78–79

Jewish resistance movement, 161

Jewish Workers' Council (Haifa), 268

Jews. *See* American Jews, European Jews, etc. *For* Palestinian Jews, see *Yishuv*

John XXIII, Pope, 391

Johnson, Lady Bird, 302

Johnson, Lyndon, 299, 342, 373

Joint Distribution Committee, 55, 226, 250

Jordan, 286, 376, 383; and Arab terrorists, 339, 383; armistice (1949), 246; fedayeen bases in, 281; Geneva talks, 438; Jerusalem, shelling of, 262; and Six-Day War, 343, 351 ff.; War of Attrition, 370; and War of Independence, 222–23, 228

Joseph, Dr., 180

Kaddar, Lou, 233, 236, 241, 246, 336, 388, 394, 395, 396, 408, 413

Kaplan, Eliezer, 203, 258–59

Katznelson, Berl, 90, 113, 118–23, 138, 145, 149, 150, 162, 164–65

Kaunda, Kenneth, 323, 324

Keating, Kenneth, 411–12

Kennedy, Jacqueline, 301

Kennedy, John F., 122, 299–301, 302, 303

Kenya, 321, 323, 326, 328, 330

Kenyatta, Jomo, 323

Keren Hayesod, 135

KGB, 235

Khartoum, 422; murder of U.S. diplomats in, 425

Khartoum summit conference, 356

Kibbutzim, 45, 81–82, 93–96, 168, 330, 331. See also specific kibbutzim

Kiev, Russia, 12, 14, 17

Kinneret kibbutz, 163

Kiryat Arba, 390

Kiryat Shmonah, 266–67

Kishon, Ephraim, 359

Kissinger, Henry, 377, 415, 427; cease-fire talks, 422, 424, 427–29, 431; Israeli-Syrian disengagement talks, 438, 442

Knesset, 251, 253, 264, 270, 278, 280, 337, 363, 380, 424, 433–34, 441, 442; first elections to, 231; move from Tel Aviv to Jerusalem, 261

Kofer Hayishuv, 138

Konnenut, 344, 349

Kopelov, Yossel, 48, 64, 68, 73, 75, 81

Korngold, Chaim (GM's nephew), 64, 76, 81, 87

Korngold, Judith (GM's niece), 47, 64, 69, 76, 81, 87

Korngold, Shamai (GM's brother-in-law), 23–25, 32, 33–34, 38–40, 42, 45, 60, 64–65, 67, 68, 76, 77, 81, 92, 96, 230

Korngold, Sheyna (GM's sister). See under Mabovitch

Kosygin, Aleksei, 343, 421

Kreisky, Bruno, 147, 148, 400–4

Kropotkin, Peter, 42

Kupat Holim (Workers' Sick Fund), 137

Kuwait, 423

Labor, Ministry of, 264–65

"Labor Battalion," 100

Labor movement, 118, 119, 121, 125 ff., 138, 139, 168, 273–74; unification of, 337–38, 360. See also Histadrut; Mapai

Labor Party, 121. See also Mapai

Labor Zionism, 30, 51–52, 54–59, 62, 66–68, 79, 80, 125–26, 134–35, 226, 307; in United States, 124–25

Laird, Melvin, 378

Land Acquisition law, 267

Lapland, 388–89

La Spezia incident, 184–86

Latin America, 309

Lavon, Pinchas, 277 ff.

Lavon Affair, 148, 277–78, 335, 338

Law of the Return, 251, 443

League for Labour Palestine, 112

League of Nations, 78

Lebanon, 210; and Arab terrorists, 362, 385; armistice (1949), 246; fedayeen bases in, 281; and War of Independence, 222–23

Lehi (Stern Group), 166, 188, 197

Levavi, Arieh, 237, 246

Levin, Shmarya "Shmaryahu," 51–52

Liberal Party, 370

Liberia, 309–11, 313

Libya, 323, 423; Boeing 727 tragedy, 398

Lior, Yisrael, 366, 397, 410

Lodge, Henry Cabot, 295, 296

Lydda Airport, Arab terrorist attack at, 384

Ma'abarot, 255, 266, 269

Ma'alot, 384, 425

Ma'arach, 360, 380, 439, 440–41

Ma'avak, 146, 183

Mabovitch, Blume (GM's mother), 12–16, 18–20, 22, 24–26, 28, 32–41, 48, 49–50, 61, 64, 65–66, 95, 98, 109, 111, 130, 181; decline in health, 230; grocery store in Milwaukee, 29–31; miscarriage, 34; move to Palestine, 101–2

Mabovitch, Grandfather, 15–16, 17

Mabovitch Korngold, Sheyna (GM's sister), 12, 14, 19, 22, 25–26, 27–28, 30, 32, 32–33, 36, 37, 38, 39–41, 46–48, 49, 60, 64–65, 70, 102, 109, 111, 112, 171, 175, 228, 230, 231, 330, 335; in Denver TB hospital, 34, 38; marriage, 38; move to Palestine, 64–65, 66; parents, relationship with, 27–28, 33–34; political activities in Russia, 19–20, 22–25; political circle in Denver, 42–45; in Tel Aviv, 73–74, 75, 76, 77, 81, 86, 87, 92, 96, 98, 101, 102

Mabovitch, Moshe Yitzhak (GM's father), 12, 13–15, 16, 20, 27–41, 48, 49–50, 62, 64, 65–66, 95, 98, 130, 181; death, 230; move to America, 17, 19, 25; move to Palestine, 101–3; war relief activities, 55–57

Mabovitch Stern, Clara "Zipke" (GM's sister), 12, 15, 24, 26, 32, 35–36, 40–41, 48, 49, 63, 65, 103, 126–27, 131, 229, 231, 336, 373, 395

MacDonald, Ramsay, 128

Machakos, Kenya, 321

Machpelah, Cave of, 390

Maimon, Ada, 108

Mali, 316

Manhattan School of Music, 216

Manila, 330

Manila, University of, 330

Mapai (Labor Party of the Land of Israel), 125–26, 138, 154, 163, 212, 245, 269–70, 272, 275–76, 277, 278, 280, 333, 337, 338, 360; and Lavon Affair, 277, 278

Mapam (United Workers' Party), 125, 245, 338, 360

May Day Riots (1921), 71

Mboya, Tom, 323

McDonald, James G., 184, 233

Meany, George, 379

Mea Shearim, 99

Meir, Amnon (GM's grandson), 327

Meir, Aya (GM's daughter-in-law), 195, 261, 264, 283, 327, 329, 336, 345, 360, 364, 410

Meir, Daniel (GM's grandson), 327

Meir, Gideon (GM's grandson), 327, 329, 378

Meir, Golda Mabovitch: childhood in Russia, 11–25; move to Milwaukee, 25–26, 27–39; elementary school, 30–31, 34, 35, 36; high school, 38; move to Denver, 39–42; early political interest, 42–43; meets Morris Meyerson, 45–46; returns to Milwaukee, 48, 49 ff.; at teacher's college, 49; early Zionist influences and activities, 50–59, 62; first meeting with Ben-Gurion, 53–54; teacher at Milwaukee Jewish Center, 57–58; joins Labor Zionist Party, 59–61; decision to move to Palestine, 59–60; marriage, 61; relationship with husband, 62–63, 91–94, 107, 260; delegate to American Jewish Congress, 63; preparation for Palestine, 64–65; voyage to Palestine, 66–70; arrival in Tel Aviv, 71 ff.; at Merhavia kibbutz, 78, 79–92; agricultural school, 86; kibbutz movement delegate, 89–90; return to Tel Aviv, 92–94; pregnancy, 93; birth of son, Menachem, 93–94; move to Jerusalem, 94, 95–107; as secretary of Women's Labor Council, 106, 107, 124 ff.; failure of marriage, 107; on women and feminism, 107–9; relationship with her children, 109–10, 111, 112, 113, 124, 327–28; on being a

Meir, Golda *(cont.)*
mother, 110-11; at Socialist International, 111–12; U.S. mission to Pioneer Women, 124–26; at Socialist Women Conference in England, 127–28; at Imperial Labour Conference in England, 128; on British government, 128–29; daughter's illness, and return to U.S., 129–34, 136; editorials, 134–35; on Histadrut Executive Committee, 136 ff., 150, 158, 176; chairman of Workers' Sick Fund, 141; on Ben-Gurion, 144–48, 273; Histadrut fund raising in U.S., 148–49; at Refugee Conference at Évianles-Bains, 151–52; on British restriction of immigration, 155 ff.; at Zionist Congress in Geneva, 157–58; on War Economic Advisory Council, 161; on terrorism, 166–67, 188, 402–3; on Germany and Germans, 169–71; on Eichmann trial, 171–74; as arms trial witness, 176–81; before Anglo-American Committee of Inquiry, 183–84; hunger strike for La Spezia refugees, 185–86; as acting head of Jewish Agency political department, 188, 197; on dissident underground groups, 188; and Chaim Weizmann, 191; at Zionist Congress in Basel, 191–92; at Cyprus displaced persons camps, 194–96; U.S. fund raising tours, 204–6, 224–26, 253–54; meeting with King Abdullah, 206–11, 212, 213; at proclamation ceremony, 214–19; signs Declaration of Independence, 219; on belligerency of Arab states, 223–24; as minister to Moscow, 227–34, 235–44, 245–46; auto accident and leg fracture, 228–29; as minister of labor, 117, 245 ff., 264–67, 269–70; housing plan, 253 ff.; on difficulties of settling immigrants, 256–57; and Israel bond issue, 258–60, 360; house in Jerusalem, 263–64; on Arab exodus from Palestine, 267–69; as candidate for mayor of Tel Aviv, 270; on Moshe Sharett, 273–74; as foreign minister, 169, 276–77, 280 ff.; on Lavon Affair, 277–80; split with Ben-Gurion, 278, 279–80; on Dag Hammarskjöld, 282; Hebraization of name, 284; on Sinai Campaign, 284–96; statements to UN General Assembly, 291–98; and John Kennedy, 299–301; and Lyndon Johnson, 301–2; and De Gaulle, 302–4; African travels, 305–25, 326–29; General Assembly speech on Africa, 317–19; Asian travels, 325–32; honorary degree, 330; illnesses, 332, 334–35, 360; *Pocahontas* reunion, 333–34; first retirement, 335, 336 ff., 360; new home, 336–37; as secretary-general of Mapai, 338; unification of labor movement, 338, 360; on Six-Day War, 339 ff.; Madison Square Garden address, 347; secretary-general of Israel Labor Party, 360; as interim prime minister, 363–65, 366 ff.; cabinet leaks to press, 371–72; meeting with Nixon in Washington, 372–79; as prime minister, 380 ff.; Rumania visit, 385–87; trip to Scandinavia, 387–89; meeting with Pope, 391–94; on mistreatment of Arabs, 392–93; second Washington visit, 398; and closing of Schonau transit camp, 399–404; on Yom Kippur War, 405–37; on preemptive strikes, 411–12; Knesset addresses, 418–19, 424, 426; on Henry Kissinger, 427–28, 429; trip to Washington, 429, 431; Socialist International leadership meeting, 430–31; on Moshe Dayan, 435; and Agranat Com-

Meir, Golda (*cont.*)
 mission of Inquiry, 436; efforts to form new government, 439–41; second retirement, 397–98, 441–42; on being Jewish, 442–43; on future of Israel, 444

Meir, Menahem (GM's son), 93–94, 96, 97, 106–7, 109, 110, 112, 113, 124, 130, 131, 136, 141, 153, 174, 175, 186, 216, 218, 227, 228, 231, 261, 264, 283, 327, 329, 332, 336, 360, 364, 373, 410; birth, 93–94; at Manhattan School of Music, 216; marriage, 264

Merhavia kibbutz, 78, 79–93, 96, 97, 101, 102, 113, 307, 364

Meyerson, Morris (GM's husband), 45–46, 48, 49, 54–55, 58, 59–61, 62–63, 64, 65, 74, 75, 77–78, 80, 81, 82, 83, 90, 92–94, 95, 96, 97, 99, 102, 106–7, 113, 130, 131, 136, 175, 230, 231, 333–34, 442; death, 107, 260; dislike of kibbutz life, 87–88, 91–92

Meyerson Rehabi, Sarah (GM's daughter), 82, 97, 102, 106, 107, 110, 122, 124, 141, 186, 218, 225, 227, 228, 230, 232, 280; at Hebrew University, 397; illnesses, 111–12, 129–31, 260–61; marriage, 230–31; radio operator in Moscow, 230, 235, 241, 243; at Revivim kibbutz, 174–76, 216, 285, 327–28, 345–46, 364, 377

Mifdeh, 138

Milwaukee, 25, 26, 27 ff., 49 ff.

Milwaukee Normal School, 49, 57

Minhelet Ha'am (People's Administration), 213

Mizrachi, Eli, 397

Mizrachi Party, 219

Mobutu, Sese Seko, 323

Moetzet Hapoalot (Women's Labor Council), 106, 107–8, 124 ff., 134, 153

Mollet, Guy, 285

Molotov, Ivy, 243

Molotov, Vyacheslav, 236, 243

Monnet, Jean, 402

Monrovia, Liberia, 309–10

Montor, Henry, 224, 226, 258–59

Moroccan Jews, 248

Morgenthau, Henry J., 259

Moshavim, 331

Mossad (the Institution), 164

Mount Carmel Center, 320–21

Mount Hermon, 423

Mufti, 101, 128, 143

Munich, Arab terrorist attacks in, 384, 385

Nachlat Yehuda, 125

Nachshon shipping enterprise, 149

Nahal (Fighting Pioneer Youth), 331

Naiditch, Grandfather, 15–16

Naiditch, Grandmother, 15

Najjar, Amiel, 392, 394

Namir, Mordechai, 232, 237, 246

Namir, Yael, 232, 243

Naphtali, Peretz, 147

Nasser, Gamal Abdel, 206–7, 282, 283, 285, 291, 298, 305, 313, 339, 362, 367, 369, 370; death, 383; eviction of UNEF, 340–42; nationalization of Suez Canal, 284; reimposition of blockade against Israel, 342–43; and Six-Day War, 340–44, 345, 348, 352–54, 356; and War of Attrition, 361

National Insurance Act, 264

National Press Club, 378

National Religious Party, 408, 439

National Unity Government, 370

Nazis, 129, 152, 155, 158, 159, 161, 169–70, 393

Negev, the, 175, 243, 287, 346; and War of Independence, 234

Nehru, Jawaharlal, 286, 305

Nenni, Pietro, 326

Nesher factory, 101

Neue Freie Presse, 21

Neustadt (Noy), Mellech, 161

Neveh Zedek, 75

Ne Win, 332

New York Hospital for Joint Diseases, 228

Nigeria, 309, 324–25

Nixon, Pat, 375, 376, 377, 378, 425

Nixon, Richard M., 368–69, 371, 398, 415, 424–25, 429, 430–31; meeting with GM and Israeli arms request, 372–79

Nixon, Tricia, 377

Nkrumah, Kwame, 311–13, 317

North African Jews, 257

North Division High School (Milwaukee), 38

Northern Rhodesia, 314

Norway, 387

Nyerere, Julius, 317

Obote, Milton, 322

Ohel (Tent), 72

Old City of Jerusalem, 353, 354, 355; liberation of, 355; occupation of, by Arab Legion, 262

Olympic Games massacre, 384, 385

Operation Kadesh. *See* Sinai Campaign

Operation Magic Carpet, 250–51

Organization for Rehabilitation through Training (ORT), 265

Oriental Jews, 245, 255, 266, 396

Ottoman Empire, 389

Padmore, George, 313–14

Pakistan, 305

Pale of Settlement, 14

Palestine, 21, 23, 43–45, 52, 59–60; Arab refugees, 268–69, 290; "Black Saturday" occupation of, by British, 187 ff.; British civil administration, 65; British conquest of, 60–61; British mandate over, 72, 78, 98, 101, 140, 217; emigration from, 100; immigration to, 101, 104, 116, 120, 121, 128, 140, 147, 150, 152–53, 155 ff., 164, 181–88, 191, 192; Jewish industrial enterprises in, 101; land purchase in, by Jewish National Fund, 78; Peel partition proposal, 122, 147, 150–51;

pioneer villages, 21, 53, 79–80; UN-SCOP partition plan, 201–3, 224; during World War I, 50, 52–53; during World War II, 158–59, 160, 161–62. See also *Yishuv*

Palestine Electric Corporation, 101, 207

Palestine Liberation Organization, 339

Palestine Philharmonic Orchestra, 219

Palestine *Post*, 177

Palestinian Arabs, 142–44, 216, 376; and Peel partition proposal, 150–51. *See also* Arabs

Palestinian Jews, 52–53; in British Army, 158, 160, 162–63; parachuted into Axis territory, 121, 161–62, 168–69. See also *Yishuv*

Palmach, 178

Passfield Paper, 128

Paul VI, Pope, 391–94

Pauls, Rolf, 169–70, 171

Peel Commission, 122, 147, 150–51, 201, 261

People's Council, 214, 219

People's Relief Committee, 55–56

People's Republic of China, 305, 325–26

Peres, Shimon, 277–78, 280, 285, 364

Peretz, I. L., 43

Persian Jews, 248

Petach Tikva (The Gate of Hope), 21, 125

Petlyura, Simon, 58, 59

Phantom jets, 416, 430; Israeli purchase of, 373, 380

Philippines, 305, 330

Philosophy of a Revolution (Nasser), 284

Pineau, Christian, 285

Pinsk, Russia, 12, 15, 17–19, 22, 25

Pioneer Women, 107, 111, 124–26, 130, 131–34

Pius X, Pope, 391

Pius XII, Pope, 391

Plain of Jezreel. *See* Emek, the

"Ploughwoman, The" (Meir), 110–11
Plumer, Lord, 98
Poalei Zion (Labor Zionists), 22–23, 51, 57–58, 59
Pocahontas (ship), 64, 66–67; reunion, 333–34
Pogroms, 11, 22, 58
Poland, pogroms in, 58
Polish Jews, 161, 248
Pompidou, Georges, 392
Poverty, in Israel, 380–83
Pravda, 239
Prisoners of war, Israeli: from War of Attrition, 393, 432; from Yom Kippur War, 420–21, 438, 442
Progressive Party, 245
Public works program, 255

Qaddafi, Muamwar el-, 323

Rabin, Yitzhak, 372, 377, 425, 442
Rafi (Israel Workers' list), 280, 338, 360, 364, 440
Ramat Rachel, fedayeen attack on, 283
Rattner, Yohanan, 237
Rehahi, Sarah Meyerson (GM's daughter). *See under* Meyerson
Rehabi, Shaul (GM's grandson), 287
Rehabi, Zechariah (GM's son-in-law), 176, 216, 230–31, 232, 235, 246, 260, 287, 364, 377
Rehovot, International Conference on Science at, 319–20
Religious bloc, 270, 440
Remez, David, 93, 106, 113, 117–18, 138, 145, 146–47, 149, 185, 187
Resolution 242, 357–59, 360, 370
Resolution 338, 423–24
Revisionist Party, 138–39
Revivim kibbutz, 176, 216, 243, 260–61, 280, 287–88, 308, 327, 337, 345–46, 364
Road-building project, 255–56
Rogers, William, 368–72, 376, 377, 378
Roosevelt, Franklin D., 151

Rosenwald, Bill, 226
Rothberg, Sam, 226
Rothschild, Lord, 60
Royal Commission. *See* Peel Commission
Rumania, 385–87
Rumanian Jews, 248, 387
Russia, 11 ff.; Revolution of 1848, 32; Revolution of 1905, 51. *See also* Soviet Union
Russian Jews, 17–18, 20–22, 164, 236, 237–42, 244. *See also* Soviet Jews

Sadat, Anwar el-, 383, 386, 389, 423, 424, 425, 427
Samuel, Sir Herbert, 98
Sapir, Pinchas, 277, 279, 335, 396–97
Sasson, Eliahu, 207
Saudi Arabia, 361, 423
Schiefer, Rabbi, 238
Schonau transit camp, closing of, 399–404
Scheinfeld, Rabbi, 61
Sdeh Boker kibbutz, 144, 272–73, 274, 277, 278, 280
Second Aliyah, 118
Selassie, Haile, 328–29
Senegal, 309, 323
Senesh, Hanna, 169
Senghor, 323
Sephardim, 245
Sereni, Enzo, 162, 167–69
Sforim, Mendele Mocher, 43
Shapiro, Eiga, 232–33, 236, 241, 244
Shapiro, Henry, 243
Shapiro, Ya'akov Shimshon, 434
Sharef, Zeev, 215
Sharett, Moshe, 17, 118, 147, 162–63, 164, 165, 187, 188, 197, 219, 226–27, 229, 230, 234, 272 ff., 280–81, 286, 309, 330, 366, 391; relationship with Ben-Gurion, 273–77
Sharett, Zipporah, 163
Sharm el-Sheikh, 288, 290, 295, 296, 297; eviction of UNEF from, 341
Shazar (Rubashos), Zalman, 90, 113–15, 145, 185, 303
Sheba, Queen of, 328

Shemen factory, 101
Shimoni, Ya'akov, 329
Shprinsak, Yosef, 113
Shtetl, 16–17
Shvernik, Nikolai, 236
Sierre Leone, 317
Single tax, 137
Sinai Campaign, 277, 299, 305, 326, 328, 339, 341, 343, 373
Sinai Desert, and Peninsula, 288 ff., 341, 440; and Six-Day War, 351, 352, 353, 354, 357; and Yom Kippur War, 413, 414, 418
Sisco, Joseph, 428
Six-Day War, 99–100, 116, 170, 196, 262, 266, 301–2, 303–4, 317, 339, 340 ff., 350–55, 367, 374, 385, 389, 408, 416, 417–18, 422; administration of occupied territory, 357, 360; cease-fire violations, 361, 362; Israeli preparation for, 344–50; postwar period, 355 ff.
Skyhawk jets, 416, 430, Israeli purchase of, 373
Snowden, Mrs. Philip, 90–91
Socialist International, 112, 125, 147, 152, 392, 400, 430
Socialist Women, Conference of, 127
Socialist Zionists, 43. *See also* Labor Zionists.
Social Welfare, Ministry of, 265
Solel Boneh (Histadrut Public Works and Building Office), 92, 93, 96, 97–98, 104–6, 118
Solomon, King, 248, 328
Solomon's Temple, 99
So Sorry We Won (Dosh-Kishon), 359
Southern Rhodesia, 314, 324
Soviet Jews, and closing of Schonau transit camp, 399 ff.
Soviet Union, 229, 230, 231, 232, 235 ff., 314, 339–40, 342, 343, 358, 361, 367–69, 376, 383, 385, 429; anti-Semitism, 237–40, 244, 283–84; arms aid to Arab states, 339, 340, 367–68, 380; and Egypt, relationship with, 283, 367–68, 380; Doctors' Plot, 283; and Israeli

occupation of Sinai and Gaza Strip, 289–90; Israel, recognition of, 221–22; Six-Day War, 342–44; Yom Kippur War, 408, 412, 415, 418–22
Stalin, Joseph, 243, 283
Stavsky, Abraham, 138
Stern, Clara (GM's sister), *See under* Mabovitch
Stern, Daniel David (GM's nephew), 126, 127
Stern, Fred (GM's brother-in-law), 126–27, 131
Stern, Isaac, 377
Stern Group (Lehi), 166, 188, 197
Stockwell, Sir Hugh, 268
Suez Canal, 352, 353, 383; Anglo-French assault on, 285, 288–89; nationalization of, 284; postwar fighting along, 360–61, 367; prohibition of Israeli shipping, 246, 281; and Yom Kippur War, 412, 413, 414, 417, 421, 424
Sweden, 387–88
Syria, 210, 284, 339–40, 357; and Arab terrorists, 385; armistice (1949); bombardment of Israeli settlements, 339; cease-fire violations, 439; disengagement agreement, 442; fedayeen bases in, 281; Israeli POW's, 393, 432, 438, 442; and Six-Day War, 343, 351 ff., 357; Soviet arms aid, 367; and War of Independence, 222–23, 228; Yom Kippur War, 405 ff., 438
Syrkin, Marie, 51
Syrkin, Nachman, 51–52

Tabenkin, Yitzhak, 90
Tamir, Shmuel, 433–34
Tanganyika, 314
Tanzania, 317, 323
Tel Aviv, 71 ff., 92–93, 101, 102, 103, 104, 107, 149, 270, 355; and Six-Day War, 352; and War of Independence, 228
Tel Aviv (ship), 149
Teti (ship), 220
Thailand, 305, 330
Third Aliyah, 72

Third World countries, 305
Thorsson, Inga, 321
Tiran, Strait of, 328; Egyptian blockade of, 295, 296, 342, 343; and Six-Day War, 353
Tito, Josip, 298, 305
Togo, Ghana, 317
Toure, Sekou, 317
Trade unionism, 137, 160, 381–82
Transjordan, 206. *See also* Jordan
Truman, Harry, 183, 189, 259; recognition of Israel, 221
Tsarapkin, Semyon, 389
Tubman, William, 310, 317
Tunisian Jews, 248
Turkish Jews, 248
Turks, 52, 53, 61, 71
Tzur, Jakob, 309

Uganda, 322–23
Ukraine, pogroms in, 58
Underground, Jewish, 161–62, 163–64
Unemployment, 100–1, 137
Unemployment fund, 138
United Egyptian-Syrian high command, 286
United Jewish Appeal, 224–26, 258, 313, 347, 379; and Israel bond issue, 258–60
United Jewish Council, 127
United Nations, 246, 247, 262, 301, 318–19, 339–40, 341, 342–43, 418, 421, 425, 431–32; and Arab terrorism, 274–75; Negev debate, 243; partition vote, 201–2, 224, 250, 268; Resolution 242, 357–59, 360, 370; Resolution 338, 423–24; Sinai Peninsula and Gaza Strip issue, 288 ff.; Six-Day War cease-fire, 353; War of Independence truce attempt, 228
UN Emergency Force (UNEF), 297; eviction of, by Nasser, from Sharm el-Sheikh and Gaza Strip, 341–42
UN Special Committee on Palestine (UNSCOP), 198–99, 201, 222, 261

UN Truce Supervision Organization, 343
United Religious Front, 245
United States, 289, 305, 342, 347; alert, 424–26; Arab oil embargo, 423; Arab states, relationship with, 283; arms aid, during War of Attrition, 368–69, 373; arms aid, during Yom Kippur War, 409, 411–12, 414–16, 417, 427; Israel, recognition of, 221; and Israeli occupation of Gaza Strip, 295–96; Jewish emigration from, 333; and Nasser, 283; Soviet détente, 368–69
U.S. Department of Defense, 415
U.S. House of Representatives, Foreign Affairs Committee, 378, 398
U.S. Import-Export Bank, 373–74
U Nu, 325, 330, 332
U Thant, 282, 379; and withdrawal of UNEF from Gaza Strip and Sharm el-Sheikh, 341–43

Va'ad Hapoel (Executive Committee of the Histadrut), 136, 150, 158, 161, 167, 176, 185, 187
Va'ad Le'umi (Jewish National Council), 185–86, 187, 199, 213, 270
Vatican, 391–94
Versailles Peace Conference, 63
Villa Haroun al-Raschid, 263
Vocational training, 265

War of Attrition, 367 ff., 380, 393, 397–98, 420; cease-fire proposal, 370–71; POW's, 393, 432
War Economic Advisory Council, 161
War of the Fathers and Sons, 416. *See* Yom Kippur War
War of Independence, 146, 212, 222–23, 228, 244–45, 246, 354, 419; armistice agreement, 246,

War of Independence (*cont.*)
247; arms, manufacture of, 224; first truce, 228; formal beginning of, 220; Israeli casualties, 224; second truce, 234

War Needs and Rescue Fund, 138

Watergate, 424

Weisgal, Meyer, 190

Weizmann, Chaim, 17, 22, 188–91, 221, 261

Weizmann, Vera, 189, 190

Weizmann, Centenary Celebrations, 190

Weizmann Institute of Science, 190, 319, 320

West Bank, 351, 357, 440; Christian holy places, 391; Jewish settlement on, 389–91;

White Paper (1930) (Passfield Paper), 128

White Paper (1939), 152–54, 155–56, 158, 166, 181–82; nullification of, 186, 219

Wilson, Harold, 147, 343

Wilson, Woodrow, 42

Wisliceny, Dieter, 172

Women's International Zionist Organization (WIZO), 265

Women's Labor Council (Moetzet Hapoalot), 106, 107–8, 124 ff., 134, 153

Workers, Israeli, 381–82

Workers' Sick Fund, 141

World Jewish Congress, 56

World War I, 50, 52–53, 55, 78, 159, 165

World War II, 55, 96, 121, 138, 237, 368, 393

World Zionist Organization, 21, 188

Yadin, Yigael, 213

Yad Veshem, 170

Yagur kibbutz, 187–88

Yanait Ben-Zvi, Rachel, 53, 108, 124, 133, 145

Yariv, Aharon, 431

Yaurich, Samuel, 250

Yavor, Chanan, 309

Yemenite Jews, 257; return of, 248–51, 252

Yershov, Pavel I., 233–34

Yishuv, 52, 53, 71, 96, 110, 121, 128, 139, 140, 142, 146, 149, 152, 154, 155–56, 160, 163, 164–67, 174, 185, 188, 193, 198, 199; civil disobedience policy, 190; civilian labor force, 160; economy, 100–1, 158–59; labor movement, 90, 104, 118–19, 125–26, 162; self-defense, 165–66; unemployment, 100; and War of Independence, 420

Yom Kippur, 407

Yom Kippur War, 306, 323, 349, 351, 353, 405–37, 441; ceasefires, 422, 423, 424, 425–30, 434, 439; disengagement agreement, 431–32, 438; Geneva talks, 438; POW's, 420–21, 430, 432, 442; unpreparedness inquiry, 434–36

Yugoslavia, 201, 222

Yugoslav Jews, 248

Zaire, 323

Zambia, 316, 323, 324

Zeit Die (The Times), 62

Zerubavel, Ya'akov, 52, 53

Zhdanov, Andrei, 235, 236

Zhitlovsky, Chaim, 51

Zionism, 258; in Soviet Union, 237–38. *See also* Labor Zionism, Zionist movement

Zionist Congresses, 157–58, 189, 197, 217

Zionist Executive, 98

Zionist movement, 21, 43–45, 78, 114, 118, 120, 139, 165, 273–74, 283, 284, 391; beginnings of, 21–22

Zionist-socialist movement, 19. *See also* Labor Zionism

Zisling, Aaron, 215

Zvi Pincus, David, 219

Dell Bestsellers

- ☐ **THE MEMORY OF EVA RYKER**
  by Donald A. Stanwood $2.50 (15550-9)
- ☐ **BLIZZARD** by George Stone $2.25 (11080-7)
- ☐ **THE BLACK MARBLE**
  by Joseph Wambaugh $2.50 (10647-8)
- ☐ **MY MOTHER/MY SELF** by Nancy Friday $2.50 (15663-7)
- ☐ **SEASON OF PASSION** by Danielle Steel $2.50 (17703-0)
- ☐ **THE IMMIGRANTS** by Howard Fast $2.75 (14175-3)
- ☐ **THE ENDS OF POWER** by H. R. Haldeman
  with Joseph DiMona $2.75 (12239-2)
- ☐ **GOING AFTER CACCIATO** by Tim O'Brien ..$2.25 (12966-4)
- ☐ **SLAPSTICK** by Kurt Vonnegut $2.25 (18009-0)
- ☐ **THE FAR SIDE OF DESTINY**
  by Dore Mullen $2.25 (12645-2)
- ☐ **LOOK AWAY, BEULAH LAND**
  by Lonnie Coleman $2.50 (14642-9)
- ☐ **BED OF STRANGERS**
  by Lee Raintree and Anthony Wilson $2.50 (10892-6)
- ☐ **ASYA** by Allison Baker $2.25 (10696-6)
- ☐ **BEGGARMAN, THIEF** by Irwin Shaw $2.75 (10701-6)
- ☐ **STRANGERS** by Michael de Guzman $2.25 (17952-1)
- ☐ **THE BENEDICT ARNOLD CONNECTION**
  by Joseph DiMona $2.25 (10935-3)
- ☐ **EARTH HAS BEEN FOUND** by D. F. Jones $2.25 (12217-1)
- ☐ **STORMY SURRENDER**
  by Janette Radcliffe $2.25 (16941-0)
- ☐ **THE ODDS** by Eddie Constantine $2.25 (16602-0)
- ☐ **PEARL** by Stirling Silliphant $2.50 (16987-9)

At your local bookstore or use this handy coupon for ordering:

Dell **DELL BOOKS**
P.O. BOX 1000, PINEBROOK, N.J. 07058

Please send me the books I have checked above. I am enclosing $_____
(please add 35¢ per copy to cover postage and handling). Send check or money
order—no cash or C.O.D.'s. Please allow up to 8 weeks for shipment.

Mr/Mrs/Miss_____

Address_____

City_____ State/Zip_____

THE BENEDICT ARNOLD CONNECTION

An electrifying **super-shocker** by

Joseph DiMona

We live in a nuclear age, in a world paralyzed by terrorism. Cases of nuclear terrorism have actually occurred in the U S Here is the novel that proves it can happen anywhere anytime.

On July 2 at 6 P M. a million tons of radioactive water will explode over the Eastern seaboard. Atlantic City, Cape May and The Hamptons will all vanish into the sea. Under direct orders from the President, George Williams is to find a nuclear warhead somewhere under 300 feet of ocean within 36 hours or millions of people will die!

Dell $2.25